Understanding Quantitative History

New Liberal Arts Series

Light, Wind, and Structure: The Mystery of the Master Builders,
by Robert Mark, 1990

The Age of Electronic Messages, by John G. Truxal, 1990

Medical Technology and Society: An Interdisciplinary Perspective,
by Joseph D. Bronzino, Vincent H. Smith, and Maurice L. Wade, 1990

Understanding Quantitative History,
by Loren Haskins and Kirk Jeffrey, 1990.

This book is published as part of an Alfred P. Sloan Foundation program.

Understanding Quantitative History

Loren Haskins and Kirk Jeffrey

The MIT Press
Cambridge, Massachusetts
London, England

This book was printed and bound in the United States of America.

Library of Congress Cataloging-in-Publication Data

Haskins, Loren.
    Understanding quantitative history / Loren Haskins and Kirk Jeffrey.
        p.   cm. — (New liberal arts series)
    ISBN 0-262-08190-3
    1. Social sciences—Statistical methods. 2. History—Methodology.
I. Jeffrey, Kirk. II. Title. III. Series.
HA29.H293   1990
300'.72—dc20   89-34497
                                                            CIP

To Patti, Kathy, and Jackie
Loren Haskins

To my parents, Kirk and Virginia Jeffrey
Kirk Jeffrey

Contents

I SUMMARIZING INFORMATION

IV   PUTTING IT TOGETHER

List of Figures

List of Tables

Series Foreword

The Alfred P. Sloan Foundation's New Liberal Arts (NLA) Program stems from the belief that a liberal education for our time should involve undergraduates in meaningful experiences with technology and with quantitative approaches to problem solving in a wide range of subjects and fields. Students should understand not only the fundamental concepts of technology and how structures and machines function, but also the scientific and cultural settings within which engineers work, and the impacts (positive and negative) of technology on individuals and society. They should be much more comfortable than they are with making calculations, reasoning with numbers and symbols, and applying mathematical and physical models. These methods of learning about nature are increasingly important in more and more fields. They also underlie the process by which engineers create the technologies that exercise such vast influence over all our lives.

The program is closely associated with the names of Stephen White and James D. Koerner, both vice-presidents (retired) of the foundation. Mr. White wrote an internal memorandum in 1980 that led to the launching of the program two years later. In it he argued for quantitative reasoning and technology as "new" liberal arts, not as replacements for the liberal arts as customarily identified, but as liberating modes of thought needed for understanding the technological world in which we now live. Mr. Koerner administered the program for the foundation, successfully leading it through its crucial first four years.

The foundation's grants to 36 undergraduate colleges and 12 universities have supported a large number of seminars, workshops, and symposia on topics in technology and applied mathematics. Many new courses have been developed and existing courses modified at these colleges. Some minors or concentrations in technology studies have been organized. A Resource Center for the NLA Program, located at the State University of New York at Stony Brook, publishes and distributes a monthly newsletter, collects and disseminates syllabi, teaching modules, and other materials prepared at the colleges and universities taking part in the program, and serves in a variety of ways to bring news of NLA activities to all who express interest and request information.

As the program progressed, faculty members who had developed successful new liberal arts courses began to prepare textbooks. Also, a number of the foundation's grants to universities were used to support

writing projects of professors—often from engineering departments—
who had taught well-attended courses in technology and applied mathematics that had been designed to be accessible to liberal arts undergraduates. It seemed appropriate not only to encourage the preparation
of books for such courses, but also to find a way to publish and thereby
make available to the widest possible audience the best products of these
teaching experiences and writing projects. This is the background with
which the foundation approached The MIT Press and the McGraw-Hill
Publishing Company about publishing a series of books on the new liberal arts. Their enthusiastic response led to the launching of the New
Liberal Arts Series.

The publishers and the Alfred P. Sloan Foundation express their ap-
preciation to the members of the Editorial Advisory Board for the New
Liberal Arts Series: John G. Truxal, Distinguished Teaching Professor,
Department of Technology and Society, State University of New York,
Stony Brook, Chairman; Joseph Bordogna, Alfred Fitler Moore Professor and Dean, School of Engineering and Applied Science, University of
Pennsylvania; Robert W. Mann, Whitaker Professor of Biomedical Engineering, Massachusetts Institute of Technology; Merritt Roe Smith,
Professor of the History of Technology, Massachusetts Institute of Technology; J. Ronald Spencer, Associate Academic Dean and Lecturer in
History, Trinity College; and Allen B. Tucker, Jr., Professor of Computer Science, Bowdoin College. In developing this new publication
program, The MIT Press has been represented by Frank P. Satlow and
the McGraw-Hill Publishing Company by Eric M. Munson.

Samuel Goldberg
Program Officer
Alfred P. Sloan Foundation

Preface

The idea for *Understanding Quantitative History* emerged out of a faculty seminar held in the Department of History at Carleton College in early 1984. Members of the department met weekly with Loren Haskins of Carleton's Mathematics Department to read and critique some of the articles being published in scholarly periodicals such as the *Journal of Interdisciplinary History*. It became clear that the historians often had to rely on an author's summary of his or her findings as stated in the introduction and conclusion—they were not equipped to follow the author's statistical analysis, much less to spot possible flaws in a historian's use of such techniques as sampling, correlation, and regression.

Our colleagues, most of whom attended graduate school in the 1960s, are not unusual. The typical professional historian in the United States has had so little training in quantitative methods that he or she is not well positioned to critique articles and books that use statistics. But this problem goes beyond the issue of how professional historians ought to be trained or re-trained. As the two of us discussed the situation among professional historians, our conviction grew that statistical analysis has become so pervasive a mode of discourse in contemporary life that every educated person ought to know something about it—enough to be able to tell a good statistical argument from a dubious one, at any rate.[1]

That's why we wrote this book with two sorts of readers in mind. Our first audience is historians and apprentice historians who have little background in statistics; the second, undergraduates taking history courses, whether they are majoring in history or not. These two groups have much in common besides an interest in understanding the past. They both will encounter historical writings that analyze the past using the tools of statistics.

Our two groups of readers also have in common the fact that they are citizens of a society in which all sorts of news stories and political debates invoke statistical information, often in misleading ways. We

---

[1] A number of educators have been making this point in recent years. See, e.g., Frederick Stirton Weaver, "Introductory Statistics and General Education," *JGE: The Journal of General Education*, 33 (Winter 1982), 287-94; Fernand Brunschwig and Richard D. Breslin, "Scientific and Technological Literacy–A Major Innovation and Challenge," *Liberal Education*, 18 (Spring 1982), 49-62; Gudmund R. Iversen, "Statistics in Liberal Arts Education," *American Statistician*, 39 (February 1985), 17-19; John Allen Paulos, *Innumeracy* (New York, 1988). For survey evidence that American students do not grasp how fundamental mathematics has become in work and public discourse, see the report in *New York Times*, June 15, 1988, p. 27.

hope that *Understanding Quantitative History* will help empower readers
to follow and participate more effectively in discussions of a wide range
of public matters: pregnancy and contraceptive use among teenagers,
risks to the public from environmental pollutants, opinion surveys during
presidential campaigns, and the spread of AIDS.

Whether you are a practicing historian, a graduate student, or an
undergraduate, this book will help you gain familiarity with terms and
symbols used by "quantitative historians." It will teach you to analyze
statistical charts and tables, from the very simple to the quite complicated. It will help you learn to follow the logic of the argument and to
see where the statistical details fit into the overall structure of a work
of history.

We don't share the common American belief that math is an esoteric subject for which a person needs some special inborn talent. We
think that your interest in historical problems and willingness to dissect
statistical arguments patiently ought to get you through every chapter
of this book. You need no background in statistics to understand and
learn from it. If you have a pocket calculator and recall the basics of
high-school algebra, you're ready.

Since we began work on this book in 1985, we have been enriched by
the advice and support of many colleagues and friends. The anonymous
readers who dissected our manuscript for The MIT Press offered a number of important suggestions for tightening and clarifying the presentation. At the beginning, Clifford E. Clark, Jr., Carl N. Degler, Russell
Menard, and William F. Woehrlin offered important encouragement and
helpful suggestions; at the end, Patti Haskins read it all and pointed out
many awkward sentences and mistakes as our chapter drafts came off
the printer.

For one of us (Jeffrey), a conference on "Statistics, Epistemology, and
History" that was sponsored by the Alfred P. Sloan Foundation and held
at MIT in November 1983 proved an important catalytic event. Jeffrey
also wishes to thank those who have tried to teach him something about
mathematics, statistical analysis, and writing: Richard Jensen, Paul S.
Jorgensen, Daniel Scott Smith, and Craig Vittetoe.

Financial support from the New Liberal Arts Program of the Alfred P.
Sloan Foundation and from the Faculty Development Program at Carleton College (funded by the William and Flora Hewlett Foundation)
gave us the time we needed to prepare the first draft of the book in

1985–86. Associate Dean William C. Child helped us with many practical financial matters. Roy O. Elveton, Dean of the College at Carleton, offered counsel and support at every stage of our collaborative endeavor. We owe a special debt to Samuel Goldberg, Program Officer for the New Liberal Arts Program at the Sloan Foundation, and John Truxal, Director of the program, for their confidence and practical advice.

Acknowledgments

Grateful acknowledgment is made to the following publishers, journals, and authors for permission to reprint excerpts from the works listed:

"A Mother's Wages: Income Earning Among Married Italian and Black Women, 1896–1911" by Elizabeth H. Pleck, from Michael Gordon (ed.), *The American Family in Social-Historical Perspective*, 2nd edition (New York: St. Martin's Press, 1978), pp. 490–510. Excerpts reprinted by permission of the author.

Immigration and Industrialization: Ethnicity in an American Mill Town, 1870–1940 by John Bodnar. Excerpts reprinted by permission of the University of Pittsburgh Press. Copyright (c) 1977 by University of Pittsburgh Press.

"Economic Growth and Occupational Mobility in 19th Century Urban America: A Reappraisal" by Anthony E. Boardman and Michael P. Weber, from *Journal of Social History*, 11 (Fall 1977), 52–74. Excerpts reprinted by permission of the *Journal of Social History* and the authors.

The Female Labor Force in the United States, by Valerie Kincade Oppenheimer. Excerpts reprinted by permission of the Institute of International Studies, University of California, Berkeley.

"Police Response to Crime and Disorder in Twentieth-Century St. Louis" by Eugene J. Watts, from *Journal of American History*, 70 (September 1983), 340–58. Excerpts reprinted by permission of the *Journal of American History* and the author.

"Angels' Heads and Weeping Willows: Death in Early America" by Maris A. Vinovskis, from *Essays in the History of the American Family* (Worcester, Massachusetts: American Antiquarian Society, 1976), 273–302. Excerpts reprinted by permission of the American Antiquarian Society.

Wage-Earning Women: Industrial Work and Family Life in the United States, 1900–1930 by Leslie Woodcock Tentler. Excerpts reprinted by permission of Oxford University Press.

"The Virginia Muster of 1624/5 as a Source for Demographic History" by Irene W.D. Hecht, from *William & Mary Quarterly*, 3rd ser., 30 (January 1973), 65–92. Excerpts reprinted by permission of the *William & Mary Quarterly*.

"Families in Colonial Bristol, Rhode Island: An Exercise in Historical Demography" by John Demos, from *William & Mary Quarterly*, 3rd ser., 25 (January 1968), 40–57. Excerpts reprinted by permission of the

William & Mary Quarterly.

"The Allotment of Space for Slaves aboard Eighteenth-Century British Slave Ships" by Charles Garland and Herbert S. Klein, from *William & Mary Quarterly*, 3rd ser., 42 (April 1985), 238–48. Excerpts reprinted by permission of the *William & Mary Quarterly.*

"Time Spent in Housework" by Joann Vanek, from *Scientific American*, 231 (November 1974), 116–20. Excerpts reprinted by permission of W.H. Freeman and Company. Copyright (c) 1974 by Scientific American, Inc. All rights reserved.

"Wage Rates in Pittsburgh during the Depression of 1908" by Peter R. Shergold, from *Journal of American Studies*, 9 (August 1975), 163–88. Excerpts reprinted by permission of Cambridge University Press.

One Kind of Freedom: The Economic Consequences of Emancipation by Roger L. Ransom and Richard Sutch. Excerpts reprinted by permission of Cambridge University Press.

"Morbidity and Mortality on the North Atlantic Passage: Eighteenth-Century German Immigration" by Farley Grubb, from *The Journal of Interdisciplinary History*, 17 (Winter 1987), 565–85. Excerpts reprinted by permission of the editors of *The Journal of Interdisciplinary History* and The MIT Press, Cambridge, Massachusetts. Copyright (c) 1987 by the Massachusetts Institute of Technology and the editors of *The Journal of Interdisciplinary History.*

"Cotton, Corn and Risk in the Nineteenth Century" by Gavin Wright and Howard Kunreuther, from *Journal of Economic History*, 35 (September 1975), 526–51. Excerpts reprinted by permission of Cambridge University Press.

"Property and Politics in Atlanta, 1865–1903" by Eugene J. Watts, from *Journal of Urban History*, 3 (May 1977), 295–322. Copyright (c) 1977 by Sage Publications, Inc. Excerpts reprinted by permission of Sage Publications, Inc., and the author.

"What Ought to Be and What Was: Women's Sexuality in the Nineteenth Century" by Carl N. Degler, from *American Historical Review*, 79 (December 1974), 1467–90. Excerpts reprinted by permission of the author.

"Parental Power and Marriage Patterns: An Analysis of Historical Trends in Hingham, Massachusetts" by Daniel Scott Smith, from *Journal of Marriage and the Family*, 35 (August 1973), 419–28. Copyright (c) by the National Council on Family Relations, 1910 West County

Road B, Suite 147, St. Paul, Minnesota 55113. Excerpts reprinted by permission of the National Council on Family Relations and the author.

"The Culture of Politics in the Late Nineteenth Century: Community and Political Behavior in Rural New York" by Paula Baker, from *Journal of Social History*, 18 (Winter 1984), 167-93. Excerpts reprinted by permission of the *Journal of Social History* and the author.

"Beyond the Tenement: Patterns of American Urban Housing, 1870–1930" by Robert G. Barrows, from *Journal of Urban History*, 9 (August 1983), 395-420. Copyright (c) 1983 by Sage Publications, Inc. Excerpts reprinted by permission of Sage Publications, Inc., and the author.

"The Impact of the City on Home Ownership: A Comparison of Immigrants and Native Whites at the Turn of the Century" by Carolyn Tyirin Kirk and Gordon W. Kirk, Jr., from *Journal of Urban History*, 7 (August 1981), 471-95. Copyright (c) 1981 by Sage Publications, Inc. Excerpts reprinted by permission of Sage Publications, Inc., and the authors.

"Voter Turnout, Critical Elections and the New Deal Realignment" by David F. Prindle, from *Social Science History*, 3 (Winter 1979), 144-70. Excerpts reprinted by permission of *Social Science History*.

"The Economic Status of Women in the Early Republic: Quantitative Evidence" by Claudia Goldin, from *The Journal of Interdisciplinary History*, 16 (Winter 1986), 375-404. Excerpts reprinted by permission of the editors of *The Journal of Interdisciplinary History* and The MIT Press, Cambridge, Massachusetts. Copyright (c) 1986 by the Massachusetts Institute of Technology and the editors of *The Journal of Interdisciplinary History*.

"Children's Roles and Fertility: Late Nineteenth-Century United States" by Avery M. Guest and Stuart E. Tolnay, from *Social Science History*, 7 (Fall 1983), 355-80. Excerpts reprinted by permission of *Social Science History*.

"The Economic Emancipation of the Non-Slaveholding Class: Upcountry Farmers in the Georgia Cotton Economy," by David F. Weiman, from *Journal of Economic History*, 45 (March 1985), 71-93. Excerpts reprinted by permission of Cambridge University Press and the author.

Introduction

You sit down to read a scholarly article from the *Journal of American History* on urban disorder in the nineteenth and twentieth centuries.[2] On the fifth page you come upon a graph showing "Arrests for Drunkenness and Disorderly Conduct per 1,000 Population"; a note beneath the graph says that the data have been "smoothed with a three-year running average." What's a running average?

Moving along, you read a few more pages and find this table:

Trends in arrest rates for drunkenness and disorderly conduct: individual cities, 1860–1920

City	Slope	Significance	Period
New York City	−.79	.001	1860–1916
Philadelphia	−.26	.001	1860–1920
Brooklyn	−.09	n.s.	1860–1896
San Francisco	.16	.044	1862–1912
Buffalo	0	n.s.	1872–1920
Washington	−1.42	.001	1862–1920
Detroit	−.08	.09	1862–1918

What's a slope? What does the term *significance* mean—does it refer to historical significance or to something else?

Discouraged, you put the *Journal of American History* aside and pick up the *Journal of Social History* to read a recent article on political partisanship in a rural New York county at the end of the nineteenth century. Before many pages have passed, you encounter a table bearing the title "Party and Occupation in Schoharie County, 1894." The table shows the party preferences of farmers, mechanics, businessmen, and laborers. But the cryptic messages below the table again spoil your equanimity:[3]

Chi Square = 595.0
Significance = .000
Contingency Coefficient = .274

---

[2] Eric H. Monkkonen, "A Disorderly People? Urban Order in the Nineteenth and Twentieth Centuries," *Journal of American History*, 68 (December 1981), p. 543, Figure 1, and an excerpt from p. 548, Table 1.

[3] Paula Baker, "The Culture of Politics in the Late Nineteenth Century: Community and Political Behavior in Rural New York," *Journal of Social History*, 18 (Winter 1984), p. 172, Table 1.

Uneasiness growing, you throw down the *Journal of Social History* and grab an issue of *Social Science History* (ominous name!). An article on "Children's Roles and Fertility" in the U.S. at the end of the nineteenth century catches your eye. Skimming right past phrases like "Pearsonian correlation" and "one-tailed F-test," you finally bog down on this:[4]

Rural CEB = $7.4 - .2 \times$ (months in school)
$R^2 = .052$
Standard error of b = .048

Urban CEB = $5.9 + 1.3 \times$ (dummy variable for employed)
$R^2 = .035$
Standard error of b = .353

Serves me right for opening a journal called *Social Science History*, you think, as you pick up *American Quarterly* with a sigh. But here's an article on magazine reading in New York during the 1790s that includes five tables and an appendix entitled "Notes on Method"! In the appendix you notice phrases like "random sample" and "reliability coefficient."[5]

If you really sat down to read these scholarly articles, all published since 1981, could you do so with the same discernment you bring to your reading of nonquantitative history? Could you follow the discussion, understand how the author related statistical information to the overall argument, and distinguish a convincing conclusion from a shaky one?

An excellent way to become comfortable and competent as a reader of quantitative history is to practice on published books and articles. *Understanding Quantitative History* will introduce selections from a wide range of publications in American history, drawn from several scholarly journals and exemplifying the statistical techniques that a reader is likely to encounter most often. Some of the examples may contain logical or mathematical flaws. You will learn to spot such flaws and will judge whether they are fatal to the writer's conclusions.[6]

This book does not argue that every historian ought to convert to quantification as the one right way to do history. History is a richly

---

[4] Avery M Guest and Stewart E. Tolnay, "Children's Roles and Fertility: Late Nineteenth Century United States," *Social Science History*, 7 (Fall 1983), p. 375.

[5] David Paul Nord, "A Republican Literature: Magazine Reading and Readers in Late Eighteenth-Century New York," *American Quarterly*, 40 (March 1988), 42–64.

[6] For a somewhat similar approach, see Schuyler W. Huck, William H. Cormier, and William G. Bounds, Jr., *Reading Statistics and Research* (New York, 1974), a work that uses examples from published articles in the field of educational psychology.

diverse discipline today; we doubt that there will ever again be a single paradigm for historical writing. But precisely because of this diversity, historians and history students need to be able to read, critique, and learn from publications that use a variety of analytical techniques. Fortunately, to understand quantitative analysis you don't need advanced mathematics so much as the willingness to read and re-read quantitative historical writings with patience and care.

Historians and apprentice historians. For many practicing historians and graduate students, the ability to read discerningly the books and articles published in their field diminishes in proportion to the quantitative content of those books and articles. Often these readers are not really hostile to quantitative analysis—they simply stopped taking math courses somewhere back in high school or the freshman year in college. As one teacher of quantitative history has recently written, such readers, hostile or not, must "suspend their disbelief, ask fewer questions, and offer less criticism than they would if the author had been using traditional, non-quantitative evidence."[7]

A generation ago, a weak background in math would not have hindered one's career as a historian. There wasn't a great deal of quantitative history to read, and most of what there was employed elementary techniques of statistical analysis.[8] That has changed. Historians now use quantitative analysis every day in a variety of sub-fields in the discipline of history. The impassioned debate of ten or twenty years ago has died down. It is clear that quantifiers are not going to take over the entire discipline (nor do they want to), but many of them have published important work and they are accepted as members of the guild.

In a very few publications that use quantification, the charts and numbers are a mere sideshow—a mathematical veneer which gives the appearance of precision. But more often, the numerical data and calculations are central to the historian's argument. Hence historians, whether they are apprentices or masters of the craft, would be well served by having a sense of just what the common statistical arguments do and don't imply.

Perhaps you don't expect to use statistics in your own research and only want to become a more sophisticated reader of publications that do use statistics. But on the other hand, if you are studying statistical

---

[7]R.E. Johnson, "History by Numbers," *A.H.A. Perspectives*, 27 (February 1989), 14–18; quotation at 14.

[8]Stephan Thernstrom's *Poverty and Progress: Social Mobility in a Nineteenth Century City* (Cambridge, Mass., 1964) is a well-known case in point.

methods with the intention of using them eventually in your scholarly work, the present book can get you started. While this is just a first step, you could begin to design a research project, think about problems of gathering data, and select statistical tests appropriate to the questions you want to ask, picking up additional knowledge as you go along.

Undergraduate history students. It is obvious why professional historians need to be able to read and critique quantitative work in history and allied disciplines; but it may not be so apparent why undergraduate history students (both majors and non-majors) need to learn more about quantitative data analysis. After all, very few of them will go on to become professional historians or professional statisticians. And because of the enrollment decline in history courses in the 1970s and early 1980s, many history teachers may be reluctant to burden their courses with a set of complex mathematical methods that they suspect will be unpopular with many undergraduates.

In our view, quantitative analysis should be an important part of anyone's liberal education because an understanding of basic mathematics, especially statistics, will help equip students for more active and effective participation in contemporary society. In the humanities fields such as history, most students don't get much exposure to mathematics. They need more, and we hope that *Understanding Quantitative History* can help provide it. Students don't just need to understand statistics for the study of history; quantitative analysis crops up in many other fields too. For generations, scientists have presented their arguments in mathematical form. In recent decades, a behavioral revolution has gathered momentum in history's sister-disciplines of sociology, anthropology, political science, and economics. At many colleges and universities nowadays, you need some knowledge of statistics even to enroll in social science courses beyond the introductory level.

Mathematics is increasingly the language of inquiry not only in the social sciences but in the analysis of public policy. Statistical information about the economy and crime rates, articles about demographic subjects such as abortion and infant mortality, debates about the degree of risk that citizens incur from pesticides and nuclear power plants, appear in every issue of the newspapers and weekly newsmagazines. Spokesmen for political interest groups often try to persuade us—and our representatives in Congress—by making quantitative arguments. These days, it seems that every citizen needs to become skilled at analyzing statistical information. Yet legislators, their staff aides, and journalists often lack the background to examine carefully the arguments of lobbyists couched in quantitative terms.[9] They are in the same boat as most of their fellow-citizens.

The Japanese believe that almost any college student who wants to learn basic mathematics and statistics can do so; they don't think that it requires some special talent that only a few geniuses possess. Unfortunately, recent studies of American students' attitudes toward mathematics reveal that students in this country don't see much point to working hard in math or gaining advanced skills in the field, and that they tend to exaggerate the complexity of math. Many students may be foreclosing future opportunities for themselves through this disinclination to learn math. Those who expect that their future jobs will require little or no mathematical knowledge may be quite mistaken.[10]

We subscribe to Stephen White's point that quantitative data analysis is a fundamental "mode of thought" in the industrial world. According to White, "to believe, in this era, that a man possesses a liberal education who is ignorant of analytic skills and technological skills is to make a mockery of the central concept of liberal education and to ignore the nature of the world in which the graduate will live, and to which he hopes to contribute. . . ."[11] White might have added that the point applies to women as well as men.

The overall plan of the book. In general, *Understanding Quantitative History* presents statistical concepts and methods by introducing examples that show how American political, social, economic, and demographic historians actually use them. Each chapter begins with a brief overview and then brings in the historical problems one by one. You will be exploring real historical issues and learning statistics in the process. We introduce the statistics as needed and try to explain all mathematical concepts in ordinary language. The book asks you to memorize few definitions and no computing formulas.

---

[9]For examples, see Max Singer, "The Vitality of Mythical Numbers," *The Public Interest,* no. 23 (Spring 1971), 3–9, and Maris A. Vinovskis, *An 'Epidemic' of Adolescent Pregnancy? Some Historical Considerations* (New York, 1988). See also William Alonso and Paul Starr (eds.), *The Politics of Numbers* (New York, 1987).

[10]*New York Times,* June 15, 1988, p. 27. See also National Research Council, "Everybody Counts: A Report to the Nation on the Future of Mathematics Education" (Washington, 1989).

[11]Stephen White, "The New Liberal Arts," in James D. Koerner (ed.), "The New Liberal Arts: An Exchange of Views" (New York: Alfred P. Sloan Foundation, n.d. [1981], 1–11; quotation at 7). White's phrase "technological skills" refers to the study of computing and the role of technology generally in modern society. This book will concentrate on White's "analytic skills" rather than "technological skills."

Part I. The three chapters of Part I review the basic ways of describing the information contained in a collection of numbers. The chapters discuss tables of numbers (called frequency distributions or frequency tables), line and bar graphs, and the basic single-number summaries that you will come across: the mean or average of a list of numbers, the median, and the standard deviation. So Part I bears the title "Summarizing Information."

Probably you encounter these descriptive devices every day. All of them except standard deviations are used in newspapers and newsmagazines; they even show up in television news programs. Even though Chapters 1 through 3 cover material that you're familiar with, we advise you to read through them anyway and to work the exercises. The chapters try not only to explain these statistical techniques, but to comment on their usefulness, their limitations, and their pitfalls. The chapters may even include a few points, about something as elementary as the arithmetic mean, that you have forgotten since high-school math. Also, each chapter emphasizes through examples how historians actually use these descriptive techniques. Since some of the examples will turn up in later chapters, you should familiarize yourself with them in Chapters 1 through 3.

Part II. Historians and history students may not be equally familiar with the steps involved in presenting a statistical argument. That is hardly surprising: statistical arguments are quite different from the narratives and analyses that historians usually employ in their writing. Moreover, opinion pollsters and other people using statistics in everyday life hardly ever present formal arguments.

But you need to know something about the underlying logic of statistical argument in order to understand and critique the quantitative history that you read. So the subject of the two chapters that make up Part II is "Statistical Arguments." These chapters discuss such topics as sampling and the generating and testing of explicit hypotheses. Part II will be necessary background if you are to understand the statistical procedures covered in Part III.

Some of the steps involved in statistical sampling and testing hypotheses may strike you as cumbersome. Scientists and social scientists generally follow them nonetheless, because doing so makes it less likely that they will draw unwarranted conclusions from their data. Historians (and this goes for quantitative historians as well as others) rarely use the standard logical steps of formal statistical arguments, though it is often illuminating to examine their discussions with those steps in mind. But we will argue that in most cases it would be inappropriate for historians to present arguments in formal terms, as if they were natural scientists.

Part III. Here you will encounter more complex methods of statistical analysis. Correlation (Chapter 6) and regression (Chapter 7) are widely-used techniques for describing the association between two or more historical factors or variables—hence the title of Part III, "Relationships among Variables." As in Parts I and II, these chapters explain correlation and regression in ordinary language, provide examples from published works of history, and include questions to help you check your understanding of these techniques.

Part IV. By the time you've completed Part III, you will have examined in depth several brief excerpts from books and articles in U.S. history that use quantitative methods. If all goes well, your skills and confidence as a reader of quantitative arguments will have improved. In a sense, Chapter 8 of Part IV is your final examination. The aim of Part IV is not to introduce important new statistical methods; instead, you'll be given an entire article and asked a series of questions about the author's analysis.

The main points of the book.

- Quantitative analysis is not something esoteric; it's just an ordinary set of techniques that scholars and students are going to encounter. Some scholars use quantitative analysis with imagination and a high degree of sophistication. Some published work, on the other hand, seems seriously flawed. Readers need to be able to critique historical writing that uses quantitative analysis even if they don't intend to use quantitative methods in their own work.

- Not all historical problems can usefully be addressed through quantification, but some can. History is a broad discipline and its practitioners use a variety of methods.

- Readers sometimes hope that statistical displays of data can provide a richer, more accurate picture of the past than it is really possible to have. Not even a supercomputer can change the fact that the past happened quite awhile ago and cannot be known to several decimal places. Realistic historians generally feel that they have accomplished something if they can get a rough sense of how people lived or why events happened as they did long ago. Even a rough sense is often illuminating. At its best, statistical analysis helps us gain that rough sense of the past.

- Historians often must use data that were not gathered through random sampling. This book will argue that as long as historians are suitably cautious and diffident about their results, no great problem arises. But often they don't do an adequate job of warning their readers that a sample may not really reflect the larger population it purports to represent.

- In studying a past society, scholars may search for interesting patterns by using rather informal procedures. At other times they may formulate and test an interpretive hypothesis in a more formal way. Each style of inquiry has its uses. The reader should ask which style a historian is actually employing in a particular chapter or article and whether that style is appropriate.

- Quantitative analysis may lead to results that are statistically significant—that is, results that probably did not just happen by chance—yet have little substantive importance. Statistical significance and historical significance are two separate matters. It is up to the historian and the reader to decide whether results have historical interest, because no statistical test can do this.

- No statistical procedure can prove that factors A and B caused result C. All the statistics will do is comment on the plausibility of a possible interpretation. To claim that A and B caused C, or contributed to C, is to make an interpretation. Statistics will not liberate the historian from the burden of deciding what the data mean.

Using the Book in Courses. Because history departments attract many humanities students, yet stand somewhere close to the social sciences (indeed, history departments are often classed as part of the division of social sciences at large universities), courses in history seem good places for giving arts and humanities students some exposure to quantitative analysis.[12]

If you are an instructor in a history department, you can assign this book in part or in toto without yourself being a quantitative historian. We have consciously designed the book to be self-contained. We provide intuitive definitions of the terms that might puzzle a student, even quite

---

[12]See the discussion in Jerome M. Clubb and Maris A. Vinovskis, "Training and Retraining in Quantitative Methods of Social Research," *Historical Methods*, 17 (Fall 1984), 255–64, at 261–62.

elementary ones such as variable and median. We do not assume that the instructor or the students have a knowledge of math beyond algebra. Most of the examples we discuss can be done on a four-function pocket calculator.

We think that the material covered in this book could be used in the following courses:

> The graduate colloquium or seminar that introduces first-year graduate students to historical study. With assistance from the campus computer center the instructor could arrange to have one or more historical databases up and running on campus computers and could have students try out the ideas discussed in this book.

> The graduate or undergraduate course on quantitative methods as taught in many history departments.

> Research seminars in American history.

But the authors of this book teach undergraduate students. We strongly believe that *Understanding Quantitative History* is particularly appropriate for use with undergraduates:

> Part One and some later chapters could be used in the undergraduate survey course. Perhaps the instructor could set up one or more special discussion sections for students interested in digging more deeply into quantitative methods and assign Parts Two through Four for those students.

> The book is also appropriate for advanced undergraduate courses that presuppose the student's having completed a survey course, especially courses on the colonial era and the late nineteenth century since so many of our examples come from these two periods of American history.

> Many history departments require that undergraduate majors take a research seminar as a requirement for the major. This book may be an appropriate work to assign in such seminars, at least for students whose research or background reading will emphasize quantitative history.

We also want to emphasize that a reader can go through this book on his or her own, reading carefully and working the problems.

In a recent book entitled *Science in Action*, Bruno Latour points out that there are only three ways to read any specialized work in a technical field of knowledge. First, most readers will open the book or journal, try to comprehend the discussion, but quickly become discouraged and give up. Latour estimates that with specialized writings in science, this happens 90% of the time. Second, most of the readers who remain will read passively; they will accept the author's claims and later, perhaps, build on them. This second path is usually the one that the writer hopes a reader will follow, and much of the author's labor goes into presenting the argument and data in a way that will persuade the reader to choose it. Perhaps 90% of those who remain, who didn't go down the first path, choose the second.

But a third path is available too: a small fraction of readers will actively grapple with the author's argument, examining each step of the logic and studying each display of data. Perhaps these readers will regroup the data on a sheet of scratch paper, check some of the author's statistics, or try different statistical tests on the data.[13]

In *Understanding Quantitative History*, we try to equip you to follow that third path, should you wish to take it.

[13]Bruno Latour, *Science in Action: How to Follow Scientists and Engineers through Society* (Cambridge, 1987), pp. 60–61 and throughout Chapter 1.

I SUMMARIZING INFORMATION

1 Reading Statistical Tables

In this chapter:

This first chapter gives you practice at reading and interpreting statistical information displayed in tables. We will primarily be considering tables that summarize historical information and thus fall in the category of descriptive statistics. We begin with a fairly straightforward table and then move to progressively more complicated examples. Our main points in the chapter will be:

- A statistical table (or any other display of statistical information) has been arranged by the historian. The numbers have been selected and to some extent predigested for the reader.

- Usually the historian can choose among several ways to organize the same information. Every statistical table highlights certain patterns in the information but obscures others.

- The fact that a historian inserts some statistical tables in a book or article doesn't necessarily make the historical interpretation any more persuasive. You have to determine whether the statistical information is accurate and relevant and whether the historian is warranted in drawing the conclusions he or she draws.

- To become a skilled reader of statistical tables, you should be ready to organize the information in different ways. This is part of the process of asking what the tables are saying, just as you would ask about a conventional historical analysis written in sentences and paragraphs.

As we noted in the Introduction, we strongly urge you to answer all the questions in each section before continuing to the next section. You ought to have a pocket calculator and some scratch paper close by as you read. You will find answers to the questions at the end of the

chapter. You will also be learning some important terms that will crop
up frequently in later parts of the book. For a full list of new terms, see
the list in the section entitled "Conclusion" at the end of each chapter.

1.1   Family Income Strategies, 1911

In Harriet Arnow's novel *The Dollmaker*, an Appalachian couple move
with their children to a northern industrial city only to find despair,
violent death, and the breakup of their family.[1]

This is the stuff of standard social theory—the impersonal city con-
sumes the flood of immigrants who fuel its explosive growth. A "pro-
gressive" version with the same underlying story emphasizes that the
immigrants or their children eventually adapt to urban-industrial conditions, achieve economic security, and begin on the path of upward
mobility toward higher education, the suburbs, and middle-class status.

What these two versions have in common is the assumption that
all immigrants encountered the same set of conditions and suffered,
or adapted, in much the same way. In the past few years, historians
have been testing this model of immigrant experience through various
methods including the use of statistical methods. Historians looking at
particular cities at particular times often find limits, qualifications, and
contradictions to sweeping social theories. Our first two examples show
this process in action.

The traditional interpretation of the urban experience of blacks and
white immigrants would lead us to guess that the two groups probably
responded to similar conditions in similar ways. But did they? Social
historian Elizabeth H. Pleck[2] compared the ways in which married Italian and black women contributed to the overall income of their families
around 1900. Both groups of families, black and Italian, suffered severe
poverty in American cities at the turn of the century because the men
in these families typically held low-paying unskilled jobs and were often
unemployed. The problem for immigrant families was finding a way to
supplement the inadequate income of the husband; one strategy was for
the wife to work outside the home, but this tactic was not universally
adopted. Table 1.1, based on a table in Pleck's article, indicates the
variety of income strategies that immigrants employed.

---

[1] Harriet Arnow, *The Dollmaker* (New York, 1954).
[2] Elizabeth H. Pleck, "A Mother's Wages: Income Earning Among Married Italian
and Black Women, 1896–1911," in Michael Gordon (ed.), *The American Family in
Social-Historical Perspective*, 2nd edn. (New York, 1978), pp. 490–510.

Table 1.1
Proportion of families in various ethnic and racial groups with income contributed
by wives, children, and lodgers, various cities, 1911

Group, City	% with Wives Working	% with Children Working	% with Lodgers	(N)
Blacks, New York	51	10	27	145
Blacks, Phila.	54	13	41	71
Italians, Chicago	19	25	17	219
Italians, New York	36	19	20	333
Italians, Phila.	8	23	16	195
Italians, Boston	16	25	39	210
Germans, Milwaukee	5	28	14	163
Poles, Chicago	7	21	43	410
Poles, Phila.	7	10	60	159
Russian Jews, N.Y.	1	31	56	452
Russian Jews, Boston	15	41	40	226
Irish, Boston	27	49	18	197

Source: Based on Elizabeth H. Pleck, "A Mother's Wages: Income Earning Among
Married Italian and Black Women, 1896–1911," in Michael Gordon (ed.), *The American Family in Social-Historical Perspective*, 2nd edn. (New York, 1978), 496, Table
1.

Note: Table 1.1 pertains to families with both husband and wife present.

Tables such as Pleck's are found in virtually every book or article
you will read that makes any use at all of statistics. A historian will
use descriptive statistics to raise an interesting question about the past
or to convince you, the reader, of some particular interpretation. Thus
information in a statistical table, chart or graph is arranged information.
Somebody selected and organized these historical facts. You are not
looking at raw, unprocessed facts but at numbers packaged to make a
point.

When statisticians or quantitative historians speak of the population,
they generally are referring to the group that is being studied. Often
they are interested in comparing two or more populations. These needn't
be human populations, by the way; the population in a quantitative history project might consist of all presidential elections from 1800 to 1984.
Often the title of a table indicates what the population is. A variable
is a characteristic or an attribute that can vary from one individual or
population to another. In a study of candidates for public office, the
population might consist of the candidates and the variable might be
their wealth. Every candidate has the attribute "wealth," and it varies

in amount from one candidate to another. (Conceivably, the wealth of
a candidate could be zero or even negative.) Another example: In a
book on farmers in the South after the Civil War, an important variable
would be each farmer's race, since you would expect that black and white
farmers faced somewhat different problems. Throughout this book, we
capitalize the first letter of each word in a variable name: Race, Wealth,
Percent with Wives Working.

Here are the first of many questions you will be asked in the course of
this book:

1.   What populations are being studied in Table 1.1?

2.   How many variables are dealt with in Table 1.1? What are their
        names?

In Table 1.1, the column headed "N" tells you the number of families in each group in this study. For example, 219 Italian families in
Chicago are included. Note that Table 1.1 does not claim that these
groups of families are representative of all urban black families, Italian
families, etc., for 1911. They may be representative, but you cannot
be certain of this without knowing more about how these families were
picked for Elizabeth Pleck's study. (You'll learn more about this matter
of representativeness in Chapter 4.)

A variable may assume any of several <u>values</u>. If the variable is Sex,
the values are male and female. If the variable is Age in Years, the
values might run from zero to 85 in a population such as the residents
of a colonial town. If the variable is Birthplace, the values would be all
the states and foreign countries where members of the population had
been born.

3.   In Table 1.1, for the variable Percent with Wives Working, which
        group has the highest value and which the lowest?

What historical insight does Table 1.1 yield? As the article's title
indicates, Elizabeth Pleck wishes to compare the ways in which married
Italian and black women contributed to the overall income of their families. In the text of the article, she shows that family income for Italian
families in New York in 1911 was about the same as that of blacks, and
less than that of blacks in Philadelphia. Did black and Italian families
respond to similar situations in similar ways as the traditional interpretation would suggest?

4. Pleck makes the following statements; cite specific information from Table 1.1 supporting them, or state that the table does not contain supporting information:[3]

   (a) "In American cities few married women from any immigrant background were employed ... [in 1911]."

   (b) "Italian wives were no more confined to the home than other immigrant wives."

   (c) "Black wives were far more often breadwinners than Italian wives."

   (d) "Black and Italian wives were probably equally as likely to earn money by ... taking lodgers.... Nevertheless, among black and Italian families in the same city, there was a tendency for blacks to house lodgers more often than Italians."

5. Write a sentence or two summarizing the typical family income strategies of black and Italian families in these American cities. Emphasize the similarities within groups and the differences between the groups.

6. Maybe the differences aren't so much between groups as between cities. Perhaps more married women contributed to the family income in city A than city B because city A had more light manufacturing and clerical jobs available (women's jobs in 1911) while city B's economy focused on heavy industry. Evaluate that hunch in light of Table 1.1.

7. An alternative possibility would be that blacks and Italians had different cultural values about the proper role of the wife in a family and also about the role of children in the family. Does any evidence in Table 1.1 cast light on that hypothesis? (Of course it is tricky to infer people's values or attitudes from evidence about their behavior, so don't expect decisive evidence.)

1.2 Immigrant Workers of Steelton

Writers of history may present quantitative information in several different ways. They often incorporate numbers into conventional sentences and paragraphs, as in the following description by John Bodnar

---

[3] *Ibid.*, pp. 492, 495, 496.

of changes in the occupational structure of Steelton, Pennsylvania, a
post-Civil War steel town:

> Between 1880 and 1905 the proportion of unskilled laborers
> in the work force declined some 30%.... Whereas 66% of
> all workers were unskilled in 1880, only 37% were unskilled
> in 1905. On the other hand, the percentage of Steelton's
> wage earners in semiskilled endeavors had doubled during
> the same period. The unskilled sector of the labor force
> still comprised about 11% of the population, as it had a
> generation ago. In 1905, however, more than twice as many
> people held nonmanual jobs as in 1880.[4]

But more commonly, a historian will present such information in a
table or chart. This has two major advantages: the information is presented more compactly and it is usually easier for the reader to see
patterns in the numbers, to remember those patterns, and to refer back
to them. Bodnar himself puts the data from his paragraph into a table.
Though there is nothing wrong with the written description as prose,
notice how much more compact and orderly the presentation is in Table 1.2.

Table 1.2
Occupational distribution of the Steelton work force, 1880–1915

	1880 (N=606)	1905 (N=3338)	1915 (N=3586)
Unskilled	66%	37%	39%
Semiskilled	15	30	33
Skilled	11	12	9
Low nonmanual	6	14	12
High nonmanual	2	7	7

Source: John Bodnar, *Immigration and Industrialization: Ethnicity in an American
Mill Town* (Pittsburgh, 1977), p. 62, Table 9.

The simplest way to summarize a great deal of information about a
population is to count how often each value of a variable occurs, then
list those totals next to the name of each value. A frequency table (or
frequency distribution) shows the frequency of occurrence of each value.
It might show the actual numbers or it might use percentages as Bodnar

---

[4] John Bodnar, *Immigration and Industrialization: Ethnicity in an American Mill
Town* (Pittsburgh, 1977), p. 62.

has done in Table 1.2. The percentages shown in a frequency distribution add up to 100 percent.

8. In Table 1.2, identify the populations, the variable, and the values.

It is clear that Bodnar organized the data in Table 1.2. The federal census for 1880 and city directories for 1905 and 1915 provided the basic information about jobs in Steelton; but it was Bodnar himself who grouped the names of dozens of specific occupations into the five categories shown in Table 1.2. Unskilled jobs at the steel mill included such work as shoveling coal and ore. The semiskilled category included crane operators, blacksmiths, electricians, and the like. Jobs in the machine shop often required considerable skill and experience. By low nonmanual, Bodnar means minor white-collar positions such as clerk and draftsman. High nonmanual included the more important managers at the mill and also the independent merchants in Steelton.

Another way in which Bodnar organized his data is that Table 1.2 actually presents three frequency distributions (the columns) as snapshots from 1880, 1905, and 1915. By choosing this way to display the data, he shows very clearly that change took place over time.

The questions below include the words percentage and proportion. If 40 out of 200 people are over age 65, the percentage (or proportion) over age 65 is just 40 divided by 200, which is 0.20. Percentages or proportions can be expressed in decimal form such as 0.20, in percentage form such as 20%, and as fractions such as 1/5.

9. For each column of Table 1.2, you are given N, the actual number of workers about whom the author has information. If 11% of the workers were classified as skilled in 1880, exactly how many workers was that? When you work this out, why does the answer extend to two decimal places on your calculator—why is there a fraction of a worker?

10. Does it make more sense to add the percentages vertically or horizontally? Why?

11. Identify specific information from Table 1.2 that supports each of the following statements:[5]

(a) Bodnar says that "the percentage of Steelton's wage earners in semiskilled endeavors had doubled" between 1880 and 1905. What are the exact percentages he is referring to?

---

[5] *Ibid.*, p. 62.

(b) He also says, "In 1905, ... more than twice as many people held nonmanual jobs as in 1880." What are the proportions in this case?

(c) Here's a trickier one: Bodnar says that "between 1880 and 1905 the proportion of unskilled laborers in the work force declined some 30%.... Whereas 66% of all workers were unskilled in 1880, only 37% were unskilled in 1905." Is this correct? Calculate the decline yourself.

12. By 1915 the proportion of skilled workers in Steelton's work force had dropped from 11% in 1880 to 9%. Is the following statement true or false?

> Though the proportion of workers in Steelton who were skilled dropped from 1880 to 1915, the actual number of skilled workers in the town rose dramatically.

13. Bodnar says that "in 1905, ... more than twice as many people held nonmanual jobs as in 1880." That's true. Is the following statement also true? In 1905, more than fourteen times as many people held nonmanual jobs as in 1880.

14. Overall, would you say that the occupational distribution of workers in Steelton changed more dramatically between 1880 and 1905 or between 1905 and 1915? Back up your answer with two or three specific statements comparing the two eras.

Bodnar is interested in the changing occupational distribution in Steelton because he wants to compare the experience of native-born whites with that of Negroes and the Slavic and Italian immigrants who came to work in the steel mill. Like Elizabeth Pleck, he is out to test the old generalizations about an undifferentiated immigrant experience in urban-industrial America at the turn of the century. Table 1.3, though more complicated than the last, is still basically a set of frequency distributions. Notice that the comparisons now cut two ways: you can compare the experience of a single group at different points in time and you can compare groups with one another.

15. In 1905, what proportion of native-born whites held nonmanual jobs? What proportion of Slavic and Italian immigrants did so? How many native-born whites and how many immigrants held nonmanual jobs in 1905? What's the significance of your finding?

Table 1.3
Occupational distribution of native-born whites, Slavic and Italian Immigrants, and blacks in Steelton

	Native-born Whites			So. European Immigrants		Blacks		
	1880	1905	1915	1905	1915	1880	1905	1915
Unskilled	60%	25%	28%	79%	76%	95%	60%	70%
Semiskilled	18	37	40	5	9	3	33	26
Skilled	14	15	12	0	3	0	0	0
Low nonmanual	5	14	14	12	11	0	4	3
High nonmanual	3	9	6	4	1	2	3	1
(N)	461	1905	2617	403	616	87	300	323

Source: Bodnar, *Immigration and Industrialization*, p. 63, Table 10; p. 65, Table 11; and p. 66, Table 12.

Note: There are only two columns for the southern European immigrants because they did not arrive in Steelton until after 1890.

16. How many blacks held nonmanual jobs in 1880?

17. Between 1905 and 1915, did the proportion of immigrants who held nonmanual jobs rise or fall? By what percent? Did the number of immigrants holding such jobs rise or fall? Which is more important in your judgment: the proportion or the actual number? Why?

18. Write a sentence or two comparing the change in the proportion of native-born whites holding the two lowest kinds of jobs from 1880 to 1905 with the change in the proportion of immigrants holding such jobs from 1905 to 1915.

19. Here are several statements that purport to account for the overall lack of improvement in the occupational distribution of the immigrants from 1905 to 1915. Based on Tables 1.2 and 1.3, how plausible is each statement?

    (a) The immigrants were probably experiencing deliberate job discrimination in Steelton.

    (b) Steelton's big growth period was over by 1905; the immigrants' opportunities for advancement were severely limited by the fact that the local economy was no longer growing as vigorously as it had earlier.

(c) In ten years the immigrants couldn't be expected to have
made the gains that the native-born whites took 25 years
(1880–1905) to make.

Question 19 asks you to examine three interpretive hypotheses. A
hypothesis can be thought of as a hunch that seems plausible based on
what you know so far, but that needs further testing before its merit
can really be judged. It may be right or wrong, but it is helpful because
it offers a guide for further inquiry. In a later chapter we'll discuss
interpretive hypotheses more fully.

20.   Can you suggest a hypothesis to explain why black workers had
substantially improved their position in the Steelton labor force
by 1905 but lost ground over the next decade?

21.   A few blacks were listed in the nonmanual categories, but not
one in the skilled category in any of the three years. Suggest an
explanatory hypothesis.

Elizabeth Pleck and John Bodnar have both argued that the immigrant experience was quite varied. A historian who wants to respect
the distinctive history of the many immigrant groups (including black
Americans, who had begun to migrate to cities from the rural South)
must be open to the possibility that life for the immigrants was not the
same in Steelton as in Chicago, not the same in 1880 as in 1911, not
the same for women as for children or men, for needleworkers as for
steelworkers, for Slavs as for Italians, Poles, and blacks.

Admittedly, such findings make it much more difficult for historians
to fashion the broad generalizations that textbooks and popular surveys
depend on. By revealing something of the complexity of social patterns
in individual communities, quantitative history has shattered our clean,
neat image of life in the past. On the other hand, sweeping national
histories used to neglect the experience of immigrant workers, black
women, and others at the bottom of the social pyramid. Quantitative
methods have helped historians recover the history of specific groups
such as the Slavic immigrants of Steelton.

1.3   Who Stayed and Who Moved On?

Anthony E. Boardman and Michael P. Weber studied records from Warren Pennsylvania, another early industrial town, in order to gain a better

understanding of the processes of geographic and occupational mobility in the developing industrial cities of the late nineteenth century. "In order to understand why changes in the composition of the working force occurred," they write, "one really needs to know why some people stay, why others leave, and why new people enter a community."[6]

Table 1.4
Characteristics of workers who stayed in or left Warren, Pennsylvania, 1870–1880

| Property Status | Migration Status | |
	Stay	Leave
Low	36.11	62.71
Middle	28.33	20.34
High	35.56	16.95
(N)	180	413

Source: Based on Anthony E. Boardman and Michael P. Weber, "Economic Growth and Occupational Mobility in 19th Century Urban America: A Reappraisal," *Journal of Social History*, 11 (Fall 1977), p. 55, Table 1.

Table 1.4 is an excerpt from the first table in the Boardman-Weber article. The population consists of $180 + 413 = 593$ workers in Warren at the beginning of the 1870–80 decade. Two variables were measured on the population; we have called the variables Property Status and Migration Status.

The values of Property Status have the following meanings:

Low   = owns no property;
Middle = owns a parcel of land, a house or both;
High   = owns more than one parcel of land or more than one house.

22. Does the table say that 36.11% of the stayers were in the low-property category or that 36.11% of the low-property workers were stayers?

23. Look at Table 1.4 and comment on the hypothesis that high-propertied workers were more likely to stay than to leave.

---

[6]Anthony E. Boardman and Michael P. Weber, "Economic Growth and Occupational Mobility in 19th Century Urban America: A Reappraisal," *Journal of Social History*, 11 (Fall 1977), 52–74; quotation at 54.

Table 1.5 shows four different ways that the information in Table 1.4 might have been presented. The four methods possess the same information but some communicate better than others, depending on the point to be made. The percentages are rounded off for ease of reading.

Table 1.5
Migration data for Warren, Pennsylvania presented in four different ways

A. Numbers of Workers				B. Percentages		
Status	Stay	Leave	Total	Status	Stay	Leave
Low	65	259	324	Low	36	63
Middle	51	84	135	Middle	28	20
High	64	70	134	High	36	17
Total	180	413	593	(N)	180	413

C. Percentages				D. Percentages		
Status	Stay	Leave	(N)	Status	Stay	Leave
Low	20	80	324	Low	11	44
Middle	38	62	135	Middle	9	14
High	48	52	134	High	11	12
				(N = 593)		

Source: See Table 1.4.

Table B is the same as Table 1.4: it shows the percentage of stayers and leavers in each of the property categories. By contrast, Table C shows the percentage of low, middle, and high propertied workers in each migration category.

24.   What do the percentages in Table D mean?

In the quotation above, the authors said they were trying to explain why some people stay and others leave. Let's assume that variables such as Property Status can be taken to provide partial explanations for migration decisions.

25.   Which table, A, B, C, or D, best communicates the idea that low-property workers were several times more likely to migrate than to stay in Warren?

26.   Look at Table C and write a brief summary comment on the proposition of Question 23: that workers of high property were more
likely to stay than to leave.

1.4   Women in The Labor Force

It is much more common today for American women to work for pay
outside the home than it was at the end of the last century. Women
slowly increased their rate of participation in the labor force from 1900
to 1940; then after 1940, that rate rose enormously. What explains that
recent boom? Was it postponed marriage? High divorce rates? Fewer
children? Increased job opportunities? Valerie Kincade Oppenheimer
has written a book exploring demographic, economic, and familial factors that might help account for the change.[7]

One way to begin attacking the question is to find out just which
groups of women increased their participation and by how much. Oppenheimer says that the traditional pattern (i.e., pre-World War II) was
for young, unmarried women to work prior to marriage and that "there
was a continuous decline in labor force participation after age 30." She
later says, "While the 1940 to 1960 increases for women of all marital
statuses combined have been sizable, the increase for married women
with husbands present have been truly enormous."[8] So divorce or late
marriage don't seem to be compelling explanations.

The numbers in Table 1.6 may help you evaluate some of the explanations mentioned earlier. These statistics come from U.S. census data
and reflect the employment situation on the days the census was taken
in each year.

27.   How are the numbers in the first three columns related to the
numbers in the Percentage Change columns? For example, in the
top row of numbers, how is the number 111 under Percentage
Change related to the numbers 9 and 19 under Percentage in Labor
Force?

28.   Why don't the 1940–50 changes plus the 1950–60 changes equal
the 1940–60 changes?

29.   Contrast 1940 and 1960 with respect to the shape or pattern of
the distribution of participation rates across age groups.

---

[7]Valerie Kincade Oppenheimer, *The Female Labor Force in the United States*
(Berkeley, 1970).

[8]*Ibid.*, pp. 10, 15.

Table 1.6
Labor force participation and percentage changes by age group and census year for
married women (husband present)

Age Group	Percentage in Labor Force			Percentage Change		
	1940	1950	1960	1940–50	1950–60	1940–60
14–19	9	19	26	111	37	189
20–24	17	26	31	53	19	82
25–29	19	22	27	16	23	42
30–34	18	23	29	28	26	61
35–44	15	27	37	80	37	147
45–54	11	23	39	109	70	255
55–64	7	13	25	86	92	257
65 and over	3	5	7	67	40	133
14 and over	14	22	31	57	41	121

Source: Based on Valerie Kincade Oppenheimer, *The Female Labor Force in the
United States* (Berkeley, 1970), p. 11, Table 1.4.

Note: The three columns on the left come from Oppenheimer's book; we used them
to compute the three columns on the right. Oppenheimer used greater decimal point
accuracy and so got slightly different percentage changes.

30.   In 1960, which age group showed the greatest percentage increase
in labor-force participation since 1950? Suggest a hypothesis explaining why.

31.   Use the 14–19 group as an example, and write two sentences that
make clear the difference between: (a) the increase in the participation percentage, and (b) the percentage increase in participation.

32.   Were more women in the 25–29 group working in 1940 or in 1950?
How many more?

33.   It's a familiar notion that women get pulled into the labor force
during wartime because the men are in uniform. Does Table 1.6
offer support for that idea for World War II (1941–45)?

34.   To conclude this brief section on women in the labor force, write
a sentence or two in which you (a) identify what seems the most
striking thing in the data and (b) suggest another question for
research based on Table 1.6.

1.5   Crime Patterns or Police Priorities?

For decades, arrest rates for offenses such as disorderly conduct, drunkenness, and vagrancy have been declining in America's big cities.[9] Some historians have suggested that the decline shows that our urban centers have become more orderly since the mid-nineteenth century. Eugene J. Watts takes a different view, arguing that the arrest rates for drunkenness and disorderly behavior, as well as for prostitution, gambling, and narcotics violations, depend more on how willing the police are to tolerate such behavior than on the incidence of the behavior itself.[10]

Ever since cities created urban police departments in the nineteenth century, the police have been used as agents of social control who sweep the streets of vagrants, rowdies, prostitutes, and drunks, and also as crime fighters who identify and arrest people suspected of major crimes such as armed robbery and murder. But a police force is only so large and the officers only work so many hours per week, so they can't do everything. Emphasizing one mission tends to make it more difficult to carry out other missions. Has their role been different from time to time and place to place? Watts has examined the police department of St. Louis for evidence of a shift in police behavior from social control to crimefighting.

Tables 1.7 and 1.8 are slightly modified excerpts of a single table in Watts's article. Each row of Table 1.7 is an example of a frequency distribution; you can tell this because each row adds up to 100 percent.

35. In the first row of table 1.7, what is the population? What variable is being measured on the population? What are the values of the variable?

36. In Table 1.7, apprehensions on morals charges as a proportion of all apprehensions seem to drop over time. Does this mean that the St. Louis citizenry became better behaved?

37. Express the apprehension rates per 100,000 population for 1921–27 as rates per 1000 population. Why doesn't Watts simply list

---

[9] The arrest rate for a particular offense is usually expressed as arrests per 100,000 residents of the city.

[10] Eugene J. Watts, "Police Response to Crime and Disorder in Twentieth-Century St. Louis," *Journal of American History*, 70 (September 1983), 340–58. Watts does not deny that "public disorder" such as public drunkenness and disorderly conduct has declined since the mid-nineteenth century; he merely denies that changing arrest rates are an appropriate index of the actual behavior of people on the streets.

Table 1.7
Average annual proportions of total apprehensions, St. Louis Police Department,
1921–1948

	Proportion of Arrests for				
Period	Disorder	Morals	Major Crime	Suspicion	Other
1921–27	17.7	28.0	16.9	21.7	15.8
1928–34	21.3	28.2	10.3	14.0	26.3
1935–41	28.7	25.4	9.1	24.5	12.2
1941–48	26.3	18.2	10.0	25.7	19.8

Source: Eugene J. Watts, "Police Response to Crime and Disorder in Twentieth-
Century St. Louis," *Journal of American History*, 70 (September 1983), p. 350,
Table 1.

Table 1.8
Average annual apprehension rates, St. Louis Police Department, 1921–48
[Apprehensions per 100,000 population]

Period	Disorder	Morals	Major Crime	Suspicion	Other
1921–27	1292	2049	1235	1586	1157
1928–34	3437	4558	1668	2262	4249
1935–41	2840	2514	899	2422	1206
1942–48	1897	1311	725	1855	1431

Source: Excerpted from Watts, "Police Response to Crime and Disorder," p. 350,
Table 1.

the number of apprehensions in each crime category for each time
period?

38. Is the information in the two tables the same? Specifically, can
you compute Table 1.7 from Table 1.8? If so, how? If not, why
not? Similarly, can you compute Table 1.8 from Table 1.7?

39. In Table 1.7, apprehensions for morals offenses seem to rise hardly
at all from the first time period to the second, but in Table 1.8
there seems to be a steep jump from the 1921–27 period to the
1928–34 period. Explain how the two tables can appear to tell
different stories. Had you thought of a possibility like this when
you answered Question 36?

40. Suppose you wanted to regroup the data somewhat by combining the Morals and Disorder categories or using larger time blocks.

Would it make any sense to add the numbers across columns or rows of either Table 1.7 or Table 1.8?

One of the striking things about Table 1.8 is the fact that apprehensions are way up in almost every category in the 1928–34 period. In fact, the total apprehension rate (add up the row) is about twice the total for the other three periods shown. Notice that this flurry of recorded police activity is completely invisible in Table 1.7 because the entries in Table 1.7 are row percents. Those row percents emphasize how the apprehensions were distributed across the crime classes. In order to gain that emphasis, other patterns were sacrificed, the patterns over time within each crime category. For example, the first column of Table 1.7 does not tell you if the arrests for disorder were increasing or decreasing. Watts included the information of both Table 1.7 and Table 1.8 in a single table of his article so a reader would be able to look for patterns over time as well as within each time period.

41.   Because Tables 1.7 and 1.8 are based on only a part of Watts's evidence, they show no evidence of a shift in police priorities. To sum up this section, describe how Table 1.7 might look if it did contain clear evidence of a shift from a social control mission to crime fighting.

1.6   Conclusion

Historical data are different from the raw facts of the past. The historian gathers factual information and organizes it as data before he or she can begin to analyze it. For example, a researcher using the 1880 U.S. census of population will find that the census-takers used hundreds of job titles. The historian must group these into a few broad categories, as John Bodnar did in his book on Steelton. Deciding which category each job title belongs in is a matter of the historian's judgment. The point is that published data are at some considerable remove from the raw "facts."

Throughout Chapter 1, we've tried to show that statistical tables are arranged information: they highlight some patterns in the data while obscuring others. We've also tried to give you some practice at manipulating the data in the tables. You have done such things as finding row and column totals, changing raw numbers to percentages, organizing some of the information into new tables, and relating the data in two separate tables. Some questions also asked you to draw a conclusion or state a hypothesis based on the data in the tables.

Chapter 2 will turn from reading statistical tables to reading charts and graphs. But it will emphasize the same basic point: A show of numbers does not, in itself, make for a more convincing historical interpretation. As is true in any reading you do, you must become an active, questioning reader of statistical presentations if you want to be able to tell a strong historical argument from a weak one.

Terms Introduced in Chapter 1

1.1 population
1.1 variable
1.1 value
1.2 frequency table, frequency distribution
1.2 proportion, percentage
1.2 hypothesis
1.5 rate

1.7   Answers to Questions

1. The populations are collections of families. The table compares different populations: New York black families, Philadelphia black families, etc. (It is also reasonable to think of the entire collection of families studied as a single population, in which case Residence and Ethnic Background would be variables).

2. There are three variables: Percent of Families with Wives Working, Percent with Children Working, and Percent with Lodgers (but see the parenthetical remark in the answer to Question 1).

3. Blacks in Philadelphia have the highest value (54%) for the variable Percent [of families] with Wives Working while Russian Jews in New York City have the lowest value (1%).

4. (a) The highest proportion of wives working is only 36%, for Italian families in New York, as long as Pleck's term "immigrants" does not include black families. The other immigrant percentages fall off rapidly. Still, some readers may not be comfortable with the word "few."

(b) Between 8% and 36% of Italian wives were employed outside the home in the four cities included in Table 1.1, and these proportions match or exceed the proportions for the other immigrant groups (except blacks).

(c) In both New York and Philadelphia, over half the black wives were employed outside the home; but in the case of Italian wives, only in New York did as many as 36% work outside the home.

(d) The first part of this statement is difficult to support on the basis of Table 1.1. As for the second part, in New York the proportion of black families with lodgers exceeded the proportion for Italian families; in Philadelphia, the proportions were 41% and 16%.

5. For black families, the typical strategy to supplement the income of the husband was to have the wife take paid employment outside the home. A secondary strategy was to take in one or more lodgers. Putting the children into the work force was apparently not an option favored by blacks. In contrast, Italian immigrant families do not appear to have had a clear preference among the three methods of adding to the family income. Compared to blacks, Italians were less likely to have the wife take a job and more likely to add income from the work of one or more children in the family.

6. Black and Italian families in New York do show a greater tendency to have the wife working than their counterparts in other cities— but this does not hold for Russian Jews. For Philadelphia, the proportion of black families with the wife working is even higher than in New York—but the proportion of such Italian families is lower than in the other three cities listed. On the whole, the evidence from column 1 does not provide solid support for the idea about differences between cities. Of course, Table 1.1 wasn't intended to deal adequately with that idea.

7. Pleck argues that the evidence is consistent with such a hypothesis. About twice as high a percent of the children in Italian families as in black families held paying jobs (10% and 13% for blacks versus 19% and 25% for Italians), while the percent of wives holding paying jobs was far higher for black than for Italian families.

8. The table compares three populations: the Steelton work force in 1880, 1905, and 1915. The variable is something you might call

Occupational Level. For each year, the values are the percentages listed.

9. Eleven percent of 606 workers would be 67 skilled workers in 1880. The calculator actually shows 66.66 workers. This is the result of rounding the computations that produced the Table 1.2 percentages in the first place. If 67 workers out of 606 are skilled, that works out to 11.056106% so Bodnar rounded this off to 11%.

10. Each column of Table 1.2 adds up to 100%. In each column you see how the population of workers was distributed across the job categories (so each column is an example of a frequency distribution). It would make no sense to add the percentages across the rows of the table.

11. (a) The percentage of semiskilled workers went from 15% in 1880 to 30% in 1905, a doubling.

    (b) In 1880, 8% of the 606 workers held nonmanual jobs (6% low nonmanual and 2% high nonmanual), while in 1905, 21% of the 3338 workers held nonmanual jobs.

    (c) The decline in the proportion of the work force in the unskilled category was from 66% in 1880 to 37% in 1905, a drop of 29 percentage points. To calculate the percentage size of the decline, you divide the decline by the starting figure. That is, divide 29 by 66 to get a 44% drop in the proportion of unskilled workers between 1880 and 1905. Given the way Bodnar has been discussing the changes, he really should have reported a 44% drop in the percentage rather than a change of about 30 percentage points.

12. In 1880, 67 workers were skilled (11% of 606); in 1915, 9% of 3586 were skilled, and this works out to 323 workers. So the statement is true, because the overall size of the workforce was so much larger in 1915 than it had been in 1880.

13. In 1880, 8% of 606 or 48 workers held nonmanual jobs. In 1905, 21% of 3338 or 701 workers held nonmanual jobs, and 701 is more than 14 times as great as 48. So the statement is true.

14. Here are several such statements: The proportion of unskilled laborers in the Steelton workforce declined between 1880 and 1905 but actually rose slightly in the 1905–1915 period. The proportion

of semiskilled workers rose much more between 1880 and 1905 than between 1905 and 1915. The proportion of skilled workers did not change nearly as much in either period, though there was slightly more change in the second than in the first period. For both low nonmanual and high manual workers, the changes were more dramatic before 1905 than after. On the whole, then, greater change in the occupational distribution occurred in the 1880–1905 period than in the 1905–1915 period. Of course, those periods covered different numbers of years.

15. In 1905, 23% of native-born whites held nonmanual jobs, while 16% of Slavic and Italian immigrants held such jobs. If you glance hastily at these percentages, you might get the idea that immigrants held a pretty hefty share of the nonmanual jobs: 23% for native-born whites versus 16% for immigrants, right? But those are percentages of different base numbers. In fact, 438 whites held nonmanual jobs (23% of 1905) but only 64 immigrants (16% of 403).

16. Two blacks held nonmanual jobs in 1880. (Bodnar informs us that they were both barbers; since they were self-employed, he classified them as high nonmanual workers).

17. The proportion fell from 16% to 12%; the number rose from 64 (16% of 403) to 74 (12% of 616). There is no pat answer to the question which is more important, the proportion or the actual number; it depends on what you want to emphasize. If you want to make the point that a growing number of immigrants was making it into the ranks of the nonmanual workforce, obviously you would emphasize the actual number. If you want to make the point that immigrant workers were really not holding a larger share of the nonmanual positions, then the percentage information would be more appropriate.

18. For native-born whites, the proportion dropped from 78% in 1880 to 62% in 1905, a 20% decline. For Slavic and Italian immigrants in the 1905–15 decade, the proportion actually rose from 84% to 85%.

19. These answers represent the authors' judgment and you may disagree with them:

    (a) Certainly the discrimination explanation is possible, but from Table 1.3 alone there is no way to test this idea. Table 1.2

shows that the overall occupational distribution of the workforce changed little between 1905 and 1915, a fact that would
tend to cast doubt on this first hypothesis.

(b) Table 1.2 offers some support for this view. The overall size
of the Steelton workforce grew 7.4% in the decade, a considerably slower rate of growth than the workforce must have
enjoyed earlier.

(c) This idea has a certain plausibility, but before accepting it as
a principal explanation you would need to test other possible
explanations. This third explanation is a kind of residual one
that you can fall back on if no other interpretation seems
satisfactory.

20. If you multiply the semiskilled percentages by their N, you get the
following counts of semiskilled jobs:

	1880	1905	1915
Native-born Whites	83	705	1047
Immigrants		20	55
Blacks	3	99	84

One hypothesis is that blacks, because of racial discrimination, lost
out to the new immigrants in competition for the extra semiskilled
jobs not filled by native-born whites.

21. Remember, nonmanual workers were very likely to be independent
proprietors like the two 1880 barbers mentioned in the answer to
Question 16. That is, they may have attained their status in the
workforce by providing services to the black community in Steelton. But a skilled worker would most likely have to be hired by a
white employer, probably the Pennsylvania Steel Company. Before
or after being hired, to gain the needed skill the worker would have
had to work in an apprentice capacity with white skilled workers.
The fact that no blacks were found in the skilled category seems
strongly suggestive of job discrimination on the part of white em-
ployers and skilled workers.

22. 36.11% of the stayers were low-property workers.

23. Since 36 (really, 35.56) is bigger than 17 (16.95), it is tempting to
believe that high-property workers were more likely to stay than
to leave. But the 36 is a percentage of a smaller number (180) and

the 17 is a percentage of a larger number (413). One would have to do some arithmetic to judge the hypothesis.

24. In Table B, the columns add up to 100%; in Table C, the rows add up to 100%. In Table D, the sum of the six boxes is 100%. The numbers shown are the percentages of the entire population of 593 workers who were both low property and stayers, both low property and leavers, etc.

25. Table C seems much better than Table B at communicating the idea that low-property workers are several times more likely to migrate than they are to stay. In fact, Table B tempts the reader to the quick conclusion that low-propertied workers were less than twice as likely to leave as to stay. But, as Table C makes clear, migration was four times as probable as staying for this group.

26. Table C makes it clear that high property workers were about as likely to stay as to leave. Here the numbers are percentages of the row totals so 48 and 52 are percentages of the high-property workers who stay or leave.

27. The numbers in the Percentage Change columns express in percentage terms the amount of change from one column to the next in the Percentage in Labor Force columns. For example, in 1940 just 9% of the women in the 14–19 age group were employed while ten years later 19% of the women in that age group held employment. The change from 9% to 19% is an increase of 111%, the amount listed in the column labeled 1940–50 under Percentage Change.

28. The percentage changes in the 1940–50 column apply to different bases than the percentage changes in the 1950–60 column. For example, in the first row the change of 111% refers to the change from 9% participation in 1940 to 19% in 1950, while the 37% figure refers to the change from 19% in 1950 to 26% in 1960.

29. When the 1940 census was taken women's participation in the labor force rose to a peak in their late 20s and then fell off steadily with increasing age. In 1960 there were two peaks: a first small peak in the early 20s and a second larger one from 35 to 54.

30. Women of ages 55 to 64 had by far the largest increases in participation rate over women of those ages in 1950. First, notice that although the 55–64 group showed by far the largest increase, that age class had about the same percentage working in 1960 as several other age groups. The big percentage increase came from the fact that they started from such a small base. So one line of interpretation could be that there had been taboos against middle-aged married women's being employed; when the taboos were broken down, the middle-aged came to resemble women of other age groups. Other hypotheses are possible. Perhaps as the U.S. shifted to a service economy after World War II, more jobs were being created in fields traditionally considered "women's work." The increase in demand for women workers could have pulled this previously underemployed group into the labor force.

31. Between 1940 and 1950 the proportion of the 14–19 group that participated in the labor force rose just over ten percentage points, from 9% to 19%. Since 19 is more than twice 9, the level of participation more than doubled so the increase in the participation rate was over 100%.

32. There is no way to answer either question from this table since only percentages are given. Even though the 1950 percentage is larger, if the population of women in that age group was smaller in 1950 than in 1940, then there could have been fewer women working in 1950 than in 1940.

33. Yes. The age groups least well represented in the labor force as of 1940 (14–19, 55–64, etc.) showed the greatest percentage increase over the next decade. It's theoretically possible, but very unlikely, that all this took place between 1945 and 1950; a more likely hunch is that the growth rates for these groups was actually higher for 1940–45 (the war years) and then slipped back.

34. The most striking thing is the very rapid rate of growth in labor-force participation for women aged 35–64 over these two decades, to the point that their participation in 1960 was at about the same rate as that of younger women. Many questions remain. Why didn't the difficult economic conditions of the Great Depression bring more married women into the labor force by 1940? Does the higher proportion of married women in the labor force in 1960 challenge our image of the 1950s as the era of the Baby Boom and strong emphasis on women as homemakers? Beyond the age groupings in Table 1.5, just who were these women labor-force participants? What was their educational background, and what kinds of jobs did they find in the American economy? Were they working part-time or full-time? What proportion defined their jobs as a way to help out the family, and what proportion saw themselves as career women?

35. The population is the set of apprehensions recorded by the St. Louis Police Department for the period 1921–27. The variable might be called something like Crime Classification and the values it takes on are "Disorder," "Morals Offenses," etc.

36. Table 1.7 tells us what proportion of all apprehensions was made for each kind of offense—public disorder, morals, crimes, etc. But Table 1.7 does not show the rate of apprehensions per hundred thousand population. Remember, the proportion of arrests for one kind of offense could decline simply because the proportion of apprehensions for other offenses was rising. The sum of the proportions has to equal 100%. But let's assume that the rate of apprehensions on morals charges was also dropping. Does that show that the citizens of St. Louis were becoming better behaved? Not necessarily. As noted in the discussion before Table 1.7, the drop in recorded morals apprehensions could be due to major policy changes in the police department regarding their function; or it could be the result of trivial changes in recordkeeping rules. (Perhaps the police decided not to record an apprehension unless the person was actually booked for a crime.)

37. The rates per 1000 would be 12.92, 20.49, 12.35, 15.86, and 11.57. It would be quite misleading simply to give the number of apprehensions because the overall population of St. Louis changed from one time period to the next. If the overall number of apprehensions rose substantially (as it did from 1921–27 to 1928–34), this could have been because the population of the city rose, so that more people were at risk to be apprehended. Watts eliminates population change as a factor by giving rates per a standard number of St. Louis residents, 100,000.

38. The information is not the same. Table 1.7 shows how the apprehensions were divided up among the crime categories. It carries no information regarding the total apprehension rate. Table 1.8 could be used to compute the first table but not the other way around. For example, to compute the proportion of apprehensions for morals in 1921–27 you would add up all the apprehension rates per hundred thousand for that period (1292 + 2049 + 1235 + 1586 + 1157) to get the total apprehension rate, 7319 per hundred thousand, and then divide the morals apprehension rate by that total: 2049 / 7319 = 28.0%. But you can't work from Table 1.7 to Table 1.8 because you don't know what the base number is in Table 1.7. Morals apprehensions were 28% of ... what?

39. The overall apprehension rate was much greater in the 1927–34 period than in the 1921–27 period. But the share of apprehensions classified as morals offenses remained about the same in the two periods. Notice that the first table did not, therefore, show morals apprehensions declining at all. That would be a misreading of the first table, which is silent about changes over time within each classification and only carries information about the distribution of apprehensions within each time period.

40. You could add the numbers within a given row in Table 1.7 or Table 1.8 since the numbers within either table have the same base. In Table 1.7, all the numbers are percentages; in Table 1.8, they all are rates per hundred thousand population. Adding the numbers in a given column would make no sense, however.

41. Table 1.7 should show decreasing percentages of the department's arrests in the disorder and morals categories and increasing percentages in major crime.

2 Reading Charts and Graphs

In this chapter:

Tables aren't the only concise way to ease comprehension by compressing information. Charts and graphs can often summarize quite complicated relationships in a single image—the author's point stands in its entirety, immediate to the eye. Perhaps historians ought to use these tools even more often than they do. In this chapter we'll introduce the most common kinds of charts and graphs and give further illustrations of the points we emphasized in Chapter 1:

- Any statistical display, whether table or graph, shows the arranging hand of the historian. It may consist of numbers rather than words, but that fact by itself ought to give it no greater authority.

- Every statistical display highlights some patterns in the data but obscures others.

- It is your task as a reader to judge whether the statistical information is accurate and relevant and whether the historian draws appropriate conclusions.

- Becoming an active reader of quantitative history means being ready to poke at the data provided—playing around with a calculator, roughing out a graph on a pad of paper, doing a few mental calculations as you read along.

2.1   Life Expectancies in 1860

Many historians and social scientists used to believe that patterns of fertility, nuptuality, and mortality (birth, marriage, and death) in preindustrial Europe and the American colonies were quite different from the patterns familiar to us today. For example, it was said that people hundreds of years ago got married at very early ages, had extremely large families, and died young.

This image of the past is appealing in one important sense: it assumes that the timing of birth, marriage, and death in people's lives has changed over the centuries—that these basic events of life have a history. Demographic historians in France, England, and the United States have developed techniques to test whether most people really did marry early, have enormous families, and die young. Getting the demographic story right is important because the demographic patterns of a society do much to shape family life and the rate of population and economic growth.

The average life expectancy is an important measure of overall demographic conditions in a society. Life expectancy refers to the average number of years that a group of people born around the same time can expect to live. In a discussion of death in early America, demographic historian Maris A. Vinovskis presents Figure 2.1.[1] We'll first examine this figure as an example of a bar chart, returning later to the question of changing life expectancies in American history.

The purpose of a bar chart (sometimes called a bar graph) is to show the relationships between two variables through an easy-to-understand visual image. To create the chart, a historian begins by separating the individuals in the population into several groups that will be compared. Sometimes there is an obvious way to group the data. The historian might want to compare Italian, Polish, Irish, and black families, for example. But sometimes it isn't so easy to know the best way to group the data. That's the case with Figure 2.1. Maris A. Vinovskis was interested in comparing towns of different size, but the particular set of five groupings he used isn't the only possible way to do it.

The variable used in grouping or classifying the data is conventionally put on the horizontal axis so that the bars run vertically. In Figure 2.1, the classifying variable on the horizontal axis is population: the towns have been grouped into population categories. Notice that these categories are not all the same size. For example, the first category goes from 0 to 1000 but the fourth category goes from 5000 to 10,000.

The bars are all the same width in a bar chart; this means that the values of the variable being measured within the categories (life expectancy in this example) are proportional to the height of the bars.

---

[1] Maris A. Vinovskis, "Angels' Heads and Weeping Willows: Death in Early America," in American Antiquarian Society, *Essays in the History of the American Family*, (Worcester, Mass., 1976), pp. 273–302.

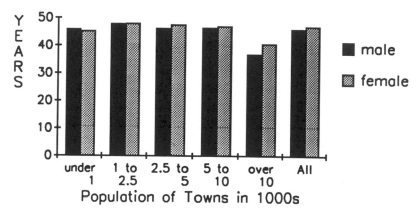

Figure 2.1
Life expectancy at birth in Massachusetts towns in 1860

Source: Maris A. Vinovskis, "Angels' Heads and Weeping Willows: Death in Early America," in American Antiquarian Society, *Essays in the History of the American Family*, (Worcester, Mass., 1976), p. 283, Figure 3.

Note: Figure 2.1 includes data on 260 towns.

1. Why do you think the author chose these particular population groupings? Why not more or fewer classes? Why not make the population range the same size in every class?

All the interesting information in Figure 2.1 is up at the top of the bars—the differences in life expectancy. Vinovskis could have emphasized those differences with a picture like Figure 2.2.

2. How does Figure 2.2 differ from Figure 2.1?

3. What are the arguments for and against Figure 2.2 as compared to Figure 2.1?

4. Demographers have sometimes argued that in preindustrial and early industrial times, life was relatively healthy in the country and unhealthy in the cities. How much support does Figure 2.1

Figure 2.2
Life expectancy at birth in Massachusetts towns in 1860

Source: See Figure 2.1

provide for this view? How would you account for the pattern that you think is suggested by Figure 2.1?

5. Does a male life expectancy at birth of around 46 mean that males born in Massachusetts in 1860 would probably die at age 46?

6. Does Figure 2.1 say that the male residents of Massachusetts in 1860 had an average life expectancy of 46 years? If not, what is it saying about those Massachusetts males of 1860?

7. Vinovskis comments that "life expectancy at birth in Massachusetts in 1860 was relatively high compared to most European countries."[2] How do you think the 1860 Massachusetts life expectancy would compare to that of the U.S. today?

8. In the U.S. today, female life expectancy is quite a bit higher than that for males, around seven years more. Why do you suppose the gender difference is so small in Figure 2.1?

_____

[2] *Ibid.*, p. 284.

9.   Figure 2.1 shows that some categories had longer life expectancies
      than others. But are the sizes of any of those differences important
      from a historical point of view?

   We've tried to emphasize that even with a simple-looking picture you
need to study it carefully: note the horizontal and vertical scales; ask
whether the differences depicted are really important. Section 2.2 gives
you additional practice with another bar chart, this one based on the
data about the workers in Steelton discussed in Chapter 1.

2.2   A Bar Chart of Steelton's Workers

Often, data presented in statistical tables might just as easily have been
presented in bar charts. Figure 2.3 presents some familiar information
on occupational distribution in Steelton, but this time as a bar chart.

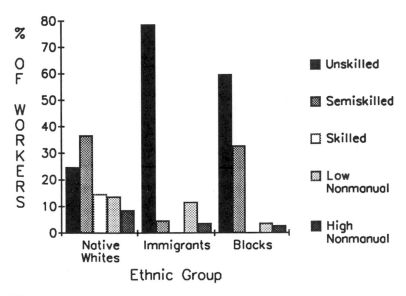

Figure 2.3
Occupational distribution of native-born whites, Slavic and Italian immigrants, and
blacks in Steelton

Source: See Table 1.3.

10.   The vertical axis in Figure 2.3 is a percentage scale. Percentages
       of what?

11.   Would it make any difference in Figure 2.3 if we changed the order
of the categories—perhaps putting blacks on the left, native-born
whites in the center, and immigrants on the right?

12.   Would it have made any difference if Vinovskis had changed the
order of the categories in Figure 2.1?

These last two questions suggest that there are different kinds of variables and that they should be handled in different ways. One important
difference between the variables in Figure 2.1 and Figure 2.3 is that
there is a natural order to numbers such as population size while the
ordering of ethnic groups is arbitrary. By arranging an ordered variable
in its natural order on the horizontal axis, one can easily spot trends—
if annual influenza rates increased with size of town, you would see an
up-sloping graph.

Variables such as Ethnic Group are called categorical variables because they divide the cases into categories, while population measured
on towns is called a numeric variable. Some categorical variables share
with numeric variables the property of having a natural order. For
example, if people are classified by wealth into groups such as poor,
moderate, and rich, then the variable Wealth is a categorical variable.
But, in contrast to Ethnic Group, the values of this categorical variable
Wealth have a natural order just as values of a numeric variable do. If
you go beyond groupings such as poor, moderate, and rich and record
the precise dollar amount of wealth for each individual, then you have
transformed Wealth into a genuine numeric variable.

We will discuss different kinds of variables more fully when we turn to
statistical procedures such as crosstabulation and correlation. For now,
note that there are both ordered and unordered categorical variables as
well as numeric variables.

13.   What type of variable is used to classify information in Figures 2.1
and 2.3?

14.   What type of variable is Life Expectancy?

15.   Give an example of an unordered categorical variable, an ordered
categorical variable, and a numeric variable; don't pick ones we
have used.

Obviously there are limits to how complex a bar chart can get. Check
back to Chapter 1 and take another look at Table 1.3. You can see that

it would be difficult to design an easy-to-read bar chart to convey all that information for 1880, 1905, and 1915.

A scholar can display information in a bar chart when one of the variables is a categorical variable, whether ordered or unordered. That was the case in both Figure 2.1 and Figure 2.3. Our next section will introduce another kind of figure, the histogram, which is used to show how concentrated a population is with respect to some variable. For example, it might show the proportion of people concentrated at each age from zero to ninety. A histogram might superficially resemble a bar chart; it's important to learn about this kind of figure so that you can properly interpret one when you encounter it. For this discussion we'll use data about the wages of Chicago working women in 1908.

2.3   Charting Women's Wages, 1908

In *Wage-Earning Women*, Leslie Woodcock Tentler studies women industrial workers in New York, Boston, Philadelphia, and Chicago in the early twentieth century. Tentler argues that women "inhabited a distinct and separate labor market, one characterized by low pay, low skill, low security, and low mobility." She shows that women workers (who were often teenagers) were usually "too shy to ask about wages when they were hired" and concludes that typical women's jobs paid half to two-thirds what men received in the same industries.[3]

In Table 2.1, Tentler presents the frequency distribution for women's wages in the men's clothing industry of Chicago in 1908. We used the data in Table 2.1 to construct the histogram shown in Figure 2.4.

At first glance, Figure 2.4 looks a lot like a bar chart. But note some important differences. First, unlike Figure 2.3, in a histogram the heights of the bars do not represent the proportion of women in each wage category. The numbers in the table tell us that 24% of the women make between $4 and $6 per week; but the top of the corresponding bar in Figure 2.4 is at 12% rather than 24%. This is because in a histogram, area, not height, stands for the percentage of cases. The base of that third bar is $2 wide (from $4 to $6) and the height is 12% per dollar. The area of a rectangle is base times height. So 12% per dollar times 2 dollars is:

$$\frac{12\%}{\$1} \times \$2 = 12\% \times 2 = 24\%.$$

[3]Leslie Woodcock Tentler, *Wage-Earning Women: Industrial Work and Family Life in the United States, 1900–1930* (New York, 1979), pp. 19, 195fn.

Table 2.1
Distribution of women's wages in the men's clothing industry, Chicago, 1908

Weekly Wage	% of Women
$0–$1.99	3%
$2–$3.99	11
$4–$5.99	24
$6–$7.99	24
$8–$9.99	19
$10–$11.99	10
$12 & up	9
Total	100%

Source: Leslie Woodcock Tentler, *Wage-Earning Women: Industrial Work and Family Life in the United States, 1900–1930* (New York, 1979), p. 190.

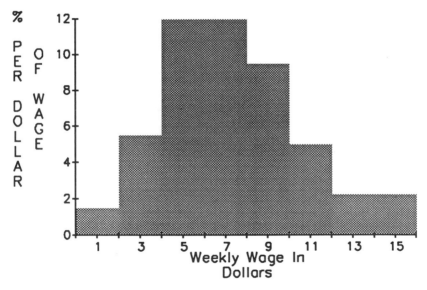

Figure 2.4
Distribution of women's wages in the men's clothing industry, Chicago, 1908
Source: See Table 2.1.

Note that 24% is the value shown in the frequency distribution. The units shown on the vertical axis of Figure 2.4 are determined by the re-

quirement that height units multiplied by width units must come out as
percent of population—area stands for percent. Percent per horizontal
unit multiplied by horizontal units comes out as percent:

$$\frac{\text{Percent}}{\text{Horizontal unit}} \times \text{Horizontal unit} = \text{Percent}.$$

Take another look at Figure 2.4. Since the last two categories of the
frequency distribution contain almost the same percentages of women
(9% and 10%), the two right-hand rectangles in the histogram should
be almost the same size. If you look at Figure 2.4, you can see that the
right-hand rectangle looks like the previous one turned on its side—the
areas are about the same.

16. Use the histogram (Figure 2.4) to find the proportion of women
who had wages between $4 and $8. Try not to look at the frequency
distribution!

17. Use the histogram to estimate the proportion of women who had
wages in excess of $10. Guess what percentage of the women
earned less than $3 per week.

18. Use the histogram to estimate the middle wage paid; that is, the
wage which half the women earned more than and half the women
earned less than.

As we have drawn it, the base of the last bar is $4 long ($12 to
$16) and the height is 2.25%, so the area is 9% ($4 times 2.25% per
dollar), again the value shown in the frequency distribution. Because a
histogram is constructed so that the area of each block is proportional
to the percentage of the population in the corresponding category, the
area under the histogram must always represent 100% of the population.

19. In the frequency distribution, the last category is $12 and over;
but we have changed it to $12–$16 for our histogram. Why did we
do something like that?

Histograms are not seen as often in published papers as other graphs
and charts, but they are an important and fundamental idea. The famous normal curve, or bell-shaped curve, is a histogram. It is area under
the bell curve that represents proportions, not the height of the curve.

One could, of course, think of the wage groupings as the categories
of a categorical variable: instead of grouping wages into intervals such

as "$2–$3.99," one could define categories called "lowest paid," "moderately paid," and "highest paid" and then make a bar chart showing the percentage of the population in each of the ordered categories. But to create a histogram, one must have categories based on some measurable attribute such as dollars, since a histogram depicts area, the product of base times height.

20.   Convert the histogram (Figure 2.4) to two bar charts, each using three wage categories as suggested in the previous paragraph:

   (a) In the first bar chart use $0 to $3, $3 to $6, and $6 & over as the three wage categories. You will have to split the area between $2 and $4 in the histogram in order to use $3 as a boundary point in your bar chart. Assign half the area between $2 and $4 to your $0–$3 category and the other half to your $3–$6 category.

   (b) In the second bar chart use $0 to $6, $6 to $12, and $12 and over as the categories.

Notice how commonsensical the class intervals seem in both (a) and (b). Imagine that you were shown just one of the bar charts. It would look in either case as though the author had divided up the horizontal axis into eminently sensible intervals. But see how different the two charts are. Clearly a naive writer or one with an axe to grind could present a striking—but misleading—visual image.

Both of the bar charts in the previous question are honest in that they report the numbers in the table reasonably accurately, provided you are also told the class boundaries. In a sense the problem is with the reader. Bar charts (a) and (b) of Problem 20 don't lie—their visual images merely tempt uncritical readers to jump to unwarranted conclusions.

21.   Convert the histogram (Figure 2.4) to a bar chart using the same boundaries that are in the histogram.

If you answered the last two questions, you understand that just as an author organizes the data in a statistical table, she controls the shape of a bar chart through the manipulation of class boundaries. The same is true for the shape of histograms. If she began with sufficiently detailed information, she could pick interval widths of a dollar, a quarter, or even one cent. But if she used one-cent interval widths, she would need 1600 intervals to get from zero up to $16. At the other extreme, if she used an interval width of $60, the entire population would fall in just one class.

Both extremes are silly. An author must choose a reasonable number of intervals, with boundaries picked so that the resulting picture honestly represents some important pattern that is actually in the underlying data.

We put one unusually wide category ($12 to $16) out at the right of Figure 2.4 instead of a couple of two-dollar categories because Tentler reported the last category as "$12 and over." We didn't know what portion of the population fell between $12 and $14. But if all the categories had been two-dollar categories, then the relative heights and areas of the bars would have been the same and Figure 2.4 would have been similar to a bar chart.

22. Suppose the last class interval had been $8 wide, i.e., $12 to $20. How tall would the histogram bar be for that interval?

23. In explaining the low wages that women received, a historian might hypothesize that women were the victims of discrimination; another hypothesis would be that women's low wages resulted from their being concentrated in unskilled jobs and was not directly because of discrimination. Can you propose a way to test these hypotheses through further quantitative analysis?

2.4 The Virginia Muster of 1624/5

In 1625, when just over 1200 persons lived in Virginia, the British authorities assumed management of the colony from the incompetent Virginia Company; as one of its first actions, the Crown ordered a census or muster of the Virginia population. In March 1622, a quarter of the settlers had died in an Indian raid. Subsequently, the population dropped still further due to food shortages and disease. The so-called Virginia Muster represented an attempt to assess the condition and prospects of the entire British effort to colonize Virginia.

A manuscript copy of the Virginia Muster survives in the Public Record Office in London, and historian Irene W.D. Hecht has analyzed it carefully to develop a profile of the struggling settlements of Virginia nearly two decades after the founding of the colony. In her article "The Virginia Muster of 1624/5 as a Source for Demographic History,"[4] Hecht presents a number of frequency distributions including the one in Table 2.2.

---

[4]Irene W.D. Hecht, "The Virginia Muster of 1624/5 as a Source for Demographic History," *William & Mary Quarterly*, 3rd ser., 30 (January 1973), 65–92.

Table 2.2
Distribution of servants in Virginia, 1624/5 [households with servants]

No. of Servants in Household	No. of Households	No. of Servants in Household	No. of Households
1	23	13	1
2	23	14	1
3	11	15	1
4	9	16	1
5	6	17	4
6	6	20	1
7	2	23	1
10	2	36	1
12	2	40	1

Total number of households with servants: 96

Total number of servants: 507

Source: Irene W.D. Hecht, "The Virginia Muster of 1624/5 as a Source for Demographic History," *William & Mary Quarterly*, 3rd ser., 30 (January 1973), p. 77, Table VI.

Note: The year is given as 1624/5 because Englishmen counted the new year as beginning in March. A date in January, February, or early March would be considered to fall in 1624 by their reckoning but 1625 by ours.

The "servants" in Table 2.2 were mostly male indentured laborers who contracted to work the land for a plantation owner for a specified amount of time (usually seven years) in exchange for passage to the New World.

24. How many servants lived in households having 13 or more servants? What proportion of servants lived in households having three or fewer servants?

25. Use Table 2.2 to answer the following questions.

(a) Table 2.2 has 18 categories. Assume you want to condense the information in the table into a smaller number of categories, say, five to eight. What categories would you use?

(b) Assume the following six categories: 1–2, 3–4, 5–6, 7–12, 13–18, 19–40. Sketch and label a bar chart in which bar height represents numbers of households.

(c) Use the categories in (b) to make a frequency distribution (a table, not a graph) showing the number of households and the percentage of households in each category. Why are the household counts and percentages almost the same?

Now we shall reveal an additional bit of information about the households of Virginia Colony. While Table 2.2 shows that 96 households had one or more servants, an additional 213 households had no servants. This presents the chart-maker with the problem of how to design a bar chart with a vertical scale running from 1 to 213.

26. What would be the problem with compressing the vertical scale so as to add a new zero-servant category to the bar chart of Problem 25 (b)? What's the best way to handle the problem?

27. From the information given in Table 2.2 and the text, what inferences can you draw about the social structure of Virginia Colony in the 1620s?

We next turn to a different sort of histogram called an age pyramid. Using data from another colonial town, Section 2.5 introduces the concept of a population's age structure and gives you some practice at analyzing this special kind of histogram. Age pyramids are probably the form in which you will most often encounter histograms in historical writing.

2.5   Age Structure and Age Pyramids

Occasionally, historians are fortunate enough to discover a list of some sort that provides a snapshot of a community at a single moment in time. The Virginia Muster is such a document, but for a number of other colonial towns there exist local censuses, lists of taxpayers and the taxes they paid, or lists of men enrolled in the militia with their ages.

In 1774, colonial officials ordered a census for the entire colony of Rhode Island. Historian John Demos has studied these census data for one Rhode Island community, the seaport town of Bristol.[5] The Bristol population was 1209, of whom 1079 were whites. Demos was able to estimate a variety of demographic statistics for Bristol, such as the average family size and life expectancy, by combining the 1774 census information with birth records showing the year of birth of many whites living in the town (about 65% of the total white population). A

---

[5] John Demos, "Families in Colonial Bristol, Rhode Island: An Exercise in Historical Demography," *William & Mary Quarterly*, 3rd ser., 25 (January 1968), 40–57.

particularly interesting part of his analysis concerned the age structure of Bristol.

In bar charts and histograms, the bars almost always run vertically. But in an age pyramid, such as Figure 2.5, the bars always run horizontally. As usual, the information could be presented in tabular form— Demos used a table, in fact. But it is often easier to grasp in the form of a picture.

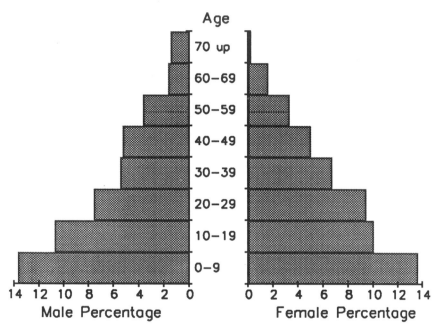

Figure 2.5
Age Structure of Bristol, Rhode Island, in 1774

Source: Based on John Demos, "Families in Colonial Bristol, Rhode Island: An Exercise in Historical Demography," *William & Mary Quarterly*, 3rd ser., 25 (January 1968), p. 53, Table VIII.

28. Satisfy yourself that an age pyramid is very similar to two histograms (one for males, one for females) set base to base. One difference is that the areas in each histogram do not add up to 100%, but the sum of the two figures is 100%. If you were to turn the female half of the age pyramid into a histogram, what label would you put on the vertical axis? How tall would you make the longest bar, the one with 13.7% of the total population?

29. The final age category in the table from which we constructed Figure 2.5 is "70 and over." What is the justification for arbitrarily cutting that category off at 79 as we have done here?

30. From Figure 2.5, roughly what proportion of the males was under ten years of age in Bristol? What proportion of the females was between 20 and 49? For people 60 and over, what is the size of the gap between the proportion of men and that of women? Which sex has a larger proportion of its members in the 60 and over category?

An age pyramid is a demographic snapshot of a population at a particular moment in time. Actually, the pyramid is not static. You can think of each half of the pyramid as a kind of escalator. As time passes, the members of each age group move upward toward the top of the pyramid—the teenagers move into the 20s, and so forth. The mortality and fertility conditions of the community as a whole determine the length of the bars at each age-level. But note that if you constructed a pyramid for Bristol in 1774 and another pyramid in, say, 1794, the second pyramid would not comprise exactly the same individuals as the first. Some 1774 residents of various ages would have moved away and some newcomers would have moved in. So while the pyramid describes the relative size of age-groups, the individuals in those groups may come and go.

The terms mortality and fertility refer to the rates of death and birth in a community or society. From Section 1.5, remember that a rate is defined as the number of events in a period of time divided by the population at risk to experience the event. So a mortality rate would be the number of deaths in a year divided by the population. Since men, young girls, and older women are not at risk to give birth, the fertility rate is often calculated as the number of births in a year divided by the number of women aged 15–45. Demographers also calculate age-specific fertility and mortality rates—for example, the mortality rate for males aged 60–64 would be the number of deaths of males aged 60–64 divided by the total number of males in that age-group.

31. Explain how an increase in mortality among middle-aged men or an increase in fertility would cause the bar representing men 50–59 to shrink.

32.   In a preindustrial society with high mortality among infants and
children, there might be quite a gap between the bottom bar and
the one just above it. Can you suggest two possible explanations
for such a pattern?

In a twentieth-century industrial society where most children survive
to adulthood, successive bars near the bottom of the pyramid will shrink
only a small amount. In fact, a bar can actually be longer than the one
just below it. But mortality will take a more and more severe toll as age
increases; as this happens, the top bars shrink toward zero.

33.   What could cause a bar in an age pyramid to be longer than the
one just below it?

By way of contrast with the Bristol age pyramid for 1774, Figure 2.6
presents the age pyramid for the entire United States in 1978. The next
few questions ask you to compare the two age pyramids. But be aware
that the sex ratio and perhaps also the age structure of Bristol were
not representative of the American colonies as a whole on the eve of
the American Revolution. Overall, the white population of Bristol was
53.3% female in 1774. This would be a typical pattern for an established
community now far removed from the frontier, but not for the colonial
population as a whole.

34.   What proportion of the Bristol population was under 20 years
of age in 1774? How would you account for the difference between that proportion and the corresponding number for the U.S.
in 1978?

35.   What proportion of the population was 60 and over in the U.S. in
1978? Again, how would you explain the difference between that
number and the Bristol proportion?

36.   Make a rough estimate of the median age of the population in
Bristol in 1774 and in the U.S. in 1978. (The median is the middle
age, so that half the population is younger and half older than the
median age.)

37.   Knowing that Bristol had been in existence for over a century
and was a long way from the frontier of settlement in the colonies,
would you predict that the town's population had a higher median
age than a frontier settlement or a lower? Why?

38.   Write a paragraph summarizing the main characteristics of the white population's age structure in Bristol; compare Bristol with the U.S. in 1978 when appropriate.

In the next section, we use an article discussing crowding on eighteenth-century slave ships to introduce a very commonly encountered kind of statistical display called the line graph. We'll briefly examine several different kinds of line graphs, some of which may be new to you.

2.6   Crowding on Slave Ships, 1790s

What conditions did newly captured slaves encounter as they crossed the Atlantic from Africa to the New World colonies? How big were

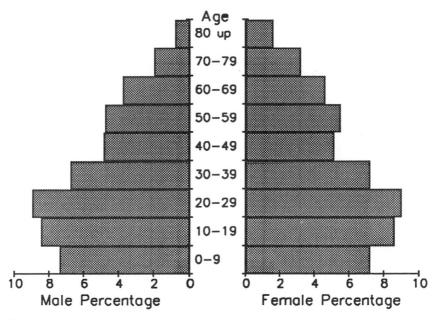

Figure 2.6
Age Structure of the United States in 1978

Source: U.S. Department of Commerce, Bureau of the Census, *1980 Census of Population*, Vol. 1: *Characteristics of the Population*, Chapter B, Part 1: "United States Summary," Table 44, pp. 1–37, 1–38 (Washington: GPO, May 1983).

these slave ships, and how much space was each slave allotted? Did the captains of slave ships deliberately pack their human cargo as tightly into their vessels as they could?

Historians of the African slave trade have raised such questions repeatedly. Unfortunately, little is known about the dimensions and other construction details of the sailing ships that carried Africans to the colonies. In eighteenth-century reports and debates, the one bit of information that is regularly reported is the tonnage of ships. Most accounts therefore relate the number of slaves on board a ship to the tonnage of the ship—but tons per slave is an unsatisfactory measure of the actual space available for each slave.

Recently Charles Garland, a naval architect, and Herbert S. Klein, a historian, have examined this problem using information about 48 British slave ships of the 1790s. Their principal purpose was to develop some estimate of the amount of square footage that each slave was allotted on these voyages. Garland and Klein also note that a 1799 act of Parliament, the Dolben Act, decreed that each slave should have a minimum of eight square feet. How well did British slave-ships measure up to that standard (a horrendously low one, to be sure)?[6]

We have grouped the authors' data on the 48 ships into categories by tonnage. First consider Figure 2.7, a bar graph showing how many slaves traveled in ships of various tonnages.

39. About what proportion of the ships was between 101 and 250 tons?

40. Roughly what proportion of the slaves was transported on those ships between 101 and 250 tons?

You can convert this bar graph to a line graph by drawing lines connecting the top centers of the bars and then erasing the original figure. It is clear from the method of construction that this line graph, called a frequency polygon (Figure 2.8), will look quite a bit like the corresponding bar graph. In both, the variation on the vertical axis is shown by height.

A less trivial modification of the bar graph can be obtained by accumulating the numbers of slaves (adding them up) as you go. In tabular form, this procedure yields Table 2.3.

---

[6] Charles Garland and Herbert S. Klein, "The Allotment of Space for Slaves aboard Eighteenth-Century British Slave Ships," *William & Mary Quarterly*, 3rd ser., 42 (April 1985), 238–48.

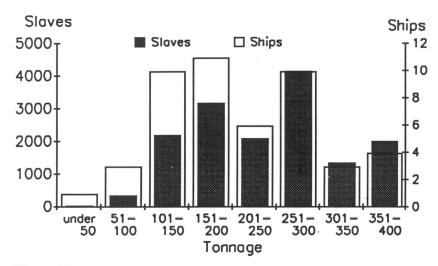

Figure 2.7
Number of slaves carried on 48 British slave ships of different tonnage categories,
1790s

Source: Based on Charles Garland and Herbert S. Klein, "The Allotment of Space for
Slaves aboard Eighteenth-Century British Slave Ships," *William & Mary Quarterly*,
3rd ser., 42 (April 1985), pp. 244–46, Table III.

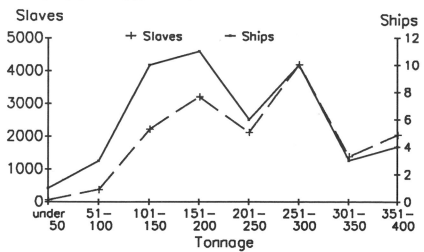

Figure 2.8
Number of slaves carried on 48 British slave ships of different tonnage categories,
1790s

Source: See Figure 2.7.

Table 2.3
Cumulative frequency distributions for numbers of ships and slaves in each tonnage category

Tonnage	No. ships	Cum. no. ships	Cum. % ships	No. slaves	Cum. no. slaves	Cum. % slaves
under 50	1	1	2.1	52	52	0.3
51–100	3	4	8.3	373	425	2.7
101–150	10	14	29.2	2207	2632	17.0
151–200	11	25	52.1	3195	5827	37.6
201–250	6	31	64.6	2111	7938	51.2
251–300	10	41	85.4	4174	12112	78.1
301–350	3	44	91.7	1367	13479	86.9
351–400	4	48	100.0	2029	15508	100.0
totals	48			15508		

Source: See Figure 2.7.

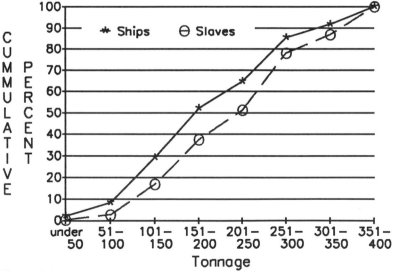

Figure 2.9
Cumulative percentage of ships and slaves in each tonnage category

Source: See Table 2.3.

41. From Figure 2.9 estimate what proportion of the slaves were transported on ships of 300 tons or less.

42. Explain why a cumulative frequency polygon (graph) like Figure 2.9 is at height zero on the left side of the graph and rises to 100 but no higher on the right.

43. Could a cumulative frequency graph ever slope downward from left to right? Could it ever be flat after it starts to rise? What causes its slope to be steeper in some places than others?

The idea behind a cumulative frequency polygon such as the ones depicted in Figure 2.9 is that the height of each point on the graph represents the cumulative proportion of all cases occurring in categories at and to the left of that point.

The data we have presented to this point do not really address our initial question. What did tonnage imply about the deck area available for each slave? Garland and Klein used Lord Liverpool's roster of 48 slave ships because he provided unusually detailed information about their dimensions; they were therefore able to work out an estimate of the total deck area of each ship. The details need not concern us here; the important thing is that they come out with an estimate of the square footage available to each slave on each of the 48 ships (Table 2.4).

Table 2.4
Area per slave in ships of different tonnage categories

Tonnage	No. ships	No. slaves	Area per slave in sq. ft.
under 50	1	52	11.8
51–100	3	373	7.1
101–150	10	2207	5.7
151–200	11	3195	5.4
201–250	6	2111	5.4
251–300	10	4174	5.0
301–350	3	1367	5.0
351–400	4	2029	5.1
totals	48	15508	5.3

Source: Based on Garland and Klein, "The Allotment of Space," pp. 244–46, Table III.

44. Out of the 48 ships, how many provided at least the minimum deck space required by the Dolben Act?

45. Draw a bar chart titled "Proportion of slaves with different amounts of deck space." Choose a set of categories for area per slave and show those on the horizontal axis. On the vertical axis, show proportion of slaves in those deck-space categories. Notice that the proportion of slaves enjoying the minimum area required by the Dolben Act is even smaller than the proportion of ships meeting those requirements.

2.7 Time Spent in Housework

Many people believe that "labor-saving technology" has liberated American homemakers from much of the drudgery of housework and meal preparation in the twentieth century. The homemaker no longer has to make clothes for the family or preserve foods for the winter months. And now that electricity is available in almost all homes, homemakers have an array of modern appliances at their command—refrigerators and electric ranges, clothes washers and dryers, vacuum cleaners. In addition to changes in household technology, the chores of child-rearing are presumably lighter because the typical American family includes fewer children than a century ago. It stands to reason, then, that homemakers must spend less time in housework than their great-grandmothers did; technology has done much to liberate women for jobs and other activities outside the home.

But is this really so? Social scientist Joann Vanek tested this popular belief about technology and the homemaker by gathering data on homemakers' actual use of their time.[7] She discovered that quite a number of research studies in home economics, dating back as far as the 1920s, had gathered statistical information on this very question. Figure 2.10 summarizes the main findings of these studies.

A set of data ordered chronologically is known as a <u>time series</u>. In a time series, a long-term rise or fall in the line is called a <u>trend</u>, while short-term, irregular rises or falls are known as <u>fluctuations</u>. Fluctuations that recur at regular intervals are called <u>cycles</u> or cyclic fluctuations.

When historians want to present time-series data, they often do so by means of line graphs, as in Figure 2.10. This figure actually represents changes in the average amount of time spent by women in five major household tasks; thus it includes five time series. Notice that the hor-

---

[7] Joann Vanek, "Time Spent in Housework," *Scientific American*, 231 (November 1974), 116–20.

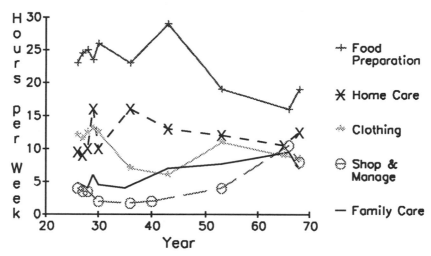

Figure 2.10
Time spent in housework by nonemployed American women, 1926–68

Source: Joann Vanek, "Time Spent in Housework," *Scientific American*, 231 (November 1974), p. 119.

izontal axis is marked in years. Why would a historian make such a graph? We think the answer will become evident as you consider the following questions:

46. From Figure 2.10, does it appear that Joann Vanek has information on women's use of time for each year from 1926 to 1968? For how many years does she appear to have data? What are the years?

47. For the five domestic activities graphed in Figure 2.10, about how much total time was spent in 1926? In 1968? Try a year in between, too—1936, 1943, or 1953 perhaps.

48. In Figure 2.10, identify one household task where the trend was downward from 1926 to 1968 and one where the trend was toward more time spent. How would you account for the fluctuation in the "Food Preparation" line in the early 1940s?

49. Statistical displays often raise questions that need to be answered. For the three tasks that actually were taking more time in the late 1960s than in the mid-1920s, formulate some suggestions as to why there might have been an increase rather than a decrease.

An important point about Figure 2.10 is that a historian doesn't need data for every year in order to develop a useful time series. Vanek has only a few points, but they are sufficient to demonstrate her most dramatic finding: that the total number of hours per week that nonemployed women spent on housework rose slightly from the 1920s to the late 1960s. Of course, it would be helpful to have more points from more time-budgeting studies. The more such studies, the more of a check we have on the overall findings of the historian. Also, more studies might reveal interesting peaks and valleys in the lines. What happened as more consumer appliances became available in the years after World War II, for example?

50.   What would be the bare minimum number of points this particular study could get away with, in your judgment?

Figure 2.10 leaves us with an interesting puzzle. If the time nonemployed women spend in housework did not drop significantly, what about the millions of married women who began to earn outside income through part-time or full-time jobs in the postwar era? How much time did they spend in housework, and how did the housework get done? Vanek mentions one interesting statistic: in the late 1960s, employed women spent only 26 hours per week in housework. She suggests several hypotheses: the homes of employed women were maintained at a lower standard of order and cleanliness; husbands shared the housework with their employed wives; with their earned income, employed wives were able to purchase more labor-saving technological devices (microwave ovens) and services (day-care, paid housekeepers); nonemployed women were spending far more time in housework than they really needed to, perhaps as a way to call attention to the importance and dignity of their household work.

2.8   Conclusion

Chapter 2 has covered a lot of ground: we have introduced bar charts, histograms, and line graphs, as well as two specialized applications of those figures, the age pyramid and the time series. In the process of covering those topics, we have also introduced several important concepts from the field of demography: life expectancy, age pyramid, and fertility and mortality rates. Our overall point really hasn't changed from Chapter 1. It is that you, the reader, must study tables, charts, and graphs with a questioning and even somewhat skeptical outlook.

In Chapter 3 we stay with descriptive statistics, but our focus changes from displays of data to ways of summarizing the information in a body of data using single numbers such as means, medians, and standard deviations.

Terms Introduced in Chapter 2

2.1 bar chart
2.1 demography
2.1 life expectancy
2.2 categorical variable, both ordered and unordered
2.2 ordinal variable
2.2 numeric variable
2.3 histogram
2.5 age pyramid
2.5 mortality and fertility rates
2.6 line graph
2.6 frequency polygon
2.6 cumulative frequency distribution
2.7 time series
2.7 trend
2.7 fluctuation
2.7 cyclic fluctuation
2.9 cohort

2.9   Answers to Questions

1. The study covers 260 towns. We speculate that Vinovskis divided the smaller communities into several categories so as to demonstrate to the reader that these categories don't make much difference—that the only really significant difference is between the cities of 10,000 or greater population and everywhere else. One reason he couldn't make the population ranges the same for all categories is that the last category, 10,000 and up, included Boston—which had over 100,000 people in 1860.[8]

2. Figure 2.2 essentially magnifies the part of Figure 2.1 where differences among the bars may be seen—between 37 and 49 on the

---

[8]See Maris A. Vinovskis, "Mortality Rates and Trends in Massachusetts Before 1860," *Journal of Economic History*, 32 (March 1972), 194–213, at 211.

vertical axis—and cuts off the rest of the bars. Notice that the vertical scale begins at 37, not at zero.

3. Figure 2.2 does bring out the differences among the bars more dramatically; but the casual reader might miss the fact that only the top bit of each bar is shown. Figure 2.2, in our judgment, creates a misleading impression about the degree of difference in life expectancies from one size place to another in Massachusetts. For example, unless you pay close attention to the numbers on the vertical scale, you might conclude that the life expectancy for women in towns under 1000 was more than twice as great as for women in towns over 10,000. In general, as we note in the text, the differences depicted in a bar chart ought to be proportional to the height of the bars. Figure 2.2 violates that principle.

4. If a city is defined as a place with 10,000 or more population, then Figure 2.1 provides some support for this view. For both sexes, the life expectancy at birth in Massachusetts towns of 10,000 and up was several years lower than the life expectancy in smaller places. [9] A possible explanation for the lower life expectancy in larger towns would focus on public health. We can speculate that with people crowded close to one another, there would have been problems with polluted drinking water and easy spread of contagious diseases.

5. Life expectancy at birth can be defined in this way: one thousand men born in Massachusetts in 1860 could expect to live a total of 46,400 years, or an average of 46.4 years per man (see the left-hand bar in Figure 2.1). This does not mean that most would die at age 46; probably very few would die at 46. In fact, some would die in infancy and some at every age from 1 to 100. Nor would half the men die before age 46 and half after. Rather, if you averaged the ages at which these 1,000 men died (by adding up their ages at death and dividing by 1,000), the average would be 46.4. For more on averages (means), see Chapter 3.

6. Figure 2.1 is saying that males born in 1860 had a life expectancy of about 46 years. Males born earlier, say in 1820 or 1830, and living in the state in 1860, might have had quite different life expectancies at birth. (A group of people sharing a common experience at the same point in time, such as birth in 1860, is known in demography as a cohort.)

---

[9] *Ibid.*, 210.

7. An American male born in 1978 had a life expectancy at birth of 69.5 years; a female, one of 77.2 years.[10] So life expectancy at birth in Massachusetts in 1860, while high compared to European countries, was low compared to the U.S. today. The point is that there is no absolute standard for "high" or "low"; these terms take on meaning only when you can compare one population with another.

8. One hypothesis would be that women died in childbirth at much higher rates in 1860 than they do today.

9. The only difference that looks very important is that between towns of 10,000 and up and any other group of towns. But the difference between, say, a life expectancy for males of 46.2 and one of 46.8 doesn't appear very important. One reason is that these figures could be off by a little bit due to misreporting of data. The number "46.2" looks very precise, but you are probably safer to read it as "around 46."

10. Each bar represents a percentage of all workers in that ethnic or racial group. So the tallest bar in Figure 2.3 says that about 79% of immigrant workers were unskilled. In effect, Figure 2.3 presents three bar charts side by side.

11. No, it wouldn't make any difference; there is no logical progression or sequence for these three ethnic/racial categories.

12. In that case it made sense to order the categories as Vinovskis did. There is a logical sequence from small to middle-sized to larger towns, though you could still read the chart if the bars were in a different order.

13. In Figure 2.1 we have an ordered categorical variable (sometimes called an ordinal variable); in Figure 2.3, an unordered categorical variable (sometimes called a nominal variable).

14. Life Expectancy is an example of a numeric variable.

15. Unordered categorical: An individual's political party preference (Democratic or Republican); whether he or she is literate (yes or no); whether he or she is over 21 years of age (yes or no).

---

[10]U.S. Department of Commerce, Bureau of the Census, *Current Population Reports*, Series P-23: Special Studies, No. 138: "Demographic and Socioeconomic Aspects of Aging in the United States" (August 1984), p. 48.

Ordered categorical: An individual's opinion about a policy of the government (strongly support, moderately support, neutral, moderately oppose, strongly oppose); his or her degree of literacy (cannot write name, can write name, can write name and read at 3rd-grade level, can write name and read at 8th-grade level); his or her age-group (child, teenager, young adult, middle adult, young-old, old-old).

Numeric: The number of acres of land an individual owns or has improved; the number of children in a family; the individual's age in years.

16.   48% had wages between $4 and $8:

$$(\frac{12\%}{\$1} \times \$2) + (\frac{12\%}{\$1} \times \$2) = 24\% + 24\% = 48\%.$$

17.   For over $10, $(5\%/\$1 \times \$2) + (2.5\%/\$1 \times \$4) = 10\% + 10\% =$ about 20%; the actual figure is 19%.

To make the under $3 guess, visually split the second area in half and add it to the first. You would get a guess of around 9% (8.5% is correct).

18.   The middle (median) wage falls in the $6–7.99 category, probably about halfway through it, so the middle wage was about $7.

19.   Each category in a histogram must be a finite interval; otherwise it would not be possible to calculate the height of the bar. We think that only a negligible proportion of the women shop workers earned more than $16 per week, if any did at all. Hence it seems okay to cut the category off at $16 since few, if any, workers would be incorrectly categorized. But this is a judgment call on our part.

20a.   % Women in wage classes

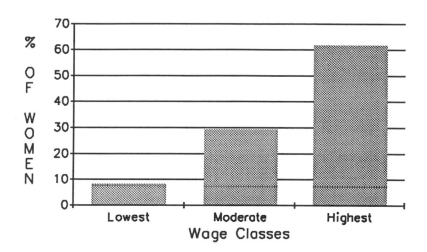

20b.   % Women in wage classes

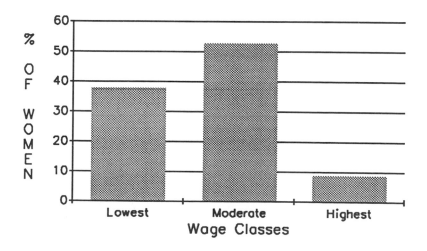

21.   Women's pay

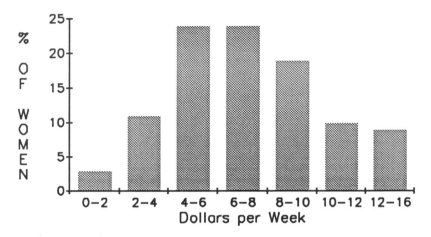

22.   If the last interval extended from \$12 to \$20, the bar would be twice as wide as in Figure 2.4 so it ought to be half as high to keep the area the same. Dividing 2.25 by 2 gives 1.125. Note that eight dollars wide times a height of 1.125% per dollar does give an area of 9%.

23.   You could eliminate the effects of skill level by comparing only women and men who had very similar jobs requiring the same amount of skill. If you still found that women's wages were substantially lower, this would be strong evidence of discrimination.

24.   245 servants lived in households having 13 or more servants $(13 + 14 + 15 + 16 + (4 \times 17) + 20 + 23 + 36 + 40 = 245)$. Of the 507 servants, 20.1% lived in households having three or fewer servants $(23 + (2 \times 23) + (3 \times 11) = 102$ servants, and $102 \div 507 = 20.1\%)$.

25.   **(a)** One possibility is 1–2, 3–4, 5–7, 10–15, 16–23, and 36–40.

(b) Servants in Households

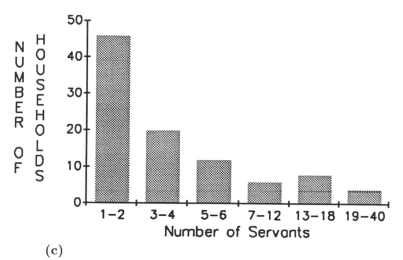

(c)

No. of Servants in Household	No. of Households	Percent of Households
1–2	46	48
3–4	20	21
5–6	12	13
7–12	6	6
13–18	8	8
19–40	4	4

The household counts and percentages are similar only because the population size 96 (the number you divide by to get the percent) is very close to 100.

26. If you compressed the vertical scale, you would also be squeezing down the other bars so that many would hardly be visible at all and it would be difficult to tell the difference between bars one or two units high or between bars nine and eleven units high. One solution to the problem is to do as Irene W.D. Hecht did and simply omit the information about households with no servants. As long as the text of the article includes the information, the reader is not misled. Another solution would be to begin drawing the vertical bar for "no servants" but to end it with an arrow pointing upward and a note explaining that it goes up to 213.

27. The information strongly suggests extreme variation in wealth. A few households had large numbers of servants while two-thirds of the households had none. Also, the colony had two persons classified as servants for every three non-servants. We know this because 1200 persons lived in the colony of whom 507 were servants.

28. Since you want to produce a histogram, the vertical axis must be percent per unit of the variable shown on the horizontal axis. In this case it would be percent per year of age. If you are working with just the left half of the population pyramid you have to adjust for the fact that the histogram applies only to males and the area under the histogram has to be 100%. If you add up all the male percentages, you find that 49.7% of the total population was male. 13.7 divided by 49.7 is 27.6%, the proportion of the males in the youngest category. Thus the area of the first bar must be 27.6%; and since it is ten years thick, its length must be 2.76% per year of age.

29. As with the earlier histogram depicting women's wages (Figure 2.4), we need to have a finite interval; by convention, the intervals in an age pyramid are of equal width, usually ten years. Very few people are misclassified by assuming that all those 70 and over were under 80.

30. In the portion of Bristol's white population included in this age pyramid, the sexes are about evenly divided, so we'll assume a 50–50 split. We see that males under ten comprised 13.7% of the population, so they comprised about 27.4%(13.7×2) of the male population alone. Similarly, females 20–49 comprised 21.1% of the total population and about 42.2% of the female population. Males 60 and over represented 3.2% of the total population, and 1.7% of the total population is females 60 and over; so the gap is $(3.2 - 1.7)$ or 1.5%. But you could express the gap more dramatically by saying that there were nearly twice as many males 60 and over as women (3.2 is nearly twice as large as 1.7). (Actually, Demos in the article on Bristol points out that the sex ratio for the entire white population was 504 men to 575 women—women comprising 53.3% of the population. So women are underrepresented in the sample of 701 individuals included in the age pyramid, where they comprise only 50.4%).

31. If the population experienced a rise in mortality among middle-aged men, some of the men 50–59 would die and the proportion of this group in the larger population would decline. Less obviously, an increase in fertility would raise the proportion of the population in the youngest age-category. Since the sum of all the proportions has to equal 100%, if one gets bigger, the others get smaller.

32. This might happen because many people die in childhood, or because the fertility rate for the community had suddenly risen so that this higher rate was apparent only for the youngest age-group. The first explanation is more plausible since mortality rates for infants and children tended to be high in preindustrial communities while fertility in the eighteenth century, being uncontrolled, probably would not change suddenly.

33. A decline in fertility would be one possibility.

34. In 1774, (13.7 + 10.8 + 13.6 + 10.0) or 48.1% of the population was under 20. In the U.S. in 1978, 32.0% of the population was under 20. The much higher proportion of young people in the 1774 Bristol population was due to the higher fertility rate of Bristol.

(An interesting sidelight is that the proportion of young people would have been higher still if Bristol had enjoyed the mortality conditions that prevail in the U.S. today. An improvement in mortality conditions from better diet or the control of contagious diseases historically benefited infants and children more than adults since the young were most at risk to die of malnutrition or such dangerous diseases as measles and smallpox. Other things being equal, a decline in fertility lowers the proportion of young people in a population while a decline in mortality raises the proportion.)

35. In 1978, 15.7% of the U.S. population was 60 and over while only 4.9% of the Bristol population in 1774 was 60 and over. The population of Bristol had a shorter life expectancy than we enjoy today, but it also had a higher fertility rate. A high fertility rate tends to mean that a high proportion of the population will be found in the lower age-groups.

36. For Bristol in 1774, 48.2% of the population was 0–19 years of age so the median age was about 20. For the U.S. in 1978, 49.7% of the population was 0–29 years of age so the median age was probably about 30.

37. A reasonable prediction would be that an older town like Bristol would have a higher median age than a frontier settlement. The frontier attracted the young, not the old.

38. A pyramid heavily loaded toward the bottom, like Bristol's in 1774, indicates that a high proportion of the population is in the youthful age-categories. So the average age in Bristol would have been lower than the average age for the U.S. population in 1978. A second interesting feature of the Bristol pyramid is that in age groups 20–29 and 30–39 one notes an excess of women, but this more or less disappears for those in their 40s, 50s, and 60s. In the oldest age group, there is a heavy excess of males. Again, the contrast with the U.S. in 1978 is striking. The reasons for these disparities would have to be sought in the history of migration into and out of Rhode Island.

39. Twenty-seven of 48 ships, or 56%, fell in the range from 101 to 250 tons. If you said "a little more than half" or something like that, that is an excellent estimate from a bar graph.

40. The proportion transported on these ships was 48.4%; again, "a little less than half" would be an excellent estimate.

41. The correct answer is 78.1%; if you said something like "three-quarters," that's fine.

42. A cumulative frequency polygon starts at height zero somewhere on the left because no matter what your horizontal categories are, for a finite population there will be some number small enough so that no cases are included to the left of that number. For example, in Figure 2.9, zero percent of ships displaced minus ten tons or less. The graphs rise only when you get your first cases between zero and fifty tons. Since the vertical scale represents percentages, clearly you can't go past 100%.

43. A cumulative frequency polygon can only rise or stay flat because you keep adding to what you have already accumulated as you move from left to right. The graph is flat as you cross categories with zero cases. The slope of the graph is steepest as you encounter categories containing the largest percentages of the cases.

44. One ship.

45.   Area per Slave

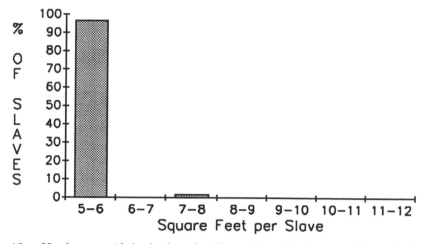

46.   No, because if she had such information, the lines would probably
have a more jagged quality with more peaks and valleys. For the
top line (time spent in food preparation), Vanek appears to have
data for 1926, 1928, 1929, 1930, 1936, 1943, 1953, 1966, and 1968
(and perhaps 1927). The line was simply drawn from one point
to the next. Some of the other lines in Figure 2.10 seem based on
studies done in a different set of years, but in no case does Vanek
have more than eight or nine points from which to plot a line.

47.   It appears that in 1926 women spent about 4 hours per week in
shopping and managerial tasks, 4.5 in family care, 9.5 in home
care, 12 in clothing and linen care, and 23 in food preparation for
a total of 53 hours. In 1968 the total comes out to about 53.5
hours, at least as we read the graph. To take one intermediate
point, the year 1953, we get $4 + 7.5 + 11 + 11.5 + 19 = 53$ hours.
These estimates may be off a bit; the point is that there has been
no drastic decline overall.

48.   Food Preparation and Clothing & Linen Care show downward
trends; the trends for the other three tasks are upward. The jump
in time spent on food preparation during the early 1940s coin-
cides with World War II; a hypothesis might be that some prepared foods, as well as kitchen appliances and implements, were
not readily available during wartime so that women had to revert
to older practices of food preparation.

49. The three activities taking more time were home care, family care, and shopping and managerial tasks.

    (a) For home care, homes are larger and standards of cleanliness may be higher today; homemakers are less likely to have paid domestic servants than they did in the 1920s.

    (b) For family care, Vanek suggests that standards of child care have risen since World War II: "Today's mother is cautioned to care for the child's social and mental development in addition to the traditional concerns of health, discipline and cleanliness."[11]

    (c) Shopping and managerial tasks is the category showing the greatest percentage change, a doubling in time spent from the 1920s to the late '60s. People's larger discretionary incomes, the great variety of products on the market, and the expansion of advertising may all have contributed to women's spending more time at shopping. Certainly the notion of women as the principal family consumers has become embedded in American life. Also, it may take women longer to reach the goods they want to buy. The neighborhood market has become a thing of the past; peddlers no longer bring their wares down the street. Instead, women drive from store to store or to suburban shopping centers.

50. Two points, for 1926 and 1968. But then we could only see the change from 1926 to 1968 and could say nothing about fluctuations in between. The intervening years could show steady rise or such large fluctuations that the observed difference between 1926 and 1968 would seem tiny.

---

[11] Vanek, "Time spent in Housework," p. 117.

3 Mean, Median, and Standard Deviation

In this chapter:

As an alternative to printing an entire table of data or displaying its features with a graph, authors often try to capture the most essential features of a distribution by using just one or two summary numbers. You can see the intellectual gain if just a couple of numbers can abstract out the critical idea from a large, complicated array. The purpose of this chapter is to explain the most commonly used of such summaries. Those single-number summaries will be introduced in the context of historical examples so you can see not only how the summaries are calculated but also how they can be used to aid historical interpretation. The main points will be:

- Averages are often used to compare different groups. However, averages can sometimes mislead if they are used alone; it is always necessary to be clear about both the variable being averaged and the variable over which the average is taken.

- It is very useful to know how data are spread out around the average. An important measure of spread, called the standard deviation, reports a representative distance between data points and the average. The range of values for a variable (the distance from the smallest to the greatest value) and the square of the standard deviation, called the variance, are also measures of spread.

- Index numbers often replace the real variable of interest when one wishes to track changes over time.

- Medians are similar in some ways to what is usually called the average, but the information they report is different enough that they should sometimes be used instead of the average, and often would provide a useful supplement to the average.

The first section introduces the most familiar number in statistics, the common average, also called the mean.

3.1   Workers' Incomes in 1910

In Chapter 1 we gave some examples of the dynamic character of historical images—how new research can modify or overthrow previously accepted pictures of the past. In particular we discussed the image of the new industrial city as destroyer of immigrant culture. To continue that theme a bit, we return now to the book on Steelton, Pennsylvania, by John Bodnar. Bodnar challenges the idea that there was a standard process that immigrant groups experienced: first the destruction of familiar ways and values, and then the opportunity for social mobility and full participation in the larger community. Instead, he believes that immigrants simultaneously defended their heritage and accommodated to a relatively static, immobile social structure "by fabricating ethnic communities which enabled them to define a place for themselves in the industrial town."[1]

Table 3.1 is one example of the kinds of materials with which Bodnar builds his case that Steelton offered immigrant workers little opportunity for upward mobility. Bodnar uses the table to suggest that background overwhelmed individual traits and skills in determining wages. For example, compare the average earnings of German and Serbian immigrants. Bodnar takes the persistence of such wage patterns (and also of job classifications) decade after decade to be evidence against the theory that immigrants participated in a common labor pool with non-immigrant workers.

1.   What proportion of the workers in Table 3.1 could be classified as Eastern European immigrants?

2.   How do the earnings of workers with northern European backgrounds (immigrants or those with foreign fathers) compare to earnings of workers with southeastern European heritages?

In order to weigh Bodnar's evidence, you need to understand averages, particularly the limitations of averages. The averages shown in this table

---

[1] John Bodnar, *Immigration and Industrialization: Ethnicity in an American Mill Town, 1870–1940* (Pittsburgh, 1977), p. xix.

Table 3.1
Average yearly earnings in Steelton by nativity, 1910

	Average Earnings	Number of Workers
Native-born white with native father	$ 402	46
Native-born white with foreign father		
English	556	21
German	426	34
Irish	504	38
Foreign-born		
Irish	457	20
German	324	104
Bulgarian	179	46
Slovenian	381	48
Croatian	256	123
Serbian	175	112

Source: John Bodnar, *Immigration and Industrialization: Ethnicity in an American Mill Town, 1870–1940* (Pittsburgh, 1977), p. 159, Table A.

are <u>means</u>. There are several kinds of <u>averages</u> so we need different names for them, but most people are referring to the mean when they use the word average. The mean for each group was obtained by adding the 1910 earnings for all persons in that group and then dividing the sum by the number of persons in the group. The mean, then, is the sum of a list of numbers divided by how many numbers there are in the list. For example, the mean of 9, 4, and 8 is $(9 + 4 + 8) \div 3$, which equals 7.

3. What is the mean of the list: 3, 46, 7, 28, 1?

4. If a list of six numbers has a mean of 8, what is the sum of the six numbers? Can you say exactly what the six numbers are?

Means are commonly used to summarize information when one wants to compare groups. If Bodnar had listed the income of each of the 123 Croatians and 112 Serbians in his study, there would be far too much information for us to comprehend—235 incomes. When he suppresses the details by boiling each list down to just one number, mean income, then you can easily compare the earnings of the Croatians and Serbians.

Averaging is a process that destroys information for the sake of simplicity; it thereby highlights a pattern from a complex jumble of data.

5. How did Bodnar calculate the average or mean earnings of Steelton's Irish-born workers in 1910?

Note that each average yearly income in Table 3.1 is expressed in units of dollars per person—numerator units per denominator units. The units accumulated in the numerator of an average (dollars, in this case) are the units of the variable being averaged, while the units of the denominator (persons) are the units of the variable over which the average is taken.

Means are always fractions or ratios—one number divided by another. That is why you use the language you do when reporting them. You wouldn't say "The average was 26 miles"; you would say "The average (gas consumption) was 26 miles per gallon" or "The average (speed) was 26 miles per hour." In Section 3.2 you will see a problem in which the issue of denominator units is important and a bit tricky.

6. Suppose a 100-block neighborhood of a large city contained 40,000 people and experienced 200 deaths from cholera during the outbreak of cholera in 1832. What was the average rate of cholera in this neighborhood?

7. Suppose list A has nine numbers with mean 4 while list B has eight numbers with mean 5. (a) What is the sum of all 17 numbers? (b) What is the mean of all 17 numbers?

Question 7 introduces the concept of a weighted average. To understand that term, consider this question about Table 3.1:

8. To calculate the average earnings of all native-born white workers with foreign-born fathers, which procedure would be better?

   (a) Add up the average earnings for workers with English fathers, German fathers, and Irish fathers and divide by three.

   (b) Add up the earnings of the 21 workers with English fathers, the 34 with German fathers, and the 38 with Irish fathers. Then divide this sum by the total number of workers in all three groups.

Suppose Bodnar had wanted to lump the Serbian and Croatian immigrant workers together as one group and find the mean earnings of the

235 workers in that new group. It would not be correct simply to add the mean Serbian income to the mean Croatian income and divide by 2, because this method assumes that the two groups are to be weighted equally. There were more Croatian than Serbian workers; the mean income for Serbs and Croats together has to reflect that fact.

The mean earnings of that combined group could be correctly computed in two different ways. First, one could add up the 112 Serbian incomes and the 123 Croatian incomes and divide by the total number of incomes, $112 + 123$ or 235 incomes.

But there is a simpler way to accomplish the same thing without adding up 235 numbers. The Serbian mean income, $175, is the sum of the earnings of the Serbian workers divided by 112, so the sum of Serbian earnings must be 112 multiplied by $175. Similarly, the sum of all Croatian earnings has to be $123 \times \$256$. Then the total earnings for the two groups together must be $(112 \times \$175) + (123 \times \$256)$. Now you can divide that total income of all 235 persons by 235 to get the mean for the combined group, $217 per person. The following calculation:

$$\frac{(112 \times \$175) + (123 \times \$256)}{235} = \$217 \text{ per person,}$$

is called taking a weighted average because you get the combined mean for the two groups of workers by weighting (i.e., multiplying) the mean for each group by the number of individuals in the group and then dividing by the sum of the weights. In our example, the weights were population sizes.

9. What's wrong with simply adding $175 and $256 and dividing by 2 to get $215.50 as the mean yearly earnings for the workers in those two groups? After all, $215.50 is close to the $217 from the weighted method. Won't the two methods always produce similar results?

10. Use the weighted average procedure to find the average 1910 income of native-born white workers with foreign fathers.

A few paragraphs back, we said that finding the average (the mean) of a list of numbers is a process that destroys information for the sake of simplicity. But alas, simplicity is not always clarity; averages can sometimes mislead instead of inform. For an example, do the following problem.

11.   Compute means for the following two groups of numbers. Are these groups alike?

> A: 2, 3, 5, 30
> B: 8, 9, 11, 12

To see this issue in the context of Table 3.1, suppose that all the 123 Croatian workers (average income, $256 a year) had earnings within five dollars of their mean (i.e., between $251 and $261) and that, similarly, all the 104 German workers earned within five dollars of $324. In that case, you would have no trouble asserting that the mean annual income for Croatian workers was a good approximation of the income of any individual Croatian worker, with the same true of the German workers. You would also feel comfortable saying that being Croatian rather than German was significantly related to the level of one's income. That's because knowing whether a man was German or Croatian would enable you to guess his annual income within $5.

But now suppose, instead, that both German and Croatian incomes ranged all over between $50 and $1000 while still averaging $324 and $256 respectively, as in Table 3.2. In this case, ethnicity wouldn't seem as significantly related to income as when all the individual incomes were clustered tightly around their means. Averaging the incomes of a number of individuals and reporting only the means doesn't tell you whether the incomes are quite similar to one another (clustered close to the mean value) or quite disparate (spread out away from the mean). In Section 3 of this chapter, you'll be introduced to another statistic, the standard deviation, that measures how tightly the numbers in a list are clustered around their mean value.

12.   Make up an example of two groups with five workers in each. Let group A have mean earnings of $100 and group B have mean earnings of $120; but pick numbers so that four of the five in group B earn less than everyone in Group A.

13.   Would you expect to find incomes of the various ethnic groups at Steelton clustered rather closely around their means, or widely dispersed as in the hypothetical example just given?

Recall that Bodnar's point was that the racial and ethnic backgrounds of Steelton's workers made a clear difference in how much they could earn. But in order to draw that conclusion, you need to assume that the means are representative of the underlying data. As you now know,

Table 3.2
Yearly income of German-born and Croatian-born workers (hypothetical data)

A. German-born workers

Worker	Income	Worker	Income
1	$ 515	6	$ 180
2	92	7	893
3	50	8	80
4	210	9	130
5	350	10	60

Mean: $ 256

B. Croatian-born workers

Worker	Income	Worker	Income
1	$ 665	6	$ 325
2	109	7	516
3	835	8	110
4	226	9	55
5	75	10	324

Mean: $ 324

that may or may not be true. As a reader, you should come to demand that authors provide more than just means.

You may sometimes come across tables that give mean values but don't make it clear what they are means of. The next section examines such a table from the article on crowding in eighteenth-century slave ships.

3.2   Slave-Ship Crowding: Another Look

In Section 3.1 you learned that a mean score is a kind of ratio: units of the variable being averaged are divided by units of the variable over which the average is taken. Take a look at Table 3.3. The title seems straightforward: the authors want to know how much deck space each slave was allotted on average. It's obvious how to calculate that for each ship: the variable being averaged will be a ship's slave area in square

feet and the variable over which the average is taken will be the number
of slaves on that ship. So if Table 3.3 had listed the 48 ships as Charles
Garland and Herbert S. Klein did in their original table, it would have
included 48 numbers in a column entitled "Area per slave."[2]

Table 3.3
Area per slave on ships of different tonnage categories

Tonnage category	No. ships in category	Average no. slaves	Average slave area per ship (sq. ft.)	Average area per slave (sq. ft.)
over 250	17	445	2250	5.1
151–250	17	309	1672	5.5
101–150	10	217	1246	5.8
under 100	4	106	814	8.3
overall average		323	1725	5.6

Source: Garland and Klein, "The Allotment of Space for Slaves," pp. 244–46, Table
III.

But Garland and Klein did something more. They also grouped the
ships into four tonnage categories and for each category gave the average
number of slaves per ship, the average slave area per ship, and the
average area per slave per ship. That's the information we've reprinted
in Table 3.3—those averages for the four tonnage groups, omitting the
individual data for the 48 ships.

In the table, it's not completely obvious how the averages were calculated because the authors grouped the ships into categories.

14. For the "over 250" category, explain how the average number of
slaves and the average square footage were derived. Since means or
averages always are expressed per something, what is that something in this case?

The column labeled "average area per slave" presents trickier problems. For the ships in one of the tonnage categories, say the "under 100"
category, the authors could have proceeded in either of two ways. First,

---

[2]Charles Garland and Herbert S. Klein, "The Allotment of Space for Slaves aboard
Eighteenth-Century British Slave Ships," *William & Mary Quarterly*, 3rd ser., 42
(April 1985), 238–48.

they may have aggregated (added up) the number of slaves on the four ships in that category, aggregated the area for slaves on the four ships, and then divided the total slave area by the total number of slaves:

$$\frac{\text{total slave sq. ft. on 4 ships}}{\text{total slaves on 4 ships}} = \text{average area per slave.}$$

By this method, they would have gotten:

$$\frac{3256 \text{ sq. ft.}}{425 \text{ slaves}} = 7.7 \text{ sq. ft. per slave.}$$

But the table gives a figure of 8.3 sq. ft., not 7.7. How did the authors derive that substantially higher average? Their method used the following formula:

$$\frac{\text{sum of areas per slave}}{\text{number of ships}} = \text{average area per slave per ship.}$$

The right-hand column in Table 3.3, then, ought to bear the label "average area per slave per ship." In other words, the two averaging formulas just discussed yield different results because they produce two entirely different averages. The first formula is easy to understand: it reveals how much space the average slave was allocated in the four ships of the "under 100" tonnage category. The second formula is a bit trickier: it reveals how much space the average ship provided for each slave.

The two results differ because one ship in the group of four—its name was *Flora*—had a small number of slaves (only 52) and a very high square footage per slave: 11.8 sq. ft., the most space per slave on any of the 48 ships. (Perhaps this ship was not fully loaded.) With *Flora* counted in the group of four, it's no surprise to find that the average ship in the group provided 8.3 sq. ft. per slave. That one ship bumped up the average for the group. But most slaves did not travel on *Flora*. Its cargo, 52 slaves, was the smallest for any ship in the entire group. Most slaves were carried across the Atlantic on ships providing far less square footage per slave than *Flora*. That explains why the average small-tonnage ship provided 8.3 sq. ft. per slave, yet the average slave traveling on one of the small-tonnage ships received only 7.7 sq. ft.

15. Which average, 8.3 or 7.7, do you think the authors should have given? How would you label the right-hand column of Table 3.3?

16. How did the authors derive the "overall average" figure of 5.6 for the right-hand column of Table 3.3? Explain the meaning of this average and comment on whether it seems appropriate.

Section 3 of this chapter gives you some additional practice with weighted averages, this time by focusing on workers' wages during an economic downturn.

3.3   Wages in the Depression of 1908

We turn from the fate of slaves on eighteenth-century slave ships to consider briefly what happens to wages during depressions. With banks collapsing, factories cutting production, and workers being laid off in industry after industry, you might expect wages to go down. There was a brief but sharp depression in 1907–09; historian Peter R. Shergold[3] decided to test the conventional wisdom by looking at wages in one city hit hard by that depression.

Table 3.4
Mean indices of hourly wage rates in Pittsburgh, 1901–1913, base year 1907

Year	Unweighted Mean	Weighted Mean
1901	84.1	85.3
1902	89.8	92.3
1903	93.0	94.2
1904	92.5	90.2
1905	92.9	92.2
1906	96.9	94.9
1907	100.0	100.0
1908	101.4	100.6
1909	102.3	100.5
1910	107.2	107.1
1911	108.0	107.8
1912	114.7	109.8
1913	119.1	117.8

Source: Peter R. Shergold, "Wage Rates in Pittsburgh during the Depression of 1908," *Journal of American Studies*, 9 (August 1975), p. 171, Table 2.

The steady increase of the index numbers from 1905 to 1910 in

---

[3]Peter R. Shergold, "Wage Rates in Pittsburgh during the Depression of 1908," *Journal of American Studies*, 9 (August 1975), 163–88.

Table 3.4 is Shergold's evidence that wages did not go down during the depression of 1907–09. This table of means is more complicated than Bodnar's, for several reasons. First, the numbers being averaged are indices; second, there may be two levels of averaging going on: averaging the workers' incomes within each occupation followed by averaging the means of all 25 occupations; and third, both weighted and unweighted means are shown.

What are mean indices? In preparing the table, Shergold used data from 25 occupations: bricklayers, plumbers, railway conductors, etc. For each occupation and for each year, it appears that he had a fairly accurate estimate of the typical hourly wage for the workers in that occupation; he may even have known the mean hourly wage for each occupation. He set this 1907 hourly wage equal to 100. Then, for example, if the bricklayers' hourly wage in 1908 was 2% greater than their 1907 wage, the 1908 index for bricklayers would be 102 (2% greater than the 1907 index of 100). Shergold did this because the changes in hourly wages are easier to understand when they are given in index terms than when given in dollars and cents. If the bricklayers' typical hourly wage had been $ 0.35 in 1907 and had risen to $ 0.37 in 1908, the reader would have to do some arithmetic to figure out how great a percentage change that was. Indexing the hourly wage figures saves the reader that trouble.

Indexing the numbers in a time series thus means expressing each value in the series as a proportion of the value for one year (called the base year) in the series. Typically, the index value for the base year is set at 100. While the first year in the series is usually chosen as the base year, this is not necessary. The Consumer Price Index is a well-known indexed time series in American life. Currently, the *Economic Report of the President* uses 1967 as the base year: the average price level for that year is indexed at 100. For December 1987, the CPI stood at 345.7.

After finding the annual index for each of the 25 Pittsburgh occupations being studied, Shergold next computed the mean over the entire 25 occupations. That is, within each year he added up the 25 indices and divided by 25 to get the unweighted mean index for that year. Those are the numbers in the center column of Table 3.4.

17. Do the unweighted mean indices in Table 3.4 offer support for the view that wages always decline in depressions? Cite specific evidence from the table.

18. What assumption about the labor force of Pittsburgh would you be making if you relied exclusively on the unweighted mean index?

19.   Briefly describe how you think the right-hand column of weighted means was calculated.

20.   Why do you think Shergold shows the second set of means, weighted means?

21.   If hourly wages remained steady or rose during the depression of 1908, does that prove that workers were as well off during the depression as before? Does it mean that the depression had no negative effect on wages?

A few paragraphs ago, we said we weren't sure whether Shergold knew the mean hourly wage for each occupation in each year of his study, or whether he was working with estimates of the "typical" hourly wage. For example, he tells us that Pittsburgh had 459 plasterers in 1910. It doesn't seem likely that he had sources listing the hourly wage of each individual plasterer in 1910. So he must have relied on one or more sources that told him that the typical wage for a plasterer was so much per hour. Perhaps for some occupations such as railroad engineers, Shergold had employer records showing what such workers received per hour. For other occupations, he must have used estimates made at the time by economists, social workers, journalists, and other observers.

Whatever his source, the author ought to inform his readers how solid his numbers really are. And you, as a reader of quantitative history, must try not to be too quickly swayed by apparently impressive arrays of data with numbers carried out to the tenth of a percentage point. In the case of Table 3.4, the numbers are reliable if they are built on actual means of the hourly wages paid men in each occupation in each year. If the numbers are built on estimates, then the table is an example of spurious accuracy: it gives the appearance of greater precision than is warranted. However, Table 3.4 doesn't need precision to one decimal place in order to illustrate the author's point that wages didn't fall during the depression years 1907–09. If the right-hand column of the table had been stated only to one or two whole numbers, you would still see the pattern: a jump from about 95 in 1906 to 100 in 1907, stability in the index at about 100 for a couple more years, then a substantial jump to about 107 in 1910.

In Table 3.4, you saw a quantitative historian using statistical evidence organized as a list of mean values to suggest that the past was more complex than some of the broad generalizations allow for. The next few sections of the chapter introduce a couple of new and important historical problems: the reasons for the rise of the cotton economy in the South after the Civil War, and mortality patterns in Philadelphia just before the American Revolution. In the process you'll encounter some more complex examples of means and we'll introduce a new single-number summary of information, the standard deviation, an important complement to the mean.

3.4 Roots of Southern Poverty

An old saying tells us that we can't have our cake and eat it too. In the language of economists, "what is consumed cannot be invested." According to Roger L. Ransom and Richard Sutch, "this simple fact explains why probably the most significant cause of persistent poverty in the world today is poverty itself."[4] Ransom and Sutch, two economic historians, present Table 3.5 as part of their argument that black farmers had to "eat their cake" each year: that discrimination against blacks in the post-Civil War South trapped blacks in a system that prevented them from accumulating the capital needed to break out of a cycle of debt and poverty.

Table 3.5
Number of acres of cropland per worker on family farms, by race and tenure, Cotton South: 1880

Form of Tenure	Acres of Crops per Worker	
	White	Black
Owner-operated	12.5	6.6
Rented	14.5	7.3
Sharecropped	11.7	8.0
All Farms	12.4	7.5

Source: Roger L. Ransom and Richard Sutch, *One Kind of Freedom: The Economic Consequences of Emancipation* (Cambridge, Eng., 1977), p. 184, Table 9.6.

Table 3.5 is intended as persuasive evidence that black farmers were severely disadvantaged. You should ask how strong you think this evidence is. First, here are some questions to check if the table is as clear as it seems.

---

[4]Roger L. Ransom and Richard Sutch, *One Kind of Freedom: The Economic Consequences of Emancipation* (Cambridge, Eng., 1977), 186.

22. How much more productive would an average black renter have to be in order to obtain the same total farm output as an average white renter?

23. Explain how you think the averages in Table 3.5 were probably calculated.

24. Are the all-farms averages (bottom row of Table 3.5) the means of the three numbers just above them? How do you think those all-farm means were computed?

Table 3.5 shows that black farmers, on the average, had fewer acres of cropland than white farmers in 1880. Going on from this finding, Ransom and Sutch provide evidence suggesting that although black workers were able to produce more <u>per acre</u> than whites ("more" meaning greater dollar value), the differences in number of acres farmed were great enough to trap blacks in a bondage of debt and dependency. No matter how well the average black farmer's land produced, they conclude, it was very difficult to break even because he had only seven or eight acres of crop.[5]

The authors are probably correct. But we want to point out why presenting only means in Table 3.5 makes their argument less powerful than it might have been. Suppose there were only six white workers on owner-operated farms and the acreages they worked are given by this list:

2, 2, 2, 2, 2, 65.

In this fictional Cotton South, imagine there were also four black workers on owner-operated farms: two who worked 6 acres and two who worked 7.2 acres. Note that in our hypothetical example, all blacks have at least three times the acreage of almost all whites.

25. In this fictional example, what would be the mean acres per worker for blacks and whites? On the basis of these averages, would you be able to make a persuasive case that black farmers suffered economic handicaps unique to them?

This little example shows the limitations of information provided by averages. Since the authors gave us only averages in Table 3.5, we are able to say that their table fails to show that most black farmers were worse off than most white farmers.

---

[5] *Ibid.*, p. 184.

26.   You have now seen several examples in which comparing means
was misleading because the mean for a group was not at all representative of the numbers used to calculate that mean. What
essential feature of those examples caused the means to be unrepresentative?

Suppose Ransom and Sutch had said that the average acreage for
white owner-operated farms was 12.5 and the average white farmer
worked within two acres of 12.5 (between 10.5 and 14.5), and furthermore almost no white farmers worked more than 16.5 or fewer than 8.5
acres. If they had also gone on to provide similar information about the
black farmers, showing how the acreages worked clustered around 6.6,
then you would have a much fuller picture of the disadvantage of the
blacks and would be more impelled to accept the authors' interpretation
of the numbers.

A common way to describe how a list of numbers clusters near the
mean value or spreads out away from it is to give a summary statistic
called the standard deviation along with the mean. Section 3.5 introduces the standard deviation.

3.5   Smallpox in Colonial Philadelphia

As part of a larger study of German immigrants in the eighteenth-
century American colonies, economic historian Farley Grubb inquired
whether the contagious disease smallpox was an epidemic or endemic
killer in Philadelphia before the American Revolution.[6] (An epidemic
disease appears sporadically and sweeps through a population, killing a
great many; an endemic disease is always present in the population and
kills some people each year without dramatic swings up and down.) Using data for one parish in Philadelphia between 1747 and 1775, Grubb
found that on the average, 12.28% of the deaths each year, or about one
death in eight, could be attributed to smallpox.

But this mean annual value doesn't show whether smallpox was epidemic or endemic. If smallpox was epidemic, you would expect to find
that the proportion of deaths fluctuated a great deal from year to year
and was particularly high in years when there was a high total number of
deaths. On the other hand, if smallpox was endemic, you would expect

---

[6]Farley Grubb, "Morbidity and Mortality on the North Atlantic Passage:
Eighteenth-Century German Immigration," *Journal of Interdisciplinary History*, 17
(Winter 1987), 565–85.

that the number of deaths and the proportion attributed to smallpox did not change dramatically from one year to the next. But you would expect to find some degree of year-to-year fluctuation. The problem, then, boils down to distinguishing normal or expected fluctuation from unusual fluctuation.

To state the problem in mathematical terms, you know the mean annual percentage of deaths attributed to smallpox for a 29-year period, but you also want to know how far each annual percentage deviated from the mean, on average. If 12.28% was the average proportion of deaths annually caused by smallpox, did the annual percentages vary between, say, 10% and 15% or did they range all the way from zero to 50%? Did the values cluster close to the mean value or were they widely scattered?

Table 3.6
Smallpox in Christ-Church Parish, 1747–1775

Year	Percent of All Deaths Attributed to Smallpox	Year	Percent of All Deaths Attributed to Smallpox
1747	1.18	1762	15.00
1748	0	1763	29.79
1749	m	1764	4.20
1750	m	1765	31.32
1751	29.38	1766	18.69
1752	9.29	1767	0
1753	6.54	1768	3.31
1754	0	1769	20.74
1755	0	1770	m
1756	52.58	1771	m
1757	7.84	1772	6.62
1758	0	1773	24.58
1759	m	1774	6.63
1760	18.54	1775	6.51
1761	2.11		

Mean = 12.28%

Source: Adapted from Farley Grubb, "Morbidity and Mortality on the North Atlantic Passage: Eighteenth-Century German Immigration," *Journal of Interdisciplinary History*, 17 (Winter 1987), p. 583, Table 4.

Note: m = missing data.

It helps to look over the list of annual percentages and to note the range of values, i.e., the highest minus the lowest. For Philadelphia's

Christ-Church Parish between 1747 and 1775, the highest percentage of deaths attributed to smallpox in any one year was 52.58% (in 1756) while the lowest was zero (in 1748 and four other years). So the range was 52.58%.

Certainly Table 3.6 suggests that rather large fluctuations occurred from year to year in the proportion of deaths caused by smallpox; but how large were those fluctuations, on average? What you want to know about the list is the <u>standard deviation</u>, a second summary statistic. Grubb provides it:

Std Dev = 13.48%

The standard deviation is an average distance between numbers in a list and their mean. For example, consider a very short list of just two numbers: 4, 8. This list has a mean of 6. Since each of the numbers is distance 2 from the mean, their average distance from the mean, the standard deviation, is also 2. Just as means summarize the size of numbers in a list (e.g., incomes, suicide rates, crop yields), standard deviations summarize the amount of variability in such lists. If the standard deviation is small, then the average distance from the mean is small and the numbers tend to cluster around their mean; if the standard deviation is large, the numbers tend to be spread out away from their mean—the variability is large.

27. Without attempting a complete calculation, state which of the following lists has the larger standard deviation:

    A: 16, 20, 18, 15, 14, 19 with mean = 17

    B: 12, 2, 4, 0, 8, 10 with mean = 6

28. Again without attempting a calculation, make a reasonable estimate of the standard deviation of the following list:

    1, 3, 4, 5, 7 with mean = 4

29. To measure deviations from the mean, why don't you simply subtract the mean from each number and then average those differences? Try this for the list in Question 28.

You may recall our saying, earlier in this chapter, that there is more than one kind of average. The mean is just one way to compute an average. We just said that the standard deviation is an average of the

deviations from the mean value of a list of numbers. That is true, but
the standard deviation is not the mean deviation.

Here is how to calculate the standard deviation: square the deviations
first to get rid of the cancellation of positive and negative deviations
and then average those squared values. But this gives you the average
squared deviation, not the average deviation, so you take the square root
and that result is known as the standard deviation.

Numbers in Question 28	Mean	Deviations From Mean	Deviations Squared
1	4	−3	9
3	4	−1	1
4	4	0	0
5	4	1	1
7	4	3	9

Averaging the squared deviations gives:

$$(9 + 1 + 0 + 1 + 9) \div 5 = 4$$

Now taking the square root of 4 yields the standard deviation, 2.

30. What is the standard deviation of the list: $1, 5, 7, 9, 13$?

The units in which standard deviations are measured are the same as
the units in the underlying data. If you have a list of dollar incomes
with a standard deviation of 122, you should really say the standard
deviation is 122 dollars. If you have a list of bushels of corn per acre
produced in Arkansas in 1890, the standard deviation is so many bushels
of corn per acre.

If one just wants some measure of how spread out the data are, why not
save a step by reporting the average of the squared deviations and calling
that the standard deviation? If you simply square the deviations −3,
−1, 0, 1, 3 in Question 28 and take the average of those squares, you get
the number 4 which you could use to describe spread. But if the original
list had been a list of dollar amounts, this answer is really four square
dollars (or dollars squared), which doesn't make any intuitive sense.
Also, the average squared deviation could come out much larger than
any distances between numbers in the original list—again, it wouldn't
have an obvious intuitive meaning as a measure of spread.

But in spite of its lack of intuitive meaning, the average squared deviation has a common name—the variance. The word "variance" is pep-
pered throughout almost all writing with a strong statistical component.

It comes from the commonsense idea of variation, how the numbers in a
list differ from one another. The variance is just the square of the standard deviation. The number 4 in the previous paragraph is the variance
of the list in Question 28. The square root of the variance, i.e., the
standard deviation, is expressed in the same units as the mean and the
original measurements.

Now you are in a better position to evaluate Grubb's data on smallpox
in Philadelphia. A standard deviation of 13.48% means that on average,
the annual proportion of deaths attributed to smallpox was not very
close to the mean figure of 12.28%. When a standard deviation is larger
than the mean, that's a good indication that the numbers in the list are
widely dispersed so that the mean alone doesn't describe those numbers
adequately by itself.

In the data for Christ-Church Parish, the distance from the mean to
zero is smaller than the distance from the standard deviation to zero.
That shows that there wasn't much room for the numbers to spread away
from the mean toward zero. You can infer, then, that some very large
numbers, quite a bit larger than the mean, are the source of the large
standard deviation; those very large numbers would indicate likely years
of smallpox epidemics. A glance at Table 3.6 shows that this inference
is correct.

31.   Which is better to know: the mean or the standard deviation?

32.   Grubb also found that between 1747 and 1775, an average of
        11.59% of deaths annually in Christ-Church Parish were attributed
        to consumption (tuberculosis), with a standard deviation of 4.96%.
        Interpret the meaning of these two summary statistics.

When you are dealing with a list of numbers such as a list of ages
at first pregnancy for 200 women or a list of the proportion of eligible
voters who voted in 100 towns, it is clear how to interpret the standard
deviations—they are the average distances from the individual ages or
voting proportions to the means of the lists. However, the standard
deviation also arises in a less intuitive context, when individuals (say,
women or counties) have merely been classified as having or not having
some property. For example, instead of knowing the age at first pregnancy for each of 100 women, suppose you only knew whether or not
their first pregnancy occurred before age eighteen.

Imagine that 20% of a population of 200 women first became pregnant
before age eighteen. You could make up a variable called Young Pregnancy, which would receive the code "1" if the individual first became

pregnant before age eighteen and "0" otherwise. So now you have a list of 200 Young Pregnancy numbers, each number a one (for yes) or zero (for no). This list of 200 numbers has a mean and a standard deviation.

To compute the average of the 200 numbers you would add them all up and divide by 200. Well, when you add up zeros and ones, the sum you get is simply the number of ones. So the sum is the number of women who became pregnant young; when you divide by two hundred to get the average, you are clearly computing the proportion of women who became pregnant young. In this example, the mean of the zeros and ones would be 0.20 or 20%. So the average of a 0/1 list used for classifying has commonsense meaning—the percentage of ones, the proportion of the population with the given property.

Once you have the mean, 0.20, you can compute the standard deviation. Each of the ones is a distance of 0.80 from that mean and each zero is a distance of 0.20 away from the mean. Now, as before, you square the distances, average those squares, and then take the square root to find the standard deviation:

$$\frac{40 \times (0.8)^2 + 160 \times (0.2)^2}{200} = \frac{(40 \times .64) + (160 \times .04)}{200} = \frac{32}{200} = 0.16.$$

The square root of .16 is .40, which is the standard deviation of the proportion. But the average distance from the zeros and ones to the mean of 0.20 has no obvious, commonsense interpretation, so why bother to calculate it? You will see in Chapter 5 that knowing this particular standard deviation is vital when one is trying to estimate proportions in a large population, say, the proportion of women or the proportion of smokers.

To review, it is useful to know several summary numbers about lists of numbers such as annual deaths from smallpox or the size of farms in the Cotton South. Most writers give the <u>mean</u> of a list of numbers if they provide any summary at all. But when you know the mean, you still don't know whether the numbers in your list are similar to one another (clustered around the mean value) or dissimilar. The <u>range</u> doesn't tell much about the list as a whole because it gives you only the highest and lowest numbers in the list. The <u>standard deviation</u> provides much more information: it tells you how far each number in your list is, on average, from the mean.

33. It is often said that the mean is a measure of central tendency while the standard deviation is a measure of dispersion. Explain what you think these phrases mean.

The next section continues with our discussion of farming in the cotton South after the Civil War; it shows how historians can use means together with standard deviations to describe a body of statistical information more clearly than would be possible using means alone.

3.6 Cotton or Corn in the Postbellum South

Some historians have asserted that Southern farmers, black and white, would have been better off if they had resisted a widespread shift away from corn and into cotton following the Civil War. According to this view, the shift into cotton cost the farmers their self-sufficiency without increasing their income. Cotton demand was weak; when Southern farmers increased their cotton production, this merely helped drive down world cotton prices, so farmers' cash incomes failed to increase. At the same time, growing more cotton meant growing less food—with the result that the farmer experienced an overall loss of real income. Corn, a basic food for farm livestock as well as farmers and their families, is thus used as a measure of self-sufficiency.

Gavin Wright and Howard Kunreuther use Table 3.7 as part of their effort to explain the apparently irrational behavior of Southern farmers.[7] Wright and Kunreuther argue that Southern farmers were interested in improving their economic position but could not have done so by sticking to corn because average corn yields per acre were less than average cotton yields. They make the point, however, that cotton yields were more volatile than corn yields (that is, they fluctuated more year-to-year) so that growing cotton was riskier for the farmer than growing corn in spite of cotton's returning a higher mean yield. Yet for a variety of reasons, farmers were willing to gamble on cotton despite the risk.

A good way to begin examining Table 3.7 is to figure out the meaning of the variables that have been averaged. Corn yield is measured in bushels per acre. The underlying historical sources (reports of the U.S. Department of Agriculture) included estimates by state of annual corn production and acres planted to corn for each year from 1866 to 1900. Similarly, there is some record of the number of bales of cotton produced and acres planted to cotton for each state in each year; from these data the authors calculated cotton yield.

Wright and Kunreuther were faced with the problem of comparing

---

[7]Gavin Wright and Howard Kunreuther, "Cotton, Corn and Risk in the Nineteenth Century," *Journal of Economic History*, 35 (September 1975), 526–51.

Table 3.7
Estimated mean yields per acre, 1866–1900 (in corn-bushel equivalents)

	Means		Standard Deviation		% of Years Corn Exceeds
	Cotton	Corn	Cotton	Corn	Cotton
Alabama	13.64	12.37	4.86	1.43	51.4
Arkansas	36.37	18.90	14.16	2.13	5.7
Georgia	13.36	10.30	6.75	1.38	37.1
Louisiana	24.71	15.12	8.41	1.62	11.4
Mississippi	20.44	14.26	6.21	1.86	11.4
No. Carolina	20.81	12.34	7.19	1.50	11.4
So. Carolina	14.43	9.76	7.19	1.50	25.7
Tennessee	33.29	20.79	13.18	2.06	8.6
Texas	34.75	20.32	19.28	3.95	0.0
Unweighted Average	23.57	14.91	9.59	1.93	18.1
Weighted Average	22.94	14.82	10.16	2.15	20.1

Source: Gavin Wright and Howard Kunreuther, "Cotton, Corn and Risk in the Nineteenth Century," *Journal of Economic History*, 35 (September 1975), p. 537, Table 5.

Note: Weighted averages used 1885 cotton output.

unlike units: bales of cotton and bushels of corn. Their solution was to convert one of them to the other; in this case, bales of cotton to bushels of corn. For example, if the market value of a cotton bale in Alabama in 1866 was sufficient to buy six bushels of corn in Alabama in 1866, then each bale of cotton per acre is the equivalent of six bushels of corn per acre. This is where the phrase "corn-bushel equivalents" in the table's title comes from. Note that this sort of conversion is possible because the two kinds of yield can be expressed in a common medium, dollars.

34. Was there even one state in which the mean corn yield exceeded the mean cotton yield? What state had the largest ratio of cotton yield to corn yield? What states had the greatest and least cotton yields?

The title of the table says that the entries are mean yields for 1866–1900. Therefore, the 12.37 at the top of the second column is the mean of 35 annual corn yields for Alabama. One way the authors might have arrived at that number 12.37 is to add up the 35 annual yields and then divide the sum by 35. A second way would be to weight the yield for each year by the total number of bushels of corn produced that year and so calculate a weighted average. You can't tell from the table which they did. In any case, the variable Annual Corn Yield was averaged over the variable Years to produce Average (mean) Yield per Year—that's what the two columns under the heading "Means" are expressing. The list of the 35 annual corn yields for Alabama may have been quite varied—a mixture of good, bad and normal years.

Notice that each annual yield for Alabama was itself an average. Perhaps a single annual yield was computed like this:

$$\text{annual yield} = \frac{\text{total bushels of corn}}{\text{total acres planted to corn}} \, .$$

Annual Yield is an average: Bushels is the variable being averaged and Acres the variable over which the average was taken. There would have been a lot of acre-to-acre variability even over a single growing season. An acre down by the creek would have produced much more corn than one on a rocky hill (but not in a year of flooding). The number 12.37 in the top row of Table 3.7 thus masks two levels of variability, year-to-year and acre-to-acre. A third level of variability, state-to-state, gets covered over when mean yields for states are averaged to produce the grand mean 14.82 (or 14.91) at the bottom of the second column.

35. State A had an average corn yield of 20 bushels per acre and a total corn output of 100,000 bushels. State B had an average corn yield of 30 bushels per acre and a total corn output of 50,000 bushels.

   (a) What is the unweighted mean yield for the two states?

   (b) What is the weighted mean yield, using output as weights?

   (c) Why is the unweighted mean larger than the weighted mean?

36. To answer the following question, examine the unweighted and weighted means (23.57 and 22.94) at the bottom of the first column of Table 3.7. The note at the bottom of the table says weighted means were computed using 1885 output as weights. In 1885 did the states that produced the most cotton tend to do so because they produced the most cotton per acre?

37. Is there any tendency for high corn yield to go with high cotton yield? Use a line graph to answer this question. On the horizontal

axis order the states from lowest to highest by cotton yield and
then graph the corn yield for each state.

The authors have explicitly shown the nine separate state means so
you can see how much state-to-state variability is associated with the
grand mean, 14.82. But instead of explicitly showing year-to-year variability, they summarize year-to-year variability by printing standard deviations.

The standard deviation 1.43 shown for corn yield in Alabama is an
average of the list of 35 deviations or distances between the 35 annual
Alabama corn yields and their average, 12.37. The example in Table 3.8
may make this clear. The numbers in the right-hand column show how
far each of the yields in the middle column is from the mean yield. The
standard deviation in this hypothetical example, 1.43, is an average of
the list of deviations (2.17, 2.63, ..., 0.90).

Table 3.8
Corn yield per acre in Alabama (hypothetical data)

Year	Bushels	Deviation From the Mean of 12.37
1866	10.20	2.17
1867	15.00	2.63
1868	12.84	0.47
⋮	⋮	⋮
1900	13.27	0.90

Note: The dots mean that the full table would include data for all the years between
1868 and 1900.

Mean annual yield per acre: 12.37 bushels

Standard deviation: 1.43 bushels

The commonsense definition of standard deviation as an average deviation enables the reader to interpret Table 3.7. Over the 35-year period,
Alabama corn yields were on average much closer to their mean of 12.37
than Alabama cotton yields were to their mean of 13.64. You know
this because the standard deviation for cotton, 4.86, is more than three
times larger than the standard deviation for corn. That is, the 35 annual
cotton yields were, on average, over three times as far away from 13.64
as the corresponding numbers for corn were from 12.37.

38. Look at the columns of standard deviations in Table 3.7. Compare the smallest cotton standard deviation with the largest corn standard deviation. Summarize the relationship between the variability in corn and cotton yields throughout the Cotton South between 1866 and 1900.

Well, so what? What did Wright and Kunreuther make of these differences in standard deviations between cotton and corn yields? Their point is that the average gain from cotton was greater, but cotton was riskier. There would be good years, say when cotton yield was an entire standard deviation or more above the mean ($13.64 + 4.86 = 18.5$), but also bad years when cotton yield was a standard deviation or more below the mean ($13.64 - 4.86 = 8.78$). Corn yield, on the other hand, tended to wobble up and down less, though at a lower level overall ($12.37 + 1.43 = 13.8$ and $12.37 - 1.43 = 10.94$). Notice that the last column says that although the mean yield from cotton was greater than that for corn, more than half the time, in 51.4% of the years, the yield of corn in Alabama was actually greater.

If Southern farmers sensed the pattern described above, they would have found themselves facing a proposition which, in modern terms, goes something like this:

> You can have a mean annual income of $15,000 over the next twenty years, but some years you might get nothing, even for several years in a row, and some years you can make a bundle, but you will never know in advance.
>
> Alternatively, you can have an average income of $12,500 over the same period, never making less than $11,000 and never more than $14,000.

39. Wright and Kunreuther argue that large numbers of farmers took the riskier bet. Can you think of a reason farmers would do that?

3.7 Size of Families in Colonial America

Historians and social scientists used to believe that in preindustrial times, most families included a great many children—a dozen or more on the average—in contrast to present-day families, which average only two children in the United States. To test this image of the way things used to be, John Demos, one of the pioneer historians of American family life, once published a table (numbered Table 3.9 here) giving information on

Table 3.9
Children per family in Bristol, Rhode Island, 1688/9

												Total
Number of children	0	1	2	3	4	5	6	7	8	9	10	226
Number of Families	7	10	11	12	9	8	6	4	1	0	1	69

Source: John Demos, "Families in Colonial Bristol, Rhode Island: An Exercise in Historical Demography," *William & Mary Quarterly*, 3rd ser., 25 (January 1968), p. 45, Table II.

the number of children in 69 families in the colonial town of Bristol, Rhode Island in 1688/9.[8]

By grouping the families according to how many children they had, Demos has already begun the process of organizing the data. Still, it's a little difficult for a reader to get a quick grasp of the information in Table 3.9. A summary number would be useful; let's first consider the mean.

You can try to guess where the mean will be before you compute it. Notice that the bulk of the families have between zero and six children; also notice that there are a few cases strung out to the right that are not balanced by cases on the left. Those extra cases on the right will cause the mean, which is like a balance point, to lie farther to the right than might be expected. If the most extreme case had been a family of 20 children instead of only ten, or if there had been several families with ten children, then the mean would be pulled far to the right in order to be at the balance point of the distribution. In the case shown, you would probably guess the mean to be around three children per family.

40. Use the idea of weighted averages to compute the mean number of children per family shown in Table 3.9.

The exact value of the mean number of children per family in Bristol, based on the data in Table 3.9, was, of course, 226 divided by 69 or 3.28.

Another number that expresses the central tendency of a list of numbers is the <u>median</u>. In some situations, the median effectively supplements the information supplied by the mean. The median is simply the middle number when a list has been ordered by size.

[8] John Demos, "Families in Colonial Bristol, Rhode Island: An Exercise in Historical Demography," *William & Mary Quarterly*, 3rd ser., 25 (January 1968), 40–57, at 45.

For example, 6 is the median in the list: 3, 3, 4, 6, 8, 8, 10. The list 2, 3, 5, 9 has no middle number so you take the mean of the two middle numbers to get a median of 4. The median has the property that half the other numbers in the list lie above it and half below. The mean often does not have that property. The mean of 1, 1, 1, 1, 16 is 4 although 80% of the cases lie below 4 with only 20% above. In fact, it would be possible for almost 100% of the numbers in a list to be on one side of the mean.

41. What are the medians of the following lists?

    (a) 1, 2, 3, 50, 90

    (b) 1, 2, 30, 60

    (c) 1, 1, 1, 1, 16

Suppose you want to find the median number of children per family in colonial Bristol. Imagine putting the 69 counts of children in order to get a list beginning with seven zeros, then ten ones, etc., and ending with an eight and a ten. The middle of that list of 69 numbers would be the 35th entry and you can see from the table that the 35th entry would be 3. So the median number of children per family is 3, quite close to the mean number.

Will the mean and the median always lie close to each other? In her article on the Virginia Muster of 1624/5, Irene W.D. Hecht compares the 69 families of Bristol, Rhode Island in 1688/9 with 189 Virginia families in 1624/5.[9] That comparison is shown in Table 3.10.

42. Would either or both of the distributions in Table 3.10 have their mean dragged to the left or right of their median?

43. Find the mean and the median number of children for the Virginia families and compare them to the mean and median for the Bristol families.

44. How would you state a comparison of the two groups in Table 3.10 if you had only the means and medians but not the underlying data?

45. For each distribution in Table 3.10, describe what you would make of the difference between the mean and the median if you did not have the underlying data.

[9] Irene W.D. Hecht, "The Virginia Muster of 1624/5 As a Source for Demographic History," *William & Mary Quarterly*, 3rd ser., 30 (January 1973), 65–92.

Table 3.10
Children per family in Virginia, 1624/5, and in Bristol, Rhode Island, 1688/9

Number of Children	0	1	2	3	4	5	6	7	8	9	10
Number of Families in Virginia	102	62	17	6	2	0	0	0	0	0	0
in Bristol	7	10	11	12	9	8	6	4	1	0	1

Source: Adapted from Irene W.D. Hecht, "The Virginia Muster of 1624/5 as a Source for Demographic History," *William & Mary Quarterly*, 3rd ser., 30 (January 1973), p. 90, Table XI.

46. For each distribution in Table 3.10, make a guess (an educated guess that depends on just a little calculating) as to the sizes of the standard deviation and variance.

47. What light does Table 3.10 cast on the traditional view that preindustrial families typically had very large numbers of children? Can you identify a reason why the table is not entirely adequate for answering that question?

For a considerably more challenging attempt to interpret means, medians, and standard deviations, we next turn to a historian's analysis of the wealth of winning and losing candidates for public office in an American city.

3.8 Wealth and Officeholding in Atlanta

A general problem in political history has to do with how different ethnic groups and social classes organized and competed to gain political power. In an article entitled "Property and Politics"[10] Eugene J. Watts considers city politics in Atlanta from 1865 to 1903. He looks at differences in property holdings between those who became candidates and those who didn't and also between winning candidates and losing candidates.

Watts observes that "few decisions of city government fail to involve property rights in some way or other...." In Atlanta, campaign rhetoric

---

[10]Eugene J. Watts, "Property and Politics in Atlanta, 1865–1903," *Journal of Urban History*, 3 (May 1977), 295–322.

"after the Civil War often suggested a battle between the rich and the poor." If Atlanta politics was class warfare along property lines, Watts wants to know who won.

Table 3.11
Average property holdings of winning and losing candidates in Atlanta, 1865 to 1903

Office	Mean Property Holding	Standard Deviation
Mayor:		
Winners	$47,435	$58,293
Losers	20,987	36,119
Alderman:		
Winners	27,808	34,150
Losers	12,362	13,541
Councilman:		
Winners	18,730	38,338
Losers	10,772	19,461
All Candidates:		
Winners	21,850	39,878
Losers	11,776	20,851

Source: Eugene J. Watts, "Property and Politics in Atlanta, 1865–1903," *Journal of Urban History*, 3 (May 1977), p. 302, Table 2.

Take a few moments to examine the means and standard deviations in Table 3.11; look for striking or puzzling features. Here are a few questions about the candidates for the office of alderman, a more important office than councilman. Aldermen were elected to represent the entire city and served for three years while councilmen were elected from wards, two to a ward (though the structure of city government changed during the time period studied).

48. Is this statement true or false? "Among the men who ran for the office of alderman in this period of nearly 40 years, the value of winners' property holdings averaged more than twice that of losers." Does the statement apply to candidates for any other offices?

49.   For both winners and losers, the value of holdings seemed to go up
with the importance of the office, so that losing candidates for the
office of mayor had more property than did winners for the office
of councilman. Can you suggest a possible reason for this pattern?

50.   Notice also that even losers for the least important office seemed to
hold substantial property on average. Perhaps all candidates for
office were more prosperous than the ordinary citizen. If this was
so, what significance (if any) do you think that fact would have?

51.   Do you think the means in Table 3.11 are probably representative
of the property values from which they were calculated, or not?

For every mean in Table 3.11, the standard deviation is bigger than
the mean. That's somewhat surprising, but you saw the same thing
earlier in the article on smallpox in Philadelphia. Recall that there it
indicated the presence of a few numbers that were much greater than
the mean. If you think about the distribution of property values in any
community, you might guess there would be many people with little or
no property, and only a few people with a lot of property. That pattern
would be consistent with the standard deviations in Watts's table.

The large standard deviations in Table 3.11 tell us that the underlying
numbers were well spread out around their means. But the distance from
the mean values to zero isn't very great; notice that it's a lot less than
the size of the standard deviations. That shows that there wasn't much
room for the numbers to spread away from the mean toward zero. You
can infer, then, that some very large property holdings among candidates
are the source of the very large standard deviations.

If that's the case, then it is going to be difficult to conclude from
just the means that successful candidates were richer in property than
losers. Recall the previous table showing average crop yields in Alabama.
Over a 35-year period, mean cotton yield was greater than mean corn
yield despite the fact that in over half the years, corn yield was actually
greater. In the same way, it is at least possible that for most contests for
public office in Atlanta, losers were wealthier in property than winners
but that the winners' mean property holdings were dragged up by a few
extremely big property holdings. In fact, the large standard deviations
warn us that the data are not adequately summarized by their means.

Here is an artificial example using four contests to make the point.

Contest	1	2	3	4
Winner's Property Holdings:	$100	$200	$300	$39,400
Loser's Property Holdings:	$4,000	$5,000	$5,000	$6,000

The winners' mean is $10,000 and the losers' is $5000—but almost all losers have substantially more property than almost all winners. Since the standard deviations in Table 3.11 tell us to be wary of the means, it is clear that you need more information than Table 3.11 provides in order to draw conclusions about property wealth and politics.

52. The trivial four-contest example above fails to mimic Table 3.11 in that the standard deviation for losers is relatively small while in the real case there was considerable spread in property holdings for both winners and losers. Could you have made up an example with the same message if you had to spread out the holdings for both winners and losers?

A variable with the pattern described in Question 52—many cases with small values, a few with very large values—would be described as skewed to the right. If you made a histogram, the bulk of the cases would be plotted to the left with a few extreme scores shown far to the right of the main body of the data—so the distribution is skewed to the right.

53. Give an example of a variable, other than wealth or income, that might be of interest to some historian and would show the above pattern of many small values, a few very large values.

54. Repeat Question 53 for a variable that would show many large values and relatively few small values. Such a variable would be said to be skewed to the left because of the stretched-out left-hand tail of the distribution.

55. In a list of numbers, are half of the numbers below average?

The large standard deviations in Table 3.11 caused us to wonder if the means could be misleading as to whether winning candidates really held more property than losing candidates. Watts anticipated that question and printed medians along with the means and standard deviations. Table 3.12 is Watts's version of Table 3.11.

In Table 3.12 the median property holdings for the winners, like the means, are much greater than the median holdings for the losers. Does

Table 3.12
Property holdings of winning and losing candidates in Atlanta, 1865 to 1903

	Mean	Median	Standard Deviation
Mayor:			
Winners	$47,435	$25,738	$58,293
Losers	20,987	7,991	36,119
Alderman:			
Winners	27,808	16,423	34,150
Losers	12,362	7,708	13,541
Councilman:			
Winners	18,730	8,975	38,338
Losers	10,772	4,538	19,461
All Candidates:			
Winners	21,850	9,482	39,878
Losers	11,776	4,975	20,851

Source: See Table 3.11.

this rule out peculiar possibilities such as shown in our hypothetical four-contest example? Yes. By knowing the median holdings, you are able to say that half of the winning mayoral candidates had property worth more than $25,738. Half of the losing candidates, on the other hand, had property worth less than $7991. Most of the time, winners held more property than losers, probably much more.

By the way, notice that for every column of Table 3.12, the mean is considerably larger than the median. This shows, as you would guess, that lists of candidates' property holdings would include a few candidates with extremely large holdings. There must be a small number of large holdings in every category dragging the balance point, the mean, to the right of the median, which is in the middle.

56. Apparently large property holders defeated smaller ones in Atlanta. Does this show that they won by outspending their opponents on campaigns?

Statisticians have other ways, beside the standard deviation, to summarize the spread of numbers around their mean. To understand why another measure might be helpful, consider the following two trivial lists: A: 1, 9 and B: 741, 749.

57. What are the mean, median, and standard deviation for lists A and B just above?

Although the spread or variation is the same within A and B, the variation is much larger relative to the sizes of the numbers in A than it is relative to the numbers in B. The standard deviation (4) is 80% of the mean (5) of list A while in list B the standard deviation is less than 1% of the mean.

It seems it might be useful to have some way to express the idea of variation that takes into account the size of the numbers in a list. Unless one can make this correction, it's difficult to compare the standard deviations of lists containing different sized numbers. To measure the size of the spread in a list relative to the size of the numbers in the list, you divide the standard deviation by the mean; the result is known as the <u>coefficient of variation</u>.

58. Use Table 3.12 to find the coefficient of variation for winners and losers within the three offices sought.

There is a simple technical point that will help you understand the coefficient of variation as well as rates and, indeed, averages themselves. The technical point has to do with what happens to units of measurement when you do arithmetic. Here is a familiar example. You drive 20 miles per hour for 3 hours. How far did you go? Obviously the answer is 60 miles. But look closely at what goes on with the units of measurement, miles and hours.

$$\frac{20 \text{ miles}}{\text{hour}} \times 3 \text{ hours} = 60 \text{ miles}.$$

The word hours canceled from the numerator and denominator as if it were a number.

Similarly, think of how you compute averages such as the following:

$$\frac{80 \text{ miles}}{4 \text{ gallons}} = 20 \text{ miles/gallon} \quad \text{or}$$

$$\frac{80 \text{ miles}}{4 \text{ hours}} = 20 \text{ miles/hour}.$$

Here too, you are, in effect, doing arithmetic on the units of measurement as well as on the numbers.

The coefficient of variation is: (standard deviation) ÷ mean.

But the standard deviation and the mean have the same units, so the coefficient of variation is what is called a unitless variable—dividing will cancel the common units as hours were canceled above.

What's the advantage of a unitless variable? Well, there are many choices of units in which to measure variables. For example, weight could be measured in ounces, pounds, tons, or grams. The numeric size of the mean or standard deviation would be different for different units of measurement, but the coefficient of variation would always be the same. The coefficient of variation doesn't depend on the scale you happen to choose.

3.9   Conclusion

To sum up, consider the different things that means and medians reveal about a list of numbers. A major characteristic of the mean is that the mean is more sensitive to changes in a small part of the data. Take a look at this list, for example:

2, 3, 10

Here the mean is ~~7.5~~ 5 and the median is 3. If the 10 were changed to 19, the mean would jump to 8 but the median would remain the same. Means are sensitive to changes in the largest and smallest numbers. This is important when measuring phenomena like wealth where there are likely to be a few extreme cases that render the mean quite unrepresentative of the body of data.

The median, by contrast, sits solidly in the middle of the list of data and budges not at all whether you double the largest or halve the smallest number—it is still in the middle. But just as the mean has limitations, this stability of the median is also a limitation. Its stability comes from the fact that it does not contain as much information about the numbers as the mean does.

Our conclusion reiterates a point made earlier in the book: there is no one descriptive statistic that tells you everything you need to know about a body of data. When a historian shows you means in order to point out interesting differences between groups, you should also be provided supporting information such as standard deviations, medians, the data itself, or at least verbal assurances, so you can judge whether the impression you get from the means is truly warranted.

Terms Introduced in Chapter 3

3.1 mean
3.1 weighted average
3.3 indexing
3.3 spurious accuracy
3.5 standard deviation
3.5 variance
3.5 central tendency
3.5 dispersion
3.8 median
3.8 skewed distribution
3.8 coefficient of variation

3.10 Answers to Questions

1. Of 592 workers, 329 (55.6%) hailed from Bulgaria, Serbia, Slovenia, or Croatia, all areas of southeastern Europe.

2. As a group, English, Irish, and German average earnings are greater than the earnings of the others, although there is some overlap—the German $324 is less than the Slovenian $381. You might guess that most of the northern Europeans earned more than most of the southeastern Europeans but you really need more information to be sure of that.

3. Adding the five numbers and dividing by 5 gives the mean of 17.

4. Since many sets of six numbers could add up to 48, so knowing N and the mean for a list doesn't enable you to reconstruct the list.

5. He had at least an estimate of the earnings of each of the 20 Irish workers. He added those earnings and divided by 20.

6. You could divide 200 deaths by 100 blocks and get an average of two cholera deaths per block. But you could also get the following averages: 200 deaths per year, five deaths per 1000 persons.

7. (a) As in the answer to Question 4, the A and B sums must be
    36 and 40 respectively so the grand sum is 76.

    (b) $\dfrac{(9 \times 4) + (8 \times 5)}{9 + 8} = \dfrac{76}{17} = 4.47$.

8. The trouble with method (a) is that there are more workers with
    Irish fathers than with English fathers so the $504 and $556 av-
    erages should not be treated equally. Method (b) is equivalent to
    the method of Answer 7 and is the correct way to compute the
    average.

9. As you'll recall from the text, averaging the averages only gives the
    overall mean when the groups are the same size. If groups have
    different sizes you should use a weighted average as in Answer 7
    (b). The reason the two methods gave such similar numbers for
    Serbo-Croatian earnings is that the two groups were almost the
    same size. But if there had been only 10 Serbians, the weighted
    average would have come out close to the Croatian mean of $256.

10. $\dfrac{(21 \times 556) + (34 \times 426) + (38 \times 504)}{21 + 34 + 38} = \$487.23$.

11. A: Sum = 40 so mean = 10. B: sum = 40 so mean = 10. These
     groups are not alike. Group B numbers are all close to their mean
     and are therefore well represented by their mean. But the group A
     numbers are spread out and are unlike their mean. Notice that 2,
     3, and 5 are below the mean and 30 is far above so that the mean
     is not in the middle of the numbers.

12. Here's one possibility: A: $100, $100, $100, $100, $100 and B: $80,
     $80, $80, $80, $360.

13. One plausible conjecture is that members of an ethnic group would
     have been tracked into similar jobs. If this is true, you would
     expect clustering of the wages. But another plausible conjecture
     is that immigrants would have arrived at different times and those
     with more years in Steelton would be making considerably more
     than new arrivals. This ambiguity suggests that when you are
     given a mean you should also be given some sense of the extent to
     which it represents the numbers that were averaged.

14. For "average number of slaves," the authors divided the total num-
     ber of slaves on the 17 ships by the number of ships. For "average

slave area," they divided the total square footage allotted to slaves on the 17 ships by the number of ships. In both cases, the averages are expressed per ship.

15. We think 7.7 should have been given because it summarizes the experience of the average slave, not the average ship. What the slaves experienced is, after all, the question most readers care about. Therefore the right-hand column already bears the correct label. The problem is that the authors used an inappropriate method for generating the averages listed in that column.

16. They weighted each average in the right-hand column by the number of ships in that category, added the weighted averages, and divided by the total number of ships, 48:

$$\frac{(5.1 \times 17) + (5.5 \times 17) + (5.8 \times 10) + (8.3 \times 4)}{48} = 5.6$$

This figure, 5.6, represents the average square footage per slave per ship for the 48 ships as a group. As we noted above, we think it would have been more appropriate to show the average square footage per slave—the total square footage available for slaves divided by the total number of slaves. If you work that out, you get a figure of 5.3 sq. ft., not 5.6.

17. The wage indices 96.9, 100.0, 101.4, and 102.3, which span the depression, rise steadily and do not support the theory that wages must decline during a depression.

18. You would be making the assumption that for each year being studied, the 25 occupations all had the same number of workers—that there were just as many bricklayers as carpenters, carpenters as bakers, bakers as ironworkers, etc. That's because the unweighted mean index in effect gives exactly the same weight to all the occupations.

19. The index for each of the 25 occupations would have been multiplied by the number of workers in that occupational category. Those products would be added up and the grand sum would be divided by the sum of the weights, that is, the total number of workers in the 25 occupations.

20. Suppose the very small occupations (those with few workers) experienced large increases while the large occupations had decreases.

Then a straight average across the occupations could show the index going up while the wages of the average worker went down. Shergold uses the weighted averages to make it clear that nothing like that happened—the average wage across all 25 occupations did go up.

21. Not at all. Many workers may have been laid off, and others may have had their work hours reduced even if wages per hour did not decline. Also, the rate of wage increase during the depression was lower than the rate of increase before or after, so the depression may have had a negative effect on wages by keeping them from rising as much as they otherwise might have.

22. Since the average black renter farmed half as much land as the white renter, he would have had to be about twice as productive to achieve the same total output.

23. Ideally, there would have been an accurate list of all family farms in the Cotton South with information on the size of each farm, the nature of the tenancy, and the race of the tenant family. Then the authors would have assembled that vast list into six categories by race and tenancy in order to compute the averages. In fact, as soon as you are sure that the population is large, such as all farms in the Cotton South, you know the information must have been partial. Ransom and Sutch used a sample taken from the 1880 agricultural census. If the sample was properly constructed, it represents the farms throughout the Cotton South reasonably accurately. It is worth noting, however, that for Table 3.5, they included only farms reporting both acreage of cropland and number of laborers. (We discuss sampling in Ransom and Sutch's book *One Kind of Freedom* further in Chapter 4.)

24. These must be weighted averages. The weights would have been the number of farms in each of the three tenancy categories.

25. The white mean is 12.5 acres per farm and the black mean is 6.6 acres per farm. If you were given just the means, you might be convinced that whites' acreage tended generally to be significantly greater than blacks' acreage, even though that's not true. Averages alone may be suggestive, but you need to know more about the nature of the distribution before they are persuasive.

26. A few extreme values, far from the bulk of the numbers, distorted the mean—dragged it away from typical or representative values.

27. In list A, the deviations from the mean are −1, 3, 1, −2, −3, and 2; in list B, they are 6, −4, −2, −6, 2, and 4. Since the standard deviation is an average of the size of the deviations and the B deviations are clearly larger, the standard deviation for B must be greater than that for A.

28. The mean for this list of five numbers is 4. The deviations are −3, −1, 0, 1, and 3, so if you ignore the minus signs the sum of the five deviations is 8. The standard deviation must be around 8/5ths, a little less than 2. This is a quick estimate of the approximate size of the average deviation; it is not a formula for computing the standard deviation.

29. In Question 28, the list 1, 3, 4, 5, and 7 has mean 4 so the deviations of the numbers from their mean are −3, −1, 0, 1, and 3. Those deviations have a mean of zero since they add up to zero. In fact, in any list, the deviations from the mean always add up to zero. So the standard deviation is not calculated by averaging the deviations.

30. The sum of the five numbers is 35, so the mean is 7. Therefore:

Number in list	Deviation from Mean	Deviation Squared
1	−6	36
5	−2	4
7	0	0
9	2	4
13	6	36

The sum of the squared deviations is 80, so the standard deviation is $\sqrt{\frac{80}{5}}$, or 8.9. 4

31. Neither is better; they summarize two different properties of a list of numbers. It is useful, and often vital, to know both properties.

32. The mean proportion of deaths attributed to consumption, 11.59%, was very close to the mean for smallpox, 12.28%. But the standard deviations were very different; the small standard deviation for consumption suggests that the proportion didn't fluctuate much from year to year. Here's an additional thought: since the sum of all the proportions in a given year is 100%, a plausible guess would be that the proportion of deaths from consumption was

low in years when the smallpox proportion was high. That hunch is based on the following reasoning: the number of deaths from consumption probably remained fairly steady from one year to another. In years when Christ-Church Parish had a particularly high number of deaths, the extra deaths were due to epidemic diseases like smallpox, not to an increase in consumption deaths. If the number of consumption deaths remains constant but the number of deaths overall rises, the proportion of deaths caused by consumption will be lower.

33. If you think of the numbers in a list as distributed along a line, the standard deviation gives some sense of how clustered or dispersed the numbers are and the mean is the point around which they are clustered or dispersed.

34. Mean cotton yield exceeded mean corn yield in every state. Arkansas had the greatest ratio of cotton yield to corn yield and also had the greatest cotton yield. Mean cotton yield for Arkansas was close to three times as great as that for the state with the lowest yield, Alabama.

35. **(a)** The unweighted mean is $(20 + 30) \div 2 = 25$.

(b) For the weighted mean:
$$\frac{(100,000 \times 20) + (50,000 \times 30)}{150,000} = 23.33.$$

(c) The unweighted mean is larger because the state with the larger total output had the smaller average yield.

36. The unweighted average yield is larger than the weighted average yield found using output as weights. That means there was some tendency for the large-weight states (those with large total cotton outputs) to have smaller yields per acre than the other cotton states.

37. Graph of Corn and Cotton Yields

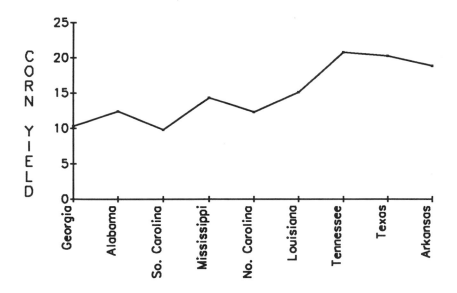

38. Comparison shows that the smallest cotton standard deviation (4.86) is significantly greater than the largest corn standard deviation (3.95). In the postbellum cotton South, the year-to-year variation in cotton yield was three to six times as great, depending on the state, as the year-to-year variation in corn yield.

39. The authors say that many of the farmers had little to lose. Sticking with corn would only keep them safely in poverty, but it provided no hope of escape. By planting cotton they were taking a gamble, and sometimes a gamble will pay off big.

40. You have to weight each of the child counts (0, 1, etc.) by the number of families that had those counts; then divide by the total number of families. The equation looks more complicated than it really is:

$(7 \times 0) + (10 \times 1) + (11 \times 2) + (12 \times 3) + (9 \times 4) + (8 \times 5) + (6 \times 6) + (4 \times 7) + (1 \times 8) + (0 \times 9) + (1 \times 10)$, all divided by 69.

This equals: $(0 + 10 + 22 + 36 + 36 + 40 + 36 + 28 + 8 + 0 + 10)/69$ or 229/69, which equals 3.28, the weighted mean.

41.   (a) 3; (b) 16; (c) 1.

42.   In both distributions the mean would be to the right of the median. That is, more than half the cases would be below the mean.

43.   Virginia: the mean is .65 and the median is 0.
Bristol: the mean is 3.28 and the median is 3.

44.   From the medians, you know that half the Bristol families had three or more children while half the Virginia families were childless. Both the Virginia mean and median are less than 1 while the Bristol values are 3 or more—that's quite a contrast. There must have been a dramatic difference between the two communities with regard to family life. This shows unambiguously in the summary numbers; you wouldn't have to see the actual distribution of children.

45.   In both groups, the mean has been pulled to the right of the median by a few families with many children. In Virginia, four children was a lot. The difference between the mean and median shows that the distributions are skewed as opposed to being symmetrical around the mean.

46.

Virginia Mean approx. 0.65		Bristol Mean approx. 3.25	
Deviations from Mean	No. of Families	Deviations from Mean	No. of Families
0.35	62	0.25	12
0.65	102	0.75	9
1.35	17	1.25	11
2.35	6	1.75	8
3.35	2	2.25	10
		2.75	6
		3.25	7
		3.75	4
		4.75	1
		6.75	1

The standard deviation is an average of the deviations. In Virginia, scanning the list of deviations might lead to a guess not far from that frequent deviation of .65 since there are 62 deviations smaller than that, but close, and 25 deviations bigger than that, but further away. Bristol is harder to see, but the median deviation is 1.75. The mean will be pulled to the right of 1.75 by the few large values and the standard deviation will be a bit bigger than that—2.0 or 2.5 would be reasonable ballpark guesses. The actual standard deviations are: Virginia, 0.85 children per family; Bristol, 2.23 children per family.

47. The table shows that in Virginia, most families had no children while in Bristol 64 years later, about half the families had about the number of children that you would expect to see in a family today, zero to three. Clearly, the old notion of the very large family in colonial times may be invalid. The reason you must be cautious about this conclusion is that both the Demos and Hecht studies counted the number of children at a particular point in time, not over the life of the families. A married couple in Bristol might have had four or five children, but perhaps only the first had been born by the time of the 1774 census.

48. True for the office of alderman and for the mayor's office.

49. Perhaps there was a tendency to begin political life with lesser offices. Accumulation of assets may take place over time as one's political career progresses. Possibly powerful, propertied cliques were more successful in securing the city-wide offices for their own than they were in more local contests where there would be closer contact between the candidate and the electorate.

50. If the candidates uniformly have greater investment in property than the electorate, then certainly the lawmakers will too. Much local law has to do with creating, protecting, and changing property rights. The citizens are not going to be represented by officials whose situations are representative of their own.

51. The large standard deviations indicate that the values are greatly spread out around the means and that the means are probably not typical values.

52. Yes. For example, Winners: $100, $100, $100, $59,700 and Losers: $2000, $2000, $2000, $34,000.

53. Years of schooling for Americans in 1820, age distribution of slaves in Virginia in 1700; population of urban centers in nineteenth-century America; distance from son's household to father's household in eighteenth-century Connecticut.

54. Age at death for American college graduates of 1870; years spent in school for post-World War Two American 18-year olds; years spent in active politics for first-time candidates to the U.S. Senate.

55. No. If this answer is not obvious to you, look back at the distinction between the mean and median.

56. Not necessarily. Perhaps they were more prominent in the community, perhaps older, better established and with a wider network of contacts. Perhaps they were associated with other powerful persons in the community who supported them.

57. A: mean =   5,   median =   5,   standard deviation = 4.
B: mean = 745,   median = 745,   standard deviation = 4.

58.

Coefficient of Variation		
Office	Winners	Losers
Mayor	1.23	1.72
Alderman	1.23	1.10
Councilman	2.05	1.77

II STATISTICAL ARGUMENTS

4 Populations and Samples

In this chapter:

Historians often face the problem that the information available to them is not the result of a designed sampling procedure but consists of whatever information happens to exist in the record. When that occurs, under what conditions or with what qualifications is it reasonable to draw conclusions as though a population of interest had been sampled? In order to consider such a question, it is necessary to have a sense of the basic principles in sampling and some familiarity with the ideas behind common sampling strategies. The key points in this chapter are:

- Samples are distinguished from populations. There are sound reasons why a researcher might choose to study a sample rather than an entire population.

- The goal in sampling is to pick a relatively small number of individuals from a larger population in such a way that the sample is representative of the sampled population.

- Sometimes scholars appear to confuse the roles of samples and populations. They will gather information about a population but then treat that population as though it were a sample of a larger population. Is this a valid procedure?

- Major considerations in choosing a sample are preventing bias in the selection process and estimating the possible size of random errors.

- Some methods of collecting samples are much better than others in dealing with bias and error estimation.

- There is a connection between the size of a sample and its accuracy; some situations demand a much bigger sample than others.

4.1   Population or Sample?

Historians have discovered that some slave populations in the New World grew by natural increase, an excess of births over deaths. This was true in most parts of the American South, at least from the eighteenth century on. But in other slave societies—Jamaica would be an example—more deaths occurred than births. These populations failed to grow except when more slaves were introduced from outside. Why was this? Why did births exceed deaths among some slave populations but not others? "One of the many factors invoked by historians as a possible determinant of slave mortality and fertility," historian John Campbell writes, "is the role of the work regime and the severity of field labor." Focusing on the years 1840 to 1860, Campbell asked whether pregnant slave women were required to perform heavy labor far into pregnancy or whether they were given time off. Did heavily-worked women fieldhands experience a higher risk of miscarriage and stillbirth? To explore this question, Campbell studied the experience of pregnant slaves on one plantation— the Georgia plantation of a slaveowner named George Kollack.[1]

Now, suppose that Campbell's information did show that a powerful and undeniable association existed between the number of weeks pregnant slaves worked in the fields and the likelihood that they would miscarry. Suppose babies usually survived when slave women were given substantial time off early in pregnancy but otherwise usually died. Even if the connection appeared to be obvious and important, a reader would still ask the question: does this interesting pattern show up only on the Kollack plantation, or is Campbell saying that his findings apply to a larger group of slave women? To what population does this discussion apply? What group of women is Campbell really writing about? All slaves everywhere in the Western Hemisphere? All slaves in the Cotton South between 1840 and 1860? Or merely the slaves on the Kollack plantation?

The word <u>population</u> refers to the entire collection of individuals under consideration, as distinguished perhaps from only those individuals on whom data are available. The individuals comprising the population

---

[1] John Campbell, "Work, Pregnancy, and Infant Mortality among Southern Slaves," *Journal of Interdisciplinary History*, 14 (Spring 1984), 793–814; quotation at 793.

might be people, time periods, countries, or any units for which the variables are defined.

1. If you were discussing differences in birth rates among Alabama counties in 1920, who or what would the individuals in your study be, and what would the population as a whole be?

2. If you asserted that your conclusions about birth rates (based on your analysis of patterns in Alabama counties) applied to the entire United States, then what would your population be?

The vital point is that the historian should identify the population, the units under consideration, as explicitly as possible. The reader should not be left in the dark about this. From one point of view, Campbell's data pertain to a very limited population, the pregnant slaves of George Kollack between 1840 and 1860. But Campbell wished to draw broader conclusions; hence he treated the pregnant Kollack slaves as a sample of all pregnant slaves in the New World. In his essay, he suggests that what was true for his sample may also have been true for this larger population. Can he make this extrapolation?

It is perfectly legitimate to use a data set in more than one role. However, if a scholar moves from discussing a population to treating it as a sample of a larger group, then you, the reader, need to ask whether this is a justified thing to do. The key issue is whether the small population—the sample—is truly representative of the larger one. What must be true of the sample in order to justify that leap? The only requirement is the obvious one, that the sample be representative of the population with respect to the variables being examined. The sample and the population don't have to resemble each other in all respects, just in those respects that are being studied. Still, historians should explain why it is reasonable to believe that the variables being studied are alike in the sample and the population.

3. Suggest one or two ways in which pregnant slave women might have differed in different parts of the New World that are irrelevant for the kind of investigation that Campbell was carrying out.

4. Briefly defend John Campbell's suggestion that it may be reasonable to treat the work and pregnancy experience of slave women on the Kollack plantation as a sample of the experience of New World slave women generally.

5. Suppose that data from 200 households in Boston in 1850 revealed
    that the usual relationship between age and income was inverted
    so that, on average, younger heads of households tended to have
    larger incomes than older heads of households. Imagine that the
    200 households were all located in a single neighborhood and were
    all headed either by Irish immigrants or by the American-born
    children of Irish immigrants. Is it reasonable to think of these 200
    households as a sample of some larger population insofar as the
    relationship between age and income is concerned?

6. If you are tempted to think of the households in Question 5 as a
    sample from some larger population, give examples of one or two
    larger populations you have in mind.

The distinction between populations and samples may seem too obvious to mention. But look over Tables 4.1 through 4.3 and ask yourself
whether the issue is really so simple.

Table 4.1
Characteristics of workers who stay or leave: Warren, Pennsylvania, 1870–1880

Property Status	Stay	Leave
Low	36.11%	62.71%
Middle	28.33	20.34
High	35.56	16.95
N	180	413

Source: See Table 1.4

In Table 4.1, which you also saw in Chapter 1, would you say the
authors, Anthony E. Boardman and Michael P. Weber, were discussing
sample data or population data? From one point of view, Table 4.1 displays population data. The numbers summarize information assembled
about the residents of Warren, Pennsylvania, in the 1870s. But just
as Campbell did with his data from the Kollack plantation, Boardman
and Weber argue that the patterns they discovered in Warren represented patterns in a much larger population. "The growth experiences
of this community," they tell us, "closely paralleled the 19th-century
American pattern. Moreover, the similarity of workers' experiences in
Warren, South Bend [Indiana], and Waltham [Massachusetts] illustrate
the importance of the Warren case as a representative sample of worker

mobility in 19th-century urban America." [2]

Once you recognize that the authors want you to treat the Warren data as a sample, you must then ask whether they have given you good reason to believe that the workers in Warren were indeed similar to other nineteenth-century workers with respect to the variables being studied, mobility and property status. How about Table 4.2, which you encountered first in Chapter 3?

Table 4.2
Children per family in Bristol, Rhode Island, 1688/9

Number of Children in Family	0	1	2	3	4	5	6	7	8	9	10	Total 226
Number of Families	7	10	11	12	9	8	6	4	1	0	1	69

Source: See Table 3.9

This is as close to a historical description of an entire population as you are likely to come. First, the original census included all the residents of Bristol, not just a sample of the residents. But beyond that, historian John Demos restricted his conclusions to the Bristol population, the same group on which he had full information. Table 4.2 does not represent a sample of some larger population. Interestingly, both the tables just discussed—from Boardman and Weber's analysis of Warren, Pennsylvania and Demos's of Bristol, Rhode Island—summarize the experience of an entire town. The difference between them lies not in the way the data were gathered but in the breadth of the authors' conclusions.

We are discussing the difference between populations and samples because it is fundamental to the distinction between descriptive and inferential statistics. Descriptive statistics is the use of statistics to describe a body of data without implying that the observed patterns extend beyond the cases at hand. If you summarize John Demos's Bristol data using means, medians, and standard deviations or graphs, you are using descriptive statistics.

If, however, you decide to use the Bristol data to draw conclusions about a larger population, you are crossing the line into the field of inferential statistics. The average number of children per family in

---

[2] Anthony E. Boardman and Michael P. Weber, "Economic Growth and Occupational Mobility in 19th Century Urban America: A Reappraisal," *Journal of Social History*, 11 (Fall 1977), 53.

Bristol in 1688/9 was about 3.27 (226 ÷ 69). That's a description. But if you go on to claim that Bristol was similar to other towns in 1688/9 and that 3.27 is a good guess as to the average number of children throughout the English colonies at the time of the Glorious Revolution, that's an inference. The distinction is important because inferences have to be defended. Much of the material that we will introduce in this chapter and the next three focuses on this problem of defending the claim that one can infer things about a larger population from examining a small sample.

Table 4.3
Proportion of black and Italian families with income contributed by wives, children, and lodgers, New York and Philadelphia, 1911

Group, City	% with Wives Working	% with Children Working	% with Lodgers	(N)
Blacks, New York	51	10	27	145
Blacks, Phila.	54	13	41	71
Italians, New York	36	19	20	333
Italians, Phila.	8	23	16	195

Source: See Table 1.1.

Consider Table 4.3, a third example from earlier in the book: Elizabeth H. Pleck's analysis of family income strategies in 1911. In Table 4.3 Pleck clearly does not have information on all black and Italian families in the two cities. She has a sample. Even if she wished to restrict the conclusions to Philadelphia and New York, she must make the case that the sample is representative of the larger populations. Take the two rows pertaining to Philadelphia: the author should describe the procedure that was used for selecting those particular 71 black and 195 Italian families and should explicitly defend the implication that those small groups are representative of all black and Italian families in Philadelphia with respect to family work patterns and the taking of lodgers.

7. Make up or find an example, using real current groups and current variables of interest, in which a researcher might have data on some population and wish to use that population as though it were a sample in order to make inferences about a larger group.

8. For the same large group and the same variables you used in your answer to Question 7, how feasible would it be to gather data on the entire population? How do you think a researcher could find a sample that truly reflected the entire population?

To sum up, we have discussed three possible situations:

- Sometimes a historian has data on all the individuals in some population and limits the discussion to just that population. When this happens, no question of sample representativeness arises.

- Sometimes a historian has data on all the individuals in some population but extends the conclusions to some larger population. Here you should look for a justification of the assumption that the one population can be treated as a representative sample of the other. This is a situation in which justification is often lacking in articles and books.

- Finally, sometimes a historian has a body of data obtained by deliberately sampling some large population. Here you should expect an explanation of the sampling method and some assurance that the method is consistent with the goal of representativeness.

9. For the three historical writings mentioned in this section: Boardman and Weber, Demos, and Pleck, state which of the three situations applies to each example.

4.2 Sampling for an Ethnic History Project

In creating a sample, an investigator selects some cases from the population he or she is studying in order to reduce the sheer amount of information that has to be examined; but if all goes well, sampling will not seriously compromise the accuracy of the results. The statistical results arrived at for the sample will closely resemble the results that would have been obtained by studying the entire population.

At a state historical society in the 1970s, researchers undertook a study of the national origins of the state's residents in 1880. Because the project director was uneasy about taking a sample, it was decided to record information from the U.S. census of population about every person residing in the state in 1880. This amounted to more than 781,000 individuals. Was the decision not to sample a prudent one?[3]

---

[3]Records of the Minnesota Ethnic History Project, Minnesota Historical Society Archives, State Archives, St. Paul, Minnesota; interviews with researchers who had assisted on the project. The major publication arising from the project was June D. Holmquist, ed., *They Chose Minnesota: A Survey of the State's Ethnic Groups* (St. Paul, Minn., 1981). For the information about Hungarians mentioned below, see p. 424.

You could make a case that a research project of this sort needed to gather data about all residents. Some small ethnic groups—the 356 persons of Hungarian origin listed in the 1880 census, for example—might have been missed entirely in a sample. Since the overall aim of the research project was to call attention to the state's rich ethnic heritage, it seemed particularly important to gather information about marginal groups.

On the other hand, you could make an argument that these scholars should have drawn a sample of several thousand families from the 1880 population of the state. Because the state legislature had appropriated limited funds for the project, the research team was able to record only a handful of pieces of information about each resident of 1880, even though the source, the U.S. census, contained information about many other matters as well. The team chose to record each resident's sex, place of residence, and place of birth, as well as the birthplaces of the individual's mother and father. That's five variables. Five times 781,000 equals 3,905,000 items of data for this project—an immense, almost unmanageable number.[4] Even so, the project did not record such things as the individual's age, occupation, or marital status, how many people were in the family, or whether the individual could read and write. Thus the decision not to sample the 1880 population resulted in a database of limited use.

Before you make up your mind about this example, it may be helpful if you have more information about how a quantitative historian draws a sample, the different sampling strategies available, and the pitfalls of sampling. We'll therefore proceed with our discussion of these matters and will return to the ethnic history project in Section 4.9.

Historians and social scientists frequently use samples rather than investigating an entire population. Several reasons come to mind. First, counting a large group in its entirety could well be impossible. Imagine trying to find the political preferences of all American males aged eighteen and over. By the time a researcher had located and queried everyone who had been eighteen and over when he began the project,

---

[4] At the time this project was under way, scholars using census returns commonly encoded the information by hand onto ruled sheets of paper (coding sheets) and later had the long rows of numbers keypunched onto punchcards. A cardreading machine would read the card's information into a computer's temporary memory each time the database was to be used. The two steps of hand coding and keypunching inevitably gave rise to many errors. Today, by contrast, a research assistant would almost certainly type the data directly from the microfilmed census returns into a microcomputer. Reducing the number of steps has reduced the risk of making transcription and keypunching errors.

some of those men would have died and some seventeen-year-olds would have turned eighteen. Perhaps the researcher would have died too, of old age.

Second, samples enable a scholar to work much more efficiently. Suppose you had the budget, time, and computing resources to make and process 100,000 observations about a population. If your study must include every individual from a population of 100,000 people, then you will be able to handle only one piece of information per person. But if you can take a sample of size 2,000 from the population of size 100,000, you can deal with fifty pieces of information about each individual and thereby explore a range of interesting historical questions.

So it is often desirable and sometimes essential to work with samples. Since this is so, you must be alert to the possibility (in fact, it's a near certainty) that a sample contains errors. But even an imperfect sample can serve a useful purpose if the historian and the reader have some idea of the nature and consequences of the imperfections. The remainder of this section and the next three sections will discuss four sources of error:

- Limitations in the original sources

- Processing errors

- Systematic bias, the result of a poorly designed sample

- Random sampling error

We can address the first two problems fairly briefly:

Limitations in the original sources. Some of the information in the original sources may be only approximately correct; some may be wildly incorrect. Information may not have been recorded for some individuals (the perennial problem of missing data). In using a nineteenth-century manuscript U.S. census, for example, researchers encounter a myriad of errors such as misspellings of names and incorrect information about the age and family relationships of some persons. Many sources such as censuses and city directories were less careful in recording information about blacks and members of immigrant communities than in recording information about white, middle-class families. Also, it often happened that Americans misinformed the census-takers who came to their doors. A man might state the ages of his children incorrectly or forget to mention the lodger renting an upstairs room. For that matter, some people simply refuse to give any information at all. For all these reasons, the idea of a complete count, a full and accurate census, is an idealization that is never more than approximated in any large population.

10. Suppose that John Demos had excluded 10% of the families in Bristol, Rhode Island from Table 4.2 because it was unclear how many children they had or even if they had any children at all. How might the missing data have influenced the resulting pattern? Would Demos have been justified in leaving out those families? (This is a hypothetical situation—Demos didn't really omit 10% of the families.)

Processing errors include the accidental miscoding or miscopying of data from the historical sources by the persons doing this work, ambiguous instructions to staff, deliberate falsification of information, machine malfunctions, overlooking one of the microfilm reels containing the census returns—in sum, any breakdown in carrying out the study as it had been planned.

Note that these first two sources of error, flaws in the original sources and processing errors, will be a problem when working with complete populations as well as with samples. In fact, processing errors may be less of a problem with a sample than with a large population because a small project will typically involve fewer, more highly trained staff members whose work will be easier to supervise and control. Also, with fewer bits of information, there are fewer opportunities to make a mistake. The Current Population Survey, published once a month by the U.S. Bureau of the Census, has been superior in several respects to the complete census of the American population taken every ten years. This is because the CPS works with samples of the population.

11. Comment on the following statement made by a project assistant in the ethnic history project discussed earlier: "The figures we have derived will not usually correspond to the published census figures.... The published census figures are based on a sample; ours are the actual figures.... In this sense, we have more accurate figures than the census itself."[5]

The third and fourth sources of error, **bias in sample design** and **sampling error**, are not present in a complete census. These are the possible cost you might pay if you decide to use a sample instead of an entire population. Bias is discussed in the next two sections while sampling error is the topic of Section 4.5.

---

[5] Minnesota Historical Society Archives, box 369.

4.3   The Literary Digest Poll of 1936

Our third potential source of error in a sample is **systematic bias** resulting from a poorly designed sample, one that over-represents or under-represents some groups in the larger population. Picking a valid sample (a sample that truly represents the attributes of the larger population) can be a tricky problem. On occasion, a mistaken sampling strategy has led to hilarious results.

As a cautionary tale, statistics textbooks often tell the story of a famous episode in the early history of opinion surveys.[6] A magazine called the *Literary Digest* predicted in the autumn of 1936 that Republican presidential candidate Alf Landon would win 57% of the popular vote and defeat incumbent president Franklin Roosevelt in the election coming up that November. The *Digest*'s prediction was based on a sample of nearly two and a half million people. That's hundreds of times larger than the sample size a pollster would use today, and it made the prediction appear very plausible indeed.

But Landon did not defeat Roosevelt. Instead, FDR was re-elected with 60.8% of the popular vote—one of the greatest landslides in American history. How could the *Digest* have gone so wrong? The problem was that despite its great size, the sample was biased: the voters in the sample were not representative of the general electorate with respect to presidential preferences. The extreme bias-error resulted from the manner in which the *Digest*'s researchers had chosen the sample. First, they had compiled a list of 10 million people from sources such as telephone books. But in the midst of the Great Depression of the 1930s, millions of poor Americans did not have telephones. The sample of 10 million thus tended to include a far higher proportion of prosperous voters than the proportion in the American population at large.

Then the *Digest* mailed a questionnaire to the 10 million people on the list; the magazine received back about 2.4 million responses. But this second step tended to heighten the bias toward prosperous, high-status voters.

12.   Explain how a mailed questionnaire might be biased.

The lesson of this famous story is that when one is sampling a population, the sample must be representative of the larger population from which it is drawn with respect to the variable being studied. If you are

---

[6]David Freedman, Robert Pisani, and Roger Purves, *Statistics* (New York, 1978), pp. 302–04.

studying the height of male adolescents, don't take your sample in the basketball team's locker room.

4.4 Readers of the New-York Magazine

In principle, it's easy to create an unbiased sample: all one has to do is ensure that every individual in the population stands an equal chance of being picked for the sample. That's the purpose of simple random sampling. A simple random sample is one that resembles drawing numbered slips out of a hat. That eliminates bias because no individual has a greater chance of getting into the sample than any other.

Here's a recent example of a historian's taking a random sample. David Paul Nord, who is interested in reading habits in the United States during the era of the early republic, found that in 1790 the *New-York Magazine* had published its list of 370 subscribers, 298 of whom lived in New York City. From city directories and other sources, Nord gathered information such as occupation and street address for 265 of the 298 New York City subscribers. Nord wanted to compare subscribers to the *New-York Magazine* living in New York City to residents of the city generally. Did magazine subscribers differ from other New Yorkers, and if so, in what ways? Since New York City had thousands of residents, Nord "drew a simple random sample of 400 from the 1790 city directory."[7]

13. In Nord's study, what was the population from which the sample of 400 was drawn?

14. Without knowing exactly how the author drew the sample, but knowing that it was a simple random sample, what can you infer about the relationship of the sample to the population?

Ensuring that a sample is truly drawn randomly, so that each individual has an equal chance of inclusion in the sample, is an intriguing challenge. Bias in the design of a sample can be very subtle and hard to spot. In an essay describing a procedure for selecting a sample of older Americans from the U.S. census of 1900, historian Daniel Scott Smith lists several biases that tended to creep into the sample. Because Smith sampled older people in households, the proportions of single

---

[7]David Paul Nord, "A Republican Literature: A Study of Magazine Reading and Readers in Late Eighteenth-Century New York," *American Quarterly*, 40 (March 1988), 42–64; quotation at 47.

males and of persons over age 75 were lower in his sample than in the entire population. He discovered that the single males and the very old were more likely to be institutionalized and therefore under represented in the households. But more subtle still, Smith reports that because of the technical details of how census information was laid out on the microfilm pages, it made a difference if his research assistants read the pages from top to bottom or bottom to top.[8]

15. Imagine the case of a historian who wants to draw a sample of 500 families from a Boston city directory of 1830 that she knows to contain the names of all 50,000 residents of the city, listed by family. (Assume that the 50,000 residents comprise 10,000 families.) Comment on whether each of the following procedures gives all families an equal chance of being picked for the sample; for those that are biased, identify the nature of the bias, if possible.

(a) She takes the first 500 families in the directory.

(b) The directory has 1000 pages, so she takes the first family listed on each even-numbered page.

(c) She makes a list of all the family names in the directory. Then she invites some undergraduates to circle the names on the list that they happen to like. The first 500 families with those names constitute the sample.

(d) She rolls a pair of dice; they show a total of nine, so she picks the ninth family in the directory. Then she rolls again and gets five, so she counts down five from the family already picked. She continues in this way until she has rolled the dice 500 times and picked 500 families.

(e) Using a computer program that generates random numbers, she obtains a list of 500 random numbers between 1 and 10,000. She numbers the families in the city directory in order, then selects for her sample those families whose numbers appear on the random-number list.

(f) She instructs her research assistant to close his eyes, open the directory, and stab his finger at a page. The family under his finger goes into the sample. She tells him to repeat this process 500 times.

[8] Daniel Scott Smith, "A Community-Based Sample of the Older Population from the 1880 and 1900 United States Manuscript Census," *Historical Methods*, 11 (Spring 1978), 67–74.

Do you understand intuitively why a random procedure is best? If you have really drawn a random sample and some attribute of interest shows up in only 10% of the individuals in the sample, that strongly suggests that the attribute exists in only about 10% of the individuals in the larger population. No other explanation (except bad luck in drawing the sample) can account for its appearing only 10% of the time in the sample.

We now consider the possibility that the "luck of the draw" might have queered the sample. Random sampling error is the last of the four possible sources of error listed earlier.

4.5   Random Sampling Error

Most people distrust samples, particularly samples that are much smaller than the population from which they are drawn. Their distrust doesn't come so much from a sensitivity to the possibility of bias in sample design as it does from the commonsense realization that, just by chance, a small subgroup might be quite different from the entire population. If you flip a coin ten times, you might get heads eight out of the ten flips just by luck and then draw the erroneous conclusion that someone had tampered with the coin. In the same way, even in a well designed sampling procedure, some group might be over- or under-represented just by the luck of the draw. **Random sampling error** is the chance error, the "bad luck," that might cause the characteristics of the sample to be different from the corresponding characteristics of the entire population—even if the sample has been selected using simple random sampling. It is the last of the four sources of error listed in Section 4.2.

Table 4.4
Ages of 40 captured Confederate soldiers (hypothetical data)

Age	N
20	30
25	10

To illustrate the problem of random sampling error, consider the made-up example in Table 4.4. Suppose that you have information about 40 Confederate soldiers who were captured in battle. Your star graduate student, Ralph, wants to know the mean age of these Confederates; but rather than do the arithmetic for the entire population, he decides to take a random sample of two soldiers. Ralph prepares 40 slips of paper and on each slip he writes the age of one of the soldiers. He puts the slips in an empty cardfile box, draws out one slip, looks at the number on it, replaces it in the box, and draws out a second. His calculation of the mean age of all the soldiers is going to be the average from the two slips he happened to draw.

16. Use Table 4.4 to compute the mean age of the 40 soldiers.

17. By drawing a sample of size two, Ralph can only get three possible average ages. What are these ages and how might he have obtained each?

18. Explain why it's impossible for Ralph to get the correct answer, which you know from having answered Question 16.

So because he sampled, Ralph is going to miss the actual mean age for the 40 soldiers, either by a little bit or by a greater amount. This error is known as random sampling error. While it might be possible to hit the true value right on the head, in most situations the probability of doing so is virtually zero—so don't worry about it. Hitting the true value on the head isn't the purpose of sampling anyway. The real danger in taking a sample isn't that the sample value is a little bit off the population value, but that it might be quite far off. You can never eliminate this risk completely. While random sampling has this imperfection, it has two major advantages that more than compensate. First, the researcher can calculate the likelihood that the sample differs from the population by some amount. Second, by raising the size of the sample, he or she can reduce (though never completely eliminate) the risk of a large sampling error.

In the case of Ralph's sample of two from a population of forty, the worst error would be to draw the age 25 from the box twice in succession. But it's not very likely that Ralph, or anyone, would do this. On any one draw, Ralph's chance of picking a slip with 25 on it is ten out of forty since ten such slips are in the box. The likelihood of picking two slips with 25 on them in succession, then, is: $10/40 \times 10/40$, or $100/1600$. This reduces to $1/16$. Ralph would come up with a sample mean of 25 about once in every 16 tries.

19. What is the probability that Ralph would get a sample mean of 20 when he draws two times with replacement from the box?

In this fictionalized example, the largest possible error wouldn't be too likely. That's the situation where Ralph might conclude that the mean age of the 40 soldiers was 25 years, a figure 3.75 years too high. But Ralph would make that large an error only once in 16 samples. In contrast, the smaller error due to pulling two slips with 20 on them would be more probable—Ralph would be this close nine times in sixteen tries. The essential task for a quantitative historian with regard to sampling error is not to eliminate all risk of error, which is impossible, but to reduce the risk of large errors.

20. What is the probability that Ralph will get a sample mean of 22.5 years?

21. Make up a simple table showing the probability of Ralph's drawing every possible combination of two slips.

The point of the above example is not that you learn how to calculate the probability of errors of different sizes. What is important is that you realize that with random sampling, one can estimate these probabilities. You can estimate the probability of a large error in the case of the imaginary Confederate soldiers only because Ralph picked blindly. If Ralph had peeked just a bit, you wouldn't have a reasonable way to know what his quick peek had done to the probability of drawing a 20 or a 25. So drawing blindly has a big advantage over peeking as a sample design.

To sum up, an ideal sampling design should have three attributes:

- It should avoid bias.

- It should enable the researcher and onlookers to estimate the chance of a large sampling error.

- It should minimize the chance of large sampling errors.

A pleasant fact about sampling is that randomization (drawing blind or employing some other chance mechanism similar in spirit to flipping a coin) accomplishes goals 1 and 2 while goal 3 can be achieved by picking the proper sample size.

22. You are studying a city of about 100,000 people in 1880 and you plan to take a sample of 1000 from the 1880 census. State which kind of error each of the following situations seems to embody, and whether the problem could crop up only in a sample or could appear in the data from an entire population:

(a) You decide that the sample will consist of the people numbered 1, 101, 201, 301, etc., in the microfilmed census returns for the city.

(b) In recording data from the microfilm copy of the manuscript census, you discover that you aren't certain how to spell some family names because you often cannot read the census taker's handwriting.

(c) Concerned that your first sampling procedure was flawed and uneasy about the illegible names, you decide to start over. This time your sample will consist of the first legible name on each page of the census.

(d) After entering the ages of the 1000 people in your computer database, you run a frequency distribution to discover how often each age was reported. You discover that ages ending in zero (10, 20, 30, etc.) and in five (5, 15, 25, etc.) show up much more commonly than ages ending in one, three, seven, or nine.

(e) In checking your database, you find a person listed as a male head of household, married and with his wife and three young children living in the home, whose occupation was carpentry, but whose age was 97.

(f) You know that there were a few black families in your population, but no such families appear in your sample.

(g) In reviewing the database, you find several individuals over 18 years of age for whom no marital status is given. In some cases you think you can guess what their marital status was by checking the age and sex of other persons in the same household. In other cases you aren't so confident.

(h) You have a clerical assistant who enters information from the census forms into a computer. Later you discover that whenever the census taker failed to check the box for "able to read" for a particular person on the 1880 census form, your assistant entered "not able to read" for that person in the computer database.

23. You want to know the mean number of children per family in Detroit in 1860. You are fortunate enough to have a complete list of all the children in that city from the 1860 census. So you randomly select 1000 children from the list; for each selected child

you determine the number of children in that child's family. What bias might result? What kind of error is being made?

In addition to avoiding sample bias, random sampling enables researchers to estimate the accuracy of predictions made from the sample and to choose a sample size that will have only a very small chance of yielding a large error. To see how sample size affects sampling error, imagine that you are going to estimate the average age of merchant seamen working out of San Francisco in the first decade of this century. Somehow you have access to a list of such men from which you can take random samples.

First, suppose you take a simple random sample of size one. About how far from the true average would you expect that one age to be? You may remember from Chapter 3 that the standard deviation of a list of numbers is the size of an average distance of numbers in the list from the mean of the list. The number you sampled is just one number from the list of ages, so, on average, you can expect the sample age to deviate from the mean age of all seamen by about the standard deviation of seamen's ages.

Now suppose you had picked a sample of four seamen instead of only one. Some of these might be further than one standard deviation from the true average and some might be closer. A typical result could look like this:

Unknown true average age, 30 years
Unknown true standard deviation, 5 years
Sampled ages: 24, 28, 35, 37

Notice that only the sample age 35 is exactly one standard deviation from the mean of 30 while the others are just a bit closer or further away. But here's the magic trick—take an average of the sample ages and you get quite close to the true mean because the numbers above and below age 30 tend to balance out. The average of the ages in the sample is 31. If you use 31 as your estimate of the age of the whole population, you would be making a sampling error much smaller than five, the standard deviation of the whole population.

You can see that by raising your sample size to four and using the sample average as an estimate of the population average, you have a reasonable hope of reducing the sampling error, which is the difference between your estimate and the true mean. The general rule (known as the sample size square root rule) is that the expected difference between the true population mean and its estimate (the average of the sample values) is the population standard deviation divided by the square root of the sample size. In statistical jargon, that expected error is called the standard error.

The similarity between the terms standard error and standard deviation is more than coincidental. Standard deviation (abbreviated SD) is the expected difference between the average score on some variable for a population and the score for one individual in that population. Standard error (abbreviated SE) is the expected difference between the average score for the entire population and the average score in the sample. The standard error for seamen's ages would vary by sample size as shown in Table 4.5.

Table 4.5
Seamen's ages: how the standard error changes with sample size

Sample Size (N)	Standard Error $(SD \div (\sqrt{N})$	Remarks
1	5.0	same as SD
4	2.5	$5 \div (\sqrt{4})$
25	1.0	$5 \div (\sqrt{25})$
100	0.5	$5 \div (\sqrt{100})$

SD = standard deviation

Notice that the standard error of 0.5 depends on the standard deviation of 5 and the sample size of 100. This relationship holds whether the number of seamen in San Francisco was 1000 or 10,000. It doesn't matter if the sample is a large fraction of the population or a small one: the sampling error is the same. What matters is the absolute size of the sample.

The message of the table on seamen's ages is that you can make very accurate estimates of population averages if you use reasonably big samples. The magic part of that message is that the accuracy of the estimate only depends on the sample size and not on the population size.

A simple random sample, such as drawing names out of a hat, is sometimes inconvenient, inefficient or impossible to carry out. The next section briefly describes four other sampling strategies that you will sometimes encounter: systematic, multistage, stratified, and cluster sampling.

4.6   Other Sampling Strategies

Systematic sampling is the alternative most like simple random sampling. If a scholar has a list of 1000 names and takes every tenth name, that would be an example of a systematic sample. If he decided in advance to start with the first name on the list and then take the eleventh, twenty-first, and so on, his sample would not have the feature that every individual in the population had an equal chance of being chosen. The ninth name would have no chance of being included in the sample while the eleventh name would be sure to be included. However, if the scholar randomly chose a number from one to ten to determine the starting point and then took every tenth name from that point on, the sample would resemble a simple random sample in the sense that, prior to the procedure, every name would have an equal chance of getting into the sample.

Claudia Goldin used systematic sampling in studying the differences in labor force participation between white and black women in 1870 and 1880. Over the last century, women's participation in the labor force has increased dramatically with profound effects on families and the economy. But Goldin points out that not all groups of women participated in the change to the same extent. "The most impressive labor market gains during this [1870–1880] period," she says, "were achieved by married white women." [9]

To compare black and white women, Goldin sampled the 1870 and 1880 U.S. population censuses. Her sampling technique proceeded something like this: for a particular city like Atlanta, she took every fiftieth page in the manuscript census returns. She then recorded the information about every person in every household that started on a chosen page, even if the record ran over to the next page. Let's assume that prior to the start of sampling, each page had an equal chance, one in fifty, of entering the sample.

24.   Describe two ways to pick one page out of fifty so that each page has an equal chance of getting into the sample.

25.   If each page has an equal chance of entering the sample, does each household have an equal chance? Note that since some households are larger than others, some pages will contain fewer household records than others.

---

[9] Claudia Goldin, "Female Labor Force Participation: The Origin of Black and White Differences, 1870 and 1880," *Journal of Economic History*, 37 (March 1977), 87–108; quotation at 87.

26.   With Goldin's method, does each woman in Atlanta have an equal chance of getting into the sample?

Sometimes historians use systematic and simple random sampling in a step-by-step fashion, first sampling systematically from a source like the census and then picking randomly from the parts of the source that had been systematically chosen. This process is called multistage sampling. Goldin could have used multistage sampling by first picking every fiftieth census page, as she did, but then picking one household randomly off each of those pages.

27.   If Goldin had used multistage sampling, would each household have had an equal chance of getting into the sample? How about each woman? Do you see any possibilities for bias if that technique had been used?

Researchers sometimes prefer cluster sampling to simple random sampling when they believe that most of the variation in the factor being studied takes place within clusters rather than between clusters. In a cluster sample, one deliberately samples particular clusters—cities, school districts, religious groups, or similar groupings. Claudia Goldin actually used cluster sampling in conjunction with the systematic sampling procedure just described. Her clusters were seven Southern cities: Atlanta, Charleston, Richmond, Mobile, New Orleans, Norfolk, and Savannah. She did not choose these cities randomly from a list of cities; she deliberately selected them because in her judgment they were typical with respect to the black/white labor patterns she wished to describe.

28.   On the basis of the sample derived in this way, Goldin estimates that in 1870, 49.5% of black women and 16.5% of white women were in the labor force. What population does the sample represent?

29.   What argument should Goldin provide to help you judge whether or not her cluster sampling technique was appropriate?

Anthony E. Boardman and Michael P. Weber, in their study of mobility in nineteenth-century Warren, Pennsylvania (Section 1.3), use the town of Warren as a cluster sample. The authors reason that Warren was representative of small, rapidly growing industrial areas and that the patterns of occupational and social mobility in Warren can stand as a general model of the connection between urban economic growth and mobility. If they are wrong, if there was considerable cluster-to-cluster (i.e., city-to-city) variation in those patterns, then a reader should not extrapolate from the experience of Warren.

Stratified sampling is a fourth common sampling technique. When Daniel Scott Smith and his associates were planning how to sample Americans over age 65 from the 1900 census, they selected a sample size of 3000 but decided not to take a simple random sample. Instead, they sampled the rural population separately from the population living in cities over 25,000. They had two reasons. First, they were interested in studying the social problems that old people faced such as poverty and isolation from relatives. They suspected that most older people experiencing such problems lived in cities—i.e., that there was an important difference between older people in rural and urban areas. However, only 21% of the older population as a whole lived in cities. A random sample of size 3000 would have included only about 630 of the urban elderly. So the research team more than doubled the size of its urban sample, ending up with 1333 cases of urban elderly people.

The second reason for beefing up the urban part of the study and reducing the size of the non-urban sample was that the urban population was much more heterogeneous. In order to get an adequate number of cases from interesting subgroups such as urban black elderly people, it was important to raise the size of the urban sample. In this way, the researchers ensured that they had an adequate number of elderly people in each stratum (rural America and urban America). They singled out this rural-urban distinction out for stratified sampling because they were already convinced that it contributed strongly to variation in the population they were studying. Because of the stratified sampling method, they could get by with a smaller overall sample size of about 3000.[10]

30.   If Smith and his colleagues had stuck with simple random sampling and also had wanted to be sure to get at least 1300 cases of older Americans from cities over 25,000, how large would their total sample of the elderly have had to be?

31.   By stratifying, Smith of course over-represented the urban elderly in the sample as a whole and under-represented the rural. In making generalizations about the United States (rather than just the urban or rural parts of the country), how would the research team have corrected for this deliberate imbalance?

---

[10]Smith, "A Community-Based Sample," pp. 67–68.

With cluster sampling, the underlying assumption is that most of the interesting variation is within the clusters, not between them. With stratified sampling, by contrast, the assumption is that the strata are quite different with respect to the variable being studied. If you were studying primary school children in Iowa to see how their heights changed as they moved from grade to grade, you might be justified in using cluster sampling—just study a few school districts whose experience could be extrapolated to the whole state. If you were studying how well prepared the children were for reading when they first arrived at school, then you might want to use school districts as strata because the affluent suburban districts might have experience quite different from others. When the assumptions about similarity or difference prove false, a cluster or stratified sample may not be a good way to model the target population.

4.7 An Early Survey of Sexual Attitudes

Often historians are tempted to use a highly imperfect quantitative sample because it is there, and nothing better will ever be available. A historian can't go out and select a random sample from a list of all pregnant slaves in the New World in 1840. No such list could ever exist. Instead, he or she must deal with the data at hand. Statisticians call these samples of convenience; since historians are so often stuck with such samples, they need to be especially sensitive to the reasons convenience samples are attacked in virtually every elementary statistics text.

The case against using available data goes like this. Suppose you wanted to survey the alcohol consumption habits of American men. You go to the nearest busy corner, because it is convenient, and you question the men who come by about their drinking habits. If there is a popular bar on that corner, or a meetingroom for Alcoholics Anonymous, your results will obviously be very biased. But they might be biased in more subtle ways even without the bar or the AA room. Perhaps the age or income distribution or ethnic makeup of this neighborhood is not typical of the entire population, and perhaps such factors are connected to men's drinking habits. But samples must be representative, not biased, if they are to be used as a basis for generalizations. So the statistics texts urge some kind of probability sampling, whenever possible, to reduce the chance of bias. An ideal, never carried out in practice, would be to take a simple random sample of all American men.

In a famous article on women's sexuality in nineteenth-century America, Carl N. Degler of Stanford University devotes about half the essay to an analysis of questionnaires filled out by a group of women for Dr. Clelia Duel Mosher, a physician at Stanford.[11] These data were later deposited in the university archives. As far as is known, the "Mosher Survey" is the earliest compilation of data on women's sexual attitudes and behavior ever gathered in the United States.

The term "survey" may be a little misleading, however: Dr. Mosher administered the questionnaire to 45 women between the 1890s and 1920. And as Degler points out, the women filling out the questionnaire were not representative of American women generally: they were far better educated, with at least 34 of the 45 having attended a college or normal school. Nine of the women had attended Stanford. Degler concludes that the respondents "were principally middle- or upper-middle-class women" though not members of a "leisure class," since over half had worked prior to marriage, usually as teachers.[12] And other biases almost certainly crept into the sample—for example, some women may have refused to fill out the questionnaire when asked.

A historian can justify using a convenience sample of some larger population. In the example of men's drinking habits, the key issue is not that the men arrive on the street corner through a random process, but rather than their presence on the corner be completely independent of their drinking habits. Randomization is a device to ensure independence. So first, the historian ought to try to describe the circumstances that caused some individuals to be included in the available data set and others to be excluded. Next, he or she needs to make a case that it is likely that the causes of inclusion and exclusion were independent of the patterns found in the data.

If an archaeologist finds nine ancient coins during a lengthy dig on a Greek island, he may be able to infer that the factors that led to his finding those particular coins are independent of the variables of interest, say the coins' silver content, inscriptions, or weight. He may thus conclude that he can use the found coins as a random sample of all ancient coins on the island. Of course, you as a reader can never be certain that "found data" are unbiased, and no historian could prove definitively that no bias existed. But certainty is not demanded, only plausibility and reasonableness. Specifically, does Degler set out the

---

[11] Carl N. Degler, "What Ought to Be and What Was: Women's Sexuality in the Nineteenth Century," *American Historical Review*, 79 (December 1974), 1467–90. Degler's discussion of the Mosher data is found at pp. 1479–90.

[12] *Ibid.*, 1482.

circumstances that led some kinds of women to be included and others not to show up in the Mosher Survey? Does he make a case that these biases were independent of the patterns found in the questionnaires—i.e., that they had no bearing on women's sexual attitudes and behavior?

Table 4.6
Response to the query: "Do you always have a venereal orgasm [during intercourse]?"

Response	N	Percentage
No response	2	4.4%
"No" with no further comment	5	11.1
"Always"	9	20.0
"Usually"	7	15.5
"Sometimes," "Not Always," or		
"No" with instances	18	40.0
"Once" or "Never"	4	8.8

Source: Carl N. Degler, "What Ought to Be and What Was: Women's Sexuality in the Nineteenth Century," *American Historical Review*, 79 (December 1974), p. 1484, Table 1.

Mosher asked some twenty-five questions, about half of them dealing with sexuality. Degler summarizes responses to one query in Table 4.6. While conceding that the number of women surveyed was small and that as a group they were unrepresentative of American women generally, Degler vigorously defends using the Mosher Survey:

> So far as I know, this is the only survey of sexual attitudes and practices in the nineteenth century.... Certainly the systematic questioning of forty-five women at considerable length ... ought to be at least as significant in shaping historians' conceptions of women's sexuality as the scraps of information ... which have been the bases of our traditional picture of women's sexual attitudes and behavior in the nineteenth century.... Obviously the Mosher Survey is not the final word.... But at the same time it ought not to be rejected because of its limited size; that would be applying a methodological standard quite inappropriate for a sensitive subject in which the evidence is always limited and fugitive.[13]

---

[13] *Ibid.*, 1481 fn.

32.   Comment on Degler's decision to use the Mosher data as part of a historical analysis of women's sexuality.

Degler's purpose in the article was to demonstrate that sexual attitudes and behavior were more varied in the nineteenth century than historians used to think, and that we therefore need to revise our stereotypes about women and the family in the Victorian era. Degler does not use the Mosher Survey to make highly specific claims about women's sexuality. He does not, for example, make any claims that half of American women, or one-tenth, or nine-tenths, or any other specific proportion, usually had orgasms during intercourse. All he needs to show is that sweeping generalizations about women's sexuality are suspect.

33.   In light of this summary of Degler's purpose, would you alter your answer to Question 32?

4.8   Assessing Sampling Strategies

In this section you will encounter a few more brief examples of historians' use of samples. The questions aim to give you some practice at judging the adequacy of sampling procedures as you will encounter them in your reading. Before you get into the examples, though, let's outline the main points you ought to look for in checking any historian's use of a sample:

(1)   What is the population that the historian is studying?

(2)   What source or sources did the historian use, and do these sources truly include all members of the target population? If you detect a bias in the sources, what groups do you think might have been over- or under-represented? Does the historian seem aware of the bias? How does he or she address the problem?

(3)   Does the historian clearly explain the steps in the sampling procedure and identify possible biases in the sample?

(4)   Does the historian use a sample of convenience? How does he or she justify this approach? Are you persuaded?

(5)   If the historian used stratified sampling, are you persuaded that the differences among the stratified groups really are substantial? If they aren't, then stratified sampling has no point.

(6) If cluster sampling was employed, are you satisfied that the clusters contain a great deal of heterogeneity with respect to important variables in the study? Recall that if the population itself is clustered into fairly homogeneous groupings that differ greatly from one another, such as ethnic neighborhoods, the historian runs a serious risk of randomly picking a set of clusters that do not represent the overall characteristics of the population.

(7) If the historian writes about just one case or a small handful of cases and claims that this "case study" reveals patterns characteristic of a larger population, how persuasive do you find his or her argument?

Table 4.7
Number of acres of cropland per worker on family farms, by race and tenure, Cotton South: 1880

Form of Tenure	Acres of Crops per Worker	
	White	Black
Owner-operated	12.5	6.6
Rented	14.5	7.4
Sharecropped	11.7	8.0
All farms	12.4	7.5

Source: See Table 3.5.

Here are some specific examples. Consider first a table introduced in Chapter 3. Roger L. Ransom and Richard Sutch produced Table 3.5 by taking a sample from the 1880 census of agriculture. The authors describe their sampling procedures and discuss sources of bias in the census in an appendix to their book *One Kind of Freedom*.[14] If they had not done so, you the reader should ask yourself how bias could creep into the numbers and how it might influence the results. Of course, you are only interested in bias bearing on the three variables shown in the table: race, farm tenure, and farm size.

34. Give a plausible example of how bias might have been introduced at the time of the original census. What effect would that have had on the results?

[14] *One Kind of Freedom*, Appendix G.

In the appendix on their data and sampling procedures, Ransom and Sutch say, "Farms that exhibited serious data deficiencies and farms where ambiguities existed with regard to the definition of the farming unit were deleted from the sample." They excluded 236 farms that had been picked for the sample "owing to ambiguities in ownership or tenure characteristics. These exclusions involved farms where more than one form of tenure was reported or where a single farm family operated more than one farm."[15]

35. Do you think the pattern of missing information is likely to be independent of the three variables the authors show in Table 3.5? If incomplete information has introduced bias, in what direction would you guess it operates—which numbers would it push up or down?

36. Does your speculation about possible bias in the original sources or in the authors' sampling lead you to disregard entirely the patterns in the table? That is, how strong are your suspicions and how strong might the bias have been relative to the sizes of the differences shown in the table?

Consider a second example. Back in Chapter 1, you explored the varying family income strategies of ethnic and racial groups at the turn of the century. For some of her data on Italian immigrant families in 1896 (not included in the shortened version of the table that appears in Section 1.1), historian Elizabeth H. Pleck relied on a report by the U.S. Commissioner of Labor entitled *The Italians in Chicago* and published in 1897. In that report, the reader learns that the Bureau of Labor gathered its statistical data by sending out one agent who canvassed selected streets of a single neighborhood and secured information on 1348 families.[16]

37. What are the major defects in the sampling procedure employed by the agent of the Bureau of Labor?

38. The Commissioner's report also says, "It is believed that the data secured for the 1,348 families visited is entirely representative of the conditions existing in all Italian families of a similar character in that city." Comment on this remark.

---

[15] *Ibid.*, 292–93.
[16] Carroll D. Wright, *The Italians in Chicago* (Washington, 1897), 11.

In Chapter 2, you examined data about 48 slave ships that plied the Atlantic between Africa and the British colonies of North America in the 1790s. Table 2.4 showed that for the 48 ships overall, the mean amount of deck space available per slave was 5.3 sq. ft. Data about the ships came from some information that Lord Liverpool gathered in 1799 to estimate the likely results of the proposed Dolben Act on the carrying capacity of British slave ships. (As passed, the Dolben Act mandated that each slave be allotted no less than 8 sq. ft. of deck space on any British slave ship.) Lord Liverpool himself was a supporter of the slave trade.

39. Do you have any reason to believe that these 48 ships are representative of other British slavers of the late eighteenth century? If they constitute a biased sample, do you think the figure 5.3 sq. ft. probably overstates or understates the mean for all British slave ships?

Consider next an example not introduced earlier in the book. Mary P. Ryan, a social historian of American women and the family, published an article on women in the religious revivals that swept upstate New York between 1800 and 1840. Since Utica, New York appeared to be a center of revivalistic activity, she decided to focus her study on the women of that city. "For nearly 20 years the women of Utica carefully prepared the soil, planted, and nourished the seeds for [evangelist Charles G.] Finney's renowned evangelical harvest of 1825 and 1826. Utica, then, is an appropriate place to begin writing the women's history of the Burned-Over District."[17]

Another important reason for Ryan's decision to examine Utica was that membership records from four of the city's churches survive. From these records she was able to see who joined each church and when, and was also able to trace many family connections among converts and other church members. Ryan was thereby able to compile "a revival population," a list of over 1400 men and women "who proclaimed their salvation during the [revival] years 1814, 1819, 1826, 1830 to 1832, and 1838."[18]

One matter of interest to Ryan is the role of family ties in the lives of women who joined the churches during the revivals. She notes "a

---

[17]Mary P. Ryan, "A Women's Awakening: Evangelical Religion and the Families of Utica, New York, 1800–1840," *American Quarterly*, 30 (Winter 1978), 602–23; quotation at 603. Upstate New York was known as the Burned-Over District because it was burned over again and again by the fires of revivalism.

[18] *Ibid.*, 603.

network of kin ties that riddled church membership lists, often link-
ing male to female in one evangelical process." Perhaps, she suggests,
the conversion experience during the Second Great Awakening was not
purely an individual's private decision and therefore not "exemplary of
youthful, independent, and individualistic Jacksonian America"; it may
have revealed, rather, the continuing influence of family in the spiritual
lives of the men and women converts.[19]

Of the 1,400 revival converts on Ryan's list, 456 joined Utica's First
Presbyterian Church during five revival years between 1814 and 1838;
of this number, she was able to find information on kinship ties for 160.
Ryan concedes that these 160 "may or may not be representative of the
bulk of converts who made a minor appearance in the annals of local
churches," but goes on to discuss them in greater detail because this
group's "more durable church ties insured a greater capacity to affect
the course of evangelism itself." She adds that "any conclusions based
solely on these fragmentary records are heuristic—rare and suggestive
tracks through an uncharted historical landscape."[20]

40.   From our summary here, outline the steps by which Ryan moved
from the Burned-Over District as a whole down to the 160 converts
in the First Presbyterian Church of Utica. For each step, identify
what kind of sample was used and explain why.

Here is an example of the kind of sampling question that arises as one
reads this article: Ryan discusses at length the converts who joined the
First Presbyterian Church during the revival of 1814. Sixty-five did so;
of these, she was able to find additional information about 31 by checking
city vital records. For those 31 converts of 1814 about whom Ryan did
find additional information, 65% were married and 23% baptized an
infant child within a year after their conversion.

41.   The author implies that these men and women were typical of the
1814 converts as a whole.[21] Would you agree?

4.9   The Ethnic History Project Revisited

Section 4.2 described the research design for an important research
project carried out at a state historical society in the 1970s. Determined to include every nationality group in the database, the project

---

[19] *Ibid.*, 611.
[20] *Ibid.*, 612.
[21] *Ibid.*, 612.

director elected not to sample the 1880 census but to include all 781,000 persons who had lived in the state at that time.[22] Could a sampling procedure have been designed that might have answered the concerns of the project director while reducing the cost and frustrations of the project? Suppose, in addition to covering all the nationality groups as of 1880, you want to create a database that includes information about all the key questions asked in the 1880 census. Instead of a database useful for one narrow purpose only, you will have invested the state's money in creating a research tool of potential use for a variety of historical projects on nineteenth-century American life. For the sample, you would probably define each person residing in the state to be a "case" or an "individual."

42. What else could you use as your individual cases, if not persons?

Table 4.8
Variables in the 1880 population study

1.	Identification number
2.	Family name
3.	Given name
4.	Sex
5.	Age
6.	Marital status
7.	Birthplace
8.	Mother's birthplace
9.	Father's birthplace
10.	Occupation
11.	Able to read and write?
12.	Relationship to head of household
13.	Family type
14.	Number of people in the household
15.	County of residence
16.	City, town, or township of residence

Suppose for each case, you decide to gather information on the variables listed in Table 4.8. Sixteen variables times 781,000 persons would be nearly twelve and a half million items of information. It's obvious why you might want to sample: you want to use the sample to

---

[22]This population figure, obviously rounded to the nearest thousand, comes from U.S. Department of Commerce, Bureau of the Census, *Historical Statistics of the United States, Colonial Times to 1970* (Washington, 1975), p. 30.

estimate the characteristics of the population. For any given variable such as Birthplace, you will know the sample distribution. You will know, for example, what proportion of the individuals in the sample were German-born and living in farm families, and from that knowledge you will estimate the proportion in the population as a whole. The accuracy of your estimate—the likelihood of random error—depends on the absolute size of the sample; it does not depend on sample size as a proportion of the population. One of the first tasks faced in sampling, therefore, is determining the optimum sample size.

43. If 50.5% of the full population was male, how many men would you expect to show up in a random sample of size 2000?

Perhaps you begin by considering a simple random sample of 1000. You're like Ralph, the graduate student who drew two slips out of a box of forty—only the box in this case has 781,000 slips and you intend to draw out 1000. (With a large population like this, you can ignore the matter of replacement after each draw. Your sample will be drawn without replacement.) You know that you always run the risk of random error in any sample. But you wonder: "A sample of 1000 looks awfully small. Should I beef the size up to, say, 3000, or perhaps even go up to 10,000? If I do, how much will I reduce the risk of error?" Recall that if you quadruple the size of the sample, you'll cut the standard error to half its former size. Remember, the phrase standard error (SE) refers to the likely magnitude of chance error in estimating a population average on the basis of a sample average.

As long as one is using fairly big samples, say more than fifty cases, and provided one is not studying extremely rare events, then it is a fact from probability theory that the average of a random sample stands about a two-thirds chance (actually 68%) of being within one SE of the population average and about a 95% chance of being within two SEs. And as discussed earlier, if you increase the size of your sample, you reduce the size of the SE because the SE is the standard deviation divided by the square root of the sample size. To cut the standard error to one-third of what it had been, you take a sample nine times as large since the square root of nine is three.

Let's see how this works in a concrete example. Suppose that in the state's population as a whole, 80% of the residents had been born in the U.S. and 20% outside the U.S. Imagine that you want to find the SE in a random sample of size 100. You know you just need to divide the standard deviation in the population by ten, the square root of 100. To find the standard deviation for the proportion of American-born people, you just multiply the two proportions and take the square root of the answer. So in this case the standard deviation is 0.4 since: $0.80 \times 0.20 = 0.16$, and $\sqrt{0.16} = 0.4$ or 40%.[23]

In your sample of size 100 the SE is 40% $\div \sqrt{100}$, which is 4%. So you have a 68% chance that the sample proportion will be within 4% of the population proportion of 80% American-born. That is, when the population percentage is 80% American-born there's about a two-thirds chance that the sample proportion will come out between 76% and 84% American-born.

44. What's the chance that the sample proportion of American-born will come out somewhere between 72% and 88%?

45. (a) If you were to boost the sample size from 100 to 1600, what size standard error would you have for the proportion of American-born?

   (b) And what would be the chance that your sample proportion would come out between 79% and 81% American-born?

46. What would happen to standard error if you reduced the size of the sample from 100 to 25?

47. Suppose the residents of large cities made up 10% of the state's population. What is the standard deviation in the population for the proportion who are residents of large cities? If you take a random sample of size 900, what SE would you have for the proportion of the population who are residents of large cities?

48. Imagine that you have a simple random sample of size 2,500 consisting of white, American-born women in the state. In the sample, the mean age of white, American-born women is 25.0. Which of the following statements best conveys the meaning of that figure, 25.0?

   (a) The mean age for white, American-born women in the state is 25.0.

   (b) The mean age for white, American-born women in the state is about 25.0, and the true mean will be close to that, probably less than one year above or below 25.

----

[23]See Section 3.5 if you want to review the standard deviation of proportions.

(c) The mean age for white, American-born women in the state is about 25.0, but the true mean may well be more than one year higher or lower than that.

49. How could you ensure a standard error of zero?

One aspect of the preceding discussion might trouble you. The true population proportion was used to calculate the random error that would occur if you took a sample in order to estimate that very same proportion. If you know the true proportion, why would you estimate it? If you don't know the true proportion, how could you get the SE in order to have a sense of the accuracy of the estimate you do make? The answer is that the true proportion is unknown: that's why you sample. So you take the sample proportion and pretend that it is the true population proportion in order to calculate the SE as was done above.

50. Suppose a random sample of 400 farmers from the 1880 census shows that half of them used at least some hired labor on their farms. What is your best guess as to the true proportion of 1880 farmers using some hired labor? Approximately what is the SE for that guess? You have a 68% chance that your guess is within how many percentage points of the true answer? You have a 95% chance that your guess is within how many percentage points of the true answer?

Random error is present in any randomly drawn sample; but with a simple random sample, you can estimate the probable size of the error quite closely and you can pick a sample size which keeps it small. Most social scientists and quantitative historians would agree that a sample size of 1,000 to 2,000 is adequate if your goal is simply to make an estimate of a few major characteristics of the state population in 1880. From such a sample, you could estimate quite closely the proportion of men and women in the population, the proportion born in the U.S. and abroad, the proportion of farmers, and the like. Suppose, however, that your project director insists that the sample must not overlook very small nationality groups.

Why is there a problem with small groups? If you answered Question 47, you found that in a population split 90/10 (say, 90% rural, 10% urban) the standard error was 1%. That's not bad if you are estimating the size of the rural population, because your claim would be that the true rural proportion is very likely to lie in a fairly narrow range, say your sample proportion plus or minus 2 SE. For example, if the sample had come out 89% rural, you would be 95% sure that the true proportion would be between 87% and 91% because there is a 95% chance that a sample estimate will come out within two SEs of the true value.

But notice that a standard error of 1% would seem huge if you were trying to estimate the size of a group constituting only a small fraction of the population. Imagine the situation with a really small group. If you came to a conclusion such as, "I am 95% sure that the Serbians made up one-tenth of one percent of the population, plus or minus two percent," you would be saying that the error in your estimate might well be twenty times as big as the estimate itself.

The important message to be taken away from all this arithmetic is that you need large samples if you want to estimate rare events. This happens because you want the SE to be very small if the chance of the event is itself very small. But in order to make the SE small, you must pick a large sample size because the SE goes down as the square root of the sample size goes up.

51. "From the published census data," the project director tells you, "I know that we had 356 people of Hungarian birth among the 781,000 residents back in 1880. How many of the Hungarians are likely to show up in a sample of 2000?" If you quadruple the size of the sample, making it 8,000, how many Hungarians are likely to show up then?

It's clear that a simple random sample of 1000, or even of 5000 or 8000, will not yield enough members of very small subpopulations to enable anyone to make interesting inferences about those subpopulations from the sample. The number of individuals captured by the sample will simply be too small.

The ethnic history project that was actually carried out in the 1970s used the entire set of 781,000 cases with five variables recorded for each case. Notice that the researchers could take a huge sample, say 100,000, and record more than twice as much information for each case, yet still end up with only one quarter as many items of information to work with.

	Cases	Variables	Total items
Original project	781,000	5	3,905,000
A possible alternative	100,000	12	1,200,000

With a sample as big as 100,000, even if some group constituted just one-tenth of one percent of the population, you would still expect to get one hundred cases from that group in the sample and you would be able to look for interesting relationships between a larger set of variables than was possible in the actual study.

4.10   Conclusion

Quantitative historians rarely enjoy the luxury of having simple random samples to work with. In this chapter, we have emphasized that working with samples of convenience, the usual kind of sample data confronting historians, is acceptable as long as the scholar and reader try to identify likely biases in the sample and remain appropriately cautious about generalizing to larger populations on the basis of this imperfect kind of sample. The simple random sample, by contrast, has two cardinal virtues: it eliminates the possibility of sample bias and it enables the researcher to estimate the probability of random errors of various sizes. For these reasons, scholars should choose simple random samples (or close approximations such as systematic samples) whenever possible. But they may not be able to do so very often.

The next chapter focuses on what we call two styles or modes of historical argument, a style appropriate for the exploratory stage of an inquiry and a style better suited for testing a clearly stated hypothesis. We also return to sampling, focusing on the question of statistical significance and its relation (if any) to historical significance.

Terms Introduced in Chapter 4

4.1 population
4.1 representative sample
4.1 descriptive statistics
4.1 inferential statistics
4.3 sample bias
4.4 valid samples
4.4 simple random samples
4.5 random sampling error
4.5 sample size square root rule
4.5 standard error
4.6 systematic samples
4.6 cluster samples
4.6 stratified samples
4.6 multistage samples
4.7 convenience samples

4.11   Answers to Questions

1. The individuals would be counties and the population would be
    the set of all Alabama counties.

2. The population would be the set of all counties in the United
    States.

3. Campbell has focused on the association between a mother's phys-
    ical stress and threats to the unborn child. Some variables such
    as nutrition level or age might be confounded with that associ-
    ation and would therefore be quite relevant to the pattern he is
    studying. Other differences might only be remotely connected, if
    at all, to that association—for example, whether the slaves tended
    to be second or third generation in the New World or whether they
    tended to be married or not at the time they became pregnant.

4. Campbell's thesis is that reproductive rates are depressed when
    pregnant women are subject to physical stress during the first half
    of their pregnancies. His mental model is of a biological mech-
    anism. One can argue that there was nothing special about the
    Kollack plantation that would cause this biological process to func-
    tion differently there than elsewhere.

5. The key issue is whether this imaginary Boston neighborhood is
    in any way special with regard to the factors that have brought
    about the income inversion. Suppose you have the following mental
    model of the causal mechanism: Immigrants were over-represented
    among the older household heads while earners born in the United
    States were predominant among the younger heads of households,
    and American-born workers had greater economic opportunities
    because of language skills and better educational opportunities. If
    (these are big ifs) your mental model is correct and if this Boston
    neighborhood is similar to other neighborhoods with respect to
    the important causal factors (the way age and opportunity vary
    with status as an immigrant or native-born American), then the
    Boston neighborhood should be representative of those others with
    respect to age and income patterns.

6. One example might be the set of all households in Boston in the
    mid-nineteenth century that were headed by immigrants or the
    children of immigrants from Ireland. That set might be enlarged
    by including other cities, other times, or other ethnic groups. The

key question is, what is the group for which the mental model of the process is appropriate? If one did generalize from the single neighborhood, one should consider testing that generalization by looking at a second, independent sample of households included in the generalization.

7. Suppose one has very complete data from a single suburban school system showing for each grade the percent of boys and girls who test below grade level in mathematics. Perhaps the pattern shown is that all the way up to high school a smaller proportion of girls than boys are below grade level, but in high school there is a dramatic shift because more girls fall behind (rather than boys' suddenly catching up). One might advance an explanatory social theory suggesting that this school district is just a sample of what is going on throughout suburban America.

8. It would be very expensive to take a random sample of all sub-urban school children in America in order to see if the different male/female math patterns held up. Fortunately, there is some middle ground between using one available school district and sampling the whole country.

9. Boardman and Weber: situation (1)
    Demos: situation (2)
    Pleck: situation (3)

10. Families for which the number of children goes unmentioned in the record would probably tend to be families that in fact had no children. To exclude such families entirely would be to risk understating the proportion of childless families.

11. We aren't certain what the project assistant meant in saying that "census figures are based on a sample"—the decennial census is an actual count of the population. But even if the published census data for 1880 had been based on a sample, the assistant shouldn't have drawn much comfort from the fact that his own project had "the actual figures." A full count is not necessarily more accurate than a sample because with a full count, there is a much greater chance of processing errors.

12. The people who responded by mailing back the completed ques-tionnaire to the magazine tended to share personal attributes such

as higher-than-average education levels, high income, and professional status. In short, the respondents tended to come from the
highest socioeconomic class. A voter's class position is obviously
strongly related to his or her party preference. Thus the second
stage of the procedure, like the first, tended to select Republican-
leaning voters who preferred Landon over Roosevelt.

13. The population was not all residents of New York City, but all
whose names appeared in the 1790 city directory.

14. You can infer that all names listed in the directory had an equal
chance of being drawn for the sample of 400.

15. (a) All families from 501 through 10,000 have no chance of being
picked, so this procedure won't yield a random sample.

(b) Families on odd-numbered pages and those farther down the
even-numbered pages have no chance of being picked, so a
random sample cannot result. This kind of procedure is often
used, though, for reasons of convenience. It can incorporate
an element of randomness—the researcher might flip a coin
to determine whether to go for the odd- or even-numbered
pages and then pick a number from a hat to decide whether
to take the first name on a page, the second, or what. Such
a procedure yields what is called a systematic sample, a kind
of sample to be discussed further in Section 4.6.

(c) Names the students like have a very high chance of appearing
in the sample while other names can't appear. No, not a ran-
domizing procedure. Notice how the sample would be biased
if the students were Irish-American and liked Irish names like
O'Malley, but didn't like East European names such as Kraca
or Dobrecak.

(d) No, this won't work either. The highest number possible in
a roll of two dice is twelve, and twelve times 500 equals 6000.
But 10,000 families appear in the directory, so even if the
historian were to roll twelve 500 times in a row, the last 4000
families would still have a zero chance of being picked for the
sample.

(e) This option will generate a random sample.

(f) This procedure won't yield a genuinely random sample. Experiments have shown that people asked to perform an activity in a random way quickly (though unintentionally) begin

to fall into patterns. In this case, for example, the research assistant might tend to open the directory around the middle, thus slighting names at the very beginning and the very end. If a right-hander, he might stab the right-hand page more often than the left-hand page. Also, families with more names will occupy more space on the page and have a greater chance of appearing in the sample.

16. The mean is $(20 \times 30) + (25 \times 10)$, all divided by 40; that's 850/40 or 21.25 years.

17. Ralph could draw age 20 twice and get a sample mean of 20; or he could draw age 25 twice and get a sample mean of 25; or he could draw a 20 and a 25 and get a sample mean of 22.5.

18. No combination of two slips can yield a mean of 21.25.

19. The probability is $(30/40 \times 30/40)$, or 9/16. In percentage terms, that's just over 56%.

20. To get a mean age of 22.5, Ralph must draw a slip with age 20 on it and a slip with age 25. He can do this in either of two ways: 20 and then 25, or 25 and then 20. The probability of drawing a 20 and then a 25 is $(30/40 \times 10/40)$ or 3/16. The probability of drawing a 25 and then a 20 is $(10/40 \times 30/40)$, which is also 3/16. So the probability of drawing one or the other is $(3/16 + 3/16)$, or 6/16.

21. Probability of Ralph's drawing various combinations of slips

Sample mean age	Probability
20.0	9/16
22.5	6/16
25.0	1/16

22. (a) Here you will have a biased sample because you are arbitrarily making it impossible for many people in the census records to be picked for the sample. This could only happen when you sample, of course.

  (b) Illegible handwriting or unclear microfilm are examples of the first kind of problem that we listed, flaws in the sources themselves. It is possible that the census taker only garbled some kinds of names—those of Czech immigrants, perhaps—so that definite biases could be built into the source itself. Or perhaps one census taker who worked one neighborhood was marginally literate or drunk so that his sheets are full of errors, while another census taker was quite complete and accurate. This problem could arise whether you are sampling or recording data about every person in the census.

(c) As just mentioned, there may be a bias in the pattern of illegibility of names.

(d) This phenomenon, known as "age-heaping," results from the fact that many people don't report ages accurately but round them off to the nearest number divisible by five or ten. Here is another flaw in the original source, a flaw that would affect anybody using a census, whether he was sampling it or not.

(e) Either the census taker of 1880 wrote down the man's age incorrectly or illegibly (an error in the source), or your research assistant made a typographical error in entering the man's age into the computer database (a processing error).

(f) Possibly the census missed the black families (a flaw in the source), or possibly it was just the luck of the draw that none appeared in the sample. If the latter, this might be considered an example of random error—the population had 1% black families, perhaps, while your sample has 0%. But if the number of black families in the population was much smaller than 1%, say 1/4 of 1%, then you ought not be surprised to find no black families in the sample.

(g) A problem with the original source, and it would crop up whether you choose to work with the population or a sample.

(h) This is a processing error, a case of faulty judgment on the part of your assistant or perhaps inadequate instructions to him on your part. (He should have entered "missing data" or "unknown" for such cases.) It would have happened had he been working with an entire population or with a sample.

23. If you selected the children randomly, then each child had an equal chance to get in the sample. That means that a six-child family had six chances to be in the sample while a two-child family only had two chances. But families are the individual cases on which

you wish to measure the number of children so your sample should
have given each family an equal chance of inclusion rather than
each child. The method described in the question is biased in favor
of large families and will completely miss families with no children.
That procedure will undoubtedly lead you to overestimate average
family size.

24. You could put slips labeled 1 to 50 in a hat, pick one slip out to
determine the starting page, and then pick every fiftieth page after
that. If you knew the total number of pages, say 1000, you could
put 1000 slips in a hat, numbered 1 to 1000, and then pick twenty
slips from the hat.

25. Each household record begins on one and only one page. Therefore
a household is selected if and only if the page its record begins on
is selected. So each household has the same one out of fifty chance
of being in the sample.

26. Yes. Each woman is listed in one and only one household. She will
be included if and only if her household begins on a selected page.
So each woman has a one in fifty chance of being in the sample.

27. With this hypothetical technique, households whose records begin
on a page with only a few others will have a greater chance of getting into the sample than those which begin on a page with many
others. If only two household records start on a page, each has a
fifty-fifty chance of selection once their page is included. But if ten
began on a page, each would only have a one-tenth chance after
their page was included. This suggests that households with very
large records on the census pages would be favored over households
with small records.

28. The population being discussed certainly includes the black and
white women in the seven cities from which the samples were
taken. However, Goldin means to include black and white women
in Southern cities generally. The first stage of sampling was the
selection of the seven cities as being representative of the rest.

29. You would want her to say why there was nothing special about
the seven cities with regard to the variables being studied. In
the absence of such an argument, the population under discussion
can only be inferred to be that of the seven cities. With such a
discussion, you may decide to believe that the conclusions apply
to all Southern cities.

30. Since 21% of the elderly population resided in cities, they would have needed a national elderly sample of 6,190 cases. Twenty-one percent of 6190 is 1300.

31. They adjusted their estimates for the rural and urban samples by weighting the sample findings by their true proportions in the population.

32. Degler carefully explains to the reader the circumstances under which the Mosher data were gathered and points out the biases in the Mosher sample. He never claims that these 45 women's attitudes represented those of American women generally. One can only commend his candor. At the same time, readers may be uneasy at the heavy emphasis that the article gives to the Mosher data.

33. Degler wishes to question broad generalizations about nineteenth-century sexuality, particularly the stereotype that women of the nineteenth century always had negative attitudes about sex. The Mosher Survey seems admissable evidence for a limited purpose of this kind.

34. Since most census efforts have undercounted the black and the poor, it is reasonable to guess that the 1880 census may have had that defect also. If the poorest blacks were missed more often than those who were better off, then Table 4.7 may be overstating the acres of crops per black worker. Of course, the census may also have undercounted the poorest whites. So the question is, would the undercounting of the poor have been more serious in one group than the other? It is not possible to guess the answer at this distance from the original sources.

35. One might speculate that the smallest farms and those operated by blacks (which tend to be smaller farms) would have incomplete data more often than the larger farms and the white farms. If that speculation is correct, the true difference between races would be even larger than that shown in the table.

36. Our hunch is that the differences shown in the table are so substantial that the general message of the table is not in error even though there must have been some error made in the many steps that led to the production of those few summary numbers.

37. Since the data came from a neighborhood canvass, those families less likely to have someone at home would tend to be missed more often than others—for example, small families or families in which the mother worked. Also, since the canvass was confined to one neighborhood, the study is biased with respect to any characteristic by which that neighborhood differed from other Italian neighborhoods in the city.

38. Essentially, the report says that the sample represents the population to which it is similar. We'll buy that.

39. It is not known how Lord Liverpool selected the ships about which he gathered data, and hence you cannot say whether they provide a fair sample of all the ships involved in the trade. If he had a conscious bias, he might have emphasized ships that provided the best conditions for the captive Africans since he was a supporter of the slave trade and would have wanted the trade to appear in the best possible light. So you might conclude that this selection of 48 ships gives a somewhat rosy picture. Of course, the selection may have been biased in other ways of which Lord Liverpool was not conscious.

40. **(a)** From the Burned-Over District to the city of Utica. Utica appears to be a sample of convenience: it was chosen because church records were available. The city was also a hotbed of revivalistic activity, so it probably was not entirely typical of the District as a whole.

(b) From Utica to the churches whose records survive. Clearly this is a case of using a sample of convenience.

(c) From the four churches to the "revival population," the list of 1400 men and women who joined during five revival periods between 1814 and 1838. This is not really a sample but apparently a complete list of all who joined the churches during revivals.

(d) From the 1400 to the 456 who joined the First Presbyterian Church during the revival years. This too appears to be a sample of convenience.

(e) From the 456 to 160 Presbyterians for whom the author was able to gather kinship data. Definitely a sample of convenience.

41. The problem is that being married or baptizing an infant probably made it more likely that a convert would show up in the group of 31 about whom additional information was available. The kind of information likely to be available was precisely a marriage or baptism record. Consider the 34 converts about whom Ryan did not find additional information. Were they just as likely to be married, except that no record of this fact exists? Or does no record exist because they were, in fact, not married? It seems perilous to claim that the 31 converts resembled the other 34.

42. You might sample families or households.

43. Fifty-point-five percent of 2000 is 1010.

44. Seventy-two percent and 88% are <u>two</u> SE's from the population mean, so there's about a 95% likelihood that the sample proportion falls somewhere within this range.

45. **(a)** Since the sample size went up by a factor of sixteen, the estimation error (the SE) will go down by a factor of four (the square root of sixteen). Four percent was the estimation error for a sample of 100, so 1% will be the SE for a sample of 1600.

  (b) With a sample of size 1600, there is a 68% chance that the sample proportion will be within one SE of the true proportion, 80%; that is, between 79% and 81% American-born.

46. SE would double to 8%, up by a factor of two since the sample size went down by a factor of four.

47. The standard deviation would be the square root of (0.9×0.1), which is $\sqrt{.09}$ or 0.3. SE is calculated as the standard deviation for the population divided by the square root of the sample size. In this case, that's $0.3 \div 30$, which equals 0.01 or 1%.

48. The best answer is (b) because the SE is surely less than one. Whatever the standard deviation for ages of women in the population is, that standard deviation is divided by 50 (the square root of 2,500) to get the SE. With a sample of size 2,500 and a standard deviation which must be no bigger than 20, your estimate will probably be accurate because the SE will be small.

49.   Don't take a sample at all. Study the entire population instead. But this strategy is guaranteed to breed other kinds of errors, notably processing errors.

50.   Since this was a random sample, your best guess is the same as the sample mean: half the farmers used hired labor. SE in this case is about 2.5%—i.e., you have a 68% chance that your estimate is within 2.5 percentage points above or below the true figure for the population, and a 95% chance that your estimate is within five percentage points above or below the true figure.

51.   Three hundred ninety is less than one two-thousandth of the state's population of 781,000. So in a sample of 2000 you still could expect to find no persons, or one person, of Hungarian birth. By quadrupling the sample size you might boost this expected number to three or four Hungarians.

5 Two Styles of Research and Argument

In this chapter:

You may have noticed that the last chapter involved a series of distinctions: populations vs. samples, descriptive vs. inferential statistics, processing error vs. bias vs. sampling error, non-random sampling vs. random sampling, and simple random sampling vs. complex sampling designs. In Chapter 5, we emphasize these main points:

- In tracing the logic of a historical argument, you should be sensitive to two additional major distinctions, namely the distinction between experiments and observational studies and that between exploratory and confirmatory research.

- In the field of history, Chapter 5 will show, the investigator cannot carry out experiments; he or she is confined to observational studies.

- The chapter will also emphasize that both the exploratory and confirmatory style of research are legitimate in the study of history, but each is appropriate to different circumstances. The historian uses the first style when exploring his data and generating hypotheses, the second when testing a previously held hypothesis.

- The results of a quantitative-history investigation usually have a probabilistic character; hypotheses cannot be proved or disproved beyond all shadow of doubt, but may seem more or less credible as a consequence of some statistical test.

- After discussing the exploratory and confirmatory styles, the chapter gives a brief introduction to the language and methods a researcher uses when formal statistical techniques are brought into the argument.

5.1   Experiment vs. Observation

An <u>experiment</u> differs from an <u>observational study</u>: an experimenter has control over at least one of the variables being studied.[1] For example, think of the debate over whether an association exists between taking vitamins and avoiding colds. If an experimenter plans to test whether vitamin C injections help prevent colds, he or she can control which individuals are to be injected with vitamin C and which injected with a placebo or not injected at all. The experimenter decides who gets treated (that's one of the key variables) but not which persons catch cold or how often they get a cold.

In contrast to the experimenter, the analogous observational researcher records information on colds for individuals who decided on their own, without regard to any study of colds, whether or not to take vitamin C. In both the experiment and the observational study you might find that taking vitamin C is associated, either positively or negatively, with catching cold. The only difference is that in the observational study, the individual (or maybe her mother) decides whether or not to take the vitamin, while in the experiment the decision is made by the experimenter.

However, this distinction is vital. In an observational study, whichever way the results turn out, the doubter has a plausible basis for attacking the conclusions. If the study shows that people who take vitamin C have more colds than others, the doubter can attribute that result to the possibility that people who tend to have many colds also tend to take vitamin C to ward off colds. On the other hand, if vitamin takers experience fewer colds, the doubter can claim that individuals who take vitamins also tend to take good care of themselves and worry a lot about their bodies and therefore have few colds because of their general good health, not because of the vitamins.

But the skeptical observer cannot make these arguments if the experimenter randomly assigned the vitamin treatment. If a person is randomly selected to get vitamins, then the taking of vitamins is strictly a matter of chance and is clearly not due to some other tendency to catch or not catch colds. So when it comes to making a convincing case for causality, an experiment with the key variable assigned randomly has a big advantage over observational studies. With the experiment, you would find it harder to argue against the conclusion that variation in one

---

[1] David Freedman, Robert Pisani, and Roger Purves, *Statistics* (New York, 1978), Chapters 1 and 2, discusses experiments and observational studies in greater depth.

variable (vitamin consumption) caused differences in another (colds).

Unfortunately, historians are stuck with observational studies. In the last chapter, when John Campbell examined slave populations in the New World he performed an observational study whose conclusions pointed to the association between the intensity of slave labor during pregnancy and infant survival. That was not an experiment because Campbell did not decide which pregnant women were to work especially hard in the field. He could only observe the patterns of work and mortality that had, in fact, existed and were revealed in plantation records. Yet he wanted his readers to draw the conclusion that the hard work had an impact on infant mortality.

A skeptical observer could claim that bias marred Campbell's investigation. The skeptic can speculate that a plantation that would force heavy labor on a pregnant woman was also a plantation more likely to mistreat her in some other way, or perhaps that plantations requiring more difficult labor were also those located in more severe climates. You might conclude, then, that Campbell's data can never prove his point and that this will always be the situation for historians since they cannot carry out true experiments.

But this is a problem, in some degree, for all sciences and social sciences. It holds true of experiments as well as observational studies. The evidence offered by a well-designed experiment is merely more convincing (because the chance of bias is less), but it is not conclusive. In the end, the critical reader must evaluate the strength of the evidence and weigh the soundness of the arguments and the reasonableness of the conclusions.

As part of that critical evaluation, you must be aware of the possibility of bias in observational studies and should look for a discussion of that possibility by the writer. Further, this principle extends beyond quantitative history. As a reader, you would have the same questions about bias if Campbell's evidence had consisted of letters from a plantation owner in which the owner recorded his impressions of the association between field labor and reproductive rates. The possibility of bias was not due to the fact that Campbell's information was numeric.

In her book *A Distant Mirror*, Barbara Tuchman describes fourteenth-century efforts to understand the terrible mystery of bubonic plague, the "Black Death":[2]

---

[2]Barbara Tuchman, *A Distant Mirror: The Calamitous 14th Century* (New York, 1978), 102–03.

In October 1348 Philip VI asked the medical faculty of the
University of Paris for a report on the affliction that seemed
to threaten human survival. With careful thesis, antithesis
and proofs, the doctors ascribed it to a triple conjunction
of Saturn, Jupiter and Mars in the 40th degree of Aquarius
said to have occurred on March 20, 1345.

The doctors were stuck with an observational study. They observed an
association between the triple conjunction and the plague and inferred
that a causal relationship was at work. Of course, prior belief led them
to look in the direction of astrology in the first place. The doctors could
not experiment because they could not reach into the sky and test what
effect different arrangements of the planets might have on the course of
the epidemic. Compare this situation with the discussion of vitamins
and colds above and note the analogies:

	Study of Vitamins/Colds	Study of Planets/Plague
Entities to be compared	individual people	different time periods
Event to be explained	occurrence of colds	occurrence of plague
Proposed explanation	vitamin treatment	planetary arrangement

To do a really careful observational study, the doctors of Paris should
have examined many time periods, checking each for the presence of
either plague epidemics or special planetary arrangements and noting
whether any pattern of association was revealed. An experiment would
have required the doctors to arrange the planets in different time periods
just as the cold experiment required that the experimenter decide which
individual got vitamins.

1. What is the reason that observational studies may be more mis-
    leading than experiments when it comes to identifying cause-and-
    effect relationships?

2. In the study of history, is it absolutely impossible to carry out an
    experiment? Explain.

This distinction between observational studies and experiments suggests a second distinction, that between causality and <u>association</u>. Usually, a researcher can make a better case for causality with an experiment than with an observational study. Variables may be strongly associated without one of them having any influence at all on the other. For human adults, thinning of hair and far-sightedness show a clear association—but would you want to argue that one causes the other? Statistics can point out the association, but the interpreter of the displayed pattern has to decide whether causality is at work. Statistical formalism never replaces the historian's common sense. However, the use of statistical techniques can sometimes suggest relationships that might otherwise have gone unnoticed.

Many observational studies have suggested that cigarette smoking damages the human body. Cigarette manufacturers say, quite correctly, that those observational studies do not constitute formal proof. But final, formal proof doesn't exist in science. Science deals only in strong or weak evidence to be evaluated by knowledgeable observers. Even though a researcher can make a better case for a cause-effect relationship if he has experimental evidence to back up his claim, observational studies, the tool to which historians are limited, do seem capable of identifying patterns that might be true. Such studies have been essential for all of science and social science. In the sciences of astronomy and geology, observational studies play an important role: scientists often work by offering interpretations of the meaning of the record left by past events, just as historians do. Although scholars and readers always need to be cautious, given the limitations of observational studies, the historian doesn't need to apologize for his or her research tool.

3. Give an example of some causal relationship you believe in even though the evidence must be based largely on the observation of evidence that happens to exist rather than on evidence provided by controlled experiments.

5.2 Exploratory and Confirmatory Styles

Quantitative historians often use a mode of argument unfamiliar and unsettling to readers familiar with traditional narrative history. In the remainder of Chapter 5, we will contrast this approach, which we refer to as the confirmatory style of research and argument, with the more familiar approach, which we call the exploratory style.

The exploratory style of research and argument (another name would be the hypothesis-generating style) involves first searching the sources, discovering and reporting a pattern in the data, and then, after having found the pattern, perhaps trying to explain why it exists.[3]

Table 5.1
Hypothetical male average age at death in pre-Civil War Georgia

	Northern counties	Southern counties
Male average age at death	48.2	41.7

Imagine that certain nineteenth-century sources contain county-by-county information on all males in pre-Civil War Georgia. Suppose that you discover different mortality patterns in different parts of the state. You organize the data in Table 5.1 and ask, why should men in northern Georgia have lived longer? You can probably generate several possible explanations: perhaps the higher elevations in the north are healthier, or diets were better, or, perhaps more realistically, the northern regions had proportionately fewer slaves and slaves experienced higher mortality than non-slaves. When a historian notes a pattern like this regional difference and tries to think of explanations that might account for it, that's the exploratory style of research.

4. Differences in average age at death would not be the only possible measure of differential mortality between two regional groups. Mention a couple of other differences a historian might search for while poking around the data.

The confirmatory style (or hypothesis-testing style) contrasts sharply with the exploratory style. Here the historian asserts the claim first—for example, he might assert before having seen the data that males in northern Georgia outlived those from southern Georgia. Where would such a claim come from? Perhaps he believes, in advance, that highlands are more healthy than lowlands and so he concludes that men should live longer in the more mountainous north. Then he looks at the evidence to discover whether it offers support for his claim or not.

---

[3]For a mathematician's discussion of exploratory research see John W. Tukey, *Exploratory Data Analysis* (Reading, Mass., 1977).

5. Suppose you wished to test the hunch that differential mortality in Georgia was being driven by differences in the concentration of slaves as opposed to differences in elevation. How might that affect the way you summarize the mortality data?

When historians and social scientists talk about "scientific method" or the "scientific-empirical model," they mean the same thing as our phrase, the confirmatory style of research. To a student in the humanities, the style may at first appear cumbersome, perhaps even pointless. Why would a historian ever put forward an interpretive idea in advance of doing research? The present chapter suggests answers to that question.

We insist on the distinction between the two styles because the human mind can always find patterns—perhaps quite a lot of patterns—in lists of numbers or collections of facts. Here is a list of five digits from a table of random digits (which in fact we picked randomly): 1, 6, 4, 0, 8. Notice that most of the numbers in this list are even numbers. (Also, none of the numbers is a prime number.) Suppose the evidence in this list causes you to assert that, generally, most numbers are even numbers. As with the Georgia example, you can even find a plausible after-the-fact explanation for the phenomenon. Every odd number can be doubled so every odd number can be paired up with a distinct even number, its double. But that leaves a lot of extra even numbers such as 8 and 4 that are not doubles of odd numbers. So there must be more even numbers than odd numbers, right?

If the mind can find a great number of patterns in a collection of information, that raises the disturbing possibility that many, perhaps all historical interpretations are plausible fictions. Somehow, one needs a method for testing the validity of the patterns one sees in the data. Let's return to the list of five numbers chosen at random. To test the hunch that most numbers are even numbers, you can switch to the confirmatory style: you gather additional information by looking at the next five random numbers in the table. You might get, as we actually did: 8, 1, 8, 9, 9. That's three odd and two even—so the new data don't support your idea. You must gather still more information and/or rethink your position.

6. We jabbed a finger into a table of random numbers and found these ten digits in sequence: 2, 2, 8, 7, 8, 0, 2, 1, 7, 9. Find some pattern in this list of numbers.

Both the hypothesis-generating and the hypothesis-testing (or exploratory and confirmatory) styles are legitimate. In fact, they complement each other and are often used interactively so that an intellectual position evolves through repeated cycles of suggesting and testing hunches.

But sometimes scholars get themselves into trouble by confusing these styles. Suppose you became confused in some convoluted argument involving the even and odd numbers and ended up testing the hunch that most numbers are even by looking a second time at your original numbers: 1, 6, 4, 0, 8. Clearly you would be guilty of circular reasoning. It is not logically legitimate to test one's interpretive hunches with the very data that generated them. Of course such data will support the hunch—that's where the hunch came from in the first place. In fact, people make this error with unfortunate frequency in published work because the complex details of real problems often obscure the underlying logical structure.

Table 5.2
Average age at death by region for males in pre-Civil War Georgia, second version (hypothetical data)

	Northern Counties	Southern Counties
Male Average Age at Death	41.02	41.03

The two modes of inquiry, exploratory and confirmatory, share a common problem. Suppose the imaginary Georgia table had looked like Table 5.2. Just as in Table 5.1, you note a north-south difference in average age at death. But in Table 5.2, the difference is so small that no historian would consider it interesting. Of course it might be interesting to a historian that male mortality was nearly the same in northern and southern Georgia. However, we want to emphasize that a huge difference such as 75 versus 42 would be interesting while a miniscule one would not be considered significant. How large does a difference have to be before you would consider it worth your attention? The answer will depend upon your sense of the practical importance of the observed difference in the real world.

7. If Table 5.2 is accurate, does that mean no difference of practical importance existed between the two regions with respect to mortality patterns?

In the remainder of Chapter 5, you will get more thoroughly acquainted with the confirmatory or hypothesis-testing style of argument in the context of an observational study done by a historian. Let's proceed by examining the genesis of a specific research project that involved the stating and testing of a hypothesis.

5.3   Modernization Theory and the Family

Historians have generally been skeptical of the idea that all societies used to be "traditional" and have become, or will become, "modern." They have several reasons for this skepticism. Talking about modernization seems deterministic: it seems to imply that History has a goal by suggesting that all societies either have modernized or will do so eventually. The modernization idea also seems to proclaim industrial societies of the West as the pinnacle of historical development, so that the goal of History is that all societies will become more like us. Also, the very terms "traditional" and "modern" were found to lack content—all they really said was that a long time ago things were very different, but now they are the way they are now. If by modernization one really means urbanization or the development of market capitalism, why not use those terms and skip modernization?[4]

Still, one can make a case for the modernization idea. Perhaps historians, in their usual work, have focused too heavily on tiny details—local developments, specific events, and individuals. Thinking about modernization means thinking about very large patterns of change in a society over long periods of time, centuries rather than decades. That's an exciting possibility. Moreover, using the theory of modernization doesn't have to mean accepting it uncritically. One can test its validity in the same sense as the simple test of the hunch that most numbers are even.

The confirmatory approach begins with a theory about relationships between variables. Here is one description of the variables involved in modernization theory. (Note that this particular definition might not be acceptable to all the social scientists who have studied and written about modernization.)

> Modernization [is] a transition, or rather a series of transitions from primitive, subsistence economies to technology-intensive, industrialized economies; from subject to partici-

---

[4]Dean C. Tipps, "Modernization Theory and the Comparative Study of Societies: A Critical Perspective," *Comparative Studies in Society and History*, 15 (April 1973), 199–226, examines the concept of modernization and reviews the principal objections to its use. See also Robert A. Nisbet, *Social Change and History* (New York, 1969).

pant political cultures; from closed, ascriptive status systems to open, achievement-oriented systems; from extended to nuclear kinship units; from religious to secular ideologies; and so on.[5]

Imagine that some historian, using this notion of modernization, has proposed the theory that modernization processes apply to all human societies. This theory is a proposition about the way the world works, stated without regard to place and time.

As a reader, you face this question: Should you accept such a sweeping claim as the one put forward in modernization theory? Suppose that a historian wants to carry out some kind of investigation in hopes that the information she derives will give her—and you, her reader—strong reasons for accepting or rejecting the theory. More than that, she wants to organize her project so that it has the greatest possible chance of coming out with a persuasive conclusion. This is exactly the situation for which the confirmatory style of investigation is appropriate.

In outline form, the basic steps include:

- The historian formulates a hypothesis, a statement claiming that particular historical circumstances do fit the conditions described in the theory. A hypothesis has the following attributes: (a) it relates a broad, general theory to the real world; (b) it could be either true or false; and (c) it is a statement that the historian proposes to test.

- She then plans a research project focused on tests that will help her decide about the truth of the hypothesis. As part of this plan, she tries to make predictions about what the research findings will look like if the hypothesis is true. But how can this be—does it make any sense to talk about predicting the past? Actually, a historian would be predicting not the past itself, but the results of her own research. A prediction takes the following form: "If the hypothesis is true, then I ought to get the following results when I examine the historical record."

- She carries out the research. This may involve some of the statistical procedures you've been examining, but not necessarily. As long as the research will yield information enabling the historian to make a judgment about the merits of her hypothesis, it doesn't matter whether she uses "quantitative methods" or not.

---

[5]Tipps, "Modernization Theory," 204.

- She examines the <u>results</u> and decides whether they confirm the predictions or not. If the researcher sticks closely to the outlined procedure, then her interpretation of the results will be reasonably persuasive. But they won't be able to compel the reader's assent. Almost always, the historian will report that his or her findings provide some reason for accepting or not accepting the hypothesis, but not overwhelming reasons.

8. Compose some hypothesis relating the theory of modernization to American history, either one that you personally believe to be true or one you believe to be false.

You must determine whether a historian is proposing a "good test" of the theoretical hypothesis.[6] Here are five criteria to help you make that judgment: for each test,

- Is the predicted finding verifiable?

- Is it improbable?

- Does the historian indicate what kinds of findings will lead to a decision to accept or reject the hypothesis?

- Does the test involve new data?

- Is the prediction logically deducible from the hypothesis and stated initial conditions?

Let's consider each of these criteria in more depth:

Is the prediction verifiable? Imagine for a moment that, as part of a study of workers' accommodation to industrial capitalism, some historian plans to select 1500 workers in 1860 and another 1500 in 1917 and study their attitudes. But there probably isn't any way to gather the needed information; no pollsters or social scientists went around surveying workers' views on industrial capitalism. Existing historical sources won't support this project. If nobody can think of a way to gather and analyze the data needed for the test, the test can't be conducted.

Even if opinion surveys from the nineteenth century did exist, you can be sure that they would provide ambiguous help at best because terms like "accommodation" and "industrial capitalism" are not historical things that can be measured directly, but concepts, abstractions

---

[6]The phrase "good test" and several of the criteria discussed in what follows are based on Ronald N. Giere, *Understanding Scientific Reasoning*, 2nd edition (New York, 1984), 101–05.

dreamed up generations later. This problem is <u>universal</u> in social-science research.

9. Go back to the definition of modernization quoted at the beginning of this section and pick from it a few abstract concepts that might be difficult to measure or otherwise clearly assess for the purposes of confirming some theory.

Since concepts usually cannot be measured directly, a historian or social scientist must substitute something that can be. In the case of workers' accommodation to industrial capitalism, a historian might, for example, argue that accommodation to capitalism can be inferred from the nature of workers' strikes and protests: if strikes focusing on limited gains within the industrial-capitalist system, such as higher wages and better working conditions in the factory, became the predominant kind of organized protest, that trend might be taken as an indication of workers' implicitly conceding that industrial capitalism had come to stay. The measureable attribute that stands for a concept is known as an <u>indicator variable</u>, or simply as an indicator.

The two key questions you should keep in mind about indicators are these: first, is the historian making a reasonable claim when he or she proposes that a particular variable is an appropriate indicator of a concept? and second, is the indicator measurable?

10. Which of the following would you classify as concepts and which as indicator variables that might be used as measurable proxies for concepts? Parental power, average age at first marriage, social class, slavery, the Radical Republicans, homicide rate, racial equality, racial segregation, democracy.

11. A history major is planning a research paper about the changing status of women students on a college campus from 1920 to the present.[7] Her specific hypothesis is that the status of women students has improved. Clearly, "the status of women" is a concept. Comment on the adequacy of each of the following as indicators of changes in women's status at the college:

(a) whether women were allowed to play on the football team;

(b) the proportion of student leadership positions held by women each year;

---

[7]This example is based on Nancy V. Hoyt, "The Changing Status of Women Students at Carleton College, 1920–1970," a senior honors thesis in the Department of History at Carleton College (1973).

(c) the overall percentage of women in the student body each year;

(d) the proportion of women majoring in traditional "women's fields" such as elementary education, nursing, and literature;

(e) whether women were required to be in their dorms by 10 p.m. each evening;

(f) the number of visiting speakers discussing women's issues each year;

(g) whether the college president was a woman.

Is the prediction improbable? Suppose that a historian has developed a hypothesis about the modernization of women and predicts that if her hypothesis is true, she expects to find that about half the population in the U.S. in 1900 was female. That's like predicting, on the basis of a hypothesis, that the sun will rise tomorrow morning. The trouble is that you don't need any complicated hypothesis to make such predictions. Anyone could have predicted the same thing.

On the other hand, suppose the same historian predicts that if the hypothesis is true, research ought to reveal that the proportion of women able to read and write rose from a very low figure in 1800 to a very high one in 1900. This prediction seems considerably more unlikely; if it turns out to be true, that gives credibility to the hypothesis.

12. Continuing with the study of the changing status of women students on a college campus, comment on the following prediction: If the status of women has improved between 1920 and 1970, you should expect to find that the number of women majoring in physics goes up over that period.

Does the historian state specifically what kinds of results will lead to a decision to accept or reject the hypothesis? The reason for trying to do this ought to be obvious. If a researcher has a hypothesis that she very much hopes will be validated by the tests, she will face a strong temptation to interpret the results in a way favorable to the hypothesis, or possibly to discard results that turned out the "wrong" way and to conduct some other test instead. But doing that would be the same as saying, "I already know the right answer to this question, and I won't accept any information that disagrees with me." To avoid this problem, it helps to state ahead of time what results will be judged to support or weaken the hypothesis.

Does the test involve new data? New data means information other than that used to generate the hypothesis in the first place. If this point is not clear to you, you should review Section 5.2, where it is discussed in detail.

Is the prediction logically deducible from the hypothesis together with stated initial conditions? This criterion is so important that the confirmatory model of research that this section is outlining has sometimes been called the "hypothetico-deductive" model. In a deductively valid argument, if the premises are true, the conclusion must also be true. Of course, the premises (in this case, the hypothesis and initial conditions) might not be true. A deductive argument states that <u>if</u> the premises are true, then the conclusion <u>must</u> be true.

The point of including this criterion for a good test is to eliminate one source of error, errors flowing from the lack of strong connection between the hypothesis and the tests that the historian proposes to carry out. But it is difficult to devise an airtight deductively valid test in historical studies; for this reason, social-science historians generally use several tests of an important hypothesis. As Daniel Scott Smith has put it, "Conclusions must rest not just on one measure but on the conformity of various indicators to some pattern."[8]

5.4   Hypothesis and Tests

Smith, a demographic historian specializing in American colonial history, employed the confirmatory style of historical analysis to test the sociologists' claim that over the past 500 years there has been a shift from a traditional to a modern family type.[9] This claim is, of course, a more specific version of the broader theory of modernization.

When Smith set out to probe the sociological theory that the family had modernized, he first had to devise a workable hypothesis. He briefly considered two hypotheses and discarded them both. The first of these, popular among social scientists a few decades ago, was the hypothesis that the family had undergone an important change in structure. But by the time of Smith's project, scholars had already established that the basic structure of the family had not altered between, say, 1500 and 1900 in Western Europe and America. The nuclear family (husband,

---

[8]Daniel Scott Smith, "Parental Power and Marriage Patterns: An Analysis of Historical Trends in Hingham, Massachusetts," *Journal of Marriage and the Family*, 35 (August 1973), 422.

[9]*Ibid.*, 419–28.

wife, and children) had been the predominant structure 500 years ago, so a hypothesis emphasizing family structure was ruled out.

Second, Smith considered one of the best-known interpretations about the history of the family: Philippe Ariés's idea that the family has become more privatized—more separated from the community—and that the child has come to occupy a central place in the modern family. Smith concluded that this interpretation focused on the changing psychology of people within the family and could not easily be tested.

Smith eventually settled on a hypothesis having to do with parental power. Here is how he stated it:

> If the American family has undergone substantial historical change, it should be reflected in the conditions of marriage formation. Were, in fact, the marriages of a significant segment of the American population ever controlled by parents at any point in our history? ... A shift in the control of marriage formation is clearly to be expected by the sociological theory of family modernization.[10]

13. Restate Smith's hypothesis in your own words and identify the key concepts that he appears to be working with.

This statement resembles an ordinary, everyday historical interpretation. But perhaps because he was writing for a social-science journal, Smith stated the hypothesis more formally than historians usually do. You can think of a hypothesis as a tentative interpretation; the historian is saying "This hypothesis states how things may have happened."[11] One virtue of the more formal approach to stating and testing hypotheses is that it brings the underlying theory out in the open for the reader to examine.

14. Briefly describe how the theoretical hypothesis given above is related to modernization theory.

15. Smith also remarked that the hypothesis was improbable "on both theoretical and historical grounds." If a shift away from strong

---

[10] *Ibid.*, 421.

[11] This suggests that behind most historical interpretations there lies some implicit theory—a point that many observers of historians have made. See, e.g., David M. Potter, "Explicit Data and Implicit Assumptions in Historical Study," in Don E. Fehrenbacher (ed.), *History and American Society: Essays of David M. Potter* (New York, 1973), 4–26.

parental authority toward a more democratic family was improbable, why put forward such a hypothesis? What is the advantage of improbability?

Smith must next test the hypothesis. Since change in parental authority (if it happened) probably took place gradually, he needed to look at a long time-span, a century at least. He proposed to study a single town, Hingham, Massachusetts, over the 240 years between 1635 and 1880—an unusually long time-span for an American historian to deal with.

How about specific predictions? Smith offered four, but in this section we consider just two of them. By way of background, Smith noted that in a preindustrial community like Hingham, "marriage was intimately linked to economic independence." Fathers had an interest in keeping their sons unmarried and living at home, since the sons provided unpaid labor and did not need to be given land. Fathers, therefore, had "something to lose—either economic resources or unpaid labor services"—when their sons married.

Smith could now offer his first prediction:

> If parents had considerable power over their children's decisions about when to marry and whom to marry in Hingham, we should find that "sons of men who die early would be able to marry before sons of men who survive into old age." Further, if the hypothesis about a decline in parental authority is true, we should find that this differential diminished over time.[12]

The author added that the reader should not expect a huge differential. "Fathers had a cultural obligation to see their children married although it was not in their short-run self-interest."

16. This first test of the hypothesis involves a concept and an indicator of that concept. Can you identify them?

Table 5.3 presents the results of Smith's research into the demographic history of Hingham.

17. In a few sentences, sum up the results of the test; focus especially on the two bottom rows that give results for 1641–1780 and 1781–1840.

18. In Table 5.3, what do the numbers in parentheses refer to?

---

[12]Smith, "Parental Power," 423.

Table 5.3
Differential in marriage age of sons by age at death of fathers

Period of fathers' marriage cohort	Fathers who died under age 60		Fathers who died at 60 and over		Differences in mean ages
	Sons' mean age at marriage	(N)	Sons' mean age at marriage	(N)	
1641–1700	26.8	(64)	28.4	(142)	+1.6
1701–1720	24.3	(30)	25.9	(130)	+1.6
1721–1740	24.7	(38)	26.7	(104)	+2.0
1741–1760	26.1	(43)	26.5	(145)	+0.4
1761–1780	25.7	(42)	26.8	(143)	+1.1
1781–1800	26.0	(71)	25.8	(150)	−0.2
1801–1820	25.7	(93)	26.5	(190)	+0.8
1821–1840	26.0	(42)	25.9	(126)	−0.1
1641–1780	25.73	(217)	26.89	(664)	+1.16
1781–1840	25.86	(206)	26.11	(466)	+0.25

Source: Daniel Scott Smith, "Parental Power and Marriage Patterns: An Analysis of Historical Trends in Hingham, Massachusetts," *Journal of Marriage and the Family*, 35 (August 1973), p. 423, Table 1.

Note: Father's age at death was divided into two categories, under 60 and 60 and over, because "over two centuries of the study 60 years was the approximate mean age of fathers at the time of marriage of their sons."

19. One of the criteria for a "good test" (Section 5.3) spoke of "initial conditions." What time-period did Smith implicitly take as setting the initial conditions for his test?

20. Comment on how well this test meets the criteria for a good test.

Smith offers a second test of the hypothesis. In preindustrial times, women were more subject to parental control than men. Therefore:

> If parents did decide when their daughters could and should marry, one might expect them to proceed on the basis of the eldest first and so on. Passing over a daughter to allow a younger sister to marry first might advertise some deficiency in the elder and consequently make it more difficult for the parents to find a suitable husband for her. If, on the other hand, women decided on the basis of personal considerations when (and perhaps who) they should marry, more

irregularity in the sequence of sisters' marriages should be expected.[13]

For this second test, again using Hingham data, Smith got the results shown in Table 5.4.

Table 5.4
Percentage of daughters not marrying in birth order in relationship to those at risk (spinsters excluded)

Time-periods when daughters become marriageable	(%)	(N)
1631–1691	8.1	86
1701–1731	11.6	138
1741–1771	18.2	176
1781–1811	14.9	214
1821–1861	18.4	298

Source: Based on Smith, "Parental Power," p. 425, Table 3. We have altered the time-periods slightly for ease of interpretation.

21. In Table 5.4 and the hypothesis accompanying it, identify Smith's prediction and the indicator variable that he measured to test the prediction.

22. Overall, are the data displayed in the table consistent with the hypothesis?

23. In discussing the test summarized in Table 5.4, Daniel Scott Smith remarks that the important question is not an either-or issue but one of how much. Explain what he means and show how his comment applies to the results presented in the table.

Smith's four tests, of which Section 5.4 has examined two, were ingenious and the results quite fascinating. But did they prove that his hypothesis about the gradual decline of parental power was true? Recall that his study was not designed to establish whether the hypothesis was true for American society generally. If Smith's hypothesis about

---

[13] *Ibid.*, 425.

parental power has been supported, it's been supported for Hingham, Massachusetts.

Here's a rule of thumb:

> If the historian has selected appropriate indicators of the concept to be tested, and if the tests meet the criteria for a "good test," and if the tests yield the predicted results, then the hypothesis is strongly supported.

This chapter has already discussed Smith's indicators and the design of the tests. Did they yield the predicted results? Consider the second test, the one that involved parental control over daughters' marriage choices. The proportion of daughters marrying out of their birth order (spinsters excluded) more than doubled between the late seventeenth century and the mid-nineteenth century (Table 5.4). Certainly if the proportions had been more extreme—if, for example, no daughters had married out of the birth order in the seventeenth century while half had done so in the nineteenth—this test would have been more impressive. But the observed change, from 8% to 18%, was in the predicted direction. Moreover, Smith offered four tests, not just one, and in every case the change was in the predicted direction.

Smith therefore seems well positioned to argue that if there was not a drastic change in the degree of parental control over children of marriage age, a genuine if gradual decline in parental power did take place. At least for Hingham, a reader can conclude that the tests provide considerable support for his hypothesis. Perhaps you could say that the hypothesis is approximately confirmed.

And you should recall that in advancing his hypothesis, Smith used deliberately loose and cautious phrasing: he spoke of a "shift in the control of marriage formation"; he avoided terms like "revolution" and never proposed simplistic dichotomous terms like "authoritarian family" and "democratic family." In effect, he never encouraged his readers to expect more than approximate confirmation for the hypothesis.

Only approximate? Could Smith have devised other tests that might have persuaded us that the hypothesis had been proved completely true? Almost certainly the answer is no. The author could add more tests, but they would be subject to the same limitations and would bring in the same kind of results as the tests he had already done. Moreover, with more tests there would be more chances for errors. Smith was wise to stop where he did.

In history and the social sciences, all theory has a probabilistic character. Tests of a hypothesis generally cannot prove or disprove the hypothesis categorically. But they can make the hypothesis seem more or less credible. When a historian conducts several independent tests, as Smith did for his hypothesis about parental power, the hypothesis looks stronger. But the world of human societies is exceedingly complicated, and is perhaps even a stochastic system—a system in which conditions at any one moment do not absolutely determine conditions at a later moment, but affect only the probability that various subsequent events will happen.

The question remains, how do the historian and his reader decide whether the results of a test offer approximate support for the hypothesis or not. In Table 5.4, what if the percentages had risen from, say, 10 to 13 instead of from 8 to 18? What if they had risen only from 10 to 11? In the end, whether to accept or reject a hypothesis is a matter of judgment, the judgment of the community of historians and their readers.[14]

5.5   Testing Statistical Significance

Daniel Scott Smith was testing hypotheses about social patterns when he asked about the meaning or implications of the data in Table 5.4. But tests of statistical significance ask quite a different question: are the women represented in Table 5.4 typical of all the women of their time—or even all the women of Hingham? Significance testing as a topic in statistics deals with the role of sampling error in generating the numbers the historian has to work with.

The subject of tests of statistical significance involves a formal jargon that you will encounter when reading quantitative history. This next section will demonstrate the steps of the statistical procedures used and introduce some of the standard phrases you will meet. It also emphasizes that the statistical methods are aimed at a very limited target—the possible role of chance. Assessing statistical significance usually constitutes one small step, although an important one, of some larger argument.

Chapter 3, Section 7 discussed family sizes in Virginia in the 1620s and Bristol, Rhode Island in the 1680s. Table 5.5 shows that information again. Let's imagine a confrontation over the meaning of this table between a Quantitative Historian (call her QH) and an inveterate critic

---

[14]Smith himself discusses why results must always be approximate in "A Mean and Random Past: The Implications of Variance for History," *Historical Methods*, 17 (Summer 1984), 141–48. See also Giere, *Understanding Scientific Reasoning*, 92–93 and 120–21.

Table 5.5
Children per Family in Virginia, 1624/5 and in Bristol, Rhode Island, 1688/9

Number of Children	0	1	2	3	4	5	6	7	8	9	10
Number of Families											
Virginia	102	62	17	6	2	0	0	0	0	0	0
Bristol	7	10	11	12	9	8	6	4	1	0	1

Source: See Table 3.10.

of hers we will call DA for Devil's Advocate.

Before you listen in on the argument, note this important point. QH and DA are not going to disagree about there being a difference in average family size between Bristol and Virginia. They both know that a difference existed. Instead, they will debate whether the difference is of a size you might reasonably expect if the Bristol and Virginia families had been drawn from a common population of origin. The proposition to be tested is that the two groups are like random samples from a common population, while the alternative proposition or hypothesis is that they are more like samples from two distinct populations so that their differences cannot be ascribed to chance.

Whether you think of the Virginia and Bristol families as having been drawn from one common population or from two distinct populations, those larger populations are purely conceptual. Some historical events led to those families being in Virginia in the 1620s or in Bristol in the 1680s. You can imagine the events as selecting the two real populations from a pool of potential populations. The question is, is it necessary to believe there was some special, oppressive process in Virginia, perhaps starvation (or a fertility enhancing process in Bristol), or can you believe that the observed difference in average family size could well be purely a matter of chance? After all, large and small families turn up in both places.

QH begins speaking carefully, knowing the critic is ready to pounce on any unwarranted assertion. She states an explicit, testable hypothesis together with an alternative and contradictory hypothesis. She intends to use Table 5.5 to choose between the two.

QH. I want to determine whether there was a substantial and possibly important difference in family size between the families of Virginia in 1624/5 and Bristol sixty years later. To do that, I'll test the null hypothesis that there was no significant difference in numbers of

children per family against the alternative hypothesis that Bristol
families averaged significantly more children per family.

Note: statistics books often use the notation H_0 for the hypothesis
being tested. This is called the null hypothesis (null for zero). In this
example, the assertion of no difference is the null hypothesis. In fact,
the null hypothesis is almost always the hypothesis of no difference or
only chance difference.

QH displays Table 5.5 and, with her critic watching closely, she com-
putes the mean number of children per family for Bristol and for Virginia, 3.3 and 0.65 respectively, using weighted averages.

QH. Clearly, 3.3 is substantially greater than 0.65; so I think we can
reject the null hypothesis, that there was no difference, in favor of
the alternative that the average number of children per family was
significantly larger in Bristol.

24. QH's argument appears so evident, such simple common sense,
that it seems even a devil's advocate won't be able to challenge
her. She predicted that there would be a difference and there was.
But try to think of some grounds on which DA might base an
objection or at least raise a question.

25. QH compared two means to test for a difference between the groups
in numbers of children per family. How else might she have used
the data in Table 5.5 to test for that difference?

The devil's advocate fussed with his pipe, pausing to phrase his response gently.

DA. Now, QH, I'm sure you're too good a historian to busy yourself
recording isolated meaningless facts. You must be bringing up
this family size business because you want to ask about the historical causes of such an important difference in family size. Perhaps
you'll be arguing that life was more prosperous in Bristol around
the time of the Glorious Revolution, so that the Bristol families
could better afford children. Or perhaps you'll be looking at cultural or social or demographic differences, or maybe you're just
raising the question for someone else to answer. But it doesn't
really matter where you're headed with this thing, because there
is a basic flaw in your thinking.

He pulled a quarter out of his pocket, flipped it nine times and wrote "H 5, T 4" on a yellow legal pad. Then he tossed it nine times again and wrote "H 6, T 3."

DA. Really, should I submit a paper to a physics journal because I got 20% more heads the second time than I did the first time? Don't you see how silly this is? Elaborate theories are not necessarily called for just because two groups of numbers fail to be identical. Imagine that you had a big pool of families in England and you selected 189 of those families randomly, like bingo numbers, and sent them to Virginia. Then, awhile later, you selected another 69 families from a very similar population and you sent that group to Bristol. Now later still, someone comes along and starts measuring these two groups of families. Sure enough, one of the groups is going to be taller on the average, or weigh more, or maybe one group will have more blue-eyed babies or, indeed, one will have more children per family. It is inevitable that they will differ in some respect or other. But it doesn't have to be due to anything but chance and no big historical explanation is called for. In any group of objects in the real world (say families in England), there is going to be quite a bit of random variability, and I think that's what you're seeing when you calculate the mean number of children for these two groups of colonial families. It's just chance. I'm still a believer in your null hypothesis.

QH. All right, let's stick with your example of selecting families from England strictly by chance. I agree that if I randomly select just one family for Virginia and one for Bristol, those families could have quite different sizes. But if I randomly picked 50 families for each place, wouldn't you think that the average sizes would tend to be closer together? After all, I would be picking both groups randomly from a common pool. Suppose that I picked 1000 families for each colony just using chance; wouldn't the two averages be closer still? In fact, if I picked large enough groups, the average of each group would be very close to the average family size of the original pool and so the two averages would also be very close to each other.

DA. That's true, but you don't have arbitrarily large groups. You only have 69 families in Bristol and 189 in Virginia. That's not many families. Furthermore, what makes you think 3.3 and 0.65 aren't close together? It may be perfectly reasonable to get averages that far apart just by chance. After all, there would have been a lot of variability in the original pool of families that we're imagining. Some of the families in the original pool could have had 15 kids while others had none.

QH. So you're saying I should simultaneously take into account how big the two selected groups are, how much variability in family size there is in the common pool, and how far apart the two group means are before I can say I have a difference in family size worth talking about. That would be quite complicated.

DA. Exactly. (He hoped she would take this positively.)

QH. Well, there is a standard statistical procedure that takes precisely those things into account.

QH whipped a diskette into a computer on her desk and, in seconds, announced:

QH. The <u>t-value</u> is 9.5.

She gathered up her papers as though that statement closed the issue.

DA. I beg your pardon? t-value?

QH. The difference between the Bristol mean, 3.3, and the Virginia mean, 0.65, is 2.65. The t-value is what you get if you divide that difference, 2.65, by an estimate of what the difference would be if you were really selecting the families randomly from a common population. The difference we're looking at is nine and a half times what we would expect by chance.

She reached over and wrote on his yellow pad,

$$\text{t-value} = \frac{2.65}{\text{Standard error for difference}} = 9.5.$$

QH. The standard error in the denominator is the average difference among the means that you would get if you selected many sets of Bristol and Virginia families randomly. The calculation of the standard error takes into account how many families there were and how variable family size is in the two groups. So what the t-value says is that the difference between Bristol and Virginia is

9.5 times bigger than the average difference you would see if only chance were operating.

To my mind, when you get a result nine and a half times bigger than you would expect by chance alone, that means the chance explanation is improbable and that it's reasonable to pursue causal explanations. It confirms my initial view that I should reject H_0 and accept the alternative hypothesis.

DA. Improbable? (The devil's advocate snorted emphatically.) So you don't rule chance out altogether?

QH. One can never do that. However....

She zinged the diskette back into the computer and in even less time than before announced,

QH. The p-value is virtually zero. This program rounds it off to 0.0000.

DA. First t-value and now p-value?

QH. The p-value is the probability of getting the t-value. For example, a p-value of .15 means the probability of finding a t as big as or bigger than the one actually found is 15%. Since our p-value is essentially zero, it means the probability of getting a t as large as 9.5 by chance is essentially zero. I think we have to deny chance as a reasonable explanation and assume that some non-random cause has produced the difference. I intend to focus my research on that question.

At this point we will allow **DA** to retire and mention two other technical phrases **QH** might have used. Instead of referring to p-value or t-value explicitly, she could have said, "The difference in means is significant at the .01 level." This is another way of referring to a p-value. Significant at .01 means that the p-value is as small as or smaller than .01. In other words, the difference is too large to ascribe reasonably to chance. A similar sentence often used is the somewhat less precise: "The difference was very significant (or highly significant)."

26. In your own words, explain the sentence "The difference was significant at the 5% level."

27. Similarly, explain "The null hypothesis was rejected at the 1% level."

28.   Here's a technical question. You will probably have to look back
at the definition of standard deviation in Chapter 3 in order to
answer it. When QH wrote the formula for the t-value on DA's
yellow pad, what did she mean in saying that the standard error
in the denominator was an average difference?

The formal procedures known as testing for statistical significance deal
with the question of chance. They enable you to judge the reasonableness of the devil's advocate claim (the null hypothesis) that observed
patterns occurred by chance. If the statistical procedures produce the
conclusion that chance was a very improbable cause, then you are justified in proceeding as though the patterns require some explanation other
than chance. It is only at this one small point, checking out chance, that
mathematics intrudes into what is otherwise conventional common sense.

Unfortunately, the words "statistically significant" encourage readers
to believe that they refer to the practical significance of a difference. To
say that a difference is highly statistically significant is only to suggest
that the given difference was not due to chance. The phrase tells you
that it would not be reasonable to think of the two groups as being like
random samples drawn from a common pool. But "statistically significant" does not say that the given difference has important consequences
or that it is worth investigating. It's up to the historian to judge, on
wholly nonstatistical grounds, the practical importance of a difference
such as the one that QH calculated from Table 5.5. The statistical procedure focuses exclusively on the devil's advocate proposition (the null
hypothesis) that only chance variation is being observed.

The following four steps represent a summary of the procedures described in the dialogue between QH and DA. Fortunately, standard tables or computer programs will do most of this for a researcher:

- Express the issue in terms of variables that can be calculated from
  the data; e.g., the issue of family size is expressed in terms of a
  difference in mean numbers of children.

- Compute a test statistic from values calculated in step 1; e.g.,
  compute t from the difference in means, the group sizes, and the
  standard deviation for the difference in means.

- Compute the probability (p-value) that chance alone would have
  produced a t-value as large as that found in the preceding step.

- If the p-value is small, reject the null hypothesis (the hypothesis stating that only chance is operating) and conclude that the

calculated values are statistically significant. If the p-value is not small, then, at least tentatively, face the possibility that observed patterns are in the range of random variability.

When one compares two means as QH did in the previous dialogue, the t-value is a helpful statistic. But one might want to compare two medians or two standard deviations or several means simultaneously. In fact, one might want to compare two entire frequency distributions instead of single numbers such as means. For each different kind of comparison, and depending on whether the data are categorical or numeric, a different statistic analogous to a t-value may be needed. So there are many such statistics.

Scholars have shown considerable imagination in comparing measurements of phenomena they care about; to introduce all the statistics you might ever encounter would make for tedious reading. The list includes statistics called Eta, chi-square, F, z, and more—too many to remember. But when you encounter them in some article or book, remember that they play approximately the same logical role. Each statistic is derived from the data in such a way that the probability is small that the statistic could be large just by chance.

Suppose an author says to you, "I found an F-score of 8.6, which is significant at the 1% level." This is similar to our example in which QH found a t of 9.5 that was significant at about 0.0000. You don't need to know the formula for F in order to understand the author's point. The author means that the contrast being examined was too large to be attributed reasonably to chance.

29. The author of an article comparing religious activity in counties of the Burned-Over District of upstate New York with activity in counties of the upper Ohio Valley writes, "This study relies on the Eta statistic.... In terms of total [number of] churches, seats, and seats held by groups not among the eight largest in the region, the Eta scores hovered around .00 in both [1850 and 1860]." She adds that such scores "suggest that no significant differences [in intensity of religious activity] existed between [the upper Ohio region] and the Burned-Over District."[15] What on earth is this historian talking about?

Up to this point, we've treated the Virginia and Bristol data as population, not sample, data. And they were in fact population data. But now

---

[15]Linda K. Pritchard, "The Burned-Over District Reconsidered," *Social Science History*, 8 (Summer 1984), 243–65; quotation at 247.

we want to introduce a new idea, closely associated with the material already covered in this dialogue, but which only comes up in discussions of sampling. So for the following few paragraphs, we ask you to imagine that Virginia and Bristol family size data came from samples of the Virginia and Bristol populations. Pretend that there had actually been a thousand or so families in each colony and that Table 5.5 is based on a random sample of 69 families from Bristol and a random sample of 189 families from Virginia.

The average number of children per family in the Bristol sample, 3.3, is clearly larger than the average in the Virginia sample, 0.65. But now, here's what a historian wouldn't know: is the average number of children in the Bristol population also larger than the average number of children in the Virginia population? Our friend the Quantitative Historian and her colleague the Devil's Advocate are about to discuss this question:

QH. Now I'm going to estimate the difference in population means from the difference in sample means. The sample means, you remember, were 3.3 and 0.65. So the difference between sample means is 2.65. My question is, what's the difference between mean number of children in the two populations, Bristol and Virginia?

DA. There is no possible way to answer that question. You only have data on a few families from each colony. Even though you found a difference between the two samples, you have no way of knowing if that same difference would show up in the underlying populations.

QH. If you mean I could never be certain, you're right. But suppose my samples were so big that they included almost everybody in the two colonies. Then I would be virtually certain that the sample difference was close to the true difference between the populations.

DA. I'll grant that, especially since your samples are not that big.

QH. On the other hand, if I had very small samples, say only one or two families from each colony, then there would be no reason to think that the sample difference approximated the population difference. So what must happen is this: as the sample sizes get bigger and bigger, I gradually move from being completely unsure to being completely sure that the sample and population differences are alike.

DA. I see it coming. You're going to say there's some magic critical sample size and that these samples are bigger than that critical size, so you can be sure the colonies really have different mean numbers of children.

QH. No, there's no "critical sample size." What happens is that you gradually become more sure that the mean numbers of children per family in the two samples actually reflect the mean numbers in the two populations. Actually, we just use that t-value of 9.5 and its p-value of 0.0000 that we calculated before.

DA. So what does that prove?

QH. Well, here's the argument:

1. If there were no difference between the Bristol and Virginia populations, then the chance of a difference as big as 2.65 between the sample means would be approximately zero.

2. But there <u>was</u> a sample difference as big as 2.65.

3. Therefore, it's unreasonable to believe that there was no difference in the populations.

DA. Wait a minute! That only defends the idea that there is <u>some</u> difference between the populations. Your argument doesn't say anything about <u>how big</u> a difference. The real population difference doesn't have to be as big as the 2.65 sample difference. Maybe the real difference is so small as to have no practical significance!

QH. Well, I didn't want to bring this up unless I had to. [She turned one last time to the computer, performed a quick calculation and said:] The 99% <u>confidence interval</u> for the population difference is from 2.1 to 3.2.

DA. Confidence interval? I'm afraid to ask.

QH. It just means that we can be pretty sure the difference in the means of the two populations lies somewhere between 2.1 and 3.2. Notice that the sample difference of 2.65 is right in the middle of those numbers. We got the confidence interval by going a little bit to each side of the observed difference of 2.65.

DA. How do you know how far to go above and below the difference in the two means?

QH. That's where the 99% comes in—its called the <u>confidence level</u>. It means that we can be 99% certain that the interval from 2.1 to 3.2 captures the real population difference. If we were willing to be less sure, we could use a 95% confidence level, which would give a smaller interval, tighter around 2.65. Because it's smaller we wouldn't be as sure it captured the true difference in average family sizes. Anyway, where this all comes out is, first, that there is convincing evidence of a real difference and, second, that the real difference is very probably at least as big as 2.1 and smaller than 3.2.

Once again we will cover the retreat of DA with some remarks. The purpose of the preceding dialogues was to introduce a handful of technical words and ideas in a context that would make their meaning clear. You will commonly encounter these words and ideas in writings that use statistics. You should check to see if you have a feel for these words and phrases: null hypothesis, alternative hypothesis, t-value, p-value, confidence interval, confidence level, and significance level.

The dialogues between DA and QH looked at three related problems. QH first asked whether an observed difference between two populations was large enough to challenge her to find a historical explanation. Then she asked if a difference between sample means really implied a difference between the corresponding population means. Finally, she asked for an estimate of the probable size of the population difference, given the sample difference.

30.   If 34.2 to 42.2 is a 95% confidence interval, which of the following could be a corresponding 90% confidence interval?

      1.   30.2 to 46.2
      2.   41.2 to 43.2
      3.   37.2 to 39.2

5.6   Conclusion

Chapter 5 has focused intensely on the confirmatory or hypothesis-testing style of research because this style involves a more formal set of rules than the exploratory style and because we believe that many of our readers will be unfamiliar with it. We are not claiming that confirmatory research is better than exploratory research. The two styles complement each other; a work of history can fruitfully employ both.

For most of Chapter 5, the examples involved entire populations. Daniel Scott Smith's article focuses on all the people who lived in Hingham, Massachusetts up to 1880. But one might ask, who really cares about Hingham except the people who live there? In making a strong case that families in Hingham experienced a gradual decline in parental power, has Smith presented an important finding? Such questions are ways of asking whether Hingham was typical of other American communities. Smith takes care not to raise anyone's hopes: "the conclusions strictly must be limited to the town of Hingham," he tells us.[16]

But at the end of the article, he reminds us that Hingham, after all, did resemble many other towns in such characteristics as size, economic activities, participation in the American Revolution, and experiencing broad demographic trends such as out-migration and the decline in fertility. These similarities give us some reason to suspect that Smith's findings can be generalized beyond Hingham.

While it is often hazardous to make the leap from a part to the whole (in this case, from one New England town to American society in general), sometimes a historian can do so with considerable confidence. As you know from having read Chapter 4, it depends on whether he or she has sampled the larger population in an appropriate way.

Here are questions you might ask yourself as you read quantitative history:

- What concepts does the author use and where did the author get them? Does the author clearly define the key concepts? Are the concepts dichotomous (yes-no) or could they be measured along a continuum? Do the concepts appear abstract enough to have broad potential relevance for different places and times, but precise enough to be measurable?[17]

- What is the model or theory that the author proposes? Does the model or theory seem suitable for quantitative testing?

- What indicator variables will the author use to represent the key concepts? Do these indicators seem reasonable to you? Will there be problems in gathering data for them or in measuring them? Will the author employ more than one indicator so that there is a check on the adequacy of any particular one?

---

[16] Smith, "Parental Power," 422.

[17] J. Rogers Hollingsworth, "Some Problems in Theory Construction for Historical Analysis," *Historical Methods Newsletter*, 7 (June 1974), 225–44, at 227. This article provides an excellent brief introduction to the role of theories and models in social-science history.

- Does the author state a <u>hypothesis</u> and offer <u>predictions</u> as to what results ought to be found if the model or theory is a good one? Does the author clearly describe how he or she proposes to <u>test</u> the hypothesis and indicate what level of results will warrant rejecting or not rejecting the hypothesis?

- Does the author choose appropriate statistical procedures for the kind of data he or she is working with? Does the author clearly explain the procedures and clearly present the results?

- What is the author's overall judgment of the meaning and significance of the test results? Are the results <u>statistically significant</u>, and if so, are they also historically interesting? What do the results mean for the original theory and model, and what further questions do they raise?

Terms Introduced in Chapter 5

5.1 experiment
5.1 observational study
5.2 exploratory or hypothesis-generating style of research
5.2 confirmatory or hypothesis-testing style of research
5.2 scientific-empirical method
5.3 theory
5.3 hypothesis
5.3 test, good test
5.3 indicator variable
5.3 hypothetico-deductive model
5.4 stochastic system
5.5 significance test
5.5 null hypothesis
5.5 alternative hypothesis
5.5 t-value
5.5 p-value
5.5 significance level
5.5 statistical significance and historical significance
5.5 confidence interval
5.5 confidence level

5.7   Answers to Questions

1. With an observational study you have to deal with the clear pos-
    sibility that an observed association between two variables may
    be due to some factors other than a connection between the vari-
    ables themselves. For example, if well educated people in the U.S.
    tend to be more prosperous than others, you must consider several
    possibilities: that education helps one attain wealth, that wealth
    helps one attain education, or that some other factors such as the
    wealth and social/economic connections of parents tend to encour-
    age both wealth and education in the offspring, or perhaps that
    there is something like general intelligence level that tends to cause
    both.

    When an experiment is possible, the experimenter can at least
    reduce the range of possible explanations for the association by
    controlling some of the variables. For example, suppose, contrary
    to fact, that the amount and quality of learning could be randomly
    assigned to young adults in the U.S. If, ten years later, the best
    learning is associated with the greatest wealth, you could no longer
    ascribe that to the wealth or connections of the parents since ran-
    dom selection would have placed both rich and poor young adults
    in both the poorly educated and well educated groups.

2. Yes, it is impossible. The key to an experiment is that the exper-
    imenter controls some of the variables in order to limit the range
    of possible explanations. The experimenter decides which rabbits
    get the drug. But the historian cannot decide which nineteenth-
    century towns get rail connections.

3. We tend to believe that some mountains were caused by volcanic
    action and others by uplift, that heavy smoking for many years is
    bad for the health of humans, and that isolating the water sup-
    ply system from the sewer system enhances the health of human
    communities.

4. One might look at the median age at death; this could be different
    from the mean because mortality patterns are skewed. Or one
    might look at the proportion of the population living into old age,
    say beyond age 60.

5. You would probably present four summary numbers instead of
    only the two shown in Table 5.1. You would show some mortality

measure for both slaves and non-slaves in each of the two geographic regions.

6. The first half of the list has larger numbers, averaging 5.4, while
    the last half averages only 3.8. This could cause you to conjecture
    that lists tend to lead off with big numbers. A second pattern is
    that all of the nonzero even numbers in the list are powers of 2.
    That's surprising since most even numbers, such as 6 and 10 and
    12, are not powers of 2. A third pattern is that the odd numbers
    tend to come late in the list. The odd numbers are in positions 4,
    8, 9, and 10.

7. Not at all. Maybe members of one group either died in infancy
    or lived to very old age while members of the other group all died
    near age 41.

8. Here are a few examples: (1) The American Revolution created
    the conditions for the modernization of the American economy.
    (2) There has been a modernization of the American "character"
    or personality type, from an inner-directed, work-oriented type
    to an other-directed, consumption-oriented type. (3) The drive
    for equal rights for women and blacks is a necessary and inevitable
    development in the creation of a modern economy in which workers
    are recruited on the basis of their talents and educational levels,
    not on the basis of ascribed characteristics such as gender and skin
    color.

9. Concepts, stated or implied, include: modernization; economy;
    primitive, subsistence economy; technology; industrialization; tech-
    nology intensive, industrialized economy; culture; political culture;
    subject political culture; participant political culture; status; sta-
    tus system; closed, ascriptive status system; open, achievement-
    oriented status system; kinship; extended kinship unit; nuclear
    kinship unit; ideology; religion; religious ideology; secular ideol-
    ogy. And there may be more.

10. We consider the following to be concepts: parental power, social
    class, the Radical Republicans, racial equality, and democracy. Of
    these, the one that may surprise you is the Radical Republicans
    (of the Reconstruction era). David Potter's comment about this
    phrase is apt: it "ascribes to an unstated number of individuals
    a common identity strong enough to justify classifying them as
    a group.... Yet, in terms of analysis historians have had great

difficulty either in defining what constituted a Radical or in proving that any given aggregate of individuals formed a truly cohesive Radical bloc."[18]

As for the other terms, we consider average age at first marriage to be an indicator variable (Smith uses it as an indicator of parental power). Homicide rate would also be an indicator variable. Slavery and racial segregation probably could be considered "facts" of history. They were complex systems of behavior universally agreed to exist in their own time and rooted in the laws and social practices of the entire society. They are not categories devised by historians after the fact.

11. (a) Not a good indicator of changes in women's status since women students probably have never played on the football team—so even if women's status were changing in other ways, it wouldn't show up in this indicator.

(b) An excellent indicator since it is clearly related to the status of women on the campus and is capable of reflecting gradual change over time.

(c) It's not clear how the proportion of women in the student body is related to women's status. So the persuasiveness of the indicator depends on whether the historian can make a compelling case on this point.

(d) As in (c), the historian should explicitly state how women's choice of majors shows something about their status.

(e) If the historian is uncomfortable with the dichotomous (yes/no) nature of this' variable, perhaps she could redefine the indicator so as to incorporate the idea of more gradual variation over time. For example, she could define the indicator as "number of hours per week that women were allowed to be out past 6 p.m."

(f) Possibly a useful indicator, though the historian might have difficulty defining "women's issues" and determining the substance of each visitor's talk.

(g) Certainly a strong symbol of the respect in which women are held at the college. But a new president is appointed so rarely, and so many factors other than gender enter into the decision

---

[18]Potter, "Explicit Data and Implicit Assumptions," 13.

of whom to appoint, that this indicator probably isn't a good one for reflecting changes in attitudes.

12. Not necessarily. If the number of women physics majors goes up, there could be other explanations such as an overall growth in the size of the student body. The <u>proportion</u> of women majoring in physics could be the same as before.

13. The hypothesis is that there has been a shift from a family type in which parental authority was strong toward a type in which family members are more equal and parental authority over older children has greatly diminished. The key concept in the quoted paragraph appears to be parental control. Marriage formation may be a second concept, but it's not clear from the paragraph alone.

14. Modernization theory suggests that in traditional times, families (like entire societies) were organized hierarchically. Parents had considerable authority over their children even after the children had reached adulthood. By contrast, in modern times the family has become more democratic. Parental authority has diminished, and older children—certainly children who have reached adulthood—make decisions for themselves, considering their own preferences without necessarily considering what is best for their family of origin.

15. Smith means that a casual observer probably wouldn't predict something like a gradual shift in the distribution of family power. In the absence of a broad theory like modernization theory, there isn't any particular reason to expect something like that. Therefore, if a shift in family power actually did take place, as Smith's hypothesis predicted, the capacity of the hypothesis to make sense of this surprising trend raises one's confidence in it.

16. Parental power is the concept, the marriage age of sons the indicator.

17. Table 5.3 shows that in the case of fathers married in the seventeenth century and up to 1780, the marriage ages of their sons dropped more than a year on average if the fathers died before age 60. By contrast, for fathers married between 1781 and 1840, the marriage age of their sons didn't change very much on average whether the fathers died before 60 or lived past 60. This suggests to Smith that the sons of the earlier cohort of fathers may have delayed marriage by more than a year, on average, past the age at which they might have chosen to marry had their fathers not been present. Sons of the later group of fathers apparently didn't have to delay marriage even if their fathers lived. This finding supports Smith's hypothesis by suggesting that the earlier group of fathers exercised some sort of parental authority in an effort to get their sons to delay marriage.

18. These show the number of sons in each category of the table. In the top row, for example, the number (64) means that Smith had information on the marriage ages of 64 men whose fathers had married between 1641 and 1700 and that the mean age at marriage of these 64 men was 26.8 years.

19. Smith's table compares an early period with a later one in the history of Hingham. Implicitly, he sets the initial conditions to be those found in the town before processes of modernization began to happen. The bottom two lines of Table 5.3 might be read to imply that marriages up to 1780 fall in the premodern or traditional era (the baseline period), with the 1781–1840 marriages representing the era of family modernization.

20. (1) Whether Smith's prediction is verifiable depends on whether you accept son's age at marriage as an indicator of parental power. Smith defends his indicator in a statement quoted before Table 5.3. You can make up your own mind about the claim, but certainly the indicator is measurable.

(2) The improbability of the predicted trend was already discussed (see the answer to Question 15).

(3) In a passage quoted just before Table 5.3, Smith clearly makes a prediction.

(4) Smith uses data not earlier employed to generate the hypothesis.

(5) The initial condition was that parents exercised strong control over key decisions of their children even into early adulthood and that the parents had an economic interest in delaying the marriage of their children. The hypothesis is that families modernized and, as Smith defined it, modernization includes families becoming more democratic. So if modernization took place, older children would have greater control over the important decisions in their lives, including when to get married.

So the prediction being tested, a recent trend to earlier marriage of sons, does seem to follow from the hypothesis and
initial conditions.

21. As before, Smith's prediction is that parental control declined over
time. In this case, he uses the order in which daughters married
as his measurable indicator.

22. Yes, the general rise in the percentage marrying out of the birth
order seems roughly consistent with Smith's hypothesis.

23. Smith is commenting on the fact that the percentages in Table 5.4
generally change in the predicted direction, but the change seems
not to be a highly dramatic one—from 8% to 18%. Actually, there
should be a tendency for birth-order marriage since older daughters
arrive at marrying ages earlier than their younger sisters. In fact,
you would never find a population in which as many as 50% of
daughters marry out of the birth order. So the 18.4% figure of
Table 5.4 is a substantial proportion.

24. The word he can pounce on is the word "significant." If one measures any two sets closely enough, one can see a difference. In
fact, if you measure the same thing twice, say the length of your
desk, being careful and accurate both times, you will come up
with a difference. The point is that a difference is inevitable so
the mere existence of a difference is not interesting. What matters
is whether the difference is "large." But what does large mean?
That's the point of the debate.

25. She might have looked at the number of families that had no children or the number of families with lots of children, say more than
four. She might have used the median instead of the mean.

26. You can think of the null hypothesis as referring to a kind of
thought experiment: it is the proposition that the Bristol and
Virginia families resemble two groups drawn from a single original population and that the difference in average number of children between the two groups has no meaning—it just occurred by
chance and needs no historical explanation. Significance at the 5%
level means that if the null hypothesis is true, then there's only a
one out of twenty chance of getting a difference in mean number
of children as big as the one observed.

27. This means that if the null hypothesis is true, then there's only a one out of one hundred chance that the observed difference would be as far as it is from the zero difference predicted by the null hypothesis. Because of this fact, QH has chosen for now to reject the null hypothesis and has accepted the alternative hypothesis that the difference in mean number of children between Bristol and Virginia families is due to factors other than chance.

28. If the null hypothesis is true, and if one repeatedly took groups of families to put into Bristol and Virginia, the average difference in mean numbers of children would be about zero. This is because the null hypothesis says that the groups are like random samples from the very same underlying population. After taking a large number of samples, one would have a long list of differences between the average number of children in Bristol and Virginia families; the mean of that list would be about zero. The standard error is the standard deviation of the differences from the mean of the list to the numbers in the list. But since the mean is zero, that distance is the average of the differences themselves. That is, the standard error is the average size of the chance difference between the mean number of children in Virginia and Bristol families.

29. It is really not very important to know exactly how the Eta statistic is calculated. All the important information is in the statistical significance or the p-value computed from that mysterious object. Statistics such as t-values, F-values, chi-square values, and so on, are only obtained as intermediate steps in order to reach the p-value or significance level. This author is saying that knowing whether a county was located in the Burned-Over District or in the upper Ohio Valley region was of little help in enabling one to estimate that county's scores on several important indicator variables such as number of church seats in the county. Whatever the differences between counties of the two regions, they were so small as not to be statistically significant—i.e., they could have happened just by chance.

30. First, a 90% confidence interval will be smaller than a 95% confidence interval. The fact that it is smaller is the reason one has less confidence that it includes the real population value. Second, we get a confidence interval by going some distance on each side of a value found from a study or experiment. So the 90% confidence interval must be symmetric in both directions from the value 38.2,

the original interval implied in the question. Only answer 3 has
those properties.

III RELATIONSHIPS AMONG VARIABLES

6 Relationships Between Two Variables

In this chapter:

Chapters 1 through 3 focused on ways to describe how a single variable was distributed over a population. For example, given a list of the landholdings of farmers in a Wisconsin county in 1870, a historian might figure out the mean, median, and standard distribution of acreage owned and might present the distribution of property holdings in a table or graph. But if the historian wanted to show the association between two variables such as acreage owned and ethnic background, he or she might want to go beyond simply showing the average acreage owned for farmers of each background.

In this chapter we introduce ways to show and summarize the relationship of two variables over a population. Instead of displaying just the average acreage for each ethnic category, the idea is in effect to show the entire distribution of either variable at each value of the other. In that Wisconsin county, the historian could present, in a single display, the joint distribution of both landholdings and ethnic backgrounds over the population of farmers.

Some important issues discussed in Chapter 6 include:

- There are different levels of data and they call for different statistical techniques. But it is sometimes possible to convert one kind of data to another, through the creation of dummy variables, in order to make use of a more powerful technique.

- Crosstabulations display patterns in the joint distribution of two or more categorical variables. In a discussion of two variables such as ethnic group and political party preference, a crosstabulation can help the reader see not only how many individuals fall into each ethnic category or each category of party preference, but also how many are in each ethnic/party category.

- A statistic called the chi-square statistic can be used to ask whether the patterns seen in a crosstabulation are too pronounced to be attributed to chance. If the data come from a sample, the chi-square statistic bears on the question of whether the sample patterns are likely to be present in the population as well as in the sample.

- Scatterplots resemble crosstabulations: both display the simultaneous distribution of two variables. But scatterplots are used when at least one of the variables is numeric.

- A single number called the correlation coefficient summarizes the extent to which the scatterplot of two numeric variables tends to look like a straight line. When the correlation coefficient is near $+1$ or -1, the plot looks like a straight line; when it is near zero, the plot does not look anything like a straight line. A researcher will use the correlation coefficient whether she is dealing with a population or with a sample.

The first section reviews different types of variables and introduces the idea of dummy variables. It emphasizes that tests of association appropriate for numeric data are not appropriate for categorical data.

6.1   Levels of Data and Dummy Variables

Variables are not all alike. Section 2.2 briefly discussed the difference between categorical and numeric variables. As a prelude to introducing several more advanced techniques of statistical analysis, we now want to extend that earlier discussion. It is common to recognize two subclasses within each of those two types of data, as shown in Table 6.1.

The names of the data types in Table 6.1 are suggestive. Of the two kinds of categorical variables, the word nominal comes from the word "name." Take a variable called Birthplace, with values such as "Germany," "Ireland," "Norway," and "U.S." This is an example of a nominal variable, or what we referred to in Section 2.2 as an unordered categorical variable. The defining characteristic here is that the values of this variable cannot be rank-ordered.

Now suppose that in the ethnic history project described in Chapter 4, the historians had coded all German-born citizens with the number 7 and all the Norwegian-born with the number 11. Those symbols "7" and "11" are not really numbers even though they look like numbers. They are simply code-names, abbreviations of the symbols "German-born" and "Norwegian-born." Even with numeric codes attached, the

Table 6.1
Types of variables

Variable type	Description	Examples
Categorical		
1. Nominal (unordered)	Gives qualitative information only	Nationality, Sex, Religion
2. Ordinal (ordered)	Ranking or order is important	Social status, Economic class
Numeric		
1. Interval	Distance between values has meaning	Year, Temperature
2. Ratio	Ratio of two values has meaning	Wealth, Age, Price

values of the variable Birthplace cannot meaningfully be rank-ordered. The type of data (nominal, ordinal, interval, ratio) is determined by the information contained in the values and not by the form of the symbol.

The word ordinal comes from the word "order" and suggests that an ordinal variable (called an ordered categorical variable in Section 2.2) contains information about ranking in addition to distinctions between categories. In the preceding example, the fact that 11 is larger than 7 had no meaning (the property of being Norwegian-born is not "larger" than the property of being German-born), so 7 and 11 are values of a nominal variable, Birthplace; they are not values of an ordinal variable. But suppose that you had an Income variable and coded all persons making $0 to $5000 a year with the numeral 1, all making from $5000 to $30,000 with 2, and all others with 3. The "1," "2," and "3" are still names, but now these names contain additional information. The numeric order of the names is the same as the order of incomes.

Referring back to Table 6.1, you'll see that an interval variable is one kind of numeric variable. In interval variables, the distances between numbers have meaning. In the income example mentioned in the last paragraph, the distance (the length of the interval) between 1 and 2 is the same as the interval between 2 and 3, namely one unit. Yet the income distance between individuals coded 1 and those coded 2 is unlike the income distance between those coded 2 and those coded 3. So the numbers 1, 2, and 3 are not values of an interval variable because they do not carry the distance information about incomes. In contrast, calendar dates are values of an interval variable. The distance between 1492 and 1500 has meaning, the same meaning as the distance between 1892 and 1900.

A ratio variable is an interval variable with the additional feature that ratios of the values are meaningful. Age of Individuals (in years) is a ratio variable: If John is age 30 and Jane is 10, it is meaningful to discuss the fraction 30/10 as when we say John is three times as old as Jane. Or consider the area of different countries in square miles: Jordan's area is 35,135 sq. mi. while Syria's is 71,498 sq. mi., so it makes sense to say that Syria is about twice as large as Jordan. Venezuela's area is 352,145 sq. mi., so it is more than ten times the size of Jordan.[1] Ratio variables have a zero value on their scale that corresponds to the absence of the property being measured. Zero wealth means no wealth, so $20,000 is twice the wealth of $10,000.

1. If you chose labels such as "low income," "moderate income," and "high income" for the values in place of the numerals "1," "2," and "3," would that transform the variable from an ordinal to a nominal variable?

2. If you wanted to take information about people's incomes and make it into a genuine interval variable rather than an ordinal variable, what would the values of the new variable be?

3. What kind of a variable is Calendar Year, with values such as 1492 and 1789?

4. What kind of variables are Annual Birthrate for a nation and Blood Type for individuals?

The reason that the above distinctions are important is that a historian must use appropriate methods of summarizing and analyzing different types of data. For example, generally one cannot average categorical data. Suppose an inattentive student had a small database consisting of ten Catholics, each given the code 7; twenty Protestants, each coded 11; and eighty non-Christians, each coded 6. Forgetting that the codes are just labels and don't carry numeric information, he might fall into a common error of beginning statistics students by trying to find the average of those codes for the group:

[1] Rand McNally & Company, *Illustrated Atlas of the World* (Chicago, 1988), pp. A-4, A-6, A-7.

$$\frac{(10 \times 7) + (20 \times 11) + (80 \times 6)}{10 + 20 + 80} = \frac{770}{110} = 7$$

5. Since 7 stood for Catholic, does that answer of 7 mean that the average religion in this group is Catholic?

If you use symbols such as 7 or 11 to compute averages and standard deviations, you will get nonsense unless the symbols carry numeric information. The source of the nonsense above is that the 6, 7, and 11 are merely names and contain no interval information. If they did carry interval information, the codes would imply that Protestants are four times further from Catholics than are non-Christians because 11 minus 7 is four times bigger than 7 minus 6.

A researcher should only do arithmetic with <u>numeric</u> variables. In this chapter and the next, you will see several statistical ideas that rely directly on arithmetic manipulation of the variables. These techniques, such as correlation and regression, are valid only for numeric variables because they assume that the variables carry at least interval information. One cannot use these methods on names (nominal variables) even if the names are disguised to look like numbers.

Special statistical methods are available to deal with different kinds of variables and with combinations of variable types. For example, a technique called analysis of variance is useful in looking for patterns of association between a categorical variable and a numeric variable when the two are measured on the same population. Bodnar's data on Steelton would have lent itself to that approach because he knew each worker's ethnic background (a categorical variable) and annual earnings (a numeric variable).

The main point is that you must know what kind of variable you have in order to decide whether a particular technique is appropriate. Don't expect a historian to work any arithmetic directly on categorical variables; on the other hand, almost any technique is O.K. if he or she has interval or ratio data.

This restriction is frustrating because some of the most popular statistical techniques, such as correlation and regression, rely directly on finding the mean value and the standard deviation for each variable. We seem to have ruled out using the most popular methods on the common situation of categorical variables. Fortunately, statisticians have devised a creative way around the problem. It consists of recoding the categorical variables as <u>dummy variables</u>.

A couple of examples can clarify dummy variables. Sex is a nominal variable that takes on the two values "male" and "female." But you could make up a new variable called Woman and code the value of Woman as 0 for each male and 1 for each female. The code 1 stands for "yes," while the 0 means "no." Now suppose that you computed the average value of the variable Woman for an adult population of 60 males and 140 females:

$$\frac{(60 \times 0) + (140 \times 1)}{60 + 140} = \frac{140}{200} = 0.70$$

This answer, 0.70, has an intuitive meaning: it means that 70 percent of this population is female. This is unlike the situation of the confused student who concluded that the "average religion" was Catholic. Here the answer makes perfectly good sense because when you add all the 0s and 1s over all the cases, the sum you get (140) is just the number of females. So adding up these 0/1 codes simply amounts to counting the number of females in the group, and that's a perfectly reasonable thing to do. Because the variable Woman has only two values, 0 and 1, the question never arises as to whether the distance between one pair of values is consistent with the distance between another pair.

Because Woman is a <u>dichotomous variable</u>, you were able to use 0/1 coding. A person either is female or is not female, so the variable only takes on the two values "yes" (coded as 1) or "no" (coded as 0). Fortunately, this strategy can be extended to categorical variables with more than two values by means of the following trick. Assume that a historian is interested in political party affiliation and his records show that each person was either a Democrat, a Republican, or Other. Thus the variable Party Affiliation takes on three values. To deal with a three-valued variable, he defines <u>two</u> new 0/1 dummy variables:

Dem, coded 1 or 0, meaning yes or no
Repub, coded 1 or 0, meaning yes or no

Notice that "Democrat" was a <u>value</u> of the nominal variable Party Affiliation while Dem is a <u>variable</u> that takes on the values 1 and 0.

These two new dummy variables contain all of the information that was in the original Party Affiliation variable. If a person was either a Democrat or Republican, one of the new variables will be coded 0 and the other coded 1. If a person was neither a Democrat nor Republican, she will be identified by being coded 0 under both Dem and Repub. So a single three-valued nominal variable, Party Affiliation, has been replaced by two 0/1 dummy variables, Dem and Repub. Similarly, a single four-valued categorical variable could be replaced by three dummy variables. The advantage of the new dummy variables is that it makes sense to do mathematical calculations on them, and they can therefore be used in statistical techniques such as correlation and regression.

6. Suppose you are examining the percentage of their incomes that different ethnic groups paid in taxes in the period from 1890 to 1899. You want to know if there is some pattern in the relationship between Ethnic Group (which takes on the values black, foreign-born white, native-born white, and other) and Percent of Income Paid in Taxes. If you want to use a technique that requires arithmetic involving the ethnic group variable, you should create some dummy variables. Give a concrete example of how to do that.

Social and political historians often use dummy variables, so it is important that you grasp the concept. Chapter 7 will introduce an example involving voting patterns during the New Deal that employs dummy variables.

6.2   Voters' Party Preferences, 1894

Historians of American politics have long tried to account for voters' party preferences in different eras of American history. In the nineteenth century, was social class the key to predicting how a man would vote? During the 1960s and 1970s, the reigning interpretations of voter behavior downgraded economic variables and emphasized the ethnicity and religion of the voters. This interpretation suggested that voters tended to prefer one party over another not so much because they believed that the party would serve their economic interests as because the party seemed to embody their "values and life styles."[2]

A major difficulty looms for anyone wishing to test these broad interpretations: public-opinion polling was nonexistent for the nineteenth century. Nobody went around gathering systematic data about the personal backgrounds and political preferences of American voters. Or almost nobody; historians, in their search for evidence about the past, have turned up a few localities where individual-level data of this sort

---

[2]Paula Baker, "The Culture of Politics in the Late Nineteenth Century: Community and Political Behavior in Rural New York," *Journal of Social History*, 18 (Winter 1984), 167–93; quotation at 167.

were compiled. In Schoharie County, in east-central New York State, the Republican Party in 1894 conducted a pre-election canvass of voters in order to identify probable Republican voters and "undecideds." The canvass listed the names, addresses, occupations, and party preferences of most voters in Schoharie—over 8000 in all. Historian Paula Baker was able to link this information to additional data supplied by other lists such as church membership rosters, city directories, tax records, and censuses; through hundreds of hours of labor in these records she built up a detailed picture of most of the 8000 Schoharie County voters whom the Republicans had contacted. Baker thus was in a position to test broad generalizations about the basis of voter preferences against data on thousands of actual individuals in the past. She first looked for evidence that voters in Schoharie divided along occupational lines. Notice that her inquiry asks about the relationship between two variables: the occupational category of the individual voter, and his party preference.

Table 6.2
Occupation and party preference: Schoharie County, New York, 1894

	Democrat	Republican	Other	Row Total
Farmer	2018	1468	230	3716
Mechanic	260	210	32	502
Businessman	412	417	52	881
Laborer	1074	677	477	2228
Column Total	3764	2772	791	7327

Source: Based on Paula Baker, "The Culture of Politics in the Late Nineteenth Century: Community and Political Behavior in Rural New York," *Journal of Social History*, 18 (Winter 1984), p. 172, Table 1. We converted Baker's percentages to counts of people and combined data from two columns to create the "Other" column.

Notes: Mechanic = blacksmith, carpenter, cooper, etc.

Businessman = storekeeper, doctor, attorney, teacher, minister, miller, hotel keeper, newspaper editor, gentleman, etc.

Other = preference for Prohibition Party or expressed no partisan preference.

Missing cases not included in Table 6.2: 1065 (occupation not listed on canvass sheets).

We present Baker's data in Table 6.2; you will generally find a table like this one referred to as a crosstabulation or contingency table. The main difference between Table 6.2 and the earlier tables you have considered is that here the table is simultaneously classifying individuals according to two variables. Instead of two separate frequency distributions, you are given a joint frequency distribution in which you can examine the relationship between the variables. When you read Table 6.2 horizontally you see the distribution of each occupation group over the party categories. Read vertically, the table shows the distribution of the members of each party over the occupation classes. The table's column and row totals are both meaningful, and the sum of the column totals equals the sum of the row totals.

7.   What are the two variables in Table 6.2? What kind of variables are they (nominal, ordinal, interval, or ratio)?

8.   The grand total is 7327. Write a sentence explaining what population this number represents.

9.   Convert the column totals of Table 6.2 into a properly labeled frequency distribution; show both the actual numbers and percentages. Do the same for the row totals.

With two single-variable frequency distributions you could see how many Schoharie County residents (or what percentage of residents) were farmers and how many residents were Democrats, but you wouldn't be able to say how many residents were both farmers and Democrats. A crosstabulation is a special kind of table that shows the number or percentage of individuals in each of several categories where the categories have been defined by the values of two or more variables. Crosstabulations are used with nominal or ordinal variables because with those kinds of variables the values do fall in discrete categories.

Paula Baker is trying to test the claim that voters tended to divide along lines of economic status; occupation would be one measure of economic status. Behind Table 6.2, then, is an implied hypothesis something like this: "If voters' political outlooks were strongly influenced by their economic status, it ought to be reflected in the party preferences of different occupational groups." If the author finds that each broad occupational group shows a decided preference for one party or another, then she will have evidence that is consistent with the hypothesis. If she fails to find such evidence in the table, she is not required to reject the hypothesis since the occupational groups shown may not be the only or best measure of what one means by economic status. But such lack of evidence might cause her to rethink the connection between the variables.

For a test of the hypothesis, it will help to change the table from counts to percentages. But what percentages should be presented? You may recall from Chapter 1 that there are three sets of percentages. One could convert the numbers in Table 6.2 into percentages of the grand total: simply divide each number in the table by the grand total. Or one could divide each entry by its corresponding row or column total in order to express the numbers of persons in the category as a row or column percentage. Since Baker is considering the influence of occupation on party preference, she wants to asks questions such as, "Are Republicans over-represented among farmers?" That is, does being a farmer lead to a greater than average tendency to be a member of the Republican party? For such questions, it seems the best way to display the information is in the form of Table 6.3, which shows row percentages.

Notice that the <u>rows</u> in Table 6.3 add up to 100%. Each row shows how an occupational group divided on the question of party preference. Take the second row, for instance: it says that 52% of the mechanics preferred the Democrats while 42% leaned toward the Republicans.

Table 6.3
Row percents, Schoharie County data

	Dem	Rep	Other
Farmer	54	40	6
Mechanic	52	42	6
Businessman	47	47	6
Laborer	48	30	21
Total Pop %	51	38	11

Source: See Table 6.2.

The row for laborers adds up to 99%, not 100%; that's because we rounded the percentages down to the nearest whole number.

10. Explain how one would derive the percentages in Table 6.3 from the information in Table 6.2.

Table 6.3 tells you that 40% of farmers supported the Republicans. But to know if 40% support is strong or weak, you need some point of comparison. The question "Are farmers over-represented among Republicans?" can't be answered until you have some sort of base line. The row labeled "Total Pop %" is not the sum of the columns in Table 6.3. Instead, the "Total Pop %" shows the proportion of the total population in each party category; that is exactly the base line or comparison distribution needed. From the bottom row you know what share of the total population supported each party, so you are able to make the following statement:

> While 38% of the Schoharie men surveyed in 1894 expressed a preference for the Republicans, 40% of farmers surveyed preferred the Republicans.

If occupation had no effect on political preference, you would expect each occupation to have about the same distribution across the political parties as the whole population does. When you ask, "Are farmers in Schoharie County over-represented among Republicans?" you look for the answer by comparing the frequency distribution for farmers with that for the entire population. In the case of Baker's data, there are 2% more Republicans among the farmers than in the whole group, 40% vs. 38%.

If you saw just the first row of the Table 6.3, you might be impressed by the fact that, as a group, farmers prefer the Democrats to the Republicans by 54% to 40%. That's true. But the base line comparison adds the information that farmers don't seem to prefer Democrats over Republicans any more than everybody else does. The ratio of 54 to 40 for farmers is a lot like the base line ratio of 51 to 38 for the whole population. There's nothing special about being a farmer in this regard. However, by comparing the farmers' row percentages to the bottom row, you would notice that there may be something special about farmers with respect to the "Other" category, which contains persons with no preference or Prohibition supporters.

From the information supplied in Table 6.2, it would be possible to turn the questions around and ask what proportion of Republican supporters were farmers. Table 6.4, which contains column percentages, would be best for such questions. Tables 6.3 and 6.4 highlight different though certainly related information. Notice that Table 6.3 says that lots of mechanics are Republicans while Table 6.4 says that very few Republicans are mechanics.

11. In Table 6.4, where are the base line percentages against which the other data can be measured?

12. Does Table 6.4 say that 15% of the businessmen leaned Republican or that 15% of the Republican-leaning voters were businessmen?

Table 6.4
Column percents, Schoharie County data

	Dem	Rep	Other	Pop %
Farmer	54	53	30	51
Mechanic	7	8	4	7
Businessman	11	15	7	12
Laborer	29	24	60	30

Source: See Table 6.2.

13. If the question had been "Are laborers over-represented among Democrats?" which table provides a more direct answer, Table 6.3 or Table 6.4? What is the answer?

Table 6.3 speaks most directly to Paula Baker's question about the effect of occupation on party preference. The most noticeable pattern seems to be the difference between the Republican preference of laborers and businessmen. The gap between businessmen and laborers on Republican preference is seventeen percentage points. Notice that that gap is largely balanced by their different levels of support for Other (which includes no preference). Is seventeen points a large enough gap to be historically important?

14. How many businessmen would one have to shift from the Republican column to the Other column in Table 6.3 to yield about the same frequency distribution as we see for the laborers?

What is the overall message of Table 6.2 and the other tables constructed from it, particularly Table 6.3? Members of different occupations do seem to have different party preferences. But only a couple of the contrasts are great enough to support interpretive conclusions. In fact, the overall impression you may get is that Democrat/Republican preference was independent of occupation. Two variables are said to be independent when an individual's score on one variable has no influence on that individual's score on the second variable.

15. Citing evidence in Table 6.3, state whether you agree that Baker's two variables are probably independent of each other.

A crosstabulation can be such a clear way to dramatize the relationships among variables that a scholar might even choose to convert numeric variables into categorical for this purpose. If he wanted to display the relationship between wealth and race, he might replace the numeric variable Wealth with a new variable, call it Net Worth, that takes on the value "low" for those individuals whose wealth is less than $10,000, "medium" for those whose wealth is between $10,000 and $100,000, and "high" for those whose wealth is over $100,000. He could then summarize the pattern of wealth distribution across race with a crosstabulation like Table 6.5.

Table 6.5
Wealth and race in a population (hypothetical data)

	Black	White	Other
Net Worth			
Low	120	300	80
Medium	60	600	70
High	20	200	30

16. What do the numbers in the body of Table 6.5 mean? What patterns do you see in the table?

17. Why would you bother creating this new Net Worth variable? Why not generate a crosstabulation using the original Wealth variable?

A scholar could transform numeric data into categorical in this way, but note that he pays a cost. The three values for the variable Net Worth in Table 6.5 don't convey as much information as the original data list, which presumably included dollar amounts for every individual. From Table 6.5 you know that 120 blacks had "low" net worth, but you don't know how low that is, or what the mean net worth of those 120 persons was. You don't know whether a lot of the blacks were close to the boundary setting "low" net worth off from "medium," or whether most were clumped down near zero net worth, or what. The table is easy to interpret but omits much information.

Also, the choice of the boundaries for the categories "low," "medium," and "high" is arbitrary. Review Question 20 in Chapter 2 and Figures 2.11 and 2.12 in the answer to that question. There you saw that different boundary choices could radically alter the number of individuals in each category.

Later in this chapter, you'll be introduced to the scatterplot, an excellent device for displaying the relationship between a categorical variable like Race and a numeric variable like Wealth.

Section 6.2 has introduced crosstabulation and given you some practice at manipulating and interpreting the information contained in this kind of table. In the next section we'll continue to use Paula Baker's discussion of voter preferences as an example in order to describe the chi-square test for independence, a statistical test that is often seen with crosstabulations.

6.3   Schoharie County: Further Analysis

Businessmen and laborers in Schoharie County differed rather sharply in their preference levels for the Republican Party. A sizable proportion of laborers (21%) also preferred neither the Democrats nor the Republicans; no other occupational group resembled the laborers in that respect. But in other ways, the occupational groups shown in Table 6.2 didn't seem to differ very much from one another in their party preferences.

The chi-square test for independence is a statistical technique that will simultaneously look at all the cells in the crosstabulation in order to summarize in a single number the tendency, or lack of one, for party preference to vary systematically with occupation. The chi-square statistic is valuable because a historian or reader needs a way to take into account relationships, such as the one Paula Baker shows, where some of the categories (e.g., Republicans among farmers) have about the same percentages as the whole group while other categories (e.g., Other among laborers) do not.

A chi-square test is based on the idea introduced in Section 6.2 of comparing cell values to a base line or set of reference values. In the chi-square test, the base line is the theoretical crosstabulation you would expect to see if the two variables were completely independent. Table 6.6 contains two sets of numbers. The numbers not in parentheses were printed earlier as Table 6.2: they show the observed number of people in each of Baker's categories so they describe the relationships that were actually observed in Schoharie County.

The numbers in parentheses in Table 6.6 show the distribution that would be expected if occupation and party preference were utterly unrelated. They are the numbers we would expect if each occupational group had the same distribution of party preferences that the whole population had. For example, if businessmen preferred the Democrats

Table 6.6
Overall frequencies, observed and expected, Schoharie County data

	Dem	Rep	Other	Row Totals
Farmer	2018 (1909)	1468 (1406)	230 (401)	3716
Mechanic	260 (258)	210 (190)	32 (54)	502
Businessman	412 (453)	417 (333)	52 (95)	881
Laborer	1074 (1145)	677 (843)	477 (241)	2228
Column totals	3764	2772	791	7327

Source: See Table 6.2.

and Republicans in exactly the same proportions as did the population as a whole, we would expect to find that 453 of the population consisted of businessmen-Democrats, 333 of businessmen-Republicans, and 95 of businessmen choosing "Other."

Here's how to calculate one of the expected numbers, that for laborers who favored the Democrats. First, you know that the fraction of laborers in the entire population is 2228/7327. If being a laborer and being a Democrat were independent, you should find that same fraction of laborers among the Democrats. Well, 2228/7327 times the 3764 Democrats yields 1145, the expected number of laborer-Democrats. Each "expected" figure in the table was calculated in this fashion.

If occupation plays a strong role in party preference, then at least some of the observed numbers in Table 6.6 should be well off of the expected numbers in parentheses. On the other hand, if occupation and party preference are independent, the observed numbers should be close to the expected numbers. The chi-square technique consists of combining all of the differences between observed and expected counts into a single summary number called the chi-square statistic.[3]

---

[3]Here are the details of the calculation: You subtract the expected value from the observed value in each cell of the crosstabulation, square each result to eliminate the effect of minus signs, divide each by the expected value to obtain results in the form

If the observed values in the table are very close to the expected numbers, the chi-square statistic will be small. If the differences between observed and expected values are large, that will be reflected in the chi-square statistic's being large. The question is, how large can a chi-square statistic be and still be consistent with the idea that the variables in the table (such as occupation and party preference) are independent?

The chi-square statistic is calculated in such a way that the following procedure is possible: first, you assume that the two variables are independent; next, you use that assumption of independence to compute the probability that chance factors would cause a chi-square statistic to be as large or larger than the one which did result from the differences in the table. For example, imagine that you get a chi-square statistic of 8 and suppose you find a 60% probability that chance alone could produce table differences substantial enough to yield that chi-square value of 8. Then that value is not large enough to be persuasive evidence that occupation influenced party preference.

The argument goes as follows:

- If occupation does influence party preference, then you should see larger differences between observed and expected table entries than chance alone would produce.

- The chi-square statistic of 8 summarizes the differences that did occur between observed and expected values.

- It is very probable (60%) that chance could produce a chi-square as big as or bigger than 8.

- Therefore, the score of 8 is not good evidence that one variable influences the other.

You have seen this logic before, in the dialogue on statistical significance testing in Chapter 5. The chi-square statistic is analogous to a t-value and the probability mentioned is the p-value associated with the chi-square. The chi-square test is thus a test of statistical significance. As usual, the null hypothesis proposes that the variables such as occupation and party preference are independent. The alternative hypothesis

of unitless numbers, and add the results. (A slightly different procedure is used for 2×2 tables because the standard procedure tends to yield inflated results.) You also calculate a number called the "degrees of freedom" of the table, which is nothing more than (the number of rows − 1) × (the number of columns − 1). With those two pieces of information, the chi-square score and the degrees of freedom, you turn to a chi-square table in the back of a statistics text to find out whether the results are statistically significant. A statistical program on a computer can do all this too.

claims that they are not independent, that there is some connection. The p-value expresses the probability of getting a chi-square as big as you got just by luck if the null hypothesis of independence is true.

For Baker's data shown in Table 6.6, the chi-square statistic turned out to be 407. A table of probabilities was used to find that the probability of getting a value as great as 407 or greater is essentially zero. That means the overall differences between observed and expected numbers in Table 6.6 are too great to be dismissed as having happened by chance. If you can't say the differences happened by chance, you must conclude that there is some systematic cause of the differences; therefore, the variation in party preference by occupation asks for interpretation or explanation.

If the probability produced by the chi-square procedure is very small, that tells you that the differences between the observed and expected percentages are statistically significant—too large to attribute reasonably to chance. In this case the historian will tend to believe there is a statistically significant relationship between the two variables. On the other hand, if the p-value is large, if the differences are well within reasonable chance range, then the historian has no reason to reject the notion that the variables are independent.

18. If Paula Baker's data in Table 6.6 had been based on a random sample from some larger population, what would it mean to say that the differences between observed and expected values in the table happened by chance?

19. If her data had been based on the entire population, what would it mean to say that the differences between observed and expected values in the table happened by chance?

Baker had information on the ethnic backgrounds of the voters as well as their occupations, so another crosstabulation is in order. To see if the ethnic groups differed in their support of the major parties you can use a crosstabulation like Table 6.7, which shows the joint distribution of individuals by ethnic group and political party. In Table 6.7, the chi-square statistic turns out to be 27.9 with 4 degrees of freedom (see footnote 3 on how it's calculated). The associated p-value is virtually zero.

Before beginning to analyze Table 6.7, let's make clear where the information about the ethnic background of voters came from. The Republican canvassers did not ask voters about their ethnic backgrounds in 1894. Paula Baker painstakingly gathered this information on many

Table 6.7
Crosstabulation of ethnicity and party preference in seven election districts of
Schoharie County, New York, 1894

	Democrat	Republican	(N)
German	488	262	750
	(443)	(307)	
Dutch	109	78	187
	(110)	(77)	
English	459	380	839
	(496)	(343)	
Irish	21	15	36
	(21)	(15)	
Scotch-Irish	4	14	18
	(11)	(7)	
Total	1081	749	1830

Source: Based on Baker, "The Culture of Politics," p. 173, Table 3.

Schoharie County voters by checking local histories and genealogies and
books on German and Palatine emigration to the United States. She
also made educated guesses about the ethnic backgrounds of some voters
based on their surnames.

A statistical display like Table 6.7 may appear neat and definite, but
you should remember that some errors have certainly crept into it despite
the historian's best efforts. This will be true for virtually all historical
tables you encounter. The existence of some errors doesn't mean that we
should ignore the Schoharie County data, only that we should consider
the results of the analysis as approximate.

20.   Name at least three different ways in which errors could have crept
      into the data on which Table 6.7 is based. Would these ways lead to
      random errors or to errors tending to bias the data in a predictable
      way?

21.   Of the total population in Table 6.7, what percentage was of Ger-
      man ethnicity? Irish?

22. True or false? A higher percentage of Republicans were Dutch than were German. Why?

23. What proportion of the population in the table expressed a preference for the Republican Party? Why does this proportion differ from the Republican proportion back in Table 6.2?

24. Assume that it was much more difficult to gather information about one of the groups, say the Irish, than the others because many Irish genealogies and other sources did not exist for Schoharie County. If true, this would imply that many voters of Irish background were omitted from Table 6.7 so that the true proportion of Irish voters in these seven election districts was higher than 2%. Would this tend to bias the results reported in Table 6.7, and if so, how?

25. Which ethnic groups in Table 6.7 seem to show a marked party preference considerably beyond what we would have predicted on the basis of the party percentages for the total population?

26. Considering the fact that members of the ethnic groups had intermarried somewhat (thereby blurring the group lines that seem so sharp in Table 6.7), and considering the percentages in the table, what would you conclude about the relation between ethnicity and political preference in Schoharie County in 1894?

27. Overall, in Table 6.7 are the two variables party preference and ethnic background statistically independent?

28. Does your answer to Question 27 reinforce or alter the view that you stated in your answer to Question 26?

In Sections 6.2 and 6.3 you have been introduced to crosstabulation as one way of looking for relationships between variables whose values can be described by discrete categories, and chi-square analysis as the appropriate way to determine whether a statistically significant relationship exists between the variables depicted in the crosstabulation.

In contrast to the variables Baker had, when a historian works with two numeric variables, he or she often finds it helpful to construct a scatterplot (also called a scatter diagram or scattergram) to get a quick sense as to whether there might be an important relationship between the variables. The scatterplot is thus another way of looking for relationships between variables. In Section 6.4, we'll introduce scatterplots through a discussion of a recent article on urban housing.

6.4   Residential Housing in Cities

Historian Robert G. Barrows studied urban housing in the 28 largest American cities for the period 1870 to 1930 to determine whether many, or most, urban Americans lived in tenement-type housing or whether the urban tenement was more or less unique to New York City. In the course of his inquiry, Barrows uncovered several rather puzzling patterns in urban housing; we will focus on one of these.[4]

When he looked at the twenty-eight largest cities together, Barrows found a great deal of construction of urban housing during the sixty-year period from 1870 to 1930. But when he compared cities with one another, he discovered "tremendous intercity differences" in the rate of new housing construction. The percentage increase in the number of housing units between 1880 and 1900 ranged from a low of 36.5% in New York City to a high of 413% in Denver. These differences could not be explained simply in terms of population growth. Some cities (Denver, Baltimore, St. Louis) built new housing at a more rapid rate than their population was increasing; others (New York, Newark, Chicago) failed to keep pace with the rate of population growth.[5]

While he did not explore fully this variability from city to city, Barrows pointed to "local economic conditions" as a probable factor. He suggested that there was probably a relationship between housing construction and the expansion of manufacturing activity in each city. One indicator of manufacturing growth would be the growth in capital devoted to manufacturing. Barrows used a scatterplot, Figure 6.1, to get a quick sense of the relationship between growth of housing and manufacturing.

A scatterplot illustrates the relation between a numeric variable and some other variable. Scales for the two variables form the horizontal and vertical axes of a graph, and each case is plotted on the graph as a single point whose coordinates are the values that case has on the two variables. Since Barrows was interested in the twenty-eight largest U.S. cities in 1890, Figure 6.1 has twenty-eight points. Note that both variables are numeric.

---

[4]Robert G. Barrows, "Beyond the Tenement: Patterns of American Urban Housing, 1870–1930," *Journal of Urban History*, 9 (August 1983), 395–420.

[5]However, very large cities with smaller percentage increases in housing units actually built more units than small cities with large percentage increases. An 11% increase in housing for New York City in the 1880s translates into a great many more units of housing than the 241% increase in Denver's housing over the same decade.

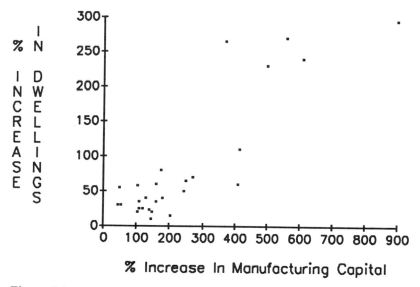

Figure 6.1
Relationships between growth of housing and manufacturing capital, 1880–1890, in 28 large American cities

Source: Robert G. Barrows, "Beyond the Tenement: Patterns of American Urban Housing, 1870–1930," *Journal of Urban History*, 9 (August 1983), p. 411, Figure 4.

29. Why wouldn't you construct a scatterplot for the data on voter preferences in Schoharie County, New York?

Scatterplots often reveal at a glance patterns not immediately evident in lists of numbers. Figure 6.1 shows that the cities separate into two groups, one in the lower left of the plot and one in the upper center and right. The scatterplot suggests the strategy of seeking common factors shared by the cities represented in the upper patch of points. Also, the plot might encourage you to ask why that one city in the upper right-hand corner seems so distinctive.

You will notice in Figure 6.1 that there seems some tendency for the points to be higher on the vertical scale as they move farther to the right on the horizontal scale. Since each point represents one city, this pattern suggests that higher percentage increases in manufacturing capital (the horizontal variable) tend to go along with high percentage increases in housing construction (the vertical variable) over the decade 1880 to 1890. However, the pattern doesn't seem to work for all the points.

30. In Figure 6.1, find two or more dots representing cities that had about the same percentage increase in manufacturing capital yet somewhat different percentage increases in housing construction. Now find two or more that had different increases in manufacturing capital but roughly the same increases in housing construction.

31. If a 50% increase in manufacturing capital was always associated with a 50% increase in housing construction, a 200% increase in manufacturing capital with a 200% increase in housing construction, etc., so that the percentages in one variable always matched the percentages in the other, what would the scatterplot look like?

32. If the two variables in Figure 6.1 were utterly unrelated, so that an increase in the value of one variable had no association with an increase in the value of the other, what would you expect the scatterplot to look like?

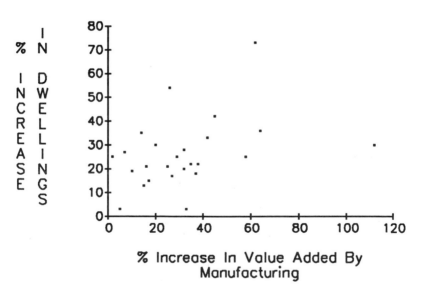

Figure 6.2
Relationships between growth of housing and value added by manufacturing, 1920–1930, for 25 large American cities

Source: Barrows, "Beyond the Tenement," p. 412, Figure 5.

In a second scatterplot, Figure 6.2, Barrows switches from 1880–90 to 1920–30, employs a slightly different measure of manufacturing activity (value added by manufacturing), and omits three cities. This plot shows two <u>outliers</u> (points standing alone, isolated from the area where most other points are located), one to the right of the rest and one well above. The plot tempts a reader to ask which cities those are and why they are out there by themselves.

33. Do the two variables in Figure 6.2 appear to be more strongly associated than the variables in Figure 6.1 or less so? Explain your answer.

Computerized statistical programs such as SPSS, SAS, and MINITAB can generate scatterplots with the greatest of ease, and they are obviously quite easy to draw with a pencil, paper, and ruler. Scatterplots are often used by themselves to suggest whether variables are associated; they are also an important preliminary step in regression analysis, a topic we will address in the next chapter.

One reminder: Even when two variables appear to be associated, a historian cannot take it for granted that they are causally associated. Take American cities again and consider this proposition: For the decade 1880–1890, a city's percentage increase in housing was associated with its distance westward from the Atlantic Ocean. The two variables show a strong association for Barrows's twenty-eight cities. Cities like Baltimore, Boston, New York City, and Philadelphia that were on or near the Atlantic also had lower rates of housing growth in the 1880s than such inland cities as Minneapolis, Omaha, and Denver.

The obvious trouble is that it's hard to see how distance from the Atlantic, in itself, could have caused different rates of housing construction. Perhaps you could show cities of the Midwest and West had more carpenters or that there was something about the bracing weather of the plains that impelled people to get out and build houses. Or more realistically, you might argue that the inland cities were smaller so that it was easier for them to show large percentage gains. The point is that even when a scatterplot suggests a relationship between two variables, that is not sufficient reason to believe that a causal relationship existed. Only the historian and the reader can decide whether the apparent association is meaningful historically.

Scatterplots are very similar to crosstabulations; they present the same kind of information in much the same way. Figure 6.3 gives a simple example to show you what we mean by that. Imagine that we

know the wealth and age of 96 individuals and we wonder if there is a
tendency for wealth to increase with age. This scatterplot has 96 points,
one for each case in the (imaginary) data set.

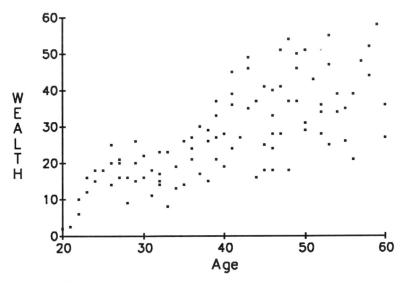

Figure 6.3
The relationship of wealth and age (hypothetical data)

Note: Wealth is given in $1,000s.

The scatterplot in Figure 6.3 conveys the visual information that
wealth tends to go up with age. You can change the scatterplot to
a crosstabulation and get exactly the same visual effect. The point is
that the two ways of presenting information are pretty much the same
thing. To transform one display into the other, change the ratio variables
Age and Wealth into ordinal variables by dividing the scatterplot into
cells with vertical and horizontal lines, as we have done in Figure 6.3.
Now if you label the rows and columns, you produce a crosstabulation
by simply counting the number of points in each cell. Here are possible
categories for the rows and columns:

Age		Wealth	
Young	Under 30	Low	Under $10,000
Middle	30–50	Medium	$10,000–$35,000
Old	Over 50	High	Over $35,000

Table 6.8
The relationship of wealth and age (hypothetical data)

	Young	Middle	Old	Total
High	0	16	10	26
Medium	17	38	10	65
Low	4	1	0	5
Total	21	55	20	96

Note: Values shown are counts of persons.

Table 6.8 shows the counts, how many individuals in each category, for the crosstabulation produced from the scatterplot. You can see the cloud of points rising left to right in the crosstabulation just as you can in the scatterplot! Notice how the numbers in the crosstabulation are large on and near the diagonal from the lower left to the upper right while the numbers off that diagonal, the numbers in the upper left and lower right corners, are small. That's the same picture that the scatterplot showed: the high ages tend to go with high wealth, the low ages with medium and low wealth.

Generally there is a loss of information and some risk of misleading readers when converting numeric to categorical variables. In this case, the conclusion you would draw from the crosstabulation is the same as from the scatterplot: there is a tendency for wealth to increase with age.

The following section includes some scatterplots; but more important, it introduces one of the most frequently used measures of the association between two numeric variables, the correlation coefficient, through a discussion of strikes in late nineteenth-century cities.

6.5   The Geography of Strikes in the 1880s

You have been learning about techniques for summarizing relationships between two variables. An ideal summary number would alert a reader to the presence of an association between two variables and help him or her gauge the form and strength of the association.

The <u>correlation coefficient</u> is the most commonly seen measure of association between two variables. It is often denoted r or R, and sometimes by the Greek r, ρ (rho). We'll use R in this book. You've already seen that the mean is not a complete summary of the properties of a list of numbers; well, the correlation coefficient, R, is not always a sufficient summary of association either, but it is useful and often used. The fact is that no <u>ideal</u> summary numbers exist.

Sari Bennett and Carville Earle, two geographers, used the correlation coefficient in a paper examining a thesis put forward by the great labor historian Herbert Gutman about the sources of labor power in the nineteenth century. Gutman argued that workers organized and fought for better wages and working conditions most effectively where they were supported by the shared values of the community as a whole. But while "the social structure of preindustrial communities [was] the solid base for labor power," Gutman went on to assert that the forces of modernization "ripped apart the fabric of preindustrial [community] culture" and thereby "assured the deterioration of labor power."[6]

Bennett and Earle were attracted to Gutman's thesis but, being careful scholars, wanted to kick the tires a few times before buying it. As Chapter 5 showed at length, one tests a hypothesis by identifying some pattern in the real world that ought to be there if the hypothesis is correct. Then one goes out to see if that pattern really is there as predicted.

Gutman's key concept, "labor power," is quite abstract; but one important sign or indicator of labor power would be the workers' willingness to go on strike for better pay and working conditions. If Gutman's thesis was correct, Bennett and Earle reasoned, then we would expect to find that strikes tended to occur in the most traditional regions and communities and tended to be absent in the most modern parts of the country. They further reasoned that traditional communities would be small, while traditional community social structure would have disappeared in the larger industrial towns and cities; hence "community scale can serve as an appropriate proxy for Gutman's notion of modernization."[7] Thus

---

[6]Sari Bennett and Carville Earle, "The Geography of Strikes in the United States, 1881–1894," *Journal of Interdisciplinary History*, 13 (Summer 1982), 63–84; quotations at 64. Gutman develops this interpretation most fully in "The Workers' Search for Power: Labor in the Gilded Age," in his *Work, Culture and Society in Industrializing America* (New York, 1976).

[7]Bennett and Earle, "The Geography of Strikes," 74–75. We want to emphasize that to test Gutman's idea adequately, a great deal more is required than the one test we are going to discuss here. Consult the full article by Bennett and Earle.

one possible test of the Gutman thesis would be to find out whether strikes became less common as the size of communities rose, as Gutman's thesis might lead one to predict.

Using reports on strikes gathered by the U.S. Bureau of Labor from 1881 to 1894, Bennett and Earle compiled information on strike frequency and community population for more than a thousand counties in the northeastern United States. Census Bureau publications provided social and economic statistics about these counties.

In testing Gutman's idea about community support and labor power, Bennett and Earle first report a correlation coefficient of +0.85 between the two variables strike frequency and size of community. Now what does that mean and does it support the Gutman thesis or undermine it?

The correlation coefficient can be computed when each individual in a population has been measured on two numeric variables. It measures the strength of association between those variables and also indicates whether the relationship is positive or negative. The correlation coefficient does not, however, say whether the relationship is significant in historical terms.

In the case of Bennett and Earle's first correlation, +0.85, the population is a collection of towns, an individual is one particular town, and the two variables measured on each town are population size and the number of strikes per year. This information is well suited for display in a scatterplot, with population on the horizontal axis and strike frequency on the vertical axis. We don't have Bennett and Earle's actual data for each town, so we've created a hypothetical example (N = 20) where $R = +0.85$, the same correlation coefficient they reported. That example is shown in Figure 6.4.

34.   In this hypothetical example, Figure 6.4, about how many strikes per year did the two largest towns have? The two smallest towns?

35.   How many towns had about 20 to 30 strikes annually?

The population in Figure 6.4 has the property that individuals (towns) with large scores on one variable show a pronounced tendency to have large scores on the other variable. In fact, your knowing a town's score on one variable would be very helpful if you wanted to make a reasonable guess as to its score on the other variable. Notice there is a tendency for the points to fall close to the straight line plotted in the figure. That line is called the <u>least-squares line</u> or regression line.

The regression line is discussed fully in Chapter 7. For now, the following brief definition will suffice: for any set of points in a scattergram,

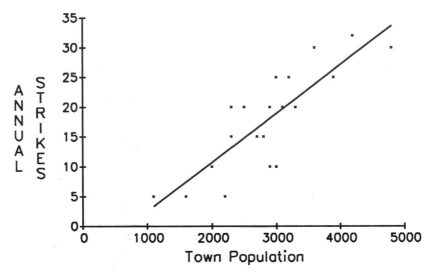

Figure 6.4
Strike frequency and community size (hypothetical data)

there exists one and only one straight line that minimizes the sum of the squared distances from the points to that line. Distance is measured by drawing a vertical line from each point up or down to the line. Since the sum of squared distances from the line to the points is minimized, you see why it is called the least-squares line.

You can think of the least-squares line as a summary description of the scatterplot in the same sense that the mean of a list of numbers is a summary description of the list. You know that the mean is a very good summary if the numbers happen to be clustered near the mean but less helpful if the numbers happen to be widely dispersed. The same is true of a least-squares line: if the points in the scatterplot fall near the line, as in Figure 6.4, then you can think of the line as a pretty good summary of all those points. That means that if you know a town's population— say 3000—and want to make a guess as to the number of strikes taking place there, you can make a reasonable guess by going out to 3000 on the horizontal axis of Figure 6.4 and then moving vertically up to the least-squares line. When you reach the line you then move horizontally over to the vertical axis; the score where you reach the vertical axis will be your guess as to the number of strikes that town experienced.

The size of R, ignoring whether it is positive or negative, measures the extent to which the points in the scatterplot cluster around a straight line. The correlation coefficient is computed in a way that forces it to stay between -1 and $+1$. If the size of R is near $+1$ or -1, then the points lie nearly on a straight line. In fact, if the size of R is 1, the points lie exactly on a line. On the other hand, if R is far from 1 and close to 0, then the points show no tendency to lie on a straight line.

The 0.85 R-value that Bennett and Earle got is remarkable for historical data and suggests that the two variables are very highly correlated. In fact, it is a little too remarkable. A moment's reflection will show you why: it stands to reason that there will be more strikes in big cities than in little villages and towns. But that's a trivial finding, like predicting that more babies will be born in Los Angeles than in Good Thunder, Minnesota. Bennett and Earle need to compare not the number of strikes but the rate of strikes per 1000 population, and that is exactly what they do next.

In the following discussion, we're going to look only at towns with populations of 5001 to 10,000. A town of 5000 might still have many of the attributes of a traditional community, but one of 10,000 is beginning to be too large to qualify. There were 194 towns between 5000 and 10,000 in Bennett and Earle's study; in testing Gutman's idea about community support and labor power, they found that the correlation coefficient between strike rate (per 1000 persons) and community population in these 194 towns was not $+0.85$; instead, it was $+0.084$, a number only one-tenth as large as 0.85.

To illustrate, we give another hypothetical scatterplot in Figure 6.5. In this one, the correlation is approximately the same R that Bennett and Earle report. They had 194 towns; in Figure 6.5 we use 25.

36. Explain why strike rate per 1000 persons per year is a better variable than number of strikes per year for purposes of this project.

In this second hypothetical example, towns with large scores on one variable do not show any pronounced tendency to have large scores on the other variable. Nor do they tend to have small scores. In fact, your knowing a town's score on one variable wouldn't be very helpful if you wanted to predict its score on the other variable.

37. Sketch a rough copy of Figure 6.5 and draw in the least-squares line as best you can. Comment on the adequacy of that line as a summary of the points in the figure.

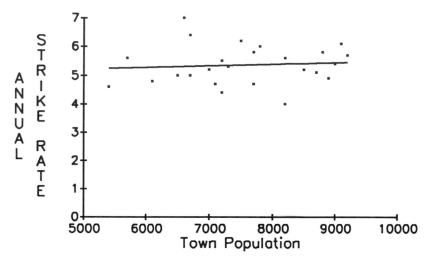

Figure 6.5
Strikes per 1000 persons in towns of 5001–10,000 population (hypothetical data)

38. Does a correlation of +0.084 support Gutman's idea that strikes (an indicator of labor power) would be found in traditional (small) communities or not?

39. If Bennett and Earle had found a correlation of +0.85 between town population and strike rate per thousand people, what would this have meant for Gutman's thesis?

40. Would a strong positive correlation coefficient (near +1) say anything about how rapidly strike rate goes up with population? That is, would it say anything about how steeply the least-squares line rises?

So far we have talked about the size of the correlation coefficient, whether it is close to 0 or close to 1. The sign of the correlation coefficient, whether it is a positive or negative number, carries the information about the direction of the relationship between two variables. In the hypothetical plots given, the fact that R bears a positive rather than negative sign shows that one variable increases as the other increases. (The score of 0.084 also is positive; but as Figure 6.5 shows, the

correlation is so slight that it hardly matters whether the sign is positive or negative.) When R has a negative sign, say $R = -0.56$, then one
variable tends to go down when the other variable goes up.

41. Give an example of a pair of variables whose relationship might be
of historical interest for which you would expect to find a positive
correlation.

Figure 6.6 shows what a negative correlation, -0.60, between population and strike rate would look like.

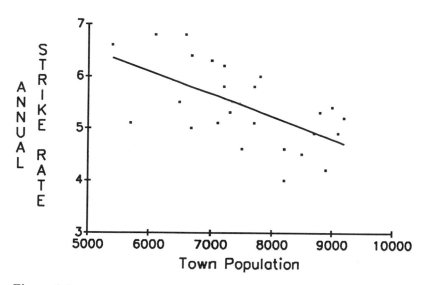

Figure 6.6
Strikes per 1000 population in cities of 5001–10,000 population (hypothetical data)

42. In Figure 6.6, the correlation coefficient is -0.60. Briefly explain
what that means with respect to strikes and how that number is
related to the scatterplot.

43. Give an example of a pair of variables whose relationship might
be of historical interest where you would expect to find a negative
correlation.

The correlation coefficient, like the mean, has limitations and can
easily be misinterpreted. Don't fall into the trap of concluding that if R

is close to 1, that means that one of the variables directly influences the other. Consider this example: In Denver, the average number of pounds of outdoor clothing worn per day by residents is highly correlated with the hardness of asphalt in the streets. However, no one would suggest that putting on an overcoat stiffens up the pavement on Colfax Avenue.

44. In the Denver example just given, what is the population on which two variables are measured?

45. Why might the weight of clothing worn and asphalt hardness be highly correlated?

Often, a pair of variables of historical interest may appear to be highly correlated; yet on reflection, the scholar or reader concludes that neither directly caused the other, but both variables are being driven by an intervening third variable. If A causes B and C, then B and C might be highly correlated without directly influencing each other. In historical studies, a commonly occurring intervening third variable to watch out for is time. If B and C both tend to rise over time, then the size of their correlation coefficient will be close to 1 regardless of any interaction or lack of interaction. Historians should be acutely conscious of the possibility that time dependence can intervene to create the illusion of a relationship.

46. Give an example of a pair of variables of historical interest that would be highly correlated because of time, even though neither directly causes the other.

Here is a second way that R can be misinterpreted. A reader might conclude that since R for two variables is virtually 0, it follows that the two variables are not closely associated. But R only indicates the presence or absence of a linear (straight line) association. The variables could be powerfully related, one could even completely determine the other as the radius of a circle determines its area, and yet the variables could have a correlation near 0 because their relationship is not linear—that is, the measurements plotted on a scatterplot would not approximate a straight line. You will see an example of this pattern in the next section.

47. Give an example of a pair of variables of historical interest that are strongly interrelated but for which the size of R (disregarding the sign) would be small. Hint: try to think of two variables whose scatterplot might resemble a sharply bent curve rather than a straight line.

Our discussion of Bennett and Earle's study of strikes in the United States leaves unresolved the question whether Herbert Gutman was on the right track with his thesis about nineteenth-century labor power and community support. All we have established, really, is that an initial correlation of strike rate with population size for middle-sized towns does not offer support for the thesis. The next section uses another study of urban housing, and presents a more complex example of how historians use correlation coefficients and introduces the concept of the coefficient of determination, R^2.

6.6   Urban Homeownership, 1900

Carolyn Tyirin Kirk and Gordon W. Kirk, Jr. have systematically built and tested a theoretical model of urban homeownership rates in large American cities in 1900. They want to develop a generally applicable explanation as to why homeownership would tend to be more or less common in one city compared with another.[8]

The Kirks are particularly interested in the homebuying behavior of immigrants. Evidence indicates that immigrants of every nationality group generally wished to become homeowners. But the rate of immigrant homeowning varied tremendously from city to city. In 1900, for example, 11% of immigrants in New York City owned their homes while 58% did so in Toledo. In their article, the Kirks examine factors such as the city's demographic profile, economic characteristics, and regional location to explain why a city had a particular homeownership pattern.

Here are just six of the factors that the Kirks thought might have an important effect on the overall rate of homeownership in a U.S. city in 1900:

- FISFD: Families in single-family dwellings. The proportion of families living in (not necessarily owning) single-family dwellings.[9]

- Density: The population density of a city, say number of persons per square mile.

---

[8]Carolyn Tyirin Kirk and Gordon W. Kirk Jr., "The Impact of the City On Home Ownership: A comparison of Immigrants and Native Whites at the Turn of the Century," *Journal of Urban History*, 7 (August 1981), 471–495.

[9]It is common for historians and social scientists to use abbreviated variable names like these when doing correlation or regression analysis. Often this is because standard statistical programs accept variable names of no more than eight characters. But using the same abbreviations in a publication adds another bit of difficulty for the reader.

- ForBorn: The proportion of a city's population that was foreign-born.

- Over 65: The proportion of the population over age 65.

- Under 14: The proportion of the population under age 14.

- Prof'l: The proportion of the labor force engaged in professional occupations.

48.   Before checking Table 6.9, think about the association that might exist between: FISFD and ForBorn, Under 14 and Over 65, FISFD and Prof'l, and Under 14 and Prof'l. State whether you think the signs of the correlations ought to be positive or negative, and why.

Although Kirk and Kirk are primarily interested in showing how these and other explanatory variables combine or interact to affect homeownership rates, they also provide a table that shows how the explanatory variables are correlated with one another. They are working with seventeen such variables, and it would be helpful to cut this number down. If they can show that some of the candidate explanatory variables are highly correlated with others (with the possibility that one is the cause of another or that both are caused by some third variable), they may be able to eliminate some of the redundant variables and base an explanation of homeownership rates on just a few.

Table 6.9
Correlation coefficients among six independent variables for the 40 cities over 100,000 in 1900

	FISFD	Density	Over 65	Under 14	ForBorn	Prof'l
FISFD						
Density	−.25					
Over 65	.03	−.12				
Under 14	−.26	.32	−.45			
ForBorn	−.65	.12	−.06	.41		
Prof'l	.41	−.42	.28	−.60	−.22	

Source: Carolyn Tyirin Kirk and Gordon W. Kirk, Jr., "The Impact of the City on Home Ownership," *Journal of Urban History*, 7 (August 1981), p. 488, Table 3.

The numbers in Table 6.9 are correlation coefficients for the variables that label the rows and columns. For example, the −0.25 at the top of the table is the correlation between the proportion of families living in single-family houses in the 40 cities (FISFD) and the population density of those cities (Density).

The reason no numbers appear in the upper right-hand part of the table is that they would just be a reflection of the numbers in the lower left portion. The correlation between ForBorn and Prof'l is the same as that between Prof'l and ForBorn. The reason no numbers appear on the diagonal of the table is that the correlation of any variable with itself is 1. So the main diagonal is understood to consist entirely of ones.

The fact that the first correlation coefficient, $R = -0.25$, is negative means that city data shows FISFD (the proportion of families in single-family housing) going down as population density goes up, which is what we would certainly have guessed. The size of that R (disregarding the sign), is 0.25, meaning that a scatterplot of FISFD against density would not show the points clustered tightly around a straight line (the size of R would be closer to 1 if they were).

49. Now reread Table 6.9 and find the correlations for the pairs of variables listed in Question 46. Which ones surprised you?

50. State briefly how you might account for the small size of the correlation between ForBorn and Density.

It is important to contrast different patterns that could cause R to be relatively small. In both Figures 6.7 and 6.8, hypothetical examples using just twenty cities, the correlation between FISFD and Density is approximately -0.25, the same number that appeared in the Kirks' table. But the patterns of association shown in the two figures are strikingly different.

In Figure 6.7, the size of R is relatively small because several cities with high density had lots of single-family housing and several cities with low density had very little single-family housing. In the Figure 6.7 scatterplot, the general pattern that FISFD goes down as density rises is often contradicted. In Figure 6.8, however, FISFD seems completely determined by population density. For cities with low densities, FISFD rises steadily with density; then the pattern reverses and FISFD falls inexorably as density increases.

Another general pattern could cause a small R to be misleading. Suppose all but two points lie virtually on a down-sloping line. Imagine that the points almost on the line would show a correlation R of -0.90, a very strong linear association. But there are two outliers far away from the line. When all the points are included in the calculation of R,

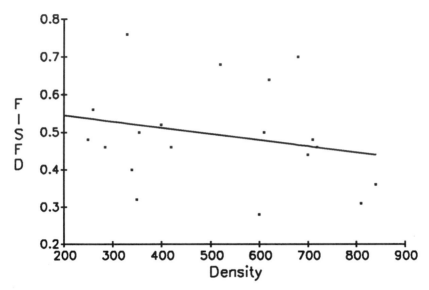

Figure 6.7
Proportion of families in single-family dwellings by population density, 20 large
cities, 1900 (hypothetical data)

it could very well come out around a weak -0.25 instead of the strong
-0.90 most of the information shows.

If the exact nature of the relationship between FISFD and Density
had been vital to the Kirks' argument, they would have given us more
information than the correlation coefficient alone; they might have presented a scatterplot, for example. The point of the above examples is
to underline a point made earlier, that a small R does not necessarily
mean weak association. On the other hand, a large R always means a
strong linear association between two variables. Some researchers make
the mistake of ceasing to pursue connections between variables when
they encounter a small value of R.

We began the discussion of correlation coefficients with Bennett and
Earle's observation that there was a correlation of 0.084 between strike
rate and town size among towns of 5001–10,000 population. Our geo-
metric interpretation of that number was that the scatterplot of strike
rate against population showed that the points, which represent towns,
had almost no tendency to cluster around a straight line. This indicated that there was no pronounced tendency for strike rate to behave

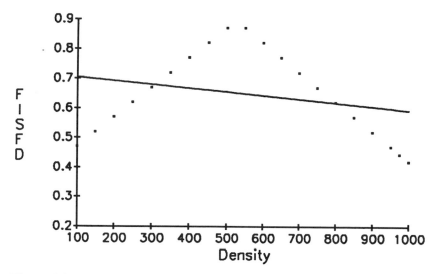

Figure 6.8
Proportion of families in single-family dwellings by population density, 20 large
cities, 1900 (hypothetical data)

predictably with respect to town population size.

There is a second common way to interpret the correlation coefficient.
If R is 0.084, then $R^2 = R \times R = 0.007$. Many writers call this number,
R^2, the <u>coefficient of determination</u>. The coefficient of determination is
interpreted as the proportion of the total variation in one variable that
is associated with variation in the other variable.

The idea is to think of the town-to-town variation in strike rate as
composed of two factors. One factor is that some towns are more pop-
ulous than others. The second factor is composed of everything else: it
includes all other possible variables that might influence strike frequency
and are themselves independent of population size.

So in the Bennett and Earle example one might say that for towns
of 5001–10,000 population, an R^2 of 0.007 means that 0.007 (or less
than 1% of the variance in strike frequency) is related to variation in
population size, while more than 99% of the variance in strike frequency
is associated with factors independent of population size.

Often, arguments employing correlations take the following form:

- If A causes B, then we would expect to find a large R.

- We do find a large R.

- Therefore, the facts are consistent with the hypothesis that A causes B.

Notice that the above argument does not pretend to be a proof that A causes B. Notice also that while the facts are consistent with the assumption that A causes B, they might also be consistent with some other assumption—for example, that A and B are both caused by C. Finally, notice that A could directly cause B without a large R if the relationship between the two variables is not a straight-line relationship.

Large values of R challenge the researcher to provide a plausible theory accounting for their existence. But a large R does not, in itself, prove anything about causation. It is up to the researcher to say whether he or she believes that the two variables are related in a cause-effect way, and the researcher needs to have some other compelling reason for making this claim besides the large value for R.

6.7 Conclusion

Chapter 6 has covered a great deal of ground. You have been introduced to four important and widely used procedures: crosstabulation, chi-square analysis, scatterplots, and linear correlation. Crosstabulation and chi-square testing are most often used when dealing with nominal or ordinal data, while scatterplots and correlation would be used with numeric data. These may appear to be quite disparate, but remember that a common theme runs through the chapter you've just completed: all these techniques are ways for a historian to gain some sense of whether an <u>association</u> exists between two variables.

In statistical literature, one encounters many measures of association similar in spirit to the correlation coefficient R described here. Some of them are designed specifically for use with categorical data. For example, Spearman's rank-order correlation is one such test.

The next chapter continues with the analysis of numeric variables. Drawing a scatterplot can help you get a sense of whether two variables are associated, and R^2 can give a more precise answer to the same question. But very often, a historian working with numeric data would like to go farther. Is a change in one variable associated with a very large change in the other or with just a small change? Is there a method for estimating the <u>relative</u> importance of several simultaneous influences on the variable whose behavior she is trying to explain? We will address these questions in Chapter 7.

Terms Introduced in Chapter 6

6.1 categorical data (nominal and ordinal variables)
6.1 numeric data (interval and ratio variables)
6.1 dummy variables
6.1 dichotomous variable
6.2 crosstabulation (contingency table)
6.2 independence (of variables)
6.3 chi-square test for independence
6.3 chi-square statistic
6.4 scatterplot (scatter diagram, scattergram)
6.4 outlier
6.5 correlation coefficient
6.5 least-squares line (regression line)
6.5 linear association
6.6 coefficient of determination

6.8 Answers to Questions

1. No, because 1 and Low Income mean the same thing, incomes of $0 to $5,000.

2. The values would be people's actual incomes in dollars, ranging from zero on up. (This variable, Income in Dollars, is a ratio as well as an interval variable.)

3. Calendar year is a ratio variable: a number like 1492 or 2001 designates the distance in time from an agreed-upon zero point, the beginning of year A.D. 1. As long as that agreed-upon starting point exists, a fraction like 1400/700 has meaning: it says that the year 1400 was twice as distant from the beginning of year A.D. 1 as the year 700.

4. Annual birthrate is a ratio variable: it does make sense to say that the birthrate in country A is three times that in country B. Blood Type is a nominal variable.

5. The "average religion" could hardly be Catholic when the Catholic group was by far the smallest of the three. The answer is just nonsense because one is attempting to do arithmetic on symbols that don't have the properties of numbers even though they have the form of numbers.

6. From the nominal variable Ethnic Group with its four values you should create three dummy variables: White, with values yes/no (1/0); Black (1/0); and Foreign-Born White (1/0). Someone in the "other" category would be coded zero on all three variables.

7. The two variables are Occupational Category and Party Preference, and both are nominal variables. For example, the variable Occupational Category has four values: farmer, mechanic, businessman, and laborer. These are simply categories; there is no logical order to them, and the distance between them can certainly not be measured on a numerical scale.

8. This number, 7327, is the number of men in Schoharie County who were questioned in the Republican Party survey of 1894 and for whom Paula Baker could find occupational information in the other records she surveyed.

9. **(a)** Occupational Distribution in Schoharie County, 1894

Occupation	Number	Percent
Farmer	3716	50.7%
Mechanic	502	6.9
Businessman	881	12.0
Laborer	2228	30.4
Total	7327	100.0%

(b) Party Preferences in Schoharie County, 1894

Preference	Number	Percent
Democrat	3764	51.4%
Republican	2772	37.8
Other	791	10.8
Total	7327	100.0%

10. One would divide the number in one of the boxes in Table 6.2 by the row total. For example, there were 412 businessmen who leaned Democratic out of a total of 881 businessmen: $412 \div 881 = 46.7\%$, which rounds to 47%, the figure found in Table 6.3.

11. The base line percentages are in the right-hand column of Table 6.4.

12. Table 6.4 says that 15% of the Republican-leaning voters were businessmen.

13. While you could answer this question from either Table 6.3 or Table 6.4, Table 6.3 provides the clearest answer. The answer is no, they weren't over-represented: 48% of the laborers preferred the Democrats, as compared to 51% of the entire population in the study.

14. Since 47 is 17 away from 30 while 6 is 15 away from 21, let's compromise and shift 16% of the businessmen to make their distribution similar to that of the laborers. Since we are working with row percents, we will take 16% of the row total, the total number of businessmen, which Table 6.2 tells us is 881. Then, $0.16 \times 881 = 141$ persons would have to change categories. That seems to be a number large enough to be historically interesting.

15. Overall, 51% of the population leaned Democratic, 38% Republican (Table 6.3, bottom row). The proportion of each occupational group leaning Democratic never varied from 51% by more than four points—the occupational groups seem remarkably similar in this respect. Of course, some other information in Table 6.3 challenges the general impression that the two variables were independent. Most important, the variation around the overall pro-Republican figure of 38% is considerably greater than the variation around the pro-Democratic figure. It ranges from a low of 30% (laborers) to a high of 47% (businessmen). Since part of the information shows considerable variability and part does not, it's difficult to make a conclusive judgment from simply scanning the numbers in the Table 6.3.

16. The numbers in the body of the table are the numbers of individuals who have both the properties indicated by their row and column titles. There were 120 persons who were both black and had low net worth. One pattern is the rapid drop-off in numbers of blacks as we move up the net worth categories. In contrast, a majority of the whites were in the middle category. The group labeled Other drops off but not nearly as rapidly as the black group.

17. If you used wealth in the crosstabulation, you would have a row in the table for every different value of wealth that occurred in the data, probably over a thousand rows. The table would go on for pages and be unreadable.

18. Imagine a table like Table 6.6, based on information about an entire population, except that the observed and expected values are exactly equal. Now suppose Baker had taken a sample from that population. What if, just by bad luck, Baker's sample isn't representative of the population from which it was drawn? When she makes up a table like Table 6.6 from her sample, it could show large differences between observed and expected values. A key question is, what's the probability that such a thing would happen?

19. Even in an entire population, you would expect to find some random variation. Suppose each individual chooses his occupation at random and also chooses his party preference at random. In this situation, it is clear that occupation and party preference would be entirely independent. Yet if you displayed a crosstabulation of these two variables, you would see some differences between the observed and expected numbers just by chance. In a population of any great size, there is going to be some random departure from the proportions calculated using the assumption of independence. So it does make sense to use the chi-square test on a population as well as on a sample.

20. Here are a few possible sources of error: The recorded responses to the original Republican survey could be wrong because the respondent answered falsely or because the response was miscoded. The matching of names between the Republican survey and the other historical information might sometimes be in error. The other historical materials such as the genealogies could contain mistakes. Some of Baker's educated guesses could have misfired.

It is quite possible that the study contains a degree of systematic as opposed to random error. For example, more complete information might have been available about one ethnic group than another. That would cause the first group to have more than their share of representatives in the study since the author is only using those cases on which she has full information.

21. Table 6.7 shows that 41% of the population was German and 2% was Irish. Note that the population for this table has 1830 cases; it is not the full population of male voters in the county.

22. False. It is true that the percentage of Dutch who were Republican is higher than the percentage of Germans who were Republican (42% vs. 35%). But the percentage of Republicans who were Dutch is found by dividing the number of Dutch who were Republican, 77, by the total number of Republicans, 749. That's about 10%. Similarly, we find that the percentage of Republicans who were German is 307/749 or 41%.

23. Of the 1830 men covered in Table 6.7, 41% preferred the Republican Party. In Section 6.2, it was noted that the preference for the Republican Party ran at 38%. This is not a huge difference and could be explained by the fact that Republican sympathizers were not evenly scattered all over Schoharie County. The seven election districts covered in Table 6.7 simply had a slightly higher concentration of Republicans than some other districts.

24. First, under-reporting of the Irish could mean that the preferences expressed by the 36 Irish voters who were included in Table 6.7 were not representative of all Irish voters in the seven election districts. The problem isn't the sample size as a proportion of the Irish population but that 36 is just too small a sample in absolute terms (unless one can be certain that the population is quite small, say 40 or 50). The possible under-reporting of the Irish would be a particularly worrisome problem if you had reason to suspect that the 36 Irish voters of Table 6.7 got into the table because they were unusual—that it wasn't just chance that led to their showing up in the records that Paula Baker checked. Perhaps they were wealthier than other Irish voters and hence were mentioned in local histories so that Baker was able to gather information about them.

Whereas the party preferences of the Irish seemed quite close to the overall preferences of the voters, the Scotch-Irish voters overwhelmingly expressed support for the Republican Party. If the Scotch-Irish had been the under-reported group (that is a hypothetical assumption, by the way), it's possible that fully including them would significantly alter the column percentage totals in Table 6.7. For example, suppose that there had actually been 300 Scotch-Irish voters in the seven election districts, not just 18. And suppose that the same proportion, 78%, of the 300 favored the Republican cause. Now we're dealing with an additional 282 voters (300 minus the 18 we already know about). That boosts the total N from 1830 to 2112; more important, since most of those extra voters fall into the Republican column, the overall percentage preferring the Republicans rises from 41% to 46%, a non-trivial increase.

The moral of this story is that historians need to be cautious about claiming that the people in their statistical tables are representative of other people not included in the tables. The claim may be valid; but before we can accept it, we need to know something of the sampling procedures that the historian used.

25. The Scotch-Irish.

26. Baker concludes (p. 173), "While a clear relationship between ethnicity and partisan affiliation existed for German voters and some of the smaller groups, it does not account for most of the voters in these districts."

27. As noted, the chi-square statistic was 27.9 with four degrees of freedom. The associated p-value was close to zero. With a p-value this small, you should reject the null hypothesis of independence.

28. One reason the p-value is so small is that the differences between observed and expected numbers in the German and English rows are quite large. That's consistent with Baker's remark quoted in the answer to Question 26. But the largest contribution to the chi-square statistic actually comes from the Scotch-Irish, a very small group.

29. The Schoharie County variables were categorical, not numeric. There was no way to place the values for those variables on a scale.

30. Here is one example of the idea. Above the mark on the horizontal axis for a 400% increase in manufacturing capital there are three points; the smallest shows about a 60% increase and the largest shows about a 270% increase in number of dwellings.

31.   All 28 points would fall on a straight line running at a 45 degree angle from the origin to the upper right corner (for positive growth); this line could be continued down to the left (for negative growth).

32.   In this case, the 28 points would be randomly distributed—they would make no pattern at all.

33.   Less so, in the opinion of the authors. In Figure 6.2 there seems some tendency for points to rise as they move to the right, which suggests that some relationship between the two variables may exist. But the points are also quite dispersed; they resemble a cloud more than a line. This suggests that the relationship between the variables is probably quite weak.

34.   The two largest towns had about thirty strikes per year while the two smallest had ten and five.

35.   Ten towns had about twenty to thirty strikes per year.

36.   Using strike rate per some unit of population eliminates the problem that you would expect big places naturally to have more strikes than little places. Gutman's thesis predicts that traditional communities (Bennett and Earle would say small communities) ought to have more strikes than you would expect while modern (large) towns and cities ought to have fewer strikes than you would expect.

37. Here is Figure 6.5 with least-squares line included. Clearly, the line is not a very good summary of the points, and no other line would be any better.

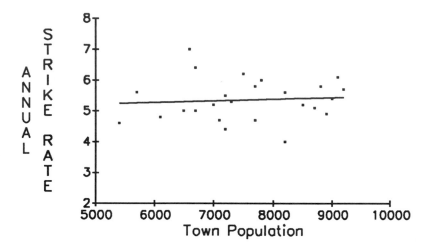

38. A correlation coefficient of 0.084 is close to zero, and this suggests that the two variables (strikes per 1000 population and population size) are hardly related at all. This finding does not support Gutman's thesis, though it does not provide decisive evidence against it either.

39. A correlation of this size between population and strike <u>rate</u> would have been powerful evidence against Gutman's thesis since it would have demonstrated that strikes occurred more commonly than expected not in small "traditional" communities but in large "modern" ones.

40. No, a correlation coefficient doesn't tell you anything about the slope of the line except whether the slope is positive or negative. What the correlation coefficient tells you is how closely the points cluster about the line. Yet the slope is also important. To get at the slope, one uses another statistical technique called linear regression; we'll get to that in the next chapter.

41. For the counties in the slave states in 1860–61, you might expect to find a positive correlation between the proportion of the county population that was enslaved and the proportion of the voters who supported secession in the special votes that were held.

42. The negative sign means that as values for one variable increase, they decrease for the other—on the scatterplot, the points tend to move downward as they move out to the right. The value 0.60 means that the two variables are correlated, though not as strongly as in the previous example (0.80). In terms of the scatterplot, this means there is some moderate tendency for the points in the scatterplot to cluster near a line.

43. To borrow an example from Elizabeth H. Pleck's article (discussed in Chapter 1), we would expect to find a negative correlation between family income in 1911 and the likelihood of a family's having a child employed. As family income rose, the need fell to put a child or children to work outside the home.

44. The population is days of the year. For each day, we have two measurements: average number of pounds of clothing worn in Denver and hardness of the asphalt on the Denver streets.

45. These two variables just might be highly correlated because both are functions of another variable, air temperature.

46. For example, the population of Atlanta and Des Moines both grew from 1900 to 1950. If you recorded the two populations for each year from 1900 to 1950 and computed the correlation coefficient, you might have an R value near 1.0. But it would be strange to say that the growth of Des Moines caused the growth of Atlanta.

47. What we want is an association that does not approximately follow a straight line. For example, a famous thesis of Malthus said that populations tend to expand exponentially while the food supplies needed to sustain them grow only linearly. Assume that Malthus had data to support this assertion, such as data on population size and numbers of acres under cultivation over a series of years. If the data followed the model he proposed, then we would have a real effect, increased population outstripping available food resources. But that effect would be understated by the correlation coefficient because the true association between acres and population is not linear. Instead, the scatterplot of one against the other would be a curve.

Here is a more concrete example. As capital is added to land in the form of herbicides, pesticides, and fertilizer, productivity per acre will go up. But as the total of such inputs continues to grow, the productivity will start to fall as the soil is damaged and loses some of its fertility. A scatterplot would first rise, then fall. Since the relationship is not linear, a correlation coefficient R would understate the strength of the relationship between those capital inputs and the productivity of the soil.

48. We guessed that FISFD would be negatively correlated with For-Born because we associate the image of crowded tenements with the rapid influx of immigrants. We guessed further that Over 65 and Under 14 would be negatively correlated because they are percentages of the same population. One proportion being large should at least tend to make the other small. FISFD should have positive correlation with Prof'l according to the stereotype. Under 14 might be negatively correlated with Prof'l if professional families tend to have fewer children than blue collar families.

49. **(a)** The negative correlation between FISFD and ForBorn is what we would have expected. It says that as the proportion of foreign-born residents rises from one city to the next, the proportion of the city's residents living in single-family dwellings tends to drop.

   (b) The negative correlation between Under 14 and Over 65 is also not a surprise. These variables measure the proportion of each group in the population; it stands to reason that as the proportion of one age-group grows, the proportions of all others would decline.

   (c) The correlation between FISFD and Prof'l is, as expected, positive. Both variables are probably indicators of the overall level of prosperity in the city: a high score for either would suggest a well-educated, well-paid populace. Certainly professionals could generally afford to live in single-family dwellings.

   (d) The correlation between Under 14 and Prof'l is strong and negative. This one is harder to figure out. One possible line of explanation would be to speculate that both variables were influenced by the level of immigration in the community. A high proportion of the population under 14 is a sign of a high proportion of immigrants in the community. Since few recent immigrants presumably were in the ranks of the professionals, proportion of immigrants would be negatively correlated with proportion of professionals.

50. This linear correlation is so small that for practical purposes, it may be considered nonexistent. Density is a variable measuring how closely packed people are in a city, on the average; it is a rough measure of their propensity to live in multiple-family or single-family housing since the kind of housing would affect the density very heavily. This low correlation is perhaps surprising since, as Robert G. Barrows suggested in his article, we tend to have an image of immigrants crowded into tenement housing in the late nineteenth century.

Several explanations for the correlation coefficient 0.12 are possible. A straightforward one is that our image is wrong; there's no strong correlation between immigrants and urban crowding. Another would be that we have a non-linear correlation here. Perhaps the scatterplot, with ForBorn on the horizontal axis and Density on the vertical, would show an s-shaped pattern: as the proportion of foreign-born people in the city population rose, density at first did not change; then it shot up, then leveled off again when it reached a maximum density figure.

7 Regression as Historical Explanation

In this chapter:

Regression models, like the crosstabulations, correlations, and scatter-plots of Chapter 6, are designed to shed light on how two or more vari-ables are inter-related. This chapter has two primary goals: first, to show you how to read regression equations (sometimes shown as tables of regression coefficients); and second, to give you practice in weighing the information in regression tables or equations against the historical arguments made in books and articles.

Because regression analysis is a more complex mathematical proce-dure than anything you have learned about in Chapters 1 through 6, we're going to adopt a somewhat different organization for the present chapter. We'll begin by briefly describing three historical problems for which historians used regression analysis. After that, we'll turn to an explanation of what regression is. We then return to the three problems introduced at the beginning; in the final section of the chapter, we ex-amine a complex regression model through the medium of what we hope is an entertaining dialogue between a professor and a student.

7.1 Regression Models: Three Examples

A. The Shift to Cotton in Southern Agriculture. There is an intriguing and important puzzle in the history of Southern agriculture that recent investigators have analyzed only to produce quite different pictures.[1] What makes their divergent visions surprising is that they

---

[1] Works referred to below include Gavin Wright and Howard Kunreuther,

use similar statistical techniques on similar data—another example, it seems, of the observation "You can prove anything with statistics."

The changes that took place in Southern agriculture following the Civil War are profoundly important for our understanding of twentieth-century America. Those changes include the transition of blacks from slavery to a free labor system and the establishment of new social and economic institutions to replace those lost to the war and the ending of slavery. The agricultural patterns that evolved in the late nineteenth century are implicated in the relative poverty of the twentieth-century South and are often given as explanations for the inability of the South to share fully in both the agricultural transformation and the industrial growth of the rest of the country.

The core of the puzzle has to do with cotton. The South still feels the effects of the time when it was dominated by cotton. As you will recall from the earlier discussion of cotton and corn (Chapter 3), the South's economy was sensitive to changes in the world demand for cotton. Before the Civil War there had been years of growth in cotton demand; yet in spite of cotton booms, Southern farmers had stayed self-sufficient by continuing to plant corn and other food crops along with cotton. Not long after the war, the demand for cotton on world markets was depressed and stagnating. Southern farmers should have moved away from cotton if they had behaved in an economically rational manner. Instead, there was a shift into cotton at the expense of corn and other foodstuffs. In fact, in the face of weak cotton demand, the farmers planted relatively so much cotton that they gave up the food self-sufficiency they had previously held onto when cotton demand had been high. They planted cotton even when it forced them to borrow at exorbitant interest rates in order to buy food.

Why would farmers react in such an apparently irrational way? No simple answer comes from comparing corn and cotton prices. The ratio of corn grown to cotton grown fell steadily from 1868 to 1890, but the ratio of corn price to cotton price stayed much the same over that period, though it oscillated from year to year. It seems a relative increase in cotton supply was driven by neither price nor demand.

"Cotton, Corn and Risk in the Nineteenth Century," *Journal of Economic History*, 35 (September 1975), 526–51; Roger L. Ransom and Richard Sutch, *One Kind of Freedom* (Cambridge, Eng., 1977); Peter Temin, "Patterns of Cotton Agriculture in Post-Bellum Georgia," *Journal of Economic History*, 43 (September 1983), 661–74; David F. Weiman, "The Economic Emancipation of the Non-Slaveholding Class: Up-country Farmers in the Georgia Cotton Economy," *Journal of Economic History*, 45 (March 1985), 71–93. See also Gavin Wright, *The Political Economy of the Cotton South* (New York, 1978).

Chapter 3 briefly considered one explanation for the puzzling behavior of Southern farmers. That was Gavin Wright and Howard Kunreuther's argument that the shift reflected farmers' changing attitudes about risk. Because cotton prices fluctuated more than corn prices, cotton offered impoverished small farmers the glimmer of a hope of occasionally enjoying a good profit and the chance to pay off debt. Planting cotton resembled buying a lottery ticket, by this explanation—the farmer had a small chance of making a handsome profit. Since many of the farmers were tenants and already in debt, they did not have much to lose if the gamble failed.

In their book *One Kind of Freedom*, Roger L. Ransom and Richard Sutch emphasize a different aspect of the shift into cotton: they argue that a new class of merchant lenders encouraged or coerced small farmers into cotton for the sake of their own profit. The merchant lender had a territorial monopoly which enabled him to demand so much cotton in exchange for the necessities of life that the farmer could end a successful growing year further in debt than when he began. Ransom and Sutch call this "debt peonage." Farmers had no other source of credit than these merchants—banks were few and far between in the South at that time. The debt peonage locked the farmer into cotton production year after year because he needed a cash crop in order to repay the merchants.

Peter Temin, a third participant in this debate, begins by denying that crop mix is a good way to look at the whole of Southern agriculture. He says that the postwar shift from corn to cotton took place in only one geographic region, the southern Piedmont, the upland country of the western Carolinas and Georgia and northern Alabama. Furthermore, this local move from corn to cotton was not caused by factors the others discuss; "it was instead related to the racial composition of the Piedmont's inhabitants." David F. Weiman, like Temin, stresses regional differences.[2] "Increasing specialization in cotton after the Civil War ... involved two regionally distinct processes." Weiman has studied the shift toward cotton in Georgia; he says that the building of railroads and the growth of new cities following the Civil War provided access to markets for a whole new class of farmers in the Georgia Piedmont or Upcountry. These farmers, far from the coast and not located on navigable rivers, had been cut off from the world cotton market. But after the war, they seized the opportunity given by market access and began to participate in commercial agriculture.

With at least four competing explanations, it seems that the reader of

---

[2]Weiman's article is reprinted in Chapter 8 of this volume.

history has a puzzle of his or her own. Whom to believe? Any of them? All of them? The obvious first step is to read the various works of history. But here a problem arises, for all the authors use <u>regression analysis</u>. So these papers can be understood fully only by those readers of history who can also read tables of regression coefficients.

Tables 7.1 and 7.2 and Figure 7.1 represent examples of what regression tables look like. Don't worry if they make no sense to you right now; the point of this chapter is to help you understand what they mean. Table 7.1 is from the 1975 article by Wright and Kunreuther. Before we explain how to read this table, we'll look at a couple of other examples of historians' use of regression.

B. What Was the New Deal Electoral Transformation? According to historian David F. Prindle, "the period 1928 to 1940 was an American political watershed.... For the first time, the federal government assumed responsibility for the nation's economic life. For the first time, the personal welfare of the population became an object of national concern."[3] He points out that this era was also a watershed in electoral politics: the Democratic Party replaced the Republican Party as the party holding the allegiance of a majority of voters.

If the congressional and presidential races of 1928 to 1940 included critical elections which marked turning points in the political life of the nation, then what were their important features? Did masses of new voters join the fray? Did large numbers of voters change ideology between elections and switch parties? Was the political watershed carved by demographic or economic forces?

Prindle uses county-level voting returns and census data for Wisconsin and Pennsylvania together with Pennsylvania registration figures to examine in some detail the process of the New Deal electoral transformation. He picked these two states because "they were sufficiently different to contain much of the relevant economic, demographic, and historical diversity of the Northern electorate of the time, but together were broadly representative of that electorate."[4] One of the statistical techniques he employs is regression; he produced a table that we've modified to create Table 7.2.

Prindle's Wisconsin Table looks quite a bit different from Wright and Kunreuther's regression results presented in Table 7.1. We want to understand exactly what this table says so that we can evaluate for ourselves the extent to which it does or doesn't provide insight into the New

---

[3]David F. Prindle, "Voter Turnout, Critical Elections and the New Deal Realignment," *Social Science History*, 3 (Winter 1979), 144–70.

[4]*Ibid.*, p. 147.

Table 7.1
Regression coefficients: Cotton South, 1860

Dependent Variable: Cotton Acreage/(Cotton + Corn Acreage)

	(1)	(2)	(3)	(4)
Constant	.342	.262	.286	.280
Soil Quality	$.0011^a$	.0000	.00025	.00028
	(3.92)	(.025)	(0.91)	(0.39)
POP/IA[b]	$-.1805^a$		$-.105^a$	$-.1820^a$
	(11.50)		(6.68)	(8.02)
IA[c]		$.00034^a$	$.00032^a$	$.00031^a$
		(21.60)	(19.32)	(19.11)
LBR/IA[d]				$.378^a$
				(4.71)
R^2	.027	.085	.093	.097
N = 5117				

Source: Gavin Wright and Howard Kunreuther, "Cotton, Corn and Risk in the Nineteenth Century," *Journal of Economic History*, 35 (September 1975), p. 534, Table 3.

t-ratios in parentheses

[a] Signifies significance at 1 percent level.

[b] On-farm population per improved acre.

[c] Improved acreage.

[d] Labor force (free males aged 15–64 plus slaves aged 15–64) per improved acre.

Dependent variable derived from cotton and corn output figures under assumption that cotton yield = 208.1 pounds per acre, corn yield = 16.81 bushels per acre. (Only the ratio of these two figures affects the result.)

Table 7.2
Wisconsin Regression: 1916/20 to 1936/40 Presidential Elections

Dependent Variable: RepTwo	Beta: .71	$p < .001$
Independent Variable: RepOne	R^2: .61	
Dependent Variable: DemTwo	Beta: .07	n.s.
Independent Variable: DemOne	R^2: .01	

Key: RepOne is the average of the Republican turnout in the 1916 and 1920 elections expressed as a percentage of all adults.

RepTwo is the comparable average for the 1936 and 1940 elections.

DemOne and DemTwo are the analogous variables for the Democrats.

Source: Based on David F. Prindle, "Voter Turnout, Critical Elections and the New Deal Realignment," *Social Science History*, 3 (Winter 1979), p. 161, Table 8.

Deal realignment.

C. The Economic Status of Women in the Early Republic.
Claudia Goldin, an economic historian whose work you have encountered earlier in this book, published an article not long ago testing the thesis that the status of women deteriorated in the nineteenth century as women were relegated to domestic roles and denied work opportunities in the marketplace. Using data from Philadelphia, Goldin inquires into the labor-force participation of women who were heads of households between 1790 and 1860.[5] Midway through her discussion, the reader encounters Figure 7.1.

What does this figure mean, and how is it related to the table on cotton and corn and the one on presidential elections in Wisconsin? The three displays aren't set up in the same way, use different notation, and refer to different statistics with cryptic names like "t" and "Beta."

So finally, let's jump into regression itself. For much of this chapter we will use yet another example, but near the end we will return to the three models already introduced. By chapter's end you will be able to read all three.

---

[5]Claudia Goldin, "The Economic Status of Women in the Early Republic: Quantitative Evidence," *Journal of Interdisciplinary History*, 16 (Winter 1986), 375–404.

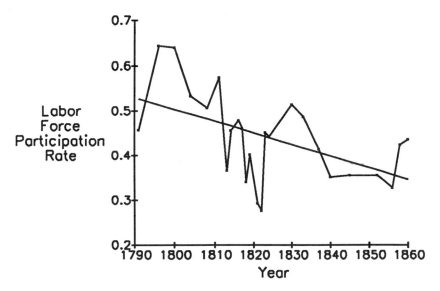

Figure 7.1
Labor force participation, female heads of households, Phil., 1791 to 1860

Labor Force Participation Rate = 0.539 − 0.0028 Time

t-value for constant = 16.26

t-value for slope coefficient = 3.20

$R^2 = 0.31$

Source: Claudia Goldin, "The Economic Status of Women in the Early Republic: Quantitative Evidence," *Journal of Interdisciplinary History*, 26 (Winter 1986),
p. 391, Figure 1.

7.2   Fertility and Children's Education, 1900

Avery M. Guest and Stewart E. Tolnay have studied variations in fertility in different parts of the United States in the late 1800s. They ask whether married couples tended to adjust the number of children they had according to whether or not the children would become economic assets at an early age or were likely to remain economic liabilities until close to adulthood.[6]

They test the well-known hypothesis that when children went into the labor force at a young age, there would be a tendency toward larger families, while smaller families would be found where children stayed in school until their late teens. The idea behind this hypothesis runs as follows: If children add to the family income by going into the fields and factories, parents will find it economically rational to have many children. But the expansion of public schooling in the late nineteenth century altered the place of children in the family economy. Once withdrawn from the labor market, children were a non-earning drain on the resources of the family and the parents had an incentive to bring fewer children into the world.

For the next several pages, we'll work with this hypothesis in order to show how regression analysis works. Later we'll return to the other historical examples introduced in Section 7.1. In effect, the hypothesis proposes that families adopted a new fertility strategy. This idea seems plausible at the outset because we know that in European nations and the United States, the spread of mass public schooling and the decline in fertility were going on at the same time. Guest and Tolnay want to find out whether there really was a connection between the two trends.

As one step in their investigation, Guest and Tolnay used a 1-in-760 sample of households from the 1900 manuscript census.[7] They further reduced the sample to include only households that included a boy aged 10 to 14 who had no siblings in the 10-to-14 age range and whose mother was over 40 years of age. They decided to analyze the rural and urban populations separately (defining "urban" as places of 2500 or more), and so ended up with a rural sample of 406 and an urban sample of 150.

---

[6]Avery M. Guest and Stewart E. Tolnay, "Children's Roles and Fertility: Late Nineteenth-Century United States," *Social Science History*, 7 (Fall 1983), 355–80.

[7]Samuel H. Preston and Robert L. Higgs, "United States Census Data, 1900: Public Use Sample," Inter-university Consortium for Political and Social Research, Ann Arbor, Michigan.

1. Think of a reason the authors might have had for each of their selection criteria: (a) boys only; (b) age range 10 to 14; (c) no siblings also 10 to 14; (d) mothers over 40.

2. Can you think of any biases their choice of selection criteria might have introduced?

3. What is the definition of an "individual" (i.e., the unit of analysis) in these samples?

4. What kind of sampling strategy was involved in the decision to analyze rural and urban samples separately?

From questions asked in these censuses, the authors define the following variables and gather information for each boy in the sample:[8]

- Children Ever Born, or CEB: the number of children ever born to each boy's mother.

- Months in School: the number of months each boy had spent attending school in the past year.

5. Which of these variables does the hypothesis specify as the dependent variable?

You can imagine that the authors' data set consisted of a table that looked something like Table 7.3.

Researchers compute regression equations from lists such as this one. The purpose of mathematical gyrations such as regression is to highlight patterns that appear in the lists; therefore, when reading a regression table, an essential first step is to imagine the lists that lie behind the table. If you can't imagine the variables being compared, you can't possibly make sense of a regression table.

From a list of data like Table 7.3, the historian could generate a scatterplot using the two numeric variables Children Ever Born in Family and Months in School. Since the data set includes 406 cases, the plot would have 406 points.

---

[8]Guest and Tolnay also defined a variable for whether the boy was in paid employment; we'll bring that into the discussion at a later point.

Table 7.3
Family and schooling information for a sample of U.S. boys, 1900 (hypothetical data)

Case No.	Months in school	Children ever born in family	Rural or urban
1	3	3	rural
2	4	5	rural
3	6	2	urban
⋮	⋮	⋮	⋮
1000	4	4	urban

Overall, those points might have a formless, cloudlike appearance like this:

(a)

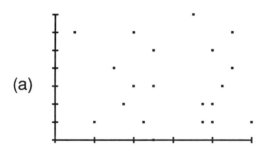

Or they might look something like this:

(b)

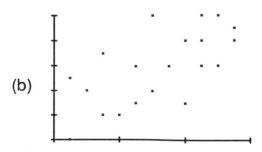

Or they might look like this:

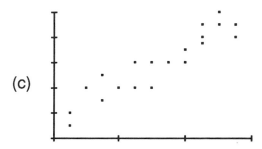

(c)

6. What would each of these shapes tell you about the likely relationship between the two variables? What other shapes could the points take?

As you saw in Chapter 6, it is desirable to go beyond a scatterplot—a visual aid—to summarize the association. That's what the correlation coefficient does, in part. A regression equation summarizes a different aspect of the scatterplot: it describes the slope of the least-squares line. Nowadays, historians use a statistical program on a computer to do the actual calculation based on the data set—it would take many hours by hand. By doing so, Guest and Tolnay obtained the following regression equations:

Table 7.4
Children ever born as a function of schooling, rural and urban households, 1900

Rural	CEB	=	$7.411 - .226 \times$ (Months in School)
	R^2	=	.052, SE of b = .048
Urban	CEB	=	$5.643 - .052 \times$ (Months in School)
	R^2	=	.003, SE of b = .081

Source: Avery M. Guest and Stewart E. Tolnay, "Children's Roles and Fertility: Late Nineteenth-Century United States," *Social Science History*, 7 (Fall 1983), p. 375.

Note: CEB means children ever born to the mother of each boy in the sample.

7. Table 7.4 shows two regression equations. Why do you think the authors separated rural and urban families in this way instead of cranking all three variables into a single equation?

The title of Table 7.4 indicates that you are considering two mathematical models in which the dependent variable Children Ever Born is to be described as a function of one other variable, Months in School. The first model applies to rural families, the second to urban. Since the two regression equations involve the same two variables, we'll focus our discussion on the first equation, the one for rural families. Let's get acquainted with it:

Recall the rural equation:

$$\text{CEB} = 7.411 - .226 \times (\text{Months in School}).$$

That equation can be written slightly differently:

$$\text{CEB} = 7.411 + (-.226 \times \text{Months in School}).$$

In this form you can see that it is a version of the familiar equation $y = a + bx$, the equation for a straight line that you probably recall from introductory algebra (hence the term <u>linear</u> regression). You should think of a horizontal and a vertical axis with a straight line cutting across them. The equation specifies where that line crosses the y-axis (the vertical axis) and what its slope is. Those two bits of information specify one and only one straight line; mathematically speaking, when you know those two things, you know everything there is to know about the line.

In the equation $y = a + bx$, the letters a and b stand for two known numbers. In this case,

$$a = 7.411 \text{ and}$$
$$b = -.226.$$

The coefficient **b**, which here is $-.226$, tells the slope of the line. It says by how many y-units (Children Ever Born) the line rises for every unit increase in the x-variable (Months in School).

The other number, **a** (7.411 in this case), is the y-intercept, the place where the line crosses the y-axis. It says that when x is zero, y is 7.411—that is, if you took the collection of boys spending zero months in school, the average number of children ever born in their families would be 7.411.[9]

Figure 7.2 shows a graph of the regression equation for rural families.

---

[9]In some cases, the x-variable could never really take on the value zero. For example, consider this made-up equation showing the relationship between height and weight for a sample of adult males: Weight $= -223 + (5.4 \times \text{Height})$. The -223 says that if you looked at the collection of adult males zero inches tall, their average weight would be -223 pounds. That is, $-223 + (5.4 \times 0) = -223$. In a case like this, the intercept value of -223 has a mathematical meaning (it defines the regression line) but no real-life meaning.

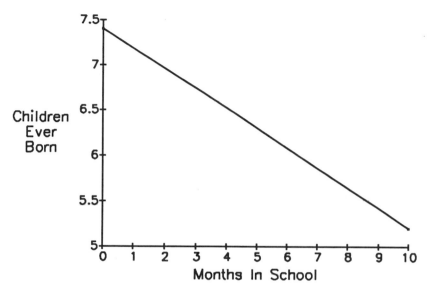

Figure 7.2
Graph of the equation CEB = 7.411 − .226 × (Months in School)

8. At what point does the line cross the y-axis? What does it mean to speak of a slope of −.226?

The regression equation that we have been considering is the equation for the <u>one</u> straight line that fits the data better than any other straight line for the 406 boys in the Guest-Tolnay rural sample—it is simultaneously closer to all the points than any other line you could draw through the cloud.[10] One reason for using least-squares fitting is that it gives the regression line the following property: if a particular value is put into the right-hand side of the equation for Months in School, then the computed value for Children Ever Born is the best estimate of the average number of children ever born in the families of those boys in the sample who attended school for the specified number of months.

For example, consider boys who attended school for six months. Now

---

[10]In more formal terms, the regression line makes the sum of the squared distances from the plotted points to the line as small as possible. The numbers are squared so that positive and negative numbers won't cancel out, then they are added up to yield an overall sense of closeness of the points to the regression line. This procedure is analogous to the method for calculating the standard deviation of a list of numbers (Section 3.5).

the rural regression equation (in our alternate version) reads:

CEB = 7.411 + (−.226 × 6).

If you solve this for CEB, you'll find that CEB = 6.055.

9.   In a sentence, explain the meaning of CEB = 6.055.

10. Estimate the average CEB for the families of those boys in the
     sample who attended school five months in the year preceding the
     census.

   Notice that each increase of one month for the variable Months in
School will yield an estimate of the average number of Children Ever
Born that is .226 lower. (Satisfy yourself of this point by plugging in
a couple of consecutive numbers for Months in School and calculating
CEB.) Because −.226 multiplies Months in School in the regression equa-
tion, any change in the number of months on the right-hand side of the
equation is multiplied by −.226 to yield the corresponding change in
Children Ever Born on the left-hand side. Therefore the coefficient of
Months in School, −.226, has the commonsense interpretation that it
is the average change in the dependent variable, Children Ever Born,
associated with every one-month change in the independent variable,
Months in School.

11. (a) What is the predicted average change in CEB associated with
          a four-month increase in Months in School?

     (b) What is the predicted average change in CEB associated with
          a six-month decrease in Months in School?

   Since the general form of the regression line is $y = a + bx$, it has
become somewhat conventional for authors to talk of "b" when referring
to regressions. When you see a reference to "b" or "B," you know that
the writer is referring to the slope coefficient, the number that multiplies
the independent variable. Sometimes in discussions of regression, the
slope coefficient is called a regression coefficient.

12. If the scatterplot were such that the regression line ran uphill from
     left to right, what could you say about the slope coefficient?

13. True or false? The slope coefficient in the regression equation and
     the correlation coefficient R that you met in the last chapter will
     have the same sign. Why?

Children Ever Born is called the <u>dependent variable</u> in this example because the researchers, Guest and Tolnay, are thinking of family fertility strategy as being at least partly caused by, and therefore dependent on, changing expectations that youngsters would be attending school rather than joining the labor force. The other variable, Months in School, goes by several names: the explanatory variable, predictor variable, or <u>independent variable</u>.

14. Without knowing anything about its historical plausibility, could you state a hypothesis that might have CEB as the explanatory variable and Months in School as the dependent variable?

Always, when scholars use regression models, they are talking about overall patterns for populations or samples; they expect the reader to understand that the pattern might not show up in every single case. Heavy cigarette smoking is positively associated with lung cancer when one looks at large populations of smokers—but we all know individuals who smoke heavily without developing cancer.

15. Can the following statement be reasonably inferred from the regression equation we have been discussing?

> Rural boys in the 1900 sample who attended school five months per year had about one child fewer in their families, on average, than rural boys who attended school one month per year.

Regression equations are usually interpreted in one of two ways. First, since a regression equation estimates the average value of the dependent variable for each value of the independent variable, the equation is often interpreted as a <u>predictive model</u>. That is, you use information about one attribute of an individual (this could be one person, one county, one farm, etc.) to make the best possible guess about some other attribute of that individual. Your guess still may not be 100% correct for any individual, but you hope that knowing one thing about the individual will enable you to make a more accurate guess than if you had known nothing about the individual at all. Figure 7.3 may help to make this clear.

16. In Figure 7.3, use the regression line to estimate visually the average weight of those men 68 inches tall.

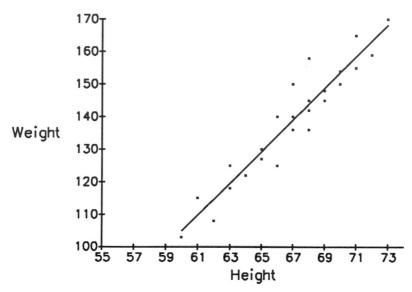

Figure 7.3
Men's weight in lbs. vs. height in inches (hypothetical data)

17. The equation of the regression line shown in Figure 7.3 is $W = -179 + (4.7 \times H)$. Identify the slope coefficient and explain why it has that name.

18. Use the equation in Question 17 to estimate the average weight of those men 68 inches tall.

You will also see regression equations being used in a slightly different way. Authors are often searching for a plausible mechanism to explain an observed historical process such as the revolutionary changes in Southern agriculture after the Civil War. They want an <u>explanatory model</u> that fits the facts. Now, a regression line is a mathematical model that best fits the data. If you tentatively advance the hypothesis that variations in family size were simply (linearly) associated with the amount of time children spent in school, then by sampling the population and calculating the regression equation, you are testing that hypothesis. If the line fits the sample data closely, you can say that the hypothesis has gained support, though it is not definitively proved. If the fit is very poor, you will have to change or discard the hypothesis. So regression equations are used to test explanatory models as well as for prediction.

19.   Would you say that Guest and Tolnay are using regression to create a predictive model or an explanatory model?

Notice how a regression model of the relationship of two variables resembles finding the mean of a list of numbers. The regression equation is a summary of the cloud of points in a scatterplot in just the same sense that the mean is a summary of the numbers in a list. The regression is a best summary of the scatterplot in the following sense: If you measure the vertical distance from each point in the scatterplot to the regression line, these vertical distances (deviations from the line) are conceptually similar to deviations of numbers in a list from their mean. The regression line is simultaneously closer to all the points than any other line you could draw through the cloud. The mean has the same feature: it is simultaneously closer to all the numbers in a list than any other number you could pick. Therefore, the regression line is to the points in a scatterplot as the mean is to the numbers in a list.

7.3   How Well Does the Model Fit the Data?

We have been talking about a regression equation as a model of the data. Guest and Tolnay's regression equations were such models. For rural families, the equation (the model) was:

$$\text{CEB} = 7.411 - .226 \times (\text{Months in School}).$$

But as a cautious reader, you have probably been thinking, "All right, that's a model—but how good a model is it, really?" The equation describes a line through the points in the scatterplot; but are the points reasonably close to the line or widely dispersed?

Take another look at Table 7.4. Beneath the regression equation you'll notice this line:

$$R^2 = .052, \text{ SE of b} = .048.$$

You might want to go back and review Section 6.6, where we discuss R^2, the coefficient of determination. R^2 is a measure of how well the model fits the actual data list—that is, how close overall the Children Ever Born predicted from the model ($7.411 - .226 \times$ Months in School) are to the actual data about the number of children in the sample families.

In Guest and Tolnay's equation, with just the one explanatory variable, Months in School, the R^2 of .052 is the square of the correlation

$(R = .23)$ between Months in School and Children Ever Born. We know
that R must fall between -1 and $+1$; so R^2 must fall between 0 and
$+1$ and will attain $+1$ only if all the data points fall exactly along the
regression line. If R^2 is near 1, the linear model is a good one, while if
R^2 is near zero, the model is poor. Alas, there is much room for debate
and judgment for middling values of this measure of fit.

As we explained in Section 6.6, R^2 has an appealing intuitive meaning
in addition to being an index of how close the data points are to the regression line. Guest and Tolnay are trying to understand why some families in 1900 had more children than others. When they regress Children
Ever Born on Months in School, they are making a model of the hypothesis that variations in schooling explain the variations observed in number
of children. In the model CEB $= 7.411 - .226 \times$ (Months in School), the
variation in CEB is totally determined by variation in Months in School.
The model predicts, in effect, that if family A's son spends six months
more in school last year than the son in family B, family A must also
have 1.356 fewer children than family B.

But in the list of 406 rural families, you know perfectly well that
some variability in the number of children is not at all associated with
schooling. For example, you might find a family with ten children in
which the son attended school for ten or eleven months. That definitely
doesn't fit the model! So some variation in the number of children can be
attributed to schooling while the rest is independent of schooling. The
number R^2 is often interpreted as the proportion of CEB variability that
can be ascribed to variability in Months in School using the model.

20.   In Tables 7.1 and 7.2, what proportion of the variability in the
dependent variables can be associated with variations in the explanatory variables?

When you read that the model (the regression line) fits the data, the
author means that the points in the scatterplot lie close to a straight
line. In Figure 7.4, the regression line fits the data very closely indeed.
For this line, R^2 is 0.88. You can see that a very large R^2 requires almost
a perfect linear fit. In contrast, Figure 7.5 shows a very bad fit. For this
example, R^2 is approximately zero.

21.   Describe a scatterplot with quite different characteristics from Figure 7.5, but for which R^2 would also be small.

22.   Does the size of R^2 say anything about the size or sign of the slope
coefficient b?

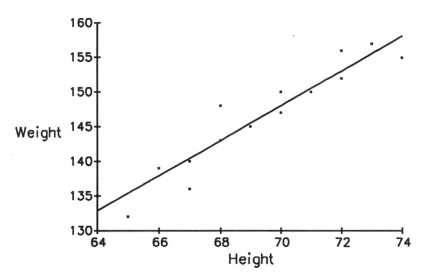

Figure 7.4
Regression of men's height and weight (hypothetical data)

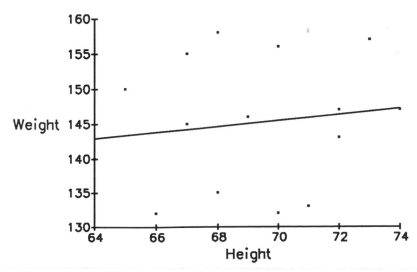

Figure 7.5
Regression of men's height and weight (hypothetical data)

In order to have an adequate sense of the relationship between the dependent and independent variables, you need to know both the slope coefficient (also called the regression coefficient) and the value of R^2. From Table 7.4, you know that the regression coefficient is $-.226$ and that R^2 is .052. You can interpret these two numbers as follows:

- Since the regression line is analogous to an average, the coefficient $-.226$ means that in the sample of 406 boys, on average, a decrease of .226 in the number of children ever born in the family was approximately correlated with an increase of one in the number of months the boy had attended school during the year preceding the census.

- Since R^2 was .052, this model using school attendance to explain the number of children in the boys' families does account for 5.2% of the variation in the number of children.

7.4   From Sample to Population

So far, we have been careful to say that the regression model with an R^2 of .052 applies not to the entire population but only to the sample of 406 families. In the sample, there was a certain tendency (expressed by the coefficient $-.226$) for CEB to decline with an increase in Months in School. But how do you know that these results were not just an accident of the sample? Maybe in the entire population of rural families, the two variables were not related at all.

23.   What is the population from which this sample of 406 was drawn?

If CEB and Months in School were truly unrelated in the population, then knowing the value of the independent variable for any family would not enable you to make a more accurate guess as to the probable value of the dependent variable CEB. If you had your statistical program calculate a regression equation using these two unrelated variables, the regression line would be horizontal—i.e., it would have a slope of zero. The equation would look something like this:

CEB = 7.411 − 0 × (Months in School).

Zero times anything equals zero, so you can simplify this equation to

CEB = 7.411.

24. In a sentence, explain what such a regression equation is telling you. Why would the slope of the regression line be zero in a case where the variables were unrelated?

Guest and Tolnay's implied null hypothesis is that the two variables are unrelated. Now, the regression model for the data in their sample came up with a slope coefficient that was not zero but −.226. If it were true that in the whole population CEB was unrelated to Months in School, then sampling error would be the explanation for the authors' finding a slope coefficient of −.226. So we can frame the question in this way: If the slope coefficient, b, is really zero in the population, how probable is it that a sample of 406 cases would yield a value for b as large as −.226?

If the probability is, say, 40% or 50%, that's just too large a chance that the −.226 is due to sampling error. On the other hand, if the chance of getting a b as far from zero as −.226 would only occur once in every hundred samples drawn from a population for which the true value of b was zero, then the fact that Guest and Tolnay did indeed get a b this far from zero strongly suggests that this −.226 wasn't just an accident of the draw but represents a real relationship in the underlying population. As you know, this one in a hundred chance is referred to as the significance level.

Guest and Tolnay provide the information a reader needs to determine quickly whether a slope coefficient of −.226 is statistically significant. If you look back at Table 7.4, you will see that below the regression equation and next to the value for R^2 there appears this cryptic statement:

SE of b = .048.

SE stands for standard error; so "SE of b" means "standard error of the slope coefficient." If Guest and Tolnay had drawn many samples instead of just one, they would have obtained many regression equations. The slope coefficients would not all have turned out exactly the same.

25. Why would they have obtained many different regression equations?

If they had a list of all those slope coefficients from the many regression equations, that list would have a mean and a standard deviation. SE of b is the estimate of that standard deviation. As you learned in Section 4.5, the standard error is the expected difference, on average, between the true population score and the sample score.

Let's use the .95 standard for statistical significance—that is, we want to be 95% certain that a slope coefficient of −.226 couldn't have happened just by chance, by random sampling error. Section 4.9 mentioned that according to probability theory, the score of a randomly chosen sample on any particular variable stands about a 95% chance of being within two SEs of the true score for the underlying population. Well, for the regression equation we've been discussing, the authors report that one SE was .048.

Figure 7.6 may help you visualize the situation (Remember, b can be interpreted as the average change in the dependent variable, Children Ever Born, associated with every one-month change in the independent variable, Months in School.) The solid line is the regression model with the slope of −.226 which Guest and Tolney found. The other lines are models whose slopes differ from −.226 by one or two standard errors.

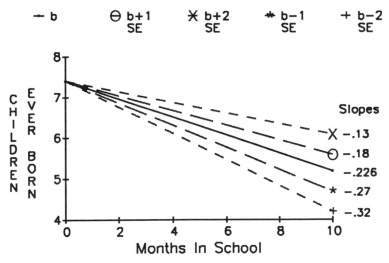

Figure 7.6
Scores within two SEs of sample b

So it is possible to say that the 95% confidence interval for b, the slope coefficient, in a regression equation for the full population, is from about −.13 to −.32. And that means we can be at least 95% sure that, with a sample size of 406, the slope coefficient is not zero.

26. What does it mean to say that b is other than zero?

27. If SE of b were 3 SEs from zero, your confidence level would be 99.73%. If it were 4 SEs from zero, the level would rise to 99.99%. How many SEs is the sample b ($-.226$) from zero? What does this mean?

28. Does the true value for b stand an equal chance of falling anywhere between $-.130$ and $-.322$ or is there a greater chance that it is close to the sample b of $-.226$ than to other scores in that range?

The next five questions pertain to the two regression equations in Table 7.4; these questions provide a checklist that you can use to test your understanding of a regression model that contains one explanatory variable. State your answers and interpretations in commonsense English rather than using technical statistical terms.

29. For the rural and urban samples, are the slope coefficients statistically significant?

30. Do the signs of the slope coefficients make sense?

31. Comment on the size of the slope coefficients.

32. Interpret the values for R^2.

33. Very briefly, what conclusions do you draw from the two regression equations in Table 7.4?

We now summarize the steps you should go through when reading a regression table:

- First, look to see if the coefficient for the explanatory variable is statistically significant. If it isn't, say t is less than 2, then there's no point in looking further because such a small t-value means that the pattern shown by the data might well be due to the luck of the draw and might not reflect patterns in the population under study.

- Second, take a moment to try to visualize the kind of data list that the writer was using to develop the regression model. These equations are formidably abstract; it's important to remember that they are no more reliable than the data from which they were calculated. If the historian doesn't let you know much about the data, that's a strike against the whole enterprise.

- Third, check the sign of the regression coefficient (the slope coefficient). If the sign is negative, then one variable goes down when the other goes up and the two variables are negatively related to one another. Now, and this is very important, ask if the direction of the effect shown in the model makes sense.

- Fourth, study the size of the regression coefficient to see if the effect is important in practical terms. For example, if the equation says

  CEB = 7.411 − .000226 × Months in School,

  then the model is estimating that an increase of, say, eight months in schooling would be associated with a decline of only two one-hundredths of one child in CEB. If the historian has a large enough sample, a tiny slope coefficient can pass our first test by being statistically significant, yet still be so small as to be, for all practical purposes, historically unimportant.

- Fifth, look at the value of R^2 to see how much of the variability of the dependent variable is explained by the model.

We will add two other items to this checklist after we discuss multiple regression.

7.5   Multiple Regression Models

We now want to discuss what additional issues are raised when a historian presents a more complicated model similar to those in a couple of the historical articles that you examined in Section 7.1. Multiple regression is the name given to such models when an investigator uses several explanatory variables instead of just one.

Suppose that for the next stage of their research on fertility, Avery M. Guest and Stewart E. Tolnay had tried to model the dependent variable Children Ever Born as a linear function of three independent variables: the son's months in school, the father's wealth, and whether the son was employed in the labor force. Notice that you might not have equal faith in the accuracy of the census data for the three variables.

The statistical program on the authors' computer might now grind out something like Table 7.5.

For convenience, we have reproduced the original regression model from Table 7.4 as column 1 in this new table, Table 7.5. In the new table, the three columns thus represent three different models; please notice that we made up the models in columns 2 and 3. For the next few paragraphs, we'll focus on column 2.

34. Satisfy yourself that column 1 of Table 7.5 contains the same information as the "Rural" row in Table 7.4.

35. Write out the information in Table 7.5, column 2, as a regression equation.

You may be wondering why the new variable Father's Wealth is expressed as wealth times 10^{-3}. What does this mean? Multiplying a number by 10^{-3} means dividing it by 10^3, or 1000. So this notation means that you don't use a father's wealth in dollars in the regression equation, but his wealth in thousands of dollars. Thus if an individual had wealth of \$7500, the number 7.5 is cranked into the equation. Of course, one could write this term of the equation as

$-.000217 \times$ Father's Wealth,

Table 7.5
Determinants of children ever born, rural households, 1900 (columns 2 and 3 are hypothetical)

	(1)	(2)	(3)
Constant	7.411	5.300	5.288
Months in School	−.226	−.013	−.008
SE of Months in School	(.048)	(.024)	(.021)
Father's Wealth $\times 10^{-3}$	−.217	−.196	
SE of Father's Wealth		(.045)	(.058)

Son's Employment
  yes = 0
  no = 1
		+.127	

SE of Son's Employment		(.049)	
R^2	.052	.149	.204
N = 406			

since that multiplies out to the same product as

$-.217 \times$ Father's Wealth $\times 10^{-3}$.

The virtue of a term like 10^{-3} is that it enables you to hold all the b, c, and d coefficients in the regression equations to the same rough order of magnitude. Since you already have a sense of what $-.226$ means in the original equation, it is easier to grasp $-.217$ in the second equation than a number like $-.000217$.

36.   Explain the meaning of that term $-.217 \times$ Father's Wealth $\times 10^{-3}$ in equation 2.

As you study this imaginary multiple regression table, begin by comparing the Months in School coefficient in columns 1 and 2. Notice that the Months in School coefficient has changed from $-.226$ in the earlier equation to $-.013$. This means that the dependent variable CEB seems to behave one way when a new variable is taken into consideration and another way when it is omitted. In fact, in real applications of regression, the variation in coefficient size from model to model can be much greater than the variation shown here. This phenomenon is at the heart of why multiple regression is so useful and so widely used.

From the earlier regression equation, we note a clear tendency for families that sent their sons to school for more months to have fewer children. But the earlier model hid the powerful effect of family wealth. From the first multiple regression model (Table 7.5, column 2) we can guess that perhaps wealthier families tended to send their boys to school for more months and to have fewer children. Taking more variables into account, the more significant factor now seems to be family wealth, not schooling.

When the variables are included together in a multiple regression model, their coefficients show the effect of each variable while taking into account the presence of the other variables. The coefficient for Months in School now becomes an estimate of the average change in CEB as Months in School changes, under the assumption that Father's Wealth is being held constant. With wealth in the model, the Months in School coefficient is estimating average CEB changes within each wealth class.

The reason multiple regression is so widely used when statistical techniques are brought to bear on historical questions is that historical processes are assumed to involve a complex web of interacting effects. Multiple regression is a mathematical tool for estimating the force of each effect in the presence of other simultaneously interacting effects.

Turning to the second multiple regression model we've made up (Table 7.5, column 3), notice that Son's Employment is not really a quantitative variable at all but a categorical variable. In such a situation, the researcher creates a dummy variable by assigning the two categories numerical values: 0 when the son is not employed, 1 when he is.[11]

In this second multiple regression model, it seems that the added variable, Son's Employment, interacts with the other two as well. It is obvious the new variable may be related to our original variable Months in School. Whether the son had a job might also have had something to do with the father's wealth, and hence might have affected Months in School indirectly as well as directly. In addition, parental attitudes about putting the children to work may have <u>directly</u> influenced attitudes about how many children to have. So Son's Employment may have affected the dependent variable, Children Ever Born, in several ways.

37. In equation 2 of Table 7.5, imagine two families of equal wealth; one sends its son to school for four months, the other for seven months. If you had to predict how far apart they were in number of children ever born, what would your prediction be?

38. In Family A the father is worth $7450 and the son is not employed; in Family B, the father is worth $2100 and the son is employed. Both families send their sons to school for five months. What is your best guess for the number of children ever born in each family?

In the third model of Table 7.5, notice that Months in School has ceased to be statistically significant—the slope coefficient, $-.008$, is closer to zero than the standard error, .021. This means that there is a substantial chance that you could have gotten this coefficient in the sample just by the luck of the draw even if the true coefficient in the entire U.S. population had been zero. Quite aside from the question of statistical significance, note also that the size of the Months in School effect in model 3 is not striking. It appears to have little practical significance now that the two new variables have been added.

39. Explain the meaning of the coefficient $-.008$ in model 3 of Table 7.5.

---

[11] See Section 6.1 if you want to review the topic of dummy variables.

40. Does the Months in School coefficient in model 3 contradict the coefficient in model 1, $-.226$?

Checking the value of R^2 in the last row of Table 7.5, you notice a significant increase in the explanatory value of the model when first one, and then a second new independent variable is added. The original model explained about 5% of the variance in CEB. When Father's Wealth is included, this jumps all the way to 14.9%. It jumps to 20.4% when the third variable, Son's Employment, comes in. (This improvement in explanatory power doesn't always happen, though. Often, adding still another variable brings little improvement in the ability of the model to explain the variation in the dependent variable.)

From the three regression equations in Table 7.5 (remember, we made two of them up out of thin air; only the first equation is taken from a published article) you could conclude that for rural families in 1900, family wealth and whether sons were employed had a more important influence on the number of children in the family than the amount of schooling that sons were receiving. You could be confident that wealth and sons' employment were important determinants of CEB but that almost four-fifths the variance in number of children remains unexplained by any of the three regression models. Since the sampling procedure was a random one, you could also conclude that the results you observe in this sample population very probably reflected the true pattern in the general rural population.

41. Suppose you wanted to use no more than two explanatory variables to produce a regression model with CEB as the dependent variable. Does Table 7.5 contain information that would help you decide which variable to discard?

A word of caution. Earlier, we said that the Months in School coefficient can be interpreted as the average change in the dependent variable associated with a one-month change in the independent variable Months in School, with analogous meanings applying to the other coefficients. You have even answered questions based on that interpretation.

The purpose of that definition of the coefficient's meaning was to test whether the model predicts that the independent variable would have an important real-world effect on the dependent variable. But in fact, you would not predict that a one-month difference in schooling would yield, on average, a .226 decline in CEB. Why not? Recall that as we put additional variables into the model, the coefficients change. As you saw in Table 7.5, when two new variables were added, the coefficient of

Months in School dropped from $-.226$ to $-.008$. Well, there could be still more explanatory variables out there that affect the coefficient in ways unknown.

So it is not reasonable to say that if you hold everything constant except Months in School, you will get a decline of .226 in CEB for every one-month increase. The problem is that each model leaves out some important influences. Perhaps additional variables would change this coefficient further—conceivably even change its sign from minus to plus. In fact, it's clear that the regression models in Table 7.5 leave much of the variation in CEB unexplained since R^2 was only .204 in the best of the three.

Don't be surprised that the best multiple regression model in Table 7.5 ended up explaining only 20.4% of the variability in CEB. If the historian were trying to account <u>fully</u> for CEB, he would have to chase down dozens of other possible explanatory factors and test their interaction with the first three variables. Diminishing returns would quickly set in. The historian might well find that even after adding ten more variables, he had only boosted R^2 to something like .35.

Moreover, adding more and more variables would result in a Rube Goldberg model: elaborate, cumbersome, and aesthetically disturbing— except to those with a fondness for the rococo. Such a model might also be inapplicable to any other historical case beyond the one for which it was fashioned, because some of the additional variables would represent factors unique to rural families in 1900. In building a regression model, scholars aim not just for explanatory power but for parsimonious explanatory power.

Life is complex. Explaining half the variance, or even 20.4%, is really quite an achievement, and most scholars would be pleased to do that well.[12] And even these rather crude regression models have a use. A regression equation is nothing more than a <u>simple model of reality</u>. It's a model derived from the real world, to be sure, but only a crude approximation of the complexities of the world. You can't use models like this to make concrete predictions. But they sometimes help you decide which explanatory variables were quite important and which were not so important.

If all three of the models in Table 7.5 strike you as hopelessly weak, consider trying to explain the fall of a feather using the mathematical model for gravitational attraction. A real feather is affected by the wind,

---

[12]For a discussion of this point see Daniel Scott Smith, "A Mean and Random History: The Implications of Variance for History," *Historical Methods*, 17 (Summer 1984), 141–48.

the temperature of the air, the moisture content of the air, and many other factors. The gravitational model fails to take any of these into account. As a result, the model cannot accurately predict the fall of the feather. Yet the gravitational model, in the form of mathematical equations, is one of the great intellectual achievements of mankind. Its utility is not that it predicts the precise behavior of a single example but that it summarizes the general nature of the relationship between acceleration, mass, and distance for all pairs of objects.

Earlier, we provided a five-item checklist that a reader should tick off when studying a regression table. That list should include at least two more items.

- Sixth, ask if some variable has been omitted that prior knowledge or theory suggests as an important determinant of the dependent variable. A small R^2 may indicate that important explanatory variables should be added. Of course, it may also indicate that no reasonable linear model will work.

- Seventh, ask if some of the independent variables are measuring almost the same thing. Suppose we are going to try to predict success in college and we take undergraduate grade point average as the dependent variable. We decide to use high school grades, IQ scores, SAT scores, and the strength of academic recommendations as the independent variables. Now we draw a sample of 500 high school students and run a multiple regression. Those independent variables are highly correlated with one another: students with good high school grades and strong academic recommendations will tend to have high SAT and IQ scores.

When independent variables are very highly correlated, it can happen that regression coefficients calculated from one sample will differ greatly from regression coefficients calculated from another sample. So the regression model you calculate from the one sample of 500 students could easily be very different if you took a second sample. This situation is clearly undesirable. You want to believe that the coefficients are not highly sensitive to the luck of the draw.

The best way for a historian to avoid the problems of highly correlated predictors and the problem of omitted predictors is to use his or her knowledge of the historical issue being studied. The historian should think long and hard about what variables to include and what variables to exclude. A historian should <u>never</u> just dump into a computer some data found near at hand and instruct the machine to calculate regression equations on every possible combination of explanatory variables.

Statistical techniques can help a little. By playing with several different models, trying different combinations of variables in the equations, computing equations from subsamples of the whole sample, and regressing independent variables against one another, you can spot variables whose information seems to be already contained in other factors. You saw that process work in the hypothetical example (Table 7.5, column 3) where the effect of one variable, Months in School, was almost wholly included in the effects of two other variables.

It is important to observe that in going through their analysis of fertility and children's roles, the historians relied not only on the numbers that occurred in the sample (and their summary in the regression table), but also on their prior knowledge about the substantive issue. There was some reason Guest and Tolnay chose to look at education as a possible predictor of fertility and not, say, father's military service.

Obviously, one never tries all possibilities. You begin by including those factors that have previously been suggested as important or that some theory predicts as important. You then use regression to test competing theories and to weigh the relative impact of plausible causes. So one could say that regression is not primarily a mathematical technique at all, but rather an exercise in building and testing theoretical models using assumptions that come from study of the field of application— history, in this case—and not from statistics or mathematics.

One should not approach regression with a bag full of numbers, expecting to find concise, definitive answers in a small set of regression coefficients. A spirit of play would be more appropriate. The game is to move back and forth between one's ideas about the substantive issue and the information in the historical record bearing on that issue. Regression might suggest new ideas or it might cause you to challenge previous ideas. Almost certainly, it will not hand you a pat answer.

The next section turns to the regressions that crop up in historical journals; those are the regressions you really want to read and understand.

7.6 Women in the Labor Force, 1860

In her analysis of the economic status of American women in the early nineteenth century, Claudia Goldin presented the figure that we reprinted at the beginning of this chapter. Here it is again as Figure 7.7.

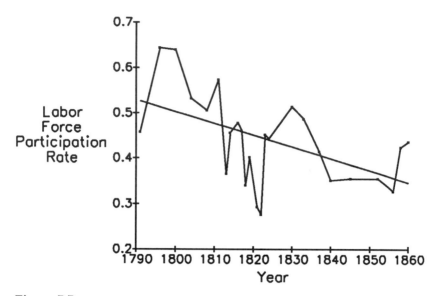

Figure 7.7
Labor force participation rates for female heads of households, Philadelphia, 1791
to 1860

Labor Force Participation Rate = 0.539 − 0.0028 Time

t-value for constant = 16.26

t-value for slope coefficient = 3.20

$R^2 = 0.31$

Source: See Figure 7.1.

The jagged line depicts time series data for various years between 1791
and 1860. Regression is often used with time series to spot and summarize long-term trends in data that show considerable short-term variability. This technique offers historians a tool that they might use even
more often than they do.[13]

In Figure 7.7, the regression line is the straight line running through
the graph. The regression equation appears below the graph. Goldin is
not using regression to create an explanatory model, but to pick out the
overall trend amidst the fluctuations in the time series data.

---

[13]For an excellent introduction to time series analysis, see Roderick Floud, *An
Introduction to Quantitative Methods for Historians* (Princeton, 1973), Chapter 6.

42. In a sentence or two, explain what relation the regression line has to the time series line with its peaks and valleys. Also, explain what relation the regression equation has to the regression line.

43. Describe the likely appearance of the data list from which Goldin constructed Figure 7.7.

44. Explain what the regression equation is telling the reader. The variable Time is measured in yearly units; what does the author mean by the term of the equation that says "−0.0028 Time"? Is that coefficient large enough to be interesting? (For this question you can ignore the numbers in parentheses beneath the equation.)

45. Comment on the sign of the slope coefficient in the regression equation.

46. Are the results statistically significant? Develop your answer in terms of the t-values that appear beneath the regression equation.

47. Explain what "$R^2 = 0.31$" means.

48. Notice the pattern of fluctuations around the trend line in Figure 7.7—the participation rate staying above the trend line for a couple of decades, then dipping below the line for several years, then climbing above it for a decade. Think of one or two hypotheses that you believe might account for this pattern.

7.7 Party Switching or New Voters?

Political historian David F. Prindle contrasts two possible mechanisms for the processes he calls the New Deal Realignment. The realignment might have happened because many persons who previously supported the Republicans switched their support to the Democratic party. Alternatively, there could have been a mobilization of new voters who joined the ranks of the Democrats. Earlier historians have debated which factor was more important. Prindle examines the regressions in Table 7.6 to see if they are more consistent with one or the other of the alternative mechanisms.

The information behind Table 7.6 is county-level population and voting figures. From this, Prindle calculated the Democratic and Republican turnout for each of the four presidential elections. A party's turnout would be the proportion of the eligible population voting for that party's

Table 7.6
Wisconsin Regression: 1916/20 to 1936/40 Presidential Elections

Dependent Variable: RepTwo	Beta: .71	p < .001
Independent Variable: RepOne	R^2: .61	
Dependent Variable: DemTwo	Beta: .07	n.s.
Independent Variable: DemOne	R^2: .01	

Source: See Table 7.2.

Key: RepOne is the average of the Republican turnout in the 1916 and 1920 elections expressed as a percentage of all adults.

RepTwo is the comparable average for the 1936 and 1940 elections.

DemOne and DemTwo are the analogous variables for the Democrats.

presidential candidate. The 1916 and 1920 were averaged to give one Democratic and one Republican score for each Wisconsin county. Similarly, the 1936 and 1940 turnouts were averaged. So the individuals in the study are Wisconsin counties.

We need to explain a couple of words or phrases in the table. First, why does Prindle say "p < .001"? Second, what does he mean by "Beta = .71"?

Instead of giving a p-value as Prindle has done, some regressions show a t-value instead. You know that when the t-values for large samples get bigger than 2, the associated slope coefficients are statistically significant. Other regression presentations make you work a bit harder, as Table 7.5 did, by giving you the coefficient b and the SE for b. Then you had to divide b by the SE for b to get the t-ratio.

Prindle made things easier instead of harder. Rather than giving you the t-value or the information you need in order to calculate it, he skipped over t entirely and just gave you the p-value, the probability of your getting that t-value if the null hypothesis were true.

49. What is the null hypothesis mentioned in the preceding paragraph?

50. Explain the meaning of Prindle's p-value of < .001 in the first model and "not significant" in the second model.

The second thing that needs explaining in Prindle's regression models is the word <u>Beta</u>. To understand Beta, try to imagine the raw data list that lies behind the regressions in Table 7.6. The following list is hypothetical as to the particular numbers but represents the kind of information that must underlie the regression.

County	Turnout 1916/20		Turnout 1936/40	
	Rep.	Dem.	Rep.	Dem.
1	2120	1470	2540	3620
2	1990	2040	1140	1760
⋮	⋮	⋮	⋮	⋮

You could take the numbers in this list and get a scatterplot of DemTwo against DemOne. Then a least-squares line fit to that scatterplot would give us a regression equation in the form

$$\text{DemTwo} = a + (b \times \text{DemOne}).$$

As before, b is the conventional symbol for the slope coefficient. But in Table 7.6, Prindle has printed the word "Beta," the Greek letter for b. Why does he say Beta instead of b? The use of the word Beta is conventional just as the use of b for the slope is. Scholars use the word Beta for the slope coefficient when they have modified the numbers in the data list before computing the regression equation. The modification of the numbers is called standardization. Prindle has created <u>standard variables</u> by first subtracting the mean of each turnout list from each individual county score on that list, and then dividing that difference by the standard deviation for that list. That is, the original list above has been turned into a list like this:

County	Turnout 1916/20		Turnout 1936/40	
	Rep.	Dem.	Rep.	Dem.
1	1.2	0.6	1.7	2.1
2	1.1	1.8	0.3	0.9
⋮	⋮	⋮	⋮	⋮

The numbers in this new list are not the turnouts themselves but rather, each turnout has been replaced by its distance in standard deviations from the mean turnout in that category. A standard score shows how many standard deviations a raw score is from the mean. Now these standard scores are put in scatterplots and fit with a least squares line to give the regression equations that are represented in Table 7.6.

Standardization gets rid of questions about units. If a variable is measured in pounds, its standard deviation is also in pounds. So when you divide by the standard deviation, the result is a unitless variable. This makes slope coefficients for different variables more comparable. We can compare one Beta against another to see which of two variables has the greater effect on a dependent variable.

Finally now, you are ready to read Table 7.6.

51. The table shows two regression equations. Very briefly, for each of the two equations go through the first five steps in the seven-step checklist we recommended.

52. Is Republican turnout in the earlier period a good predictor or not for Republican turnout in the later period?

53. Is Democratic turnout in the earlier period a good predictor or not for Democratic turnout in the later period?

54. With which of Prindle's two alternative ideas, party switching by voters or the registration of new voters, are these equations more consistent? Why?

7.8   Dialogue: Why Plant Cotton?

NOTE: In the following dialogue, we discuss sample representativeness as a problem in Wright and Kunreuther's article "Cotton, Corn and Risk." The article does not describe the sampling procedure, and we point this out; yet the authors draw conclusions about the entire population as if their sample of Southern farms in 1860 is representative. So after raising the issue, we are going to proceed as if it is indeed representative.

Student. Hello, there, professor. You know, I did read that material about regression, but it's pretty confusing. It's all spinning around in my head.

Historian. I'm not surprised. You're learning many new concepts, and it's very different from traditional history.

Student. I'll say! I thought American history would cover things like the Battle of Gettysburg and tell me why Lee's army was defeated.

Historian. Well, you won't find out today, I'm afraid. But here is a historical problem that is also quite important. I think you're ready now to analyze a difficult multiple regression table. The one I've chosen appears in the article by Gavin Wright and Howard Kunreuther on the shift from self-sufficient farming into cotton production in the South after the Civil War. On the surface, this shift seems hard to understand because world cotton prices had entered a long-term decline. Do you recall reading about this debate?

Student. Sure. Their explanation is that many small farmers changed their attitudes toward taking risk. Although cotton was a riskier crop, it held out some hope of substantial gain. Corn was safer but offered no hope of escape from poverty.

Historian. That's the one. An important logical step in the authors' argument is to establish that the risk-taking pattern changed, that it was different before the war than after the war. They assert that prior to the Civil War, the typical small Southern farmer's behavior was characterized by a "safety-first" strategy in which he would initially provide for the farm's self-sufficiency and only speculate on cotton with land or labor beyond that which was required to insure the farm's basic needs.

As one part of their discussion, Wright and Kunreuther ask what observable effects would follow if farmers in 1860 (before the war) had, as a group, employed the safety-first strategy. Do you see why that's an important question?

Student. No, I don't see what you're driving at.

Historian. Well, this notion of farmers having a "strategy" is an important underlying premise in the Wright-Kunreuther article. But how are they going to know whether farmers really had strategies? That's not the kind of thing that you'll find farmers talking about in their diaries—and anyway, not many farmers kept diaries. So how can Wright and Kunreuther suggest that farmers had a safety-first strategy, or any conscious strategy, before 1860?

Student. I don't know.

Historian. They reason that if farmers had a safety-first strategy, we should find some observable consequences. That is, the farmers' strategy leads to some consequences; if we observe the consequences, we'll take that as evidence that the strategy really was in force. Using 1860 data, Wright and Kunreuther look for two observable indicators of the safety-first strategy:

(1) If such a strategy was being practiced widely, cotton share (proportion of land planted to cotton) would show a positive association with farm size, soil quality, and labor force per acre.

(2) Also, cotton share would show a negative association with the number of people who had to be supported by the acreage.

Here's what number 1 means: You would expect that big farms, or those with superior soil or extra labor, would have resources beyond the minimum required to sustain themselves. The authors assert that these were the farms that were devoting more of their resources to cotton in 1860, while the small farms remained committed to corn production. That would be evidence that the risk-taking strategy hadn't caught on among smaller farmers yet. Now what do you make of number 2?

Student. I guess it means that the more individuals living on a farm, the more corn the farm would have to produce for the purpose of feeding those people and their animals.

Historian. Right. Now, in Table 7.7 we have a regression table that in effect paints part of a picture of Southern agriculture in 1860. You saw this table early in Chapter 7, but it was probably incomprehensible.

Student. Paints a picture? It's still incomprehensible to me.

Historian. Well, your big opportunity has arrived, because together we're going to figure it out. We will work on Table 7.7 at two levels. First, we will try to understand the literal meaning of the words and numbers. Then we can try to understand the implications of the table for the historical argument. So where do you think we should start?

Student. I'll start with the parts that are closer to being in standard English. The title to the table says that the dependent variable

Table 7.7
Regression coefficients: Cotton South, 1860

Dependent Variable: Cotton Acreage/(Cotton + Corn Acreage)

	(1)	(2)	(3)	(4)
Constant	.342	.262	.286	.280
Soil Quality	.0011[a]	.0000	.00025	.00028
	(3.92)	(.025)	(0.91)	(0.39)
POP/IA[b]	−.1805[a]		−.105[a]	−.1820[a]
	(11.50)		(6.68)	(8.02)
IA[c]		.00034[a]	.00032[a]	.00031[a]
		(21.60)	(19.32)	(19.11)
LBR/IA[d]				.378[a]
				(4.71)
R^2	.027	.085	.093	.097

Source: See Table 7.1.

N = 5117

t-ratios in parentheses

[a] Signifies significance at 1 percent level.

[b] On-farm population per improved acre.

[c] Improved acreage.

[d] Labor force (free males aged 15–64 plus slaves aged 15–64) per improved acre.

Dependent variable derived from cotton and corn output figures under assumption that cotton yield = 208.1 pounds per acre, corn yield = 16.81 bushels per acre. (Only the ratio of these two figures affects the result.)

being modeled is 1860 cotton acreage divided by the sum of 1860 cotton and corn acreage—i.e., cotton acreage as a proportion of the total acreage planted to cotton and corn. I think the measurements are taken on individual farms, because N = 5117 must mean 5117 farms. There are four explanatory variables: soil quality, farm population per improved acre, number of improved acres, and farm labor supply per improved acre.

Historian. Soil quality was calculated, according to the footnotes, from farm value and the ratio of unimproved to improved acres. A remark just above the table in the original article says that cotton and corn acreage were estimated from data on the cotton and corn output of the farms.

Now you have a sense of what the variables are. What do you do next?

Student. Wave the white flag of surrender. No, I can get one step further. The next step might be to try to imagine what the data looked like before the authors ran the regression.

Historian. Good! So what <u>did</u> the data look like?

Student. Something like this, I think. I'm just making these numbers up.

Farm	Impr. Acres	Unimpr. Acres	Value	Pop.	Labor Supp.	Cotton Output	Corn Output
1	110	50	$1320	7	4	20 bales	50 bushels
2	2050	230	$18600	51	38	500 bales	400 bushels
⋮	⋮	⋮	⋮	⋮	⋮	⋮	⋮

Historian. Good again! Since they had seven pieces of information for each farm, the authors were confronted with almost 36,000 numbers in which to find patterns which support or contradict their hypotheses. Table 7.7 may seem a bit complex, but perhaps that should be expected of such a small set of numbers that aspires to abstract a significant pattern from among the swarm of 36,000 numbers.

Student. How did they get all this data about 5117 farms? And why those particular farms—are they supposed to be a representative sample or something?

Historian. You're asking an important question. Clearly the list is restricted to farms for which the needed information is known. Could there be systematic differences, such as size or wealth, between farms with complete records and those without?

Student. You mean that maybe we have more complete data about large, prosperous farms or farms in some parts of the South, while the marginal farms or those in frontier regions are neglected?

Historian. Yes, that's what I'm wondering. There isn't any way to know from the Wright-Kunreuther article alone. And once you begin poking around, other questions might occur to you: Is it plausible that the 1860 census enumerators accurately recorded the number of free males and slaves aged 15–64 on thousands of farms, for example? And what about the authors' methods for estimating soil quality and acreage planted in cotton and corn? Overall, what is your sense of the quality of the numbers in the list? The possibility of systematic bias is more important than complete accuracy. If only random errors have crept into the record, then the effects will tend to balance out and not greatly affect our conclusions; but if the errors occur systematically they can mislead us entirely.

Student. The last footnote says that this list came from the Parker-Gallman manuscript census sample. In the title to Table 7.7, the authors say that this table refers to the entire Cotton South. But I can't tell whether their data uses all farms in the Parker-Gallman sample, a sample of the sample, or only those farms which had data recorded for all seven of the above variables. The manner in which they chose the 5117 farms could possibly bias their results, so I guess the authors should have described their selection process more fully.

Historian. Clearly, we have some uneasiness about the data on these Southern farms of 1860; but in order to get on to the regression equations, let's put aside for the moment any technical questions about the way in which the variables were obtained and assume that for each farm we know the following four independent variables: 1) how good the land was (Soil Quality), 2) how much land was improved (IA), 3) how many consumers per acre each farm had to support (POP/IA) and 4) how many workers per acre there were to produce the farm output (LBR/IA).

Now, just what are Wright and Kunreuther trying to do with all these variables?

Student. Well, as I understand it, the farms in their list had different proportions of their corn-cotton land planted to cotton. The proportions constitute the dependent variable and the problem is to explain their variability. For example, why do some farms plant, say, 80% of that land to cotton but others only 35%? I guess the broader question is, did a pattern exist that is consistent with the authors' idea that farmers were following a safety-first strategy? The regression table, if I could only read it, is supposed to show us whether we can explain part of the variability in cotton share as due to differences among the farms in the four independent variables.

Historian. You're thinking about the problem as a historian. Wright and Kunreuther happen to be econometricians, and it's my impression that they are not primarily interested in explaining cotton share. They want to support their model, which predicts the direction of certain relationships. It is enough for them that the coefficients have the right sign and are statistically significant.

But you and I must still be concerned with the size of the coefficients and the size of R^2. You have seen that coefficients can move around and even change sign as explanatory variables are moved in and out of a regression model. And if R^2 is very small, something is missing in the explanation. Does the regression model omit some variables that would strongly interact with farm size and cotton share? If so, it is hard to have confidence in either the sign or the statistical significance of the regression coefficients. Here again, we need assurance from the authors that they have thought deeply about the variables to be included in the model.

Now, let's look at Table 7.7. What do you make of equation (1)?

Student. Uh-oh. I knew we'd get to this eventually. Hmmm. Well, equation (1) is given by the coefficients in the first column of Table 7.7—the column with a (1) at the top.

Historian. Bravo! What model is it testing?

Student. Well, ... The explanatory variables in (1) are Soil Quality and POP/IA. So (1) considers the hypothesis that cotton share can be explained by the fact that some farms had better soil than others and that some farms were more densely populated than others.

Historian. And what does that mean?

Student. Presumably, the farmers on more densely populated farms would feel pressure to follow the safety-first strategy and grow food (corn), while those on farms with better soil quality could exploit that richness by planting more cotton. That's the hunch to be tested, anyway.

Historian. So far, so good. Can you write down the regression equation?

Student. Well, ummmm. How about this?

$$PC = .342 + (.0011 \times SQ) - (.1805 \times [POP/IA])$$

PC means proportion of acreage planted in cotton; SQ means soil quality; and POP/IA means on-farm population per improved acre.

Historian. Okay. Now, you have a checklist to help you find your way through one of these equations. Proceed, and I'll come to your rescue if you get lost.

Student. Step 1 is to see if the coefficients for the explanatory variables are statistically significant. The footnote references "a" beside the coefficients in model (1) tell us that both coefficients are statistically significant at the 1% level, which means it is improbable that they differ from zero only because of chance in the sampling procedure.

Historian. That's correct as long as we're assuming a random sampling procedure, by the way. Next?

Student. Step 2 is to think about the data lists and underlying sources from which the historians must have been working—we already talked about that. Checking the signs of the regression coefficients (the slope coefficients) is the third step. I'd say the signs of the coefficients are what we would have expected in advance of seeing the data. Cotton share goes up with soil quality and goes down with population density.

Fourth, I'm supposed to see if the size of the regression coefficients is enough to be interesting in historical terms. This is where I get hung up. What does .0011 mean? And −.1805? Help!

Historian. Yes, it's tough to get a sense of the practical importance of the independent variables in this model. Okay, let's take the POP/IA variable. I usually find that it helps to set up a concrete example. So imagine a fifty-acre farm that is asked to support two extra consumers (or a 500-acre farm being asked to feed 20 extra consumers). That is clearly a very significant increase in population density, right? An increase of two persons per 50 acres is an increase of 2/50ths to the variable POP/IA. Does that change yield an important change in the dependent variable? An increase of 2/50 in POP/IA gives a decrease of .1805 times 2/50 or 0.72% (less than one percent) in cotton share.

Such a small increase in cotton share can't be much beyond measurement error (how accurately do we know these numbers?) and so it is not very interesting. So I conclude that this model (1) would not be strong evidence for a theory stating that farm population density was a major force in keeping some classes of farmers out of cotton, because a significant change in POP/IA is associated with an insignificant change in cotton share.

Now why don't you try interpreting the coefficient for soil quality? You need some additional information, though. The soil quality index was computed in a way that makes reasoning about it more difficult. According to a footnote that I left out of Table 7.7, soil quality has been measured in dollars per acre using the value of the farm after adjusting for differences in value that seem to be due to the fact that some farms have a higher proportion of improved acres than others.

Student. Soil quality measured in dollars per acre ... well, if $10.00 an acre is an interesting difference in this measure, it coincides with a .0011 times ten or approximately a 1% difference in cotton share. And by the way, I notice that when we look ahead to the other equations, we see that soil quality ceases to be statistically significant.

Historian. Yes; this variable seems to be in the models more for the sake of the other independent variables than for itself. That is, we can say that these models show the relevance of the other variables having controlled for differences in soil quality. So what would you conclude about equation (1) as a whole?

Student. I guess it didn't really explain much.

Historian. Much of what?

Student. Much of the variance in proportion of acreage devoted to cotton.

Historian. I agree. Now on to equation (2)!

Student. Equation (2) considers the effect of farm size (IA, improved acres) on the cotton share, controlling for soil quality. Farm size is hugely significant in a statistical sense since the t-ratio is 21.6. The sign of the regression coefficient makes sense: it's saying that as farm size increases, the proportion of the land planted in cotton also increases.

Now let me see if I can figure out that .00034, the regression coefficient. If farm size jumps by 100 acres, the coefficient implies that cotton share rises by (.00034 × 100), which is .034 or 3.4%, on average. For farms 1000 acres larger, that would be 34%. I would say that this model (2) predicts that large plantations have a significantly greater portion of their corn-cotton land planted to cotton than small farms.

Historian. Will farm size (IA, improved acres) retain this effect when we add in the variables that measure the number of consumers the farm must support and the labor available to create the product? Maybe (3) and (4) will tell us.

Student. Equations (3) and (4) say that farm size (IA) remains statistically significant and large enough to be practically important even when the authors include all of the variables they are considering.

Historian. I think you're right. But here's something puzzling. Compare equations (1) and (3). I'm seeing an effect similar to the interaction between age and exercise in that hypothetical weight-height example that you studied last night. In the first equation, soil quality was statistically significant but in the third equation it is not. In fact, a t-ratio less than 1 means that the average error expected in this coefficient because of sampling is actually greater than the coefficient itself. Why should the effect of soil quality go away in the presence of farm size? Here's a hint: that disappearance of significance implies that soil quality may have been operating on cotton share through farm size.

Student. You mean that once we add farm size in as a variable, in equation (3), the effect of soil quality disappears?

Historian. Right. Now why would that have happened? What does it mean in commonsense terms?

Student. Let's see ... a large soil quality index must be associated with large farm size, which in turn is associated with large cotton share. Once size is accounted for, soil quality is no longer important.... I don't know. I can't see what you're driving at.

Historian. Well, one plausible explanation for this phenomenon might be that larger farms were more heavily capitalized so that soil quality, since it is really a name for adjusted farm value, would indeed go up with size.

Student. Are you saying that Wright and Kunreuther don't really have a good way to measure soil quality?

Historian. I think so. Certainly their soil-quality variable is correlated with their farm-size variable. What else is striking about equations (3) and (4)?

Student. Hey! Look how small the R^2 values are for these models! That means that none of the four equations explains much of the variation in cotton share which actually occurred in the sample data. The best is (4), but it only gets R^2 up to explaining 9.7% of the variance.

Historian. The authors mention this and suggest that one cause might be that they are using data aggregated over such a diverse geographic area. Another way to say that would be to state that the regression models should have had another independent variable, a geographic one. Then the effects of the independent variables such as farm size could have been observed taking location into account. So what do you make of that?

Student. You've pointed out that when we add additional variables to a regression model, it is possible for previously significant variables to become unimportant—that's what happened with the Soil Quality variable. If the R^2 is small in all four models, and if, as the authors admit, there are important variables missing, then how do we know that farm size won't vanish in significance as soon as geographic region (or something else) is taken into consideration?

Historian. A very shrewd comment. Now can you briefly summarize Table 7.7 using the checklist you read about?

Student.

(1) Soil quality loses statistical significance in the presence of the other variables, but the other three variables are significant in all four equations.

(2) We had some questions about the quality of the data sources and were especially uneasy about the possibility of systematic biases in the original census records.

(3) All the variables have the signs that were predicted.

(4) The coefficient on IA is large enough to have practical importance. The others are questionable.

(5) R^2 is very small.

(6) Important variables may have been omitted. You mentioned geographical region. Also, how about some measure of each farm's access to markets?

(7) Two of the independent variables may be correlated: Soil Quality and IA.

Historian. Excellent summary. By the way, I have a hunch that two other variables may be correlated: POP/IA and LBR/IA, because if the farmer had a large family or a number of hired workers living on the farm, this would increase the size of both variables. Well, now you must ask how convincing Table 7.7's regression evidence is in support of the predictions made by Wright and Kunreuther's model. But it's time for my next class. Would you stop by tomorrow and give me a brief written evaluation of how the regression evidence speaks to the authors' idea of a safety-first strategy?

Student. Okay professor. That table wasn't quite as hard to interpret as I thought it would be.

7.9   Conclusion

We've tried to emphasize one cardinal point in our discussion of regression analysis: For all the machinery of slope coefficients, standard errors, and the like, a regression equation is nothing more than a simple model of reality. We think that in the field of history, regression comes in handiest when a scholar wants to analyze time-series data (as Claudia Goldin did) or when he or she wants to sort out the most important explanatory factors from the less important (as Wright and Kunreuther were trying to do).

With this chapter on regression analysis, you have made the acquaintance of the statistical procedures and tests that you will most often encounter as a reader of quantitative history. When you come across procedures not covered in this book, such as Guttman scaling or Spearman's coefficient of rank-order correlation, we think that you will be able to figure them out by consulting a standard statistics text.

The final chapter of our book consists of a reprinted historical essay that we invite you to analyze for yourself. We have interrupted the flow of the author's argument occasionally to explain a statistical procedure not covered earlier or to ask a few questions. Good luck!

Terms Introduced in Chapter 7

7.2 linear regression
7.2 y-intercept
7.2 slope coefficient
7.2 dependent variable
7.2 independent variable, predictor variable, explanatory variable
7.2 predictive model
7.2 explanatory model
7.5 multiple regression
7.7 Beta
7.7 standard variables, standardization

7.10   Answers to Questions

1. (a) They are interested in the economic effect on the family of having children in school as opposed to employed in the labor market. There may not have been a significant market for the

labor of young girls at the turn of the century so the economic effect of the different decisions would not have shown up as strongly for girls as for boys.

(b) Children ages 10–14 would be old enough to work but not so old that a substantial number would have left home to strike out on their own.

(c) A child's role, being at work or in school, might be dependent on a sibling's role. A family might choose to have one child go to work and have another in school. The authors wanted their observations to be independent so they restricted their sample to families that had only one child in the 10–14 age range.

(d) Guest and Tolnay wanted to count the total number of children ever born to the mothers so they restricted their sample to families with a high probability of having reached their final size.

2. Larger families would be more likely to have more than one child in the age range 10–14, so the no-sibling rule would tend to put a higher proportion of smaller families into the sample than you would find in the general population. Also, the boy-only rule would bias the sample in favor of families with more boys than girls. A family with many boys would be more likely to have a boy in the 10–14 age range than a family with only one or two boys. In addition, some women over 40 would not have completed their childbearing, so the sample might understate the size of families.

3. Since the sample comprises households that include one and only one boy aged 10 to 14, you can think of the unit of analysis as being either the household or the boy. The authors speak of a sample of boys.

4. Stratified sampling.

5. CEB is the dependent variable.

6. (a) No relationship between the variables—i.e., knowing a person's score on one variable would be no particular help if you wanted to guess his score on the other.

(b) There appears to be some relationship between the variables, but not a very close one. Knowing the score on one variable would be of some help in guessing the score on the second.

(c) The two variables are closely related; knowing the score on one would help you greatly in guessing the score on the second.

7. Their preliminary analysis showed substantially different relationships between children's roles and fertility among rural and urban families. Lumping all the families together would have masked these differences.

8. The line crosses the y-axis at 7.411. As for a slope of $-.226$, the fact that it is negative means that the two variables are negatively correlated: one declines as the other grows. As you can tell from examining Figure 7.2, the size of the coefficient .226 indicates that the y-variable declines by .226 for each one-unit increase in the x-variable.

9. It means that the families in the sample with sons who attended school for six months had, on average, about six children ever born.

10. CEB $= 7.411 - (.226 \times 5) = 6.281$.

11. (a) A decline in CEB of .904. (b) An increase in CEB of 1.356.

12. It's positive.

13. True. As you learned in Chapter 6, when R is positive, that means that the least-squares line runs uphill. The phrase "the line runs uphill" means that an increase in the x-value is associated with an increase in the y-value. Because of this, students sometimes confuse the correlation coefficient with the slope coefficient—they mistakenly think that R is the slope coefficient.

14. You might claim that with more children to feed, a family might be less able to keep its sons in school, more in need of whatever income they could bring in. Thus higher fertility (measured by CEB) might cause a reduction in Months in School. The point is that a regression equation is only as convincing as the interpretive model that undergirds it.

15. Yes.

16. If you look at the height of the regression line above 68 inches, then using the scale on the vertical axis, you might estimate that height to be about 136 to 144 pounds.

17. On the regression line, every one-unit change in height yields an increase in weight of 4.7 pounds. Because the line rises 4.7 units for every one unit move to the right, we say its slope is 4.7.

18. By substituting 68 for H and solving the equation for W, we get an estimate of the average weight of 140.6 pounds.

19. An explanatory model.

20. Table 7.1 presents several regression models; R^2 varies between 2.7% and 9.7%. In Table 7.2, one R^2 listed is quite high, 61%; the other is 1%.

21. R^2 will be small when R is small. You saw in Chapter 6 that R will be small when the scatterplot is quite nonlinear, say a sharply bent curve. Also, extreme outliers from a roughly linear cloud of points can make the R small.

22. R^2 could not say anything about the sign of R (which is the same as the sign of b) because squaring a number yields a positive number whether we start with a positive or negative number. The size of b has to do with how steep the regression line is. The size of R has to do with how tightly the points are clustered around a line. Those pieces of information are independent of one another.

23. It's a sample of rural families with one boy aged 10–14 and no other children in this age-range, with both parents present and the mother over 40 years of age. But Guest and Tolnay are really making the claim that their regression model or a similar one very probably applies to rural families generally that have at least one child in this age range.

24. In a sentence, the equation is telling you that this particular regression model doesn't help you understand a thing. To elaborate: The equation says that families whose boys were in school for no months of the year have an average CEB of 7.411, and families whose boys attended for six months also had an average CEB of 7.411. So did families with boys who were in school eight, ten, and twelve months. The model is <u>not</u> saying that all these families had an identical CEB—only that knowing the variable Months in School doesn't improve your ability to predict CEB. So the equation is telling you that you need a better model involving different explanatory variables.

25. Because the characteristics of each sample would have been slightly different due to the luck of the draw.

26. It means that there is <u>some</u> mathematical relationship between the two variables—that knowing the independent variable is of some help in predicting the size of the dependent variable. Of course, it does not necessarily mean that the relationship is historically interesting or important.

27. The sample b is 4.7 SEs from zero, and that means a confidence level greater than 99.99%. From Chapter 5 recall that this ratio, the slope coefficient divided by its standard error, is known as a t-score or t-ratio.

28. There is a greater chance that it is close to the sample b.

29. Yes for the rural model, no for the urban. The urban b is less than one SE from zero.

30. They make sense if you buy the authors' suggestion that families whose children spend more time in school will be smaller than families whose children spend less time in school. In the equations, as months in school go up, the number of children goes down.

31. In the rural equation, the slope coefficient is big enough to have a meaningful effect on family size. If child A spends four more months in school than child B, then the number of A's siblings is predicted to be about one fewer than the number of B's siblings. In the urban equation, even a ten-month difference will not yield more than a half-child average difference in family size.

32. The rural R^2 is small but not zero. If you say that children's time spent in school explains 5% of the variation in family size, you may not have fully explained variation in family size but you have at least pointed to a factor with an observable impact on family size. In the urban equation, however, the R^2 is so small as to suggest that variations in Months in School have no relevance to variations in CEB. Would you bother saying you had explained less than one half of one percent of something?

33. It looks as though there may be some connection between months of schooling and family size in the case of the rural families in the study. It is not necessary to conclude from that, however, that rural families consciously decided to have fewer children because they were going to be in school. Both small family size and increased schooling could be the result of general social trends occurring in the region at that time. If there is a causal connection, it could even run the other way, with family size as the causal variable and months in school as the dependent variable. Small families might be better able to afford to send children to school, after all.

The regression equation for urban children shows no evidence of any connection between the variables studied.

35. CEB = $5.300 - (.013 \times \text{Months}) - (.217 \times \text{FW} \times 10^{-3})$. (We've abbreviated the names of the two independent variables.)

36. It means that for every increase of $1000 in a father's wealth, on average there was a decline of .217 in children ever born (while holding constant the other variable in the equation, Months in School).

37. Since the families' wealth was the same, you can ignore that term entirely. Multiply the Months in School coefficient, $-.013$, by three months (the difference in schooling between the boys in the two families) to find that the predicted difference in number of children is .039, or about four one-hundredths of a child—hardly a striking difference.

38. You plug in the numbers and get these equations:

$$
\begin{aligned}
\text{CEB(A)} &= 5.288 - (.008 \times 5) - (.196 \times 7450 \times 10^{-3}) \\
&\quad + (.127 \times 0) \\
&= 5.288 - .04 - 1.4602 + 0 \\
&= 3.786 \text{ children ever born;}
\end{aligned}
$$

$$
\begin{aligned}
\text{CEB(B)} &= 5.288 - (.008 \times 5) - (.196 \times 2100 \times 10^{-3}) \\
&\quad + (.127 \times 1) \\
&= 5.288 - .04 - .4116 + .127 \\
&= 4.9634 \text{ children ever born.}
\end{aligned}
$$

39. It means that an increase in schooling of one month for the son aged 10–14 is associated, on average, with a decline of .008 in the number of children ever born per family, when Father's Wealth and Son's Employment are held constant.

40. Not at all. In equation 1 the coefficient, $-.226$, has to do with differences in the number of children per month of schooling for all families in the rural sample. In equation 3, the coefficient $-.008$ estimates difference in the number of children per month of schooling for families in the rural sample that have the same score on both Father's Wealth and Son's Employment. Looking at the equations together tells you that schooling may have been an important factor in determining family size, but that much of its importance, in this made-up example, was due to the fact that wealthier families were better able to keep their sons in school.

41. You would almost certainly want to drop Months in School. The explanatory power of this variable in model 1 turns out to be accounted for by the other two variables added in models 2 and 3. In addition to its lack of explanatory power, the coefficient $-.008$ is much closer than one standard error to zero, so there is no good evidence that in the entire population, the coefficient is other than zero.

42. A regression line is the one line that best summarizes the time-series data as a whole, in the same sense that the mean value summarizes a list of numbers. Another way to say this is that the regression line is simultaneously closer (in a least-squares sense) to all points in the time series than any other line would be. What this means in the case of Figure 7.7 is that the regression line summarizes the overall trend while ignoring the short-term fluctuations in the time-series line. As for the regression equation, it is the linear equation whose graph is the straight line shown in Figure 7.7.

43. The title to Figure 7.7 speaks of "participation rates"; this implies that Goldin had an estimate of the number of female heads of household in Philadelphia in various years (probably from city directories) and an estimate of the number of such women who actually were employed. Her data list might have had four columns: the first column listing the years, a second column for number of female household heads in each year, a third for number of such women in the labor force, and a fourth for the participation rate in each year (column three divided by column two).

While Goldin used great care in arriving at her estimates and describes her procedure in the article, you should remember that the participation rates shown in Figure 7.7 and used to generate the regression equation are perhaps less precisely known than the figure suggests. You might ask such questions as: How complete a listing of women household heads did the city directories provide? Did completeness vary from one directory to another? Would these sources have had some systematic bias?

44. This term means that a one-year change in the independent variable, Time, is associated with a decline of 0.0028 in the dependent variable, Labor Force Participation Rate. Another way to express 0.0028 is 0.28%. Multiplying both Time and Labor Force Participation Rate by 10, the equation tells us that Labor Force Participation Rate declined by a little less than 3% with each passing decade. Since Figure 7.7 shows a seventy-year period, you can check that conclusion by multiplying 3% times seven decades. You ought to see the regression line drop about 21 percentage points from one end of the figure to the other, and indeed, you do—it drops from about 55% in 1791 to about 35% in 1860.

45. The minus sign on the slope coefficient tells you that Labor Force Participation Rate and Time are negatively correlated: as one rises, the other falls. In particular, as Time rises (i.e., as the years go by), Labor Force Participation Rate falls. The regression line in Figure 7.7 shows that relationship quite clearly.

46. Figure 7.7 doesn't give the sample size or the SE for either coefficient in the regression equation. But the t-statistics were calculated by using those numbers along with the coefficients. As a rule of thumb, remember that the chance is exceedingly small (far less than 1%) that Goldin could have gotten t-values of size 16.26 and 3.20 if there were in fact no relationship between time and labor-force participation rates in the population of Philadelphia's female heads of households. T-values of this size immediately tell you that the regression coefficients are statistically significant.

47. It means that this simple regression model accounts for 31% of the variance in the dependent variable, Labor Force Participation Rate. Figure 7.7 itself helps explain what this is all about. The regression model works quite well at describing the long-term decline in women's labor-force participation, but it isn't much good at accounting for the fluctuations in the time-series line. The time-series points bounce all over, above and below the regression line. This bouncing around, the short-term rise or decline in women's

labor-force participation, cannot be accounted for by the regression model, which, after all, has only one explanatory variable: Time. To explain more of the variance, Goldin would need to experiment with additional variables in the model. Of course, she wasn't using the regression model as an explanatory model but as a device for spotting the trend in her time-series data.

48. Goldin herself remarks, "The surge of demand in the period of American neutrality during the Napoleonic Wars generated the high figures from 1796 to about 1804, and the commercial crisis of 1818 to 1820 had the opposite effect, one of lowering employment figures to their nadir in 1822."[14] Note that if one wanted to use the regression model as an explanatory model rather than as a summary of the time series, one might boost R^2 above 31% by adding some quantitative measure of the overall performance of the economy to the regression equation.

49. Prindle's implied null hypothesis is that the variables are not related at all—that any apparent relationship might plausibly be accounted for by chance.

50. The statement "$p < .001$" means that there is less than a 0.1% probability that a Beta as far from zero as .71 could have been attained by chance. That is, the p-value suggests that there was very probably some real relationship between the variables and raises the possibility that that relationship may have been of historical interest. In the second model, we interpret the phrase "not significant" as meaning that the p-value was greater than .05—i.e., the probability was greater than 5% that a Beta score of 0.07 or larger could have occurred simply by chance. Prindle could have provided a clearer picture to his readers if he had simply given the precise p-values for both these regression models. In the second model, was p something like .05, or was it .25? The trouble with using notations like "$p < .001$," "highly significant," or "not significant" is that it implies to the reader that some magic threshold p-value exists. This is not so. Whether p is .00001 or .10, determining how acceptable the results are is a matter for the historian and the reader to judge. Judgment always enters into the situation.

---

[14]Goldin, "The Economic Status of Women in the Early Republic," 390–91.

51. **(1)** The regression coefficient is statistically very significant for the Republican equation. This is shown by the phrase "p < .001" where p is the probability of getting a beta as far from zero as .71, the slope coefficient in the standardized equation. The author states that the slope coefficient in the Democratic equation is not significant. There's not much purpose in pursuing the Democratic equation beyond this point.

(2) As noted, the data list must have consisted of county-level census data and voting returns for the years in question. Presumably the author either knew or was able to estimate the size of the population over age 21.

(3) In the Republican equation the sign of the regression coefficient is positive; that makes sense because it means that a greater turnout in the early period predicts a greater turnout in the later period.

(4) Since this equation seems to have been calculated from a standardized list of numbers, the Beta gives us no intuitive sense of the practical importance for the dependent variable of a unit change in the predictor variable. Perhaps the author could have given us both Beta and b.

(5) R^2 is remarkably large for a one-predictor equation and is certainly large for historical data. It says that the model can explain over 60% of the variation in later turnouts by the county patterns of turnout in the earlier period.

52. Yes. Since R^2 is .61, R itself must be about .78; this means that the scatterplot of points is clustered quite closely about the regression line and the line would be a good predictive model with which to approximate voting patterns in the 1936–40 period.

53. No. Beta is not significantly different from zero. That means that knowledge of the independent variable, 1916–20 turnout, provides no help in predicting 1936–40 turnout for Democrats.

54. Prindle claims that the two equations provide some support for the idea that substantial party switching did not take place. First, the pattern of Republican support was too well sustained from one period to the next. The Democratic pattern, by contrast, was not sustained at all. The level of Democratic support in a given

county in 1916–20 was of no help in guessing the support in 1936–
40. Taking the two equations together, it is easier to believe that
new voters were behind the Roosevelt sweep than to believe that
many Republicans switched to the Democrats.

IV PUTTING IT TOGETHER

8 Georgia Farmers Shift to Cotton After the Civil War

In this chapter:

8.1 The Historical Problem
8.2 David Weiman's Article
8.3 Answers to Questions

This chapter is quite different from the others in this book. Instead of being introduced to new statistical ideas or techniques, you will be asked to read and comment on an article which uses many of the methods you have already encountered. In particular:

- In David F. Weiman's article below you will run into: averages, percentages, crosstabulations, regression models, confidence and significance levels, R^2, t-statistics, and arguments explicitly in the form of statistical hypothesis testing.

- Your task is to see how these ideas function, how they fit into Weiman's argument. Are they essential to his conclusions? How strong a case do they enable the author to make?

- In order to be clear about the role the statistical methods play in Weiman's discussion, you need to be clear about what the tables say, the source of their information, and the author's purpose in including them.

- We have inserted questions throughout the article so you can stop from time to time and test your own understanding by analyzing and commenting on what you have read.

- There are additional questions at the end of the chapter which make use of Weiman's article as a place for more practice in applying statistics to the study of history.

8.1 The Historical Problem

In the 1970s and 1980s, a significant historical controversy has erupted over changes in Southern agriculture in the period following the Civil War.[1] David F. Weiman's 1985 article considers one of the major questions raised about the agricultural economy of the postbellum South: the

---

[1] See the works cited in Chapter 7, footnote 1. See also Stephen DeCanio, "Cotton 'Overproduction' in Late Nineteenth Century Southern Agriculture," *Journal of*

shift away from subsistence agriculture and into cotton as a commercial crop.

Weiman wants to explain apparently irrational aspects of the agricultural revolution in the South during the Reconstruction period. In spite of an oversupply of cotton and falling prices from 1866 to 1880, per capita production of corn and hogs fell while the relative production of cotton went up. This historical problem has come up earlier in this book—twice, in fact. Section 3.4 introduced the work of Ransom and Sutch, who explored the roots of post-Civil War Southern poverty. Later in Chapter 3 and in Chapter 7, we used an article by Wright and Kunreuther that asked why Southern farmers relied more and more heavily on cotton as a cash crop, even in the face of falling cotton prices and limited demand.

Weiman focuses on the integration of Georgia Upcountry farmers into the cotton economy. Prior to the war they had practiced diversified subsistence farming and domestic manufacture. He interprets their increased cotton specialization and declining production of food as resulting from the development of transportation and marketing institutions that allowed these farmers access to national and world markets. He emphasizes regionally distinct mechanisms for the shift into cotton, arguing that the process was driven by different forces in the Upcountry and in the Cotton Belt. In the Upcountry, cotton specialization involved the new inclusion of farmers who had previously been excluded from the cotton market, while in the Cotton Belt the shift to cotton was the result of the emancipation of slaves.

Weiman begins with crosstabulations to make the case that before the Civil War, regions of Georgia differed with respect to size of slaveholdings, acreage of farms, and farm output. He argues that these differences cannot be entirely accounted for by geographic factors such as climate and soil type. Then he presents a second set of crosstabulations to show the growing concentration on cotton in each region after the Civil War.

The timing of the shift to cotton is important for Weiman's argument. He wants to show that the major shift occurred after 1870 during a period of falling cotton prices. But that same period was one of rapidly expanding merchandising and commercial centers and railroad networks. He uses a regression equation to support his argument about the timing.

Economic History, 33 (September 1973), 608–33; and Jonathan M. Wiener, "Class Structure and Economic Development in the American South, 1865–1955," *American Historical Review*, 84 (October 1979), 970–92. David F. Weiman's article, reprinted below but with many footnotes omitted, cites a great many other books and articles in this debate.

He makes use of a second regression equation to show that the pattern of cotton specialization in the Upcountry was quite distinct from that in the Cotton Belt.

8.2 David Weiman's Article

The Economic Emancipation of the Non-Slaveholding Class: Upcountry Farmers in the Georgia Cotton Economy

David F. Weiman

Reprinted from *Journal of Economic History*, 45 (March 1985), 71–93. The author's abstract and many footnotes have been omitted, while the numbered questions and answers have been added.

In 1914, Robert Preston Brooks offered perhaps the first systematic analysis of the impact of the Civil War and emancipation on the Southern cotton economy. His study of Georgia examined familiar issues: "the destruction of the old order of master and slave, the fall of the plantation system, [and] the rise of former slaves to the position of free laborers, tenants, and landowners."

In contrast to many recent studies, however, Brooks recognized that the "readjustment" to the war and emancipation had "not been uniform in all sections of the state." "The agrarian revolution of the postbellum period," Brooks observed, "has been more profound and conspicuous in the Black Belt than elsewhere," since these regions had the largest concentrations of plantations and farms with slaves during the antebellum period. Yet, as Brooks noted, these changes extended beyond the boundaries of the plantation districts (referred to as the Cotton Belt in this article) into the region known as the Upcountry, which had been inhabited mostly by self-sufficient, white farm households before the Civil War. During Reconstruction, farm communities in the Upcountry evolved a "labor system" distinct from that in the Cotton Belt. The Upcountry farms became thoroughly integrated into the cotton economy and, in turn, into national and world markets. Hence, Brooks included "the economic emancipation of the non-slaveholding class" in his list of significant developments in the postbellum period.

The economic transformation of Upcountry Georgia is consistent with the trend of increasing specialization in cotton and declining food crop production, documented in the works of Ransom and Sutch, and Wright and Kunreuther. Regional differences in the readjustment to the war and emancipation also explain the recent findings of Peter Temin that relate changes in the levels and composition of crop output across counties in Reconstruction Georgia to the racial composition of the population. An analysis of the integration of Upcountry farmers into the cotton economy during Reconstruction reinforces the conclusion, for it identifies the specific factors that induced Upcountry farmers to shift to cotton after the Civil War and that, in turn, limited their involvement in the antebellum market system.

This article explains why Upcountry farmers moved from self-sufficiency to specialization in cotton after the Civil War. It also explains the impact of the antebellum plantation system on the Southern yeomanry.

ECONOMIC REGIONS OF ANTEBELLUM GEORGIA

Figure 8.1 identifies the principal economic regions in the cotton economy of antebellum Georgia. The core of its plantation economy was located in the Lower Piedmont and the Central Cotton Belt which together formed the Cotton Belt. The regions were well suited to cotton culture because of their moderate climate, relatively fertile soil, and level-to-rolling terrain. They were directly linked to coastal ports through an extensive system of interior rivers. These natural factors reduced the costs of producing and shipping cotton to export markets and enabled producers to cultivate cotton without making large investments in internal improvements.

Cotton could be grown in the Upper Piedmont and in the Appalachian Valley (except in the extreme northern counties), although these lands were more marginal. The cooler climate shortened the growing season and increased the risk of early frosts. The hillier terrain was more difficult to till and was vulnerable to erosion. In addition, counties in the Upcountry were located considerably above the fall line, and they contained few navigable rivers which isolated them from coastal ports. Planters and more prosperous commercial farmers bypassed these regions as they moved west. Instead, the Upcountry was settled by an independent yeomanry, who established a diversified system of production based on household self-sufficiency. Although Upcountry farmers regularly cultivated cash crops, which often included small amounts of cotton, they remained on the periphery of the market system and the cotton economy throughout the antebellum period.

The division between Cotton Belt and Upcountry counties occurred throughout the lower South, but was most clearly drawn in Georgia.

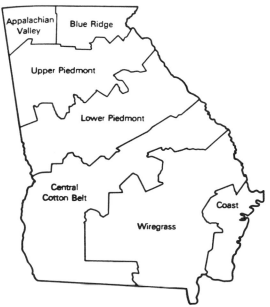

Figure 8.1
Economic Regions of Georgia

Regional differences in Georgia can therefore be discerned using the county data from the decennial census. Tables 8.1 through 8.3 compare the size distribution of slaveholdings and of farms and the levels and composition of farm production in the Cotton Belt and Upcountry for the year 1860. Additionally, they provide a reference point for the subsequent analysis of economic changes in each region during Reconstruction.

Numerous studies, beginning with those of Frank Owsley and his students, have demonstrated that plantations based on slave labor did not displace small farmers onto the periphery of the Cotton Belt. Yet, despite the intermingling of planters and farmers in the region, the size distribution of slaveholdings and of improved acreage holdings (presented in Tables 8.1 and 8.2) reveal the considerable geographical segregation between slaveholders (planters and farmers) and the non-slaveholding yeomanry. In the Cotton Belt one-half of the free households owned slaves, and slaveholdings were concentrated among planters and owners of large farms. In the Upcountry slave ownership was relatively uncommon; three-quarters of the slaveholders owned fewer than ten slaves. Similarly, over 50 percent of the farms in the Cotton Belt contained at least 100 improved acres, as compared to only 30 percent in Upcountry counties.

Table 8.1
Size distribution of slaveholdings, economic regions of Georgia, 1860

	Percentage of Slaveholders with					% of Households with 0 Slaves
	1–4 Slaves	5–9 Slaves	10–14 Slaves	15–49 Slaves	50 plus Slaves	
Appalachian Valley	52.6	25.7	11.0	9.9	0.8	80.7
Upper Piedmont	52.4	24.3	10.5	12.0	0.7	75.5
Lower Piedmont	37.9	23.5	12.3	23.0	3.4	43.1
Central Cotton Belt	39.9	22.5	11.5	21.6	4.4	52.0

Source: U.S. Census Office, Eighth Census, 1860, vol. 3, *Agriculture of the United States in 1860* (Washington, D.C., 1864), pp. 224–27, and vol. 4, *Statistics of the United States (Including Mortality, Property, &c.) in 1860* (Washington, D.C., 1866), p. 341.

Table 8.2
Size distribution of farms by improved acreage, economic regions of Georgia, 1860

	Percentage of Farms with				
	3 to 19 Acres	20 to 49 Acres	50 to 99 Acres	100 to 499 Acres	500 plus Acres
Appalachian Valley	4.6	32.2	34.0	28.3	0.9
Upper Piedmont	7.7	31.4	31.5	28.0	1.5
Lower Piedmont	3.0	14.4	21.2	48.9	12.4
Central Cotton Belt	4.0	18.4	24.7	41.2	11.7

Source: U.S. Census Office, Eighth Census, 1860, vol. 3, *Agriculture of the United States in 1860*, p. 196.

1.   Briefly state what Weiman intends to accomplish in this paper.

2.   Does Table 8.1 summarize information obtained from a sample or an entire population? To what "individuals" does Table 8.1 refer? Is Weiman going to restrict himself to describing the characteristics of just those individuals on whom Table 8.1 is based or is he going to extend his argument to some larger group?

3. What percentage of all households in the Appalachian Valley had 50 or more slaves? What is the comparable percentage for the Central Cotton Belt?

4. Compare the Upper and Lower Piedmont with respect to the percentage of all families holding 5 to 9 slaves.

5. Does Table 8.1 raise any question about statistical significance or common-sense historical significance?

6. To what "individuals" does Table 8.2 refer?

7. What is the ratio of the proportion of 500-plus acre farms in the Central Cotton Belt to the comparable percentage in the Appalachian Valley?

8. Was the number of farms of 3 to 19 acres smaller in the Lower Piedmont or in the Appalachian Valley?

9. Briefly summarize the point that Table 8.1 and Table 8.2 make and explain how this point fits into Weiman's argument.

   The output of food crops and cotton per capita among the rural population indicates the levels of production for self-sufficiency and for market on Upcountry and Cotton Belt farms. As shown in Table 8.3, levels of food crop production, measured in corn-equivalent bushels, were roughly comparable in Cotton Belt and Upcountry counties except for counties located in the Appalachian Valley. The composition of food crops, however, varied according to region. Upcountry farmers cultivated somewhat larger quantities of wheat and small grains, while in the Cotton Belt, corn, sweet potatoes, and peas and beans formed the main staples of the rural diet. In addition to producing abundant supplies of food, farmers and planters in the Cotton Belt also cultivated relatively large crops of cotton, between 0.9 and 1.2 bales per capita of the rural population. In contrast, yeoman farmers in the Upper Piedmont cultivated only a third of a bale per capita, and almost no cotton was produced in the Appalachian Valley in 1860.

10. Describe how the numbers in Table 8.3 might have been obtained. That is, what numbers may have been available at what level (farm-level? state-level?) and how were they put together to get Table 8.3? Were all of the numbers in Table 8.3 arrived at in essentially the same way or do you note considerable differences in the nature of the sources?

Table 8.3
Levels of per capita farm output (of rural population), economic regions of Georgia, 1860

	Corn	Grains	Food Crops	Net Food Supply	Cotton	Home Manufactures
Appalachian Valley	41.9	50.9	53.1	38.1	0.09	$2.0
Upper Piedmont	30.1	37.2	39.7	25.0	0.34	$2.5
Lower Piedmont	30.5	34.3	38.2	23.6	0.91	$1.0
Central Cotton Belt	36.3	37.6	43.3	28.1	1.23	$1.0

Notes: The rural population is defined as the total population less the population living in cities with at least 2,500 people.

Units for Corn: bushels.

Grains (corn, wheat, rye and oats): corn-equivalent bushels based on the nutritional value of each crop relative to corn. Food crops (grains, potatoes, and peas and beans): corn-equivalent bushels. Net food supply (food crops less seed and feed requirements for draft animals): corn-equivalent bushels.

Cotton: 400-pound bales.

Sources: U.S. Census Office, Eighth Census, 1860, vol. 1, *Population of the United States in 1860* (Washington, D.C., 1865), pp. 55–56, 120–30, and vol. 3, *Agriculture of the United States in 1860*, pp. 22–29.

11. What two types of farm output show the greatest contrast between the Upper and Lower Piedmont?

12. In the Central Cotton Belt, was the farm output of corn shown in Table 8.3 greater than or less than the output shown for cotton?

13. Identify two or three patterns in the numbers of Table 8.3 that are important for the point Weiman is making at this stage in his argument.

The lower levels of crop production, and more generally of agricultural production, in the Upcountry can be partially explained by the larger share of household labor devoted to domestic manufacturing and other nonagricultural activities. Although census agents often ignored or undervalued these forms of production, even the reported levels of domestic manufacturing indicate their importance to the household economy on Upcountry farms, as well as the greater extent of self-sufficient production in the region.

The distinct system of farm production in the Cotton Belt and Upcountry may account for other important differences in the economy and society of the two regions, such as the racial composition of the rural population and the levels and composition of wealth holdings. However, as is often assumed, these structural differences cannot simply be reduced to soil or ecological conditions in each region. Although climate, soil quality, and topography exerted an important influence on regional development, in the Upper and lower Piedmont differences in natural conditions were not pronounced. The growing season in the Upper Piedmont, for example, averaged only a week less than in the lower Piedmont and exceeded the requirement for cotton cultivation by more than two weeks.

Geographical isolation from interior and coastal markets, it seems, confined farmers in the Upper Piedmont to a marginal position in the antebellum cotton economy. The higher cost of transportation adversely affected the terms of trade for staple producers in the Upcountry. Also, merchants purchased cotton from their customers at substantial discounts to account for the risks of costly delays or of damage to shipments en route to coastal ports. While transportation improvements would have narrowed price differentials between the Upper Piedmont and coastal markets, railroad construction in Georgia essentially followed the contours of the Cotton Belt.

The one exception to this generalization was the state-financed Western and Atlantic Railroad, which in 1851 provided a long-awaited rail connection between coastal ports in Georgia and South Carolina and the Midwest. The railroad passed through the western half of the Upper Piedmont, an area known as the Cherokee Territory, and the Appalachian Valley. In the decade after its completion, cotton production in the Cherokee Territory increased from 0.33 to 0.57 bales per capita of the rural population. Producers in this region also shipped large quantities of corn, wheat, and pork to Atlanta. Not surprisingly, in the Georgia Upcountry urban and commercial development and slave population were concentrated in the Cherokee Territory.

REGIONAL PATTERNS OF SPECIALIZATION IN COTTON

According to the recent studies by Ransom and Sutch, and Wright and Kunreuther, farmers throughout the Cotton South specialized more in cotton after the Civil War. The shift to cotton, they argue, caused the decline in food production on Southern farms and increased the dependence of farm households on interregional trade for their food supplies. Regional statistics on crop production for Georgia over the period 1860 to 1880 provide evidence for these claims.

Estimates of the crop mix which is the ratio of cotton to corn production are presented in Table 8.4 and indicate that farmers in all of the principal cotton-growing regions of the state almost certainly allocated more labor and tilled acreage to the staple crop during Reconstruction. The largest shift in farm production (as measured by this index) occurred in the Upcountry and reflects the rapid spread of the cotton culture into this region after the Civil War. However, even in the Cotton Belt farmers substantially increased their cotton production relative to food crops.

Table 8.4
Changes in the crop mix, 1860 to 1880, economic regions of Georgia (bales of cotton per thousand bushels of corn)

	1860	1870	1875[a]	1880
Appalachian Valley	1.9	1.8	7.2	9.4
Upper Piedmont	11.2	10.2	23.4	34.0
Lower Piedmont	29.7	b	44.1	57.9
Central Cotton Belt	34.0	b	45.3	60.0

a: Estimates of the crop mix are derived from the statistics on crop acreage reported in the state census of agriculture in 1875 and crop yields per acre in 1880 in the federal census of agriculture.

b: Because of the deficiencies of the 1870 census, I have omitted estimates of the crop mix in the Cotton Belt.

Sources: U.S. Census Office, Eighth Census, 1860, vol. 3, *Agriculture of the United States in 1860*, pp. 23, 27; Ninth Census, 1870, vol. 3, *The Statistics of Wealth and Industry in the United States* (Washington, D.C., 1872), pp. 120–27; Tenth Census, 1880, vol. 3, *Report on the Production of Agriculture in the United States*, pp. 109–11, 218–20; and Georgia, Department of Agriculture, *Annual Report of the Commissioner of Agriculture* (Atlanta, 1875), pp. 146–47.

14. Between Tables 8.3 and 8.4 Weiman makes an argument that is very much in the spirit of "controlling for a third variable." That argument suggests why it may have been wise not to lump the entire Upcountry into a single averaged geographic region. Find that argument and explain the advantage in keeping the Upper Piedmont and Appalachian Valley separate in these tables even though he is treating them jointly as the "Upcountry" in contrast to the Cotton Belt.

15. Does Table 8.4 say that, between 1860 and 1880, cotton production went up in the Appalachian Valley, or that corn production went down, or what?

16. Divide the four 1875 crop mix numbers in Table 8.4 by their 1860 counterparts. Is there much geographic diversity in the resulting ratios? Now divide the 1880 numbers by those for 1875 and look at the geographic diversity. Were the two time periods alike with respect to how the swings in crop mix varied by region?

17. What is the historical significance of the 1870 crop mix values shown in Table 8.4? Since Weiman couldn't complete the table for the Cotton belt, why didn't he just leave 1870 out altogether?

Table 8.5
Percentage of tilled acreage devoted to cotton, economic regions of Georgia, 1875 and 1880

	1875	1880
Appalachian Valley	10.0	11.9
Upper Piedmont	24.8	30.5
Lower Piedmont	38.1	42.0
Central Cotton Belt	34.2	38.2

Sources: Georgia, Department of Agriculture, *Annual Report of the Commissioner of Agriculture*, pp. 146–47; and U.S. Census Office, Tenth Census, 1880, vol. 3, *Report on the Production of Agriculture in the United States*, pp. 109–11, 218–20.

18. In Table 8.5, divide each 1880 number by the corresponding percentage for 1875. Were swings in cotton share of total acreage similar in the four regions?

19. State two major points suggested by Tables 8.4 and 8.5 that reinforce Weiman's argument.

In the case of Georgia, statistics on crop acreage, collected by the state tax assessors in 1875 and federal census agents in 1880, clarify the nature of the change. Although the state census of agriculture probably underestimates the actual levels of crop acreage in 1875, the share of tilled acreage devoted to cotton (see Table 8.5) is consistent with trends based on crop output. Between 1875 and 1880, Upcountry farmers allocated an additional 120 percent of their tilled acreage to cotton, and in the Cotton Belt cotton acreage increased by 10 percent. Assuming that per acre yields remained constant (at their 1880 levels) over these five years, the increased allocation of acreage to cotton accounted for almost half of the change in the crop mix in both regions during the 1870s.

With the adoption of a more specialized system of farming, production of food crops per capita among the rural population declined sharply in all regions of the state. (The levels of food crop production and esti- mated food supplies in the counties of the Cotton Belt and the Upcoun- try for the years 1860 and 1880 are presented in Tables 8.3 and 8.6.) In the Cotton Belt per capita output of corn, potatoes, and peas and beans fell by 50 percent between 1860 and 1880. Despite increased production of small grains, the food supply available for household consumption was only 11.1 bushels per capita, as compared to 25.6 bushels 20 years earlier. In the Upcountry, food crop production per capita fell by 30 percent between 1860 and 1880. Still, by the end of the period, the residual food supply in Upcountry counties was 18.6 bushels per capita, and the region as a whole was self-sufficient in basic foodstuffs.

Regional analysis of crop production demonstrates that the shift into cotton was not limited geographically to the Southern Piedmont Plateau, as Peter Temin has claimed recently. Farmers in the Central Cotton Belt of Georgia also specialized more narrowly in the production of the staple between 1860 and 1880. Furthermore, an analysis of the data for the five cotton states of the Deep South shows that regions without increased specialization (as measured by the crop mix) were the exception during the period.

Nonetheless, as Temin has pointed out, regional differences in crop output qualify the direct relationship between specialization in cotton and the abandonment of self-sufficiency, as implied by Ransom and Sutch, and Wright and Kunreuther. Because the shift into cotton oc- curred during a period of declining agricultural productivity in the Cot- ton Belt, the per capita output of food crops fell more sharply there than in the Upcountry. Yet, despite the substantial reallocation of farm labor and tilled acreage into staple production, per capita output of cot- ton remained constant or declined over these two decades. (Compare the level of cotton production in 1880 in Table 8.6 with that in 1860 in Table 8.3.) In contrast, Upcountry farmers greatly expanded their pro- duction of cotton in 1880 and were still able to supply sufficient grain and other food to satisfy the subsistence requirements of rural households. Output of cotton per capita in Upcountry counties doubled between 1860 and 1880, and Upcountry farmers accounted for two-thirds of the increased output of cotton in Georgia during the period.

Table 8.6
Per capita levels of farm output (of rural population), economic regions of Georgia, 1880

	Corn	Grains	Food Crops	Net Food Supply	Cotton
Appalachian Valley	29.7	39.6	40.1	27.3	0.27
Upper Piedmont	21.6	28.2	28.8	18.6	0.73
Lower Piedmont	15.6	21.1	22.0	12.3	0.90
Central Cotton Belt	16.2	20.1	21.7	10.1	0.91

Note: See notes to Table 8.3 for definition of rural population.

Sources: U.S. Census Office, Tenth Census, 1880, vol. 1, *Statistics of the Population of the United States* (Washington, D.C., 1883), pp. 55–56; and vol. 3, *Report on the Production of Agriculture in the United States*, pp. 147–48, 183–84.

20. Why has the author expressed Table 8.6 and Table 8.3 in nutritional units (as opposed to a measure like dollar value)?

21. Consider Table 8.6 by itself (not in comparison to some other table) and comment on how its information relates to Weiman's thesis.

Increasing specialization in cotton after the Civil War, then, involved two regionally distinct processes. This explanation—overlooked by Wright and Kunreuther and misinterpreted by Temin—finds empirical support in the pattern of cotton production in the Cotton Belt and Upcountry regions of Georgia for 1880 and reconciles the divergent interpretations of this process implied in the regression analysis of these authors and of Joseph Reid.

When the regression equation explaining the share of tilled acreage in cotton, as specified by Wright and Kunreuther, is used to make estimates for the counties of the Cotton Belt and the Upcountry separately, it distinguishes the cross-sectional pattern of specialization in each region.[2]

---

[2] The regression equation tries to determine the effect of farm size and, in particular, of small farms on specialization in cotton. Using county data, the equation relates the share of tilled acreage in cotton to average farm size and the percentage of small-sized and medium-sized farms, controlling for differences in population density and the rate of tenancy. The estimated regression equations are presented in the Appendix. The results of the analysis differ substantially from those obtained by Wright and Kunreuther. Specialization in cotton is strongly correlated with the rate of tenancy only in Cotton Belt counties and with the percentage of small farms only in Upcountry counties. More generally, a Chow test rejects the hypothesis that the equations for the Cotton Belt and Upcountry were derived from the same underlying sample at a 1 percent confidence level.

In the Cotton Belt, the share of tilled acreage devoted to cotton is strongly correlated with the density of the rural population per improved acre, the percentage of medium-sized farms, and the rate of tenancy. In the Upcountry, however, the degree of specialization in cotton is positively correlated with average farm size and the percentage of small farmers. Temin's cross-sectional analysis of crop production in the Piedmont and Cotton Belt of Reconstruction Georgia affirms the regional difference in specialization in cotton. In counties with a higher density of blacks (located mainly in the Cotton Belt), farmers allocated a larger share of their tilled acreage to cotton, while the degree of specialization decreased with the density of whites per acre (which tended to be higher in Upcountry counties).

> The next few questions pertain to Table 8.9 at the end of the article that Weiman calls Appendix Table 1. That's the regression he has been referring to in the preceding paragraph and in footnote 1. Reread the above paragraph and footnote 1 and look over the table, then try to answer these questions:

22.   To what population does Table 8.9 refer (what are the "individuals" in the population)?

23.   Is Table 8.9 based on measurements of the whole population or of a representative sample?

24.   One of the independent variables in the table is Cotton Yield / Corn Yield. What are those yields? For example, are they the total output per county, per farm, per acre? Is output measured in nutritional units as in earlier tables?

25.   What would you have to know about a county in order to compute a rate of tenancy?

26.   In the first sentence of the preceding paragraph Weiman uses the phrase "the regression equation explaining the share of tilled acreage in cotton." Does he literally mean that the appendix equation explains cotton share? What does he mean?

27.   In footnote 1, Weiman has written, "a Chow test rejects the hypothesis that the equations for the Cotton Belt and Upcountry were derived from the same underlying sample at a 1 percent confidence level." You may have no idea what a Chow test is. Even so, explain what Weiman's sentence means.

28. In Weiman's last paragraph before Question 22 he lists three factors that were strongly correlated with cotton share in the Cotton Belt. Explain how Table 8.9 provides a basis for Weiman's remark.

29. Repeat the previous question, but for Weiman's analogous comment on the Upcountry.

30. The All Counties equation in Table 8.9 must be a fit to the scatterplot of all 87 points, 61 from the Cotton Belt and 26 from the Upcountry. Why does it make sense that the All Counties equation would have a lower R^2 than the Cotton Belt equation?

31. What is the purpose of Table 8.9 in this paper? What is the historical point the author wants to make or defend with those equations?

INTEGRATION OF UPCOUNTRY FARMERS INTO THE COTTON ECONOMY

The shift to cotton and the abandonment of self-sufficiency in the Cotton Belt was more a consequence of emancipation than of the Civil War. Emancipation fundamentally altered the organization of agricultural production and the system of marketing the cotton crop. As the initial experiments with wage labor revealed, the autonomy of blacks undermined the antebellum plantation system of large-scale production that had enabled planters to specialize in cotton while producing enough food to satisfy the subsistence needs of their slaves. Furthermore, emancipation created a class of free, but propertyless agricultural laborers who leased small plots of land, usually for a share of the crop, and borrowed each year from local merchants to finance current production. Tenancy, the small scale of production, and the absence of physical and human capital resulted in greater specialization in cotton and larger food deficits. This interpretation is consistent with the strong positive correlation among the share of tilled acreage devoted to cotton, population density per improved acre, the percentage of blacks in the population, and the rate of tenancy.

In contrast, commercial specialization in the Upcountry involved the integration of the region into the national and the world market. From this perspective, the change in the crop mix indicates a shift in the orientation of Upcountry farmers away from production for household consumption or sale in local markets and toward a growing dependence on the staple trade for their livelihoods. It also indicates a change in the pattern of development that economically isolated the Upcountry yeomanry.

The most common explanation for the shift of Upcountry farmers toward cotton emphasizes their increased indebtedness to local merchants during Reconstruction. After the war, households had to accumulate wealth to repair damaged homes and farms and to replenish depleted stocks of food and swine. At the same time, it is argued, the unusually high price of cotton offered farmers the prospect of large and immediate returns from the cultivation of the staple. As a result, Upcountry farmers specialized in cotton and purchased food supplies and working capital on credit from local merchants. Because of the precipitous decline in cotton prices between 1866 and 1869 and a series of bad harvests, many yeomen fell deeply into debt and became permanently tied to the cash nexus.

The need to accumulate wealth may explain why Upcountry farmers sought to expand cotton production after the Civil War. It cannot, however, account for the timing or extent of the region's economic transformation. The estimates of the crop mix in Table 8.4 indicate that Upcountry farmers did not specialize in cotton until after 1870, even though they had begun reconstruction five years earlier. Also, the degree of specialization increased throughout the 1870s despite the continued decline in the price of cotton, which eventually returned to its prewar level in 1878. While it is true that many Upcountry farmers found themselves in debt to local merchants and were forced to cultivate cotton, regional estimates of food supplies (reported in Table 8.6) imply that their dependence on the market was more limited than Cotton Belt farmers'.

While the integration of the Upcountry into the cotton economy may have required an external shock, such as the war, to change the economic orientation of farm households, it also depended on the formation of an internal marketing and transportation system to overcome the region's geographical isolation. The commercial development of the Upcountry did not begin until 1870 with the construction of new rail lines and the growth of urban and local marketing centers.

Only 180 miles of railroad had been built in Upcountry counties before the Civil War. Rail transportation was limited to farm communities along the Western and Atlantic Railroad and near Atlanta. Railroad construction during the immediate postwar period, 1866 to 1869, had little impact on the Upcountry. But, track mileage in the region tripled in the 1870s, and the geographical orientation of the transportation system shifted. The major change in the rail network, in both quantity and quality, involved construction of the Atlanta and Charlotte Air Line, which spanned the eastern half of the Upcountry and, as part of the Southern Railway Security Company, linked the region to cities in the Northeast. In addition to the new trunk line, over 200 miles of branch and connecting lines were built after 1870. More than half these smaller lines were located in the eastern segment of the Upcountry. To complete the infrastructure, telegraph lines were built parallel to the rail network and provided farm communities with a more direct means of communication.

Urban development accompanied the expansion of the transportation and communications system. The population of Atlanta more than doubled during the 1860s, while other Upcountry cities and towns stagnated. After 1870 new cities and towns sprang up along the rail lines, and town and urban population increased by 90 percent with the largest growth occurring outside of Atlanta. By the end of the decade, the Upcountry had become the most urbanized region of the state.

Transportation improvements and urbanization opened new commercial opportunities and established the basis for an internal marketing system. Unfortunately, reliable statistics on commerce in Georgia are not available before 1870. However, the assessed value of merchandise and of money and solvent debts, collected and reported by the state's comptroller general, provide a crude measure of mercantile activity over the entire period. The real value of merchandise per capita fell by over 50 percent between 1860 and 1870 and increased by approximately the same percentage during the next decade. Holdings of money and solvent debts followed a similar pattern, although the decline in the 1860s was greater in magnitude because of the collapse of the Southern banking system after the war and the effects of national banking legislation.

The growth of rural merchandising and commercial centers in the 1870s can be analyzed more systematically from the information contained in the *Mercantile Agency Reference Books* of the R.G. Dun and Company (presented in Table 8.7). Between 1870 and 1880 the number of stores in the Upcountry doubled. Despite this rapid growth, the distribution of stores according to their financial strength did not change substantially. Three-quarters of the stores in the region had less than $5000 worth of assets, while the financial strength of only 11 percent of the stores exceeded $10,000.

Locations in the Upcountry with at least one merchant (and in most cases, a post office) increased by 75 percent in the 1870s, from 114 to 199. By 1880, 31 percent of the locations had at least 5 stores as compared to only 26 percent 10 years earlier, and they contained 80 percent of the stores in the region (only 75 percent, excluding Atlanta). At the close of the decade the Upcountry contained one commercial center, Atlanta, and seven interior cotton centers.

The growth and distribution of stores in the eastern half of the Upper Piedmont (excluding Atlanta), which had no rail transportation before the Civil War, demonstrate more directly the impact of railroad construction on the commercial development of the region as a whole. The number of stores in this part of the Upcountry increased by 155 percent between 1870 and 1880, and the size distribution of stores shifted from small to medium and large firms. Large firms, those with at least $5000 worth of assets, comprised only 14 percent of the stores in 1870, but 24 percent 10 years later. One-third of the locations in this part of the Upcountry had at least 5 stores in 1880, as compared to only one-quarter in 1870.

The construction of an internal marketing and transportation system generally improves the terms of trade for local producers. In the specific case of the Upcountry, it increased the value of cotton as a cash crop to farmers. Local processing and storage facilities and rail transportation reduced the differential between the price of cotton quoted in New York and in Upcountry cities. In Rome, Georgia, for example, which was an interior center on the Eastern Tennessee, Virginia, and Georgia Railroad, cotton sold at a 5.5 percent discount, relative to the price in New York, in January 1880. Market conditions, in fact, were most favorable to local producers when their cotton could be shipped directly to New York along rail routes, as was the case in Rome. New York cotton brokers, through their Southern agents, paid higher prices for direct shipments of cotton, as they avoided unnecessary intermediaries and were able to sell the cotton to textile manufacturers in the Northeast before delivery by means of bills of lading.

Of equal importance was the availability of current market information and reliable transportation which eliminated much of the risk involved in the cotton trade for local merchants. With less uncertainty, merchants charged a smaller discount on cotton purchased from their customers (that essentially covered handling costs), so farmers received a higher price for their staple crops.

Local furnishing merchants also served as a distribution network for phosphate fertilizers and contributed to the diffusion of this new technology throughout the Upcountry. Ecological conditions and the more diversified system of farming made commercial fertilizers essential to cotton production. Not only did the use of phosphate fertilizers increase per acre yields, but it also accelerated crop growth and caused the

Table 8.7
Size distribution of stores by financial strength and store locations, Upcountry Georgia, 1870 and 1880

	Percentage of Stores			
	$1 to 4,999	$5,000 to 9,999	$10,000 plus	Number of stores
1870				
Appalachian Valley	65.2	16.1	18.8	112
Cherokee Territory	77.2	13.0	9.8	223
Eastern Upper Piedmont	78.3	8.9	12.9	248
(excluding Atlanta)	(86.3)	(6.2)	(7.5)	(146)
1880				
Appalachian Valley	73.9	12.5	13.7	176
Cherokee Territory	80.5	11.2	8.2	401
Eastern Upper Piedmont	76.8	10.1	13.1	633
(excluding Atlanta)	(75.5)	(11.3)	(13.3)	(372)

	Percentage of Locations				
	1 Store	2 to 4 Stores	5 to 10 Stores	11 plus Stores	Number of Locations
1870					
Appalachian Valley	44.0	32.0	12.0	12.0	25
Cherokee Territory	35.0	37.5	15.0	12.5	40
Eastern Upper Piedmont	46.9	28.6	20.4	4.1	49
1880					
Appalachian Valley	37.8	33.3	22.3	6.7	45
Cherokee Territory	39.7	30.9	19.1	10.3	68
Eastern Upper Piedmont	36.0	31.4	20.9	11.6	86

Notes: Stores include general, grocery, and dry goods stores. Firms without an estimated financial strength are assumed to have less than $2,000 worth of assets.

Source: R.G. Dun and Company, *Mercantile Agency Reference Books* (New York, Jan. 1870 and Jan. 1880).

cotton bolls to ripen more uniformly. Fertilizers shortened the length of the growing season and compressed the labor-intensive cotton harvest into a five-week to six-week period. These changes in the growth process translated into higher actual yields for Upcountry farmers because crop damage caused by early frosts was reduced and competition for labor from other crops was minimized.

The potential impact of this technology on staple production in the Upcountry was recognized before 1860, but the cost of imported fertilizers and inadequate transportation restricted its use to wealthier farmers and planters in the Cotton Belt. After the Civil War, the development and production of phosphate fertilizers and the construction of the Air Line railway greatly altered the economic value of this input for Upcountry farmers. The discovery of phosphate mines in Maryland and South Carolina and advances in chemical technology reduced the cost of producing fertilizers. Furthermore, rail transportation enabled manufacturers to market their products through retail merchants. This distribution network lowered sales costs, as it bypassed wholesale houses and employed merchants directly in the final stages of production, the mixing of chemical ingredients with other inputs to produce fertilizers. Also, because merchants came into direct contact with farmers, they could adapt fertilizers to the ecological conditions and methods of cultivation in their area. Over time the final product could be improved through trial and error.

To complete the argument, a regression equation, similar to the one specified by Wright and Kunreuther, has been estimated on the counties of the Upper Piedmont for the census years 1860, 1870, and 1880 to determine more precisely the timing of the economic transformation in the Upcountry. Since the census of agriculture did not report crop acreage before 1880, the dependent variable, the degree of specialization, is defined as the ratio of the value of cotton to the value of all field crops, where all crops are valued at their 1860 prices. Because the census changed its measure of farm size in 1880, small-sized and medium-sized farms are defined as those with fewer than 20 and between 20 and 49 improved acres in 1860 and 1870 and with fewer than 50 and between 50 and 99 total acres in 1880. In the second equation, a dummy variable has been included to control for regional differences between the western Cherokee Territory and the eastern half of the Upper Piedmont.

The results of the analysis, presented in Table 8.8, distinguish the cross-sectional pattern of specialization in cotton in the Upcountry in 1860 and in 1880. Although the degree of specialization is positively correlated with average farm size in both years, in 1880 it is more strongly

correlated with the percentage of small farms than with the percentage
of medium-sized producers, while in 1860 the opposite conclusion holds.
In the second equation, the dummy variable becomes negative and statistically significant in 1880 and indicates a shift in the locus of cotton
production away from the Cherokee Territory.

The two equations for 1870 explain only a small fraction of the variation in cotton production in the Upper Piedmont counties. Nonetheless,
the cross-sectional pattern of specialization in cotton is similar to that
of the antebellum period. A test for structural change over the decade
1860 to 1870 supports this claim; it fails to reject the hypothesis that the
coefficients of the two equations are equal and hence derived from the
same underlying sample. The same test, when applied to the combined
sample of counties for the years 1870 and 1880, however, rejects the hypothesis and implies that the economic transformation of the Upcountry
occurred after 1870.

32. Describe the data list that must underlie Table 8.8. That is, identify the individuals (farms, persons, cities, regions, whatever) on
which variables were measured and describe the information the
author might have had for each individual, including the units of
measurement used.

33. How many regression equations does Table 8.8 show?

34. Each equation in Table 8.8 is based on a sample. What was the
population being sampled? What was the sampling procedure?

35. In the notes beneath Table 8.8, Weiman refers to the unweighted
average of the dependent variable. To be sure you understand
what he is talking about, make up hypothetical cotton and field
crop production figures for an average county in 1880. What does
he mean when he says he took an unweighted average?

36. In Table 8.8, consider equation (1) for 1860. (a) What does that
model say about two counties whose average farm size differs by
50 acres while the other variables are the same? (b) Suppose per
capita wealth differs by $100 while other variables are the same?

37. Explain the difference between equations (1) and (2) in Table 8.8.
Particularly, explain how that Cherokee Territory variable works.
Is the Cherokee Territory coefficient of -0.07 in 1880 (2) too small
in size to have much effect?

Table 8.8
Cross-sectional pattern of specialization in cotton, Upper Piedmont of Georgia,
1860 to 1880

	Dependent variable is value of cotton per dollar of all field crops					
	1860		1870		1880	
	(1)	(2)	(1)	(2)	(1)	(2)
Constant	−0.31	−0.26	−0.52	−0.63	0.09	−0.01
	(−0.96)	(−0.78)	(−0.92)	(−1.13)	(0.32)	(−0.04)
Rural Population	−1.66**	−1.88*	0.46	0.53	−0.22	−0.08
per improved acre	(−2.04)	(−2.18)	(0.78)	(0.92)	(−0.27)	(−0.11)
Personal wealth	0.49	0.50	0.30	0.48	0.71	0.38
per capita	(1.47)	(1.47)	(0.58)	(0.93)	(0.44)	(0.26)
Average farm size	3.11	2.90	4.54	5.09	6.58*	7.50*
	(1.66)	(1.52)	(1.47)	(1.68)	(3.06)	(3.75)
Percentage of	0.84	0.59	−0.36	−0.26	0.49*	0.49*
small farms	(1.24)	(0.78)	(−0.85)	(−0.61)	(2.16)	(2.36)
Percentage of	1.17**	1.18**	0.90	1.03	0.04	0.41
medium farms	(1.85)	(1.85)	(1.11)	(1.31)	(0.09)	(0.086)
Cherokee Territory		0.04		0.08		−0.07*
		(0.86)		(−1.45)		(−2.27)
R^2	0.47	0.46	0.03	0.09	0.42	0.52
SEE	0.09	0.09	0.12	0.12	0.08	0.07

* Indicates significance at a 5 percent confidence level.

** Indicates significance at a 10 percent confidence level.

Notes: t-statistics are in parentheses.

The sample contains 23 counties in 1860 and 1870 and 26 counties in 1880.

The unweighted average of the dependent variable is 0.26 in 1860, 0.24 in 1870, and 0.58 in 1880.

Personal wealth is measured in thousands of dollars, and average farm size is measured in thousands of acres.

Sources: For agricultural data, see Table 4. Personal wealth data: U.S. Census Office, Eighth Census, 1860, vol. 4, *Statistics of the United States (Including Mortality, Property, &c.) in 1860*, p. 298; Ninth Census, 1870, vol. 3, *The Statistics of Wealth and Industry in the United States*, pp. 22–24; and Georgia, Comptroller General's Office, *Annual Report of the Comptroller General* (Atlanta, 1880), pp. 128–32.

38. Look at the statistical significance of the coefficients of the explanatory variables. Were any of the coefficients significant at the 1% level? How many were significant at the 5% level. The 10% level?

39. Look at the t-values of the coefficients in the two equations for 1870. What do you make of the fact that not one of the t-values is greater than 2? Can you suggest an explanation? (You might want to review Section 5.5, where we introduced t-values.)

40. In the 1860 model (1), two of the coefficients are assigned asterisks. Are those two coefficients really quite distinct from all the other coefficients in that equation?

41. Look at the equations numbered (2) for 1860 and 1880 and study the size of the regression coefficients. Do you note any variables that seem to have either substantial practical effect or little practical effect on the dependent variable?

42. What would be the approximate effect on the dependent variable if, in equation 1880 (2), the percentage of small farms declined by the same amount that the percentage of middle-sized farms grew?

43. Look at the coefficients and t-values for the percentage of small farms in the two equations 1860 (1) and 1880 (2). Use those examples to explain the difference between the size of a coefficient and the statistical significance of a coefficient.

44. Use the R^2s at the bottom of the table to comment on the usefulness of the six equations shown.

45. Look at equation 1860 (1). What do you make of the fact that none of the coefficients was highly significant but that R^2 is highly significant?

46. Can you think of an important omitted variable? Is there some factor, in your opinion, to which the dependent variable might respond strongly but which has not been included among the explanatory variables?

47. Has the author used as explanatory variables factors that would tend to have a strong linear relationship with one another?

48.   In two paragraphs just before Table 8.8, Weiman refers to a test of a statistical hypothesis. In your own words, outline the logical structure of that test.

49.   Explain the contribution Table 8.8 makes to Weiman's argument. Is the evidence in the table persuasive? Suggestive?

INTERNAL DEVELOPMENT OF THE POSTBELLUM COTTON SOUTH

The formation of an internal marketing and transportation system and the integration of the Upcountry into the cotton economy reveal an overlooked aspect of the profound structural changes that occurred in the Cotton South after the Civil War. Nonetheless, as several studies have shown, the transformation was clearly related to the emancipation of slaves and the breakdown of plantation agriculture in the Cotton Belt. After the Civil War, cotton factors located in interior and coastal ports could no longer control the staple output of small tenant farmers, and could not satisfy the varied demands of individual farm households. Cotton factors were gradually displaced by local furnishing merchants. Merchants moved into Upcountry counties after changes in the lien law that limited their claim over the crops of tenant farmers.

Moreover, the antebellum network of natural transportation routes, augmented by east-west railroads, was inadequate to handle the expanding trade in the interior of the Cotton South and the shipments of foodstuffs into the region from the upper South and Midwest. To increase the flow of traffic along their trunk lines and through their terminal cities, railroad companies competed vigorously for the new markets and built additional spurs into the interior and lines to cities in the upper South which often passed through Upcountry counties.

These internal improvements, however, were not induced simply by structural changes in the Cotton Belt, but were the product of intense competitive struggles over the Southern market among merchant houses and railroad companies based mainly in Northern cities. Due to the high price of cotton after the Civil War, the number of cotton brokers in New York multiplied, and many firms abandoned the traditional method of buying cotton on consignment from factors. By sending their own agents into the interior to purchase cotton directly from local merchants and large-scale producers, firms were able to reduce their costs and to gain greater control over their supplies. Competition from interior cotton buyers weakened cotton factors economically, because the factors were unable to guarantee large shipments of cotton to brokers in New York and Liverpool. Without this collateral, cotton factors had a difficult time obtaining credit to conduct other aspects of their business, such as providing advances to producers and storeowners. At the same time, wholesale houses in Northern cities, especially in the mid-Atlantic and midwestern states, actively sought to expand their share of the Southern market and sent large armies of sales agents into the South to establish contacts with local furnishing merchants. With new sources of credit and merchandise, county store owners expanded their retail trade at the expense of factors whose position was further weakened.

Competition over the Southern market also involved urban rivalries and system-building by major railroad companies. Vying for the title of "Gateway to the South," merchants in Cincinnati financed the construction of the Cincinnati Southern Railroad which provided an alternative route to the Midwest from the Lower South and diverted traffic from the Louisville and Nashville Railroad. The merchants in Cincinnati and Louisville sponsored numerous commercial conventions to attract the business of Southern retail merchants and built cotton exchanges to increase their share of the return traffic. Similarly, the Pennsylvania Railroad extended its system into the South initially through its involvement in the Southern Railway Security Company, a holding company which helped finance the construction of the Atlanta and Charlotte Air Line. After the Panic of 1873, the Pennsylvania Railroad acquired direct control over the two major trunk lines that connected the South Atlantic states to Philadelphia and New York, the Richmond and Danville System and the Eastern Tennessee, Virginia, and Georgia Railroad.

Competition among railroad companies and wholesale merchants during the 1870s and 1880s was not confined to the Southern market, but extended into every region of the country, creating a centralized distribution and marketing system, in other words, a national market. Examining the integration of the Upcountry into the cotton economy within this broader context reveals an element of continuity. Although exceptional at the time, the construction of the Western and Atlantic Railroad in the late 1840s heralded the pattern of internal improvements in the Cotton South after 1870. It simultaneously linked the South Atlantic states to the Midwest through Cincinnati and integrated farmers in the western Cherokee Territory into the cotton economy through Atlanta. The complete integration of the Cotton South, including the Upcountry, into the national economy, however, occurred only after the Civil War, when Northern railroad companies and wholesale houses sought to expand their markets beyond traditional, regional boundaries.

Table 8.9
Appendix Table 1: Cross-sectional pattern of specialization in cotton, Cotton Belt
and Upper Piedmont of Georgia, 1880

	(dependent variable is cotton acreage per tilled acre)		
	All Counties	Cotton Belt	Upper Piedmont
Constant	0.00	0.01	−0.17
	(0.00)	(0.06)	(−0.70)
Cotton yields	1.34	−0.04	5.92
over corn yields	(1.11)	(−0.04)	(1.29)
Rural population	0.52	1.06*	0.05
per improved acre	(1.64)	(3.49)	(0.09)
Average farm size	0.83	0.54	3.18**
	(1.50)	(1.11)	(2.04)
Percentage of farms	−0.17	−0.11	0.48*
3 to 49 acres	(−1.50)	(−0.90)	(2.15)
49 to 99 acres	0.22	0.44*	0.16
	(1.28)	(2.59)	(0.45)
Rate of tenancy	0.41*	0.30	−0.22
	(4.31)	(2.89)	(−0.97)
R^2	0.31	0.36	0.17
SEE	0.06	0.05	0.06

* Indicates significance at a 5 percent confidence level.

** Indicates significance at a 10 percent confidence level.

Notes: t-statistics are in parentheses. The sample contains 87 counties, 61 counties
from the Cotton Belt and 26 counties from the Upper Piedmont. Average farm size
is measured in thousands of acres. Source: See Table 6.

THIS IS THE END OF THE ARTICLE BY DAVID F. WEIMAN.

One thing that might not be clear in Tables 8.8 and 8.9 is the SEE
at the bottom of the tables. To understand that, first recall what a
standard deviation means. If you have a list of numbers, the standard

deviation is an average distance from the numbers in the list from the mean of the list. In an earlier chapter you read about the standard error for a mean. It turned out to be a kind of standard deviation. For example, suppose you take a sample of ages and compute the average age. Your sample average is going to miss the true mean age of the entire population. If you take many different samples, each sample will probably have a different average. The standard error for the average is the expected or average distance of the many sample averages from the true mean of the population. The standard error is the standard deviation in a hypothetical list of possible sample averages.

The SEE in Weiman's tables are the initials of Standard Error of Estimate. The number being estimated from the sample is R^2 instead of an average. If Weiman had taken many samples, he would have computed many values of R^2. The SEE is the standard deviation in that hypothetical list of R^2s. Here is how you use that information: In the All Counties model, R^2 is 0.31 while its SEE is 0.06. If it were true that R^2 would really be zero in a regression based on the whole population, then Weiman, just by bad luck, got an R^2 from his sample which is more than five standard deviations from that zero expected value (0.31 is more than five times as big as 0.06, the standard error).

Remember that if you go two standard deviations on each side of a sample-based estimate you have a 95% confidence interval for the true value. So a 95% confidence interval for R^2 runs from $0.31 - 0.12$ up to $0.31 + 0.12$. You are 95% sure that the true R^2 is between 0.19 and 0.43. That is, you are quite sure the regression model explains between 19% and 43% of the variation in the dependent variable.

ADDITIONAL QUESTIONS

50. Is it possible to carry out a chi-square test on the information in Table 8.2? Would there be any point in doing so?

51. Weiman wants to contrast the Upcountry (which includes the Appalachian Valley and the Upper Piedmont) with the two regions comprising the Cotton Belt. To facilitate the contrast, would it make sense to average the percentages shown in the first two rows of Tables 8.1 and 8.2 to get Upcountry percentages, and then do likewise for the Cotton Belt? How would you carry out that averaging?

52. Suppose four persons lived on a farm in the Upper Piedmont that experienced the average results shown in Table 8.3. How many corn-equivalent bushels of wheat, rye, and oats did their farm produce in 1860? How many corn-equivalent bushels of potatoes, peas, and beans did their farm produce? How many corn-equivalent bushels did they require for seed and draft-animal feed?

53. Would there have been any way, at least theoretically, to make all the categories of production in Table 8.3 comparable to one another?

54. In the text above, Weiman suggests there may have been bias in some of his sources. What numbers were those and why doesn't that bias affect his argument?

55. Table 8.3 said that in the Appalachian Valley in 1860, the per-capita corn output was 41.9 bushels and the per capita cotton output was .09 bales. How does that information about crop mix compare to the 1.9 shown in Table 8.4?

56. We filled out the following table by dividing each entry in Table 8.6 by the corresponding entry in Table 8.3. Comment on how this comparison of Table 8.6 and Table 8.3 relates to Weiman's argument.

	Corn	Grains	Food Crops	Net Food Supply	Cotton
		1880 farm output as % of 1860			
Appalachian Valley	.71	.78	.76	.70	3.00
Upper Piedmont	.72	.76	.73	.74	2.15
Lower Piedmont	.51	.62	.58	.52	.99
Central Cotton Belt	.45	.53	.50	.36	.73

57. Look at the Cotton Belt equation in Table 8.9 and consider the units of the dependent variable and the coefficient for rural population. If County A has 0.1 more persons per improved acre than County B, what is your best guess as to the difference in their cotton share? Does that make sense? Does this explanatory variable have a powerful effect?

58. What does your answer to Question 58 imply about the impact on cotton of county to county differences in population per improved acre?

59. There seems to be a "typo," a missing asterisk, in the Cotton Belt equation in Table 8.9. Why would we say that?

60. Suppose the Upper Piedmont regression equation had been based on the entire population instead of on a sample. Express as an interval your guess as to how much of the variation in cotton share would be explained by the independent variables in the equation.

61. In Chapter 4 we mentioned that a t-value is actually the regression coefficient divided by an estimate of the standard error (standard deviation) for that coefficient. What is the estimate of the standard error for the coefficient of Average Farm Size in the All Counties equation in Table 8.9?

8.3 Answers to Questions

1. His primary goal is to explain "why Upcountry farmers moved from self-sufficiency to specialization in cotton after the Civil War." He wants to establish that there were regional differences in the shift to cotton, so he must identify the specific factors operating to induce the shift in the Upcountry.

2. Weiman doesn't mention sampling when he says he used county-level data from the decennial census. So the Table 8.1 data must summarize information on the entire population of "individuals" in the four geographic regions. The individuals are households. The author says that the distinction between Upcountry and Cotton Belt extended throughout the Lower South. However, he doesn't go out on a limb with that idea and seems to focus the conclusions of this paper on the regions of Georgia.

3. In the Appalachian Valley 80.7% of the households had no slaves so 19.3% of the households had one or more slaves. Table 8.1 says that 0.8% of the households with slaves had 50 or more. Thus, $(19.3\% \times 0.8\%)$ of the Appalachian households had fifty or more slaves. This amounts to only 0.15%, about one-seventh of one percent. For the Central Cotton Belt the calculation is $48\% \times 4.4\%$ or around 2%. The ratio of those two answers, .15% and 2%, is over 13. In one region the proportion of households with very large slaveholdings was thirteen times greater than in the other.

4. Although the percentages shown in the column labeled "5 to 9
    slaves" in Table 8.1 are similar for these two regions, the percent-
    ages for all households are quite different. In the Upper Piedmont
    the calculation is $(24.5\% \times 24.3\%)$, which is around 6%. In the
    Lower Piedmont we get $(56.9\% \times 23.5\%)$, which is over 13%.

5. Since Table 8.1 is based on an entire population, there is no ques-
    tion about sampling error. Also, since it must refer to many hun-
    dreds of households, any difference worth discussing is bound to
    be statistically significant. Such differences could not lie in the
    range of chance error. And as the answers to the last two ques-
    tions make clear, the distinctions between the regions are certainly
    large enough to be "significant" in the commonsense meaning of
    that word.

6. The individuals are farms.

7. The ratio is $11.7 / 0.9 = 13$.

8. You can't answer this question because Weiman has not given N,
    the number of individuals, for each of the categories.

9. These tables support the point that the Upcountry and the Cotton
    Belt were clearly different in 1860 with respect to slaveholding and
    farm size. Weiman says that he is also going to use these tables as
    a reference point for showing how much change took place between
    1860 and 1880. They provide some evidence that the movement
    into cotton may well have had a distinct form in the Upcountry
    since 1) cotton cultivation may have been related to slaveholding
    and farm size, and 2) slaveholding and farm size were distinct in
    the Upcountry.

10. We assume that Weiman had county-level information on each of
    the outputs and on the rural population. For example, perhaps his
    sources showed 400,000 bushels of corn produced in 1860 in County
    X and showed the rural population of that county to be 10,000.
    Dividing these gives 40 bushels of corn per person in County X.
    He would then combine the equivalent figure for all counties in
    one geographic region by computing weighted averages, using ru-
    ral population as weights. While the food production numbers
    have come from the census, the net food supply is computed from
    food production by subtracting an estimate of seed and feed re-
    quirements. So net food supply is itself an estimated number. The

data used for those estimates may have come from samples instead of the full census.

11. Cotton output in the Lower Piedmont was 2.7 times as large per person as in the Upper Piedmont. For home manufactures the ratio is 2.5 in the other direction. All the other ratios are smaller.

12. You can't answer this question because the outputs for the two crops have not been expressed in comparable units.

13. The contrast between the Appalachian Valley and Central Cotton Belt in home manufactures and cotton is as prominent as the contrast we noted between the Upper and Lower Piedmont (see the answer to Question 17). Taken together, these contrasts support the author's point that prior to the Civil War, cotton was not nearly as important in the Upcountry as in the central region and that there was evidence of greater self-reliance in the Upcountry. The figures on net food supply in Table 8.3 show that all the regions, except for the Appalachian Valley, were quite similar. If the Upper Piedmont was self-sufficient with regard to food, so were the two Cotton Belt regions.

Just as with Table 8.1 and Table 8.2, Weiman is going to use these figures to contrast 1860 with 1880 in order to show the shift toward cotton.

14. In one of the paragraphs between Tables 8.3 and 8.4, Weiman addresses the reader who might be wondering about differences in climate, soil quality, and topography within the Upcountry region. Broad geographic regions are usually not completely homogeneous, this reader thinks; using average figures for an entire region like the Upcountry may obscure quite a bit of variability in climate and soil within that region. Perhaps some parts of the Upcountry resembled the Cotton Belt in climate and soil; perhaps other parts had too short a growing season for farmers even to consider cotton. In that case, comparing subregions of similar climate in the Upcountry and the Cotton Belt might cause the differential in cotton acreage to disappear.

Weiman addresses this concern by assuring the reader that the subregions of the Upcountry really were quite homogeneous with respect to climate. All had a growing season adequate for cotton. Hence he believes that there is no need to control for the climate variable when comparing the two regions. His point is that the contrast with respect to cotton production is still there even when climate is somewhat the same. So his use of four categories has "controlled for" the possible third variable, climate.

15. Since Table 8.4 only shows the ratio of cotton to corn, it can't show what happened to either crop individually. For example, if cotton production went up by a factor of 4 while corn went up by a factor of 2, the ratio would double. But the same doubling of the ratio would occur if cotton production were cut in half and corn production cut to one-fourth of the 1860 level. So if both go up or both go down the ratio could double. It could also double if one goes up while the other goes down.

The conclusions we can draw from Table 8.4 are restricted to the relative concentration on the two crops—that cotton became more important than it was before, relative to corn.

16.

	1875/1860	1880/1875
Appalachian Valley	3.8	1.3
Upper Piedmont	2.1	1.5
Lower Piedmont	1.5	1.3
Central Cotton Belt	1.3	1.3

It looks as though the two geographic regions were different with respect to changes in crop mix between 1860 and 1880. However, those regional differences occurred in the 1860 to 1875 period and not in the 1875 to 1880 period. This pattern is important for Weiman's argument about the timing of the shift toward cotton.

17. Weiman wants to fix fairly precisely the timing of the Upcountry shift toward cotton. He wants to point out that the major shift did not come immediately after the Civil War during the first few years of the reconstruction. In particular, the shift does not coincide with the high cotton prices which existed at the close of the war but comes largely after 1870, in spite of the fact that cotton prices fell sharply from 1866 to 1869.

18.

	1880/1875
Appalachian Valley	1.19
Upper Piedmont	1.23
Lower Piedmont	1.10
Central Cotton Belt	1.12

The Upcountry and the Cotton belt had quite different rates of growth in the percentage of tilled acreage devoted to cotton. Notice that in these figures a difference between 1.1 and 1.2 is quite important since a 1.1 would mean that the region experienced 10% growth while a 1.2 would mean 20% growth—twice as much.

19. One major point is that there was indeed a shift into cotton over the 1860 to 1880 period. A second point is that the Cotton Belt and the Upcountry differed in the degree of their shift into cotton, the larger shift occurring in the Upcountry. A third point is that the relative shift was greater between 1860 and 1875 than between 1875 and 1880, but that (at least in the Upcountry) it came largely after 1870.

20. His point has to do with self-sufficiency, the ability of the region to feed itself.

21. The table makes it clear that the per-capita nutritional value of farm output in the Upcountry was about double that of the Cotton Belt. So it would be possible for the Upcountry to feed itself at the same time the Cotton Belt would fail to be self-sufficient.

22. The individuals are counties. The population is apparently the set of all counties in three of the four geographic regions we have been studying (the Appalachian Valley seems to be excluded).

23. The table is based on a sample of 87 counties. We have no information on how the sample was chosen.

24. A guess would be that yield means the county's average yield per acre measured in some economic unit which would make it possible to compare cotton and corn. That would provide a sensible independent variable to test in that it is reasonable to ask if differences in the potential economic return per acre were driving the decision to plant cotton instead of corn.

25.   A rate is a fraction—for example, the number of tilled acres in
the county that were rented or sharecropped divided by the total
number of tilled acres in the county. There are other reasonable
ways to compute a rate of tenancy. One might use the ratio of
tenant farms to total farms or the number of farmers who worked
as tenants divided by the total number of farmers.

26.   Table 8.9 is a model. It is the unique linear model that best fits the
actual data and uses that particular set of independent variables
to explain the dependent variable, cotton share. There may be
other models that fit the data even better (explain more of the
variation in cotton share) and it may be that no linear model
would explain the variability in cotton share very well. Weiman is
using a conventional phrase which has only the technical meaning
that certain factors have been entered in a certain equation form
in a certain way.

27.   Weiman means that there is less than a 1% likelihood that sampling error could have caused the regression equations to be this
different if the Cotton Belt and the Upcountry counties were essentially similar. The overwhelming likelihood is that the differences
that show up in Table 8.9 reflect the fact that the two regions
really did differ. Whether those differences are historically interesting is, of course, another matter entirely; statistical significance
tests refer only to the question whether the results obtained could
have happened by chance.

28.   Weiman refers to these three variables: "density of the rural population per improved acre" (i.e., the variable labeled Rural population / improved acres); "the percentage of medium-sized farms"
(the variable labeled Percentage of farms 49 to 99 acres); and "the
rate of tenancy."

One might emphasize these three explanatory factors because of
the high t-score associated with each. Recall the rule of thumb
that a t-value larger than 2 means that the chances are extremely
likely that the true slope coefficient is different from zero (Section
7.4). I.e., there is some mathematical relationship between the
variables—knowing a county's score on the independent variables
would be of some use in predicting its score on the dependent
variable.

But the suggestions that the three factors were "strongly correlated" with cotton share does not directly refer to the t-scores but

instead to R^2 and to the impact of the three factors on the dependent variable. You can get a feel for these effects by multiplying the slope coefficients by some reasonable increment in the associated independent variables. And here the model may not be quite as powerful as Weiman's phrase suggests. For example, for the variable Percentage of Farms 49 to 99 Acres, we interpret the coefficient 0.44 to mean that a one-percent rise in the percentage of mid-sized farms was associated with a 0.44% increase in the proportion of tilled acreage devoted to cotton. Multiplying by ten, a ten-percent difference in the proportion of mid-sized farms was associated with a 4.4% difference in the cotton proportion. Does this qualify as a powerful relationship? A moderately strong one? You must use your own judgment. Question 57 examines another of the three explanatory variables that Weiman mentions.

29. In discussing the Upcountry (or Upper Piedmont) model in Table 8.9, the author emphasizes two other variables. Again, both have t-scores above 2. But as before, you must also look at the regression coefficients and R^2. The coefficient for the variable Average Farm Size seems impressive at first glance: a one-unit increase in farm size leads to a 3.18% rise in the proportion of tilled acreage devoted to cotton (holding other variables constant). But the size of a unit for this variable is 1000 acres (see the explanatory note beneath the table)! And despite a larger t-score, the other variable, Percentage of Farms 3 to 49 Acres, also has a less than impressive coefficient.

30. The model for all 87 counties includes the Upper Piedmont counties, for which the regression yielded an R^2 of only .17. This less good fit for 26 of the counties must be reducing the R^2 for the list as a whole, diluting the effect of the higher R^2 found for the Cotton Belt counties.

31. The regression estimates in Table 8.9 are based on a model proposed by Gavin Wright and Howard Kunreuther in their article "Cotton, Corn and Risk in the Nineteenth Century" (not their model for 1860 discussed in Section 7.8 of this book, however). Using Georgia data, Weiman is making the point that when you control for economic region by running separate regression models for the Cotton Belt counties and the Upcountry counties, the Wright-Kunreuther model doesn't work very well and two distinct explanations for the degree of specialization in cotton emerge.

32. The individuals in the sample in Table 8.8 consist of counties in the Upper Piedmont region of Georgia in 1860, 1870, and 1880. Since Weiman's dependent variable, stated at the top of Table 8.8, is cotton's proportion of the dollar value of all field crops, we know that he must have dollar-value estimates at the county level for all crops. He also knows the mean personal wealth per capita at the county level, the size of each county's rural population, the improved acreage, and the proportion of farms in various size categories. The note beneath Table 8.8 alerts you that some of this information was expressed in thousands of units. To come up with the actual variables for the regression models, Weiman sometimes computed new county-level data by dividing one number by another.

33. Six.

34. For each census year, the population was all Upper Piedmont counties of Georgia; so the sample consisted of some of those counties—23 in 1860 and 1870, 26 in 1880. It's not clear from the article how the sample was taken or how many counties the Upper Piedmont region had, so we can't tell the size of the entire population. Notice that in discussing these regression models, Weiman uses the terms Upcountry and Upper Piedmont interchangeably. Earlier in the article, he had indicated that the Upper Piedmont counties and the Appalachian Valley counties of Georgia together comprised the Upcountry. The counties of the Appalachian Valley may have been dropped for this analysis.

35. Take a hypothetical county, County Q, in 1880. Say that cotton production in Q was valued at $2 million; corn production at $2 million; and other crops at $1 million. The dollar value of all field crops in County Q was, then, $5 million, and cotton's share (the dependent variable) was 2/5 or 0.4. When Weiman says that the unweighted average of the dependent variable was 0.58 in 1880, he means that he found cotton's share of the dollar value of all crops for each county in the sample and calculated the mean for all 26 counties, but without weighting the scores. In the unweighted average, a county with crop production worth $1 million was given as much weight as a county whose crop production was worth $20 million.

36. **(a)** Remember that farm size is measured in thousands of acres. A change of 50 acres in Average Farm Size from one county to another would be associated with a change of $(3.11 \times .05) = .1555$, or about 15%, in the Value of Cotton per Dollar of All Field Crops, holding the other variables constant. That seems a substantial difference—but the t-value is only 1.66, strongly suggestive but not conclusive.

(b) In the case of Personal Wealth per Capita, that's measured in thousands of dollars so a change $100 in wealth would yield a predicted change of (0.49×0.1) or 4.9% in the Value of Cotton per Dollar of All Field Crops. Again that seems a change of sufficient magnitude to be historically interesting, but again the t-statistic is not conclusive.

37. Weiman explains early in the article that the Cherokee Territory was the western half of the Upper Piedmont region. (It was so called because it had been land occupied by the Cherokee Indians until their removal in the 1830s.) In the regression models numbered (2), the author has added a dummy variable that divides the Upper Piedmont into eastern and western subregions as a way of checking whether subregional differences within the Upper Piedmont were important. We presume that he coded each county 1 if it was in the Cherokee Territory, 0 if not.

For 1880, the Cherokee Territory variable tells you that if other variables are held constant, being a county in the Cherokee Territory was associated on average with a 7% lower value of cotton per dollar of all field crops than if the county had been located in the eastern part of the Upper Piedmont. That seems a historically interesting difference, especially when you compare the negative 1880 coefficient with the positive coefficient in the 1860 equation. Back in 1860, being a Cherokee Territory county meant having a slightly higher value of cotton per dollar of all field crops, on average, than in the eastern counties. Twenty years later, it meant having a lower value. As Weiman says, this change "indicates a shift in the locus of cotton production away from the Cherokee Territory."

38. Out of the 33 terms in the six equations (omitting the constant in each equation), none was significant at the 1% confidence level, six were significant at the 5% level, and three were significant at the 10% level. The other 24 terms were not significant even at the 10%

confidence level. This is not impressive. However, the author appears to be interested not in the particular features of each model with its various explanatory variables, but in gauging "the timing of the economic transformation in the Upcountry." The basic model itself he simply borrowed from Wright and Kunreuther, except that he has added the dummy variable for subregion. Weiman does not dwell on the details of each model but emphasizes that the differences between the 1860 and 1870 models are not statistically significant, while those between 1870 and 1880 are. From this, he concludes that "the economic transformation of the Upcountry occurred after 1870."

39. The low t-values warn that for each term in the 1870 equations, there is a fairly large chance that the results don't reflect patterns in the underlying population but happened from the luck of the sampling draw. From the lack of single or double asterisks in these two models, we know that this chance is at least 10% for each coefficient. You wouldn't want to rely overmuch on this model as a firm basis for conclusions about the population of all counties. One of the problems here might be the small sample size.

40. Notice that the sizes of the t-values in equation (1) are 1.24, 1.47, 1.66, 1.85, and 2.18. It is true that there is some difference between the chance of getting a 1.66 just by luck and the probability of getting a 1.85, but that difference is not very striking. The 2.18 is in the region where you would begin to consider results statistically significant. There is no sharp line with significance on one side and insignificance on the other.

41. All the variables seem important as we examine the two models. For example, in both years, but particularly in 1880, Average Farm Size appears to have a substantial effect—see the answer to Question 37 (a). Percentage of Medium-Sized Farms and Percentage of Small-Sized Farms also seem to have some practical effect. Consider our old friends County A and County B: imagine that in one, 40% of the farms are small; in the other, 28%. Regression model (2) for 1880 tells you that this twelve-point difference ought to be associated, on average, with about a six-point difference ($.12 \times .49 = .0588$) in the value of cotton per dollar of all field crops. Six percent seems large enough to be of historical interest.

42. The result would be pretty much a wash since the coefficients are quite similar, 0.49 and 0.41. A ten-percent rise in small farms and

a ten-percent decline in medium-sized farms would be associated with a change in the dependent variable of only .008, or eight-tenths of one percent, since $(0.49 \times 0.1) - (0.41 \times 0.1) = .008$.

43. In looking over this variable called Percentage of Small Farms, you may feel that it's odd that the larger coefficient, 0.84, in model (1) for 1860, has a smaller t-value than the smaller coefficient, 0.49, in model (2) for 1880. These coefficients show that Percentage of Small Farms plays a more important role in the 1860 model than in the 1880 model. But you can't compare the size of these two co-efficients directly. These coefficients are embedded in two different models applied to two very different years. Model (1) for 1860 does not include the Cherokee Territory dummy variable while model (2) for 1880 does; it thereby introduces a possibly significant additional factor. And the economy of the Georgia Piedmont had changed fundamentally in this twenty-year period that included the Civil War, emancipation, and Reconstruction. Each model applies to its own year only.

The fact that the t-value for the 1880 coefficient is larger than the t-value for the 1860 coefficient means it is less likely that the 0.49 slope coefficient is due just to the luck of the draw than that the 0.84 coefficient happened by chance. This example shows again the distinction between practical significance (indicated by the size of the slope coefficient) and statistical significance (measured here by the t-value).

44. The R^2s are impressively high for 1860 and 1880 but poor for 1870. For example, the R^2 for 1860 suggests that about half of the variation in cotton share can be attributed to independent variables in the equation. Weiman mentions in a footnote (not reprinted) that census data for 1870 may be unreliable. Other historians have reported weaknesses in this census as well. Weiman also suggests that 1870 was an aberrant year because the Georgia economy had not yet recovered from the ravages of the Civil War.

45. The low t-values indicate that the slope coefficients are not statistically significantly different from zero—i.e., that the population regression model could be "flat." That means the dependent variable doesn't tend to rise or fall much as the independent variables change.

All that the large R^2 shows is that the flat linear model fits the data points fairly well. So if a regression model can fit the data very well, R^2 will be high. But that does not necessarily mean the independent variables have a big impact on the dependent variable.

46.   A review of the literature on the post-Civil War South would be helpful here since other historians may have utilized important variables omitted in the present article. Note that in Table 8.8 Weiman is testing a model first developed by Wright and Kunreuther. This may have been a wise approach—plausible models surely need to be put through their paces more than once.

This paper by Weiman suggests that one might experiment with independent variables which would measure changes in marketing systems, transportation systems, and agricultural technology— e.g., fertilizers.

47.   Personal Wealth per Capita and Average Farm Size might be positively correlated. Average Farm Size might be negatively correlated with Percentage of Small-Sized Farms. We emphasize that these are merely speculative comments, though.

48.   The author implies a null hypothesis (H_0), which, as always, claims that the observed differences between two samples do not reflect genuine differences between two populations, but instead could have come about through random sampling error—i.e., that the samples were drawn from the same underlying population. He's asking, "Were the Upper Piedmont counties so similar economically in 1860 and 1870 that it's as if my samples for those years had been drawn from a single population?" Then he asks the question again with respect to 1870 and 1880.

In a footnote, Weiman explains that for 1860–1870, a statistical test called an F-test fails to discredit the null hypothesis. In practical terms, this implies that the counties in 1870 did indeed closely resemble those in 1860 with respect to the economic variables being studied here. For 1870–80, however, the F-test leads Weiman to reject H_0. In the decade of the 1870s, substantial economic change took place in the Upper Piedmont so that the counties in 1880 didn't resemble those in 1870 enough to warrant thinking of the two samples as drawn from a single population. Weiman is thus able to conclude that "the economic transformation of the Upcountry occurred after 1870."

49.   Weiman says that Table 8.8 helps specify the timing of the switch to cotton in the Upcountry. Certainly the models suggest much greater change between 1870 and 1880 than between 1860 and 1870. But the 1870 model is a very poor fit to the data ($R^2 < 0.10$). Therefore, Table 8.8 may be more suggestive than convincing.

50. There is no point in a chi-square test for Table 8.2 because there is no question that the results are statistically significant. Even if there were some point to it (if the table used sample data, for example), you would not be able to do it because you don't know the number of cases in each category.

51. It would not make sense simply to average the numbers shown in the tables because the sub-regions such as the Appalachian Valley and the Upper Piedmont may have had different numbers of households. You would have to weight the percentages in Table 8.1 by the number of cases in each region.

52. The column headed Grains in Table 8.3 includes corn. To get the figure for wheat, rye, and oats we have to subtract the corn output. So this average farm would produce $37.2 - 30.1 = 7.1$ bushels per person. Then the farm produced 4×7.1 or 28.4 corn-equivalent bushels of wheat, rye, and oats. Similarly, $4 \times (39.7 - 37.2)$ or ten bushels of potatoes, peas, and beans were yielded and $4 \times (39.7 - 25.0)$ or 58.8 corn-equivalent bushels of animal feed were produced.

53. To do that, one must use some measurement scale applicable to all crops and home manufactures. For example, one might use dollar value or some measure of total labor and capital inputs required for production.

54. Weiman says that the census figures for domestic manufacture may be biased because census agents frequently ignored or undervalued home manufactures. If he is correct, then the true figures would be larger than those shown in the table and would constitute even stronger support for his view of farm self-sufficiency than the numbers he shows.

55. The numbers in Table 8.4 are in units of bales of cotton per 1000 bushels of corn. Using Table 8.3 data, if 0.09 bales of cotton were produced in 1860 for every 41.9 bushels of corn, then $(1000/41.9) \times 0.09$ bales were produced for every 1000 bushels of corn. That's 2.15 bales of cotton for every 1000 bushels of corn.

Table 8.4 showed 1.9 instead of 2.15, the difference may be due to rounding and the fact that the two tables were calculated somewhat differently. Were you to check the other regions you would see that Table 8.3 and Table 8.4 are quite consistent with one another—to within 0.1 or 0.2.

56. Weiman stresses that there were two regionally distinct processes underlying the shift of crop mix toward cotton. These ratios strongly support that position. In the Cotton Belt, both kinds of agricultural production declined on a per-capita basis. But food production declined more than cotton production. In fact, food production fell so drastically that the region could not feed itself.

In the Upcountry the shift to cotton comprised a moderate decline in food production that still left the region able to feed itself, while cotton production increased two- or three-fold.

57. When you try to estimate the real-world importance of one of these regression terms, it's often a good idea to make up a plausible but imaginary example. We're considering the explanatory variable called Rural population/improved acres. Say that County B had 20,000 improved acres and a rural population of 4000. This would yield a score of 0.2 persons per improved acre (4000 / 20,000). Now, if County A had the same number of improved acres and its population per improved acre was 0.3 (that's 0.1 higher than County B's, as stipulated in the question), then County A's rural population was 6000 because (6000 / 20,000) = 0.3.

	County A	County B
Improved acres	20,000	20,000
Rural population	6,000	4,000
Rural pop/improved acres	0.3	0.2
Cotton acres/tilled acre		
Due to Rural Pop/imp acre	32%	21%

An increase from 0.2 to 0.3 persons per improved acre would lead you to predict that in County A the cotton share of acreage was about ten or eleven percent greater than in County B. But that is a fifty percent increase over the prediction for County B. That seems a very substantial difference, so it's no surprise that Weiman mentions this explanatory variable in the text. On the other hand, notice that to get such a large increase in the proportion of tilled land devoted to cotton, you had to bring in 2000 people.

58. Those counties with greater rural population density would tend to have a significantly greater share of the tilled land devoted to cotton.

59. In the cotton belt equation, the variable "Rate of Tenancy" is statistically significant since the t-value of 2.89 shown in parentheses is even greater than the 2.59 t-value just above which is marked as being statistically significant.

60. R^2 is the percentage of cotton share variability attributable to the variables in the model. The standard error for R^2 is 0.06 in the Upper Piedmont example. A 95% confidence interval for the true R^2 would be about 0.17 plus or minus 2 times 0.06. The 95% confidence interval would be 0.05 to 0.29.

61. Since $t = 0.83 \div \text{SE}$, it must be that $\text{SE} = 0.83 \div t$. Then the SE is $0.83 \div 1.5$.

Index